Lillian F. Wright   1993
State Meet at Waco, TX

TEXAS TEMPTATIONS

This cookbook is a collection of favorite recipes that we have gathered to share from members throughout the state. We do not claim them to be original. The recipes have been tested for quality and accuracy. We, as an organization, promote good nutrition and healthy living. These recipes are published as submitted. To meet your dietary needs, we have included guidelines for your use in adapting recipes to be low fat, heart healthy, etc. Please check with your County Extension Office for food preservation recommendations.

State Cookbook Committee

Fern Maxwell, Chm.	Sylvia Steen
Hazel Bray	Loretta Mahan
Joyce Cabe	Amy Adrian
Jo Ann Bone	

1993 State TEHA Officers

Charlotte Watson	President
Carrol Davig	First Vice-President
Martha Crawford	Second Vice-President
Kila Lackey	Secretary
Joan Frost	Treasurer

Texas Extension Homemakers Association

Copyright Applied For
ISBN 0-9637300-0-2

The cover, including the name, is by Dawn Riley of Rusk Extension Homemakers Club, Cherokee County, District 9.

TEHA MISSION

The mission of the Texas Extension Homemakers Association is to work with the Texas Agricultural Extension Service to strengthen and enrich families through educational programs, leadership development and community service.

VISION

We envision the Texas Extension Homemakers Association as Texas' most effective volunteer organization for supporting families through life-long learning opportunities. We will strive through education to improve family and community life for all families, reaching across ethnic, age, cultural lines and including those with disabilities.

The Family Community Leadership program will be the catalyst for leadership development of Texas women and community service activities will be the medium for the expression of charitable interests and community enrichment. Opportunities for individual growth and development will be supported by TEHA for youth and adults to help them reach their full potential through educational pursuits.

We will strengthen communication among TEHA members, with other Extension clientele and related community organizations that share common goals. We will cooperate with the Extension Service to strengthen, develop and extend adult education that improves the quality of life for Texas families and communities.

TEHA HEALTH SALAD

Start with 5 heads of lettuce:

Let us understand the goals and objectives.
Let us increase our skills.
Let us participate fully.
Let us earn respect and empowerment.
Let us understand our members' needs and wants.

Prepare 5 cups of peas:

Purpose,
Preparation,
Presence,
Promptness, and
Perseverance.

Add 3 cups of squash:

Squash gossip.
Squash criticism.
Squash indifference.

Toss in the right amount of turnips:

Turn up at meetings on time.
Turn up with a smile.
Turn up with new ideas.
Turn up with a determination to make everything count for
  something good and worthwhile.

Serving size:

Makes enough to serve an entire organization. And have
  fun...just for the halibut!

For variety:

Cut the bologna, add the beef,
watch the carrots, cut the corn,
eliminate the sour grapes,
patch the leeks, and skip the pickles.

Copied and Adapted

23RD PSALM
FOR
BUSY TEHA LEADER

The Lord is my pacesetter,
     I shall not rush
He makes me stop and rest for
     quiet intervals.
He provides me with images of stillness
     which restores my serenity.
He leads me in ways of efficiency,
     through calmness of mind,
And His guidance is peace.

Even though I have a great many things
     to accomplish this day,
I will not fret, for His presence
     is here.
His timelessness, His all-importance
Will keep me in balance.

He prepares refreshment and renewal in
     the midst of my activity by
     anointing my mind with oils of
     tranquility.

My joyous energy overflows.

Surely harmony and effectiveness
     shall be the fruits of my hours,
For I shall walk in the peace of my Lord,
     and dwell in His house forever.

A Daily Food Guide for Variety and Balance

Food Group	Major Dietary Contributions	Suggested Daily Servings
Breads, cereals and other grain products • Whole grain • Enriched	Provide starch, thiamin, riboflavin, niacin and iron. Whole grains also provide fiber, folic acid, magnesium and zinc.	**6 to 11** (Include several servings per day of whole-grain products.) 
Fruits • Citrus • Other fruits	Contribute many nutrients as well as dietary fiber. Citrus fruits, melons and berries are excellent sources of vitamin C. Deep yellow fruits are high in vitamin A. Fruits also add color, flavor, texture and sweetness to the diet.	**2 to 4** 
Vegetables • Dry beans and peas (legumes) • Starchy • Other vegetables 	Supply fiber, some starch or protein; also provide many vitamins and minerals.	**3 to 5** (Include all types regularly; use dark green leafy vegetables, dry beans and peas several times per week.)
Meat, poultry, fish and alternates (eggs, dry beans and peas)	Provide protein, niacin, thiamin, vitamins B_6, B_{12} (animal foods only), iron, phosphorus and zinc.	**2 to 3** (Total 5 to 7 ounces lean)
Milk, cheese and yogurt 	As the best sources of calcium in U.S. diets, they provide protein, riboflavin, vitamins B_{12}, A, thiamin and if fortified, vitamin D.	**2** for adults; **3** for teens and women who are pregnant or breast-feeding; **4** for teens who are pregnant or breast-feeding.
Fats, sweets and alcohol 	These foods are calorie-dense, not nutrient-dense. Fats provide 9 calories per gram; sugars, 4 calories per gram and alcohol, 7 calories per gram.	Avoid too many fats and sweets. If you drink alcoholic beverages, do so in moderation.

Food Guide Pyramid

A Guide to Daily Food Choices

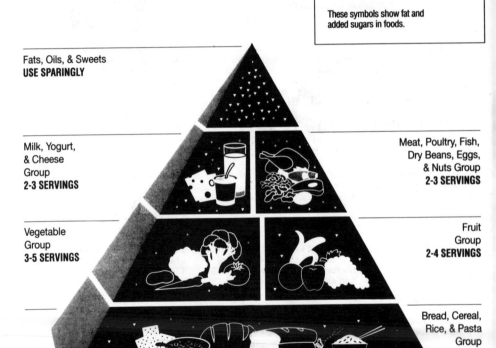

KEY

◻ **Fat** (naturally occurring and added)

▼ **Sugars** (added)

These symbols show fat and added sugars in foods.

Fats, Oils, & Sweets
USE SPARINGLY

Milk, Yogurt, & Cheese Group
2-3 SERVINGS

Meat, Poultry, Fish, Dry Beans, Eggs, & Nuts Group
2-3 SERVINGS

Vegetable Group
3-5 SERVINGS

Fruit Group
2-4 SERVINGS

Bread, Cereal, Rice, & Pasta Group
6-11 SERVINGS

What is the Food Guide Pyramid?

The Pyramid is an outline of what to eat each day. It's not a rigid prescription, but a general guide that lets you choose a healthful diet that's right for you.

The Pyramid calls for eating a variety of foods to get the nutrients you need and at the same time the right amount of calories to maintain a healthy weight.

The Pyramid also focuses on fat because most American diets are too high in fat, especially saturated fat.

How to Use The Daily Food Guide

What counts as one serving?

Breads, Cereals, Rice, and Pasta
1 slice of bread
1/2 cup of cooked rice or pasta
1/2 cup of cooked cereal
1 ounce of ready-to-eat cereal

Vegetables
1/2 cup of chopped raw or
 cooked vegetables
1 cup of leafy raw vegetables

Fruits
1 piece of fruit or melon wedge
3/4 cup of juice
1/2 cup of canned fruit
1/4 cup of dried fruit

Milk, Yogurt, and Cheese
1 cup of milk or yogurt
1-1/2 to 2 ounces of cheese

Meat, Poultry, Fish, Dry Beans, Eggs, and Nuts
2-1/2 to 3 ounces of cooked lean
 meat, poultry, or fish
Count 1/2 cup of cooked beans,
 or 1 egg, or 2 tablespoons of
 peanut butter as 1 ounce of lean
 meat (about 1/3 serving)

Fats, Oils, and Sweets
LIMIT CALORIES FROM THESE
especially if you need to lose weight

> The amount you eat may be more than one serving. For example, a dinner portion of spaghetti would count as two or three servings of pasta.

How many servings do you need each day?

	Women & some older adults	Children, teen girls, active women, most men	Teen boys & active men
Calorie level*	about 1,600	about 2,200	about 2,800
Bread group	6	9	11
Vegetable group	3	4	5
Fruit group	2	3	4
Milk group	**2-3	**2-3	**2-3
Meat group	2, for a total of 5 ounces	2, for a total of 6 ounces	3 for a total of 7 ounces

*These are the calorie levels if you choose lowfat, lean foods from the 5 major food groups and use foods from the fats, oils, and sweets group sparingly.

**Women who are pregnant or breastfeeding, teen-agers, and young adults to age 24 need 3 servings.

A Closer Look at Fat and Added Sugars

The small tip of the Pyramid shows fats, oils, and sweets. These are foods such as salad dressings, cream, butter, margarine, sugars, soft drinks, candies, and sweet desserts. Alcoholic beverages are also part of this group. These foods provide calories but few vitamins and minerals. Most people should go easy on foods from this group.

Some fat or sugar symbols are shown in the other food groups. That's to remind you that some foods in these groups can also be high in fat and added sugars, such as cheese or ice cream from the milk group, or french fries from the vegetable group. When choosing foods for a healthful diet, consider the fat and added sugars in your choices from all the food groups, not just fats, oils, and sweets from the Pyramid tip.

PRACTICAL GUIDELINES FOR CHANGING
TO A HEALTHFUL DIET

Reduce your blood cholesterol level by selecting a healthful diet low in fat, particularly saturated fatty acids and low in cholesterol. Use the following dietary guidelines as you plan your new diet.

1. To cut back on saturated fatty acids and replace part of the saturated fatty acids in your diet with unsaturated fatty acids:
   * Choose 2- to 3-ounce servings of poultry, fish, and lean cuts of meat more often; remove the skin from chicken and trim the fat from meat.
   * Bake, broil, or boil rather than fry.
   * Trim excess fat off meat before cooking.
   * Drink 2 or more servings daily of skim milk or 1% milk instead of 2% milk or whole milk. And eat cheeses with no more than 2 to 6 grams of fat per ounce (like low-fat cottage or low-fat farmer cheese) instead of processed, natural, and hard cheeses (like American, brie, and cheddar).
   * Limit the use of butter, cream, salad dressing, margarine, shortening, and oil.
   * Use tub margarine or liquid vegetable oils that are high in unsaturated fatty acids (like safflower, corn, and olive oil) instead of butter, lard, and hydrogenated vegetable shortening that are high in saturated fatty acids. Choose products that list more unsaturated fatty acids than saturated fatty acids on the label.
   * Use less cooking oil and fats than called for in recipes.
   * Cut down on commercially prepared and processed foods made with saturated fatty acids such as non-dairy creamers or oils. Read labels to choose those low in saturated fatty acids.

2. To cut back on dietary cholesterol found only in foods of animal origin:
   * Eat less organ meat such as liver, brain, and kidney.
   * Eat fewer egg yolks; try substituting two egg whites for each whole egg in recipes.
   * Eat less shellfish such as oysters.

3. To increase complex carbohydrates (starch and fiber):
   * Eat more whole grain breads and cereals, pasta, rice, and dried peas and beans.
   * Eat vegetables and fruits more often.

4. To lose weight:
   * Eat fewer daily calories (cutting back on fat in your diet will really help).
   * Burn extra calories by exercising regularly.

LOW-FAT, LOW CHOLESTEROL COOKING

Try these tasty tips to keep the lid on your total fat and calorie intake. Remember, it is not always what you eat that gets you in trouble; often it is how you cook it.

1.   In casseroles and main dishes, cut back or even eliminate added fat. For example, browning meat in added fat is unnecessary because some fat will drain from the meat as it cooks. Use a non-stick pan or cooking spray.

2.   Reduce fat by one-fourth to one-third in baked products. For example, if a recipe calls for 1 cup of oil, try 2/3 cup. This works best in quick breads, muffins, and cookies.

3.   Saute or stir-fry vegetables with very little fat or use water, wine, or broth.

4.   To thicken sauces and gravies without lumping, eliminate fat and instead mix cornstarch or flour with a small amount of cold liquid. Stir this mixture slowly into the hot liquid you want to thicken, and bring it back to a boil.

5.   Decrease the proportion of oil in home-made salad dressings. Try one-third oil to two-thirds vinegar.

6.   Chill soups, gravies, and stews and skim off hardened fat before reheating to serve. This will save 100 calories per tablespoon of fat removed.

7.   Select lean cuts of meat, chicken, fish or turkey and trim off visible fat before and after cooking. Remove skin from poultry before cooking and bake, broil, grill, steam, poach or microwave meat, poultry, or fish instead of frying in fat.

8.   Use reduced-calorie sour cream or mayonnaise. To reduce fat further, use plain low-fat or nonfat yogurt, buttermilk, or blended cottage cheese instead of regular sour cream or mayonnaise for sauces, dips, and salad dressings. If a sauce made with yogurt is to be heated, add 1 tablespoon of corn starch to 1 cup yogurt to prevent separation.

9.   Use less whole milk products, including less cheese and eggs. Use skim or low-fat milk instead of whole milk. For extra richness, try evaporated skim milk. Eat live cultured low-fat yogurt and low-fat dairy products. Avoid non-dairy creamers that have coconut oil, palm oil or palm kernel oil. These contain high levels of saturated fatty acids. Consider using substitute cheeses. Remember, however, that some substitute cheeses are high in sodium.

10. Use vegetable oils instead of solid fats. To substitute liquid oil for solid fats, use about one-fourth less than the recipe calls for. For example, if a recipe calls for 1/4 cup (4 tablespoons) of solid fat, use 3 tablespoons of oil. For cakes or pie crusts, use a recipe that specifically calls for oil because liquid fats require special mixing procedures and different proportions of sugar.

11. Use two egg whites or an egg substitute product instead of one whole egg. In some recipes, simply decrease the total number of eggs.

12. Use margarine instead of butter. While both have about the same calories, butter is higher in saturated fatty acids. Look for margarines in which liquid vegetable oil is the first ingredient. Avoid those margarines which are higher in saturated fatty acids, and lists its first ingredient as hydrogenated oil rather than a liquid vegetable oil. The process of hydrogenation turns an unsaturated fatty acid into a partially saturated fatty acid.

EATING TIPS TO HELP MANAGE CHOLESTEROL

Use water-packed canned fish. If in oil, make sure to drain and rinse with water for one minute.

Eat more cereals of whole grains and whole-grain bread, both are rich in B-complex vitamins, vitamin E, and magnesium.

Reduce your intake of refined sugar (e.g. doughnuts, cakes, etc.). Eat more complex carbohydrates such as pasta and brown rice.

Eat starchy vegetables—potatoes, winter squash, peas, corn, and lima beans.

Eat more foods containing fiber such as apples, oatmeal, legumes, and other fruits and vegetables that are eaten with the skin.

Eat more garlic and onions. Use spices, such as dried mint flakes and lemon, instead of butter or salt. Use high-fat salad dressings sparingly.

Substitute for high fat products. Use soybean based products as meat analogs, low-fat yogurt for sour cream, ice milk or frozen yogurt instead of ice cream.

SUBSTITUTIONS
(Especially for Diabetics)

Note: Substitutions will not always work — especially in baking. Taste and texture may vary from the original recipe, but the results are often pleasing.

Instead of	Use
1 cup butter -- 498 mg cholesterol	7/8 cup polyunsaturated oil -- 0 mg cholesterol
	or
	1 cup tub margarine (polyunsaturated oil, partially hydrogenated) -- 0 mg cholesterol
	or
	1 cup (2 sticks margarine (partially hydrogenated -- but lower in polyunsaturates than tub margarine) -- 0 mg cholesterol
1 cup heavy cream -- 832 calories, 286 mg cholesterol	1 cup evaporated skim milk -- 176 calories, 8 mg cholesterol
1 medium whole egg - 274 mg cholesterol	1/4 cup egg substitute -- 0 mg cholesterol*
1 cup high-fat (creamy) yogurt, plain -- 250 calories	1 cup part skim milk yogurt, plain -- 125-145 calories
1 cup sour cream -- 416 calories	1 cup Mock Sour Cream (Basic Cheese Sauce recipe) -- 180 calories
1 ounce baking chocolate -- 8.4 grams saturated fat	3 tablespoons cocoa powder -- 1.7 grams saturated fat
	plus
	1 tablespoon polyunsaturated oil -- 1.1 grams saturated fat Total: 2.8 grams saturated fat
3 tablespoons flour -- 87 calories, 18 grams carbohydrate	1 tablespoon cornstarch -- 28 calories, 7 grams carbohydrate
1 cup sugar -- 770 calories, 199 grams carbohydrate	Commercial sugar substitutes: The equivalent as suggested by the manufacturer or according to your own taste
1 teaspoon sugar -- 16 calories, 4 grams carbohydrate	1/2 packet Equal** -- 2 calories, 1 gram carbohydrate
	or
	1/2 packet Sweet 'n Low -- 2 calories
	or
	other sugar substitute

*   Some egg substitutions do not contain cholesterol. Check label to be sure.

**   Equal is a protein and loses its sweetness when cooked. It cannot be used in baking.

FOUR WAYS TO DECREASE SUGAR IN YOUR RECIPES

Sugar contains nothing but calories. Amazingly, over 130 pounds of sugar are consumed by the average person each year. Try these ways to reduce your sugar intake.

1. Decrease or eliminate sugar when canning or freezing fruits. Buy unsweetened frozen fruit or fruit canned in its own juice or water. Once the container is opened, you can always add your own sweetener.

2. Try reducing sugar by one-quarter to one-third in baked goods and desserts. Do not decrease the small amount of sugar in plain yeast breads because it provides food for the yeast and promotes rising.

3. Non-sugar sweeteners can be used in moderation to decrease your sugar intake.

4. Increase the amount of cinnamon or vanilla in a recipe to enhance the impression of sweetness.

THREE WAYS TO MAKE YOUR RECIPES LOW-CALORIE

Most of us could benefit by modifying what we eat. One way to modify your diet is to make adjustments in the types and amounts of ingredients in recipes so that the end result is just as satisfying but fits better with recommended dietary guidelines.

Very few recipes need to be followed exactly to assure a good quality product. Your chances for success are best if you understand when and how to modify recipes. Instead of giving up your favorite recipes, modify them by following these three principles:

1. Eliminate non-essentials: Leave out all non-essential ingredients. For example, butter on broiled fish can be eliminated or salt can be omitted from the water when boiling foods.

2. Reduce contents: Use less fat, sugar, or salt as much as possible by reducing the amount in preparation.

3. Substitute ingredients: Use more healthful ingredients or a lower-calorie cooking method. Replace whole milk with low-fat or skim milk. Try steaming rather than frying.

Don't be too quick to change your recipes, however. Take a look at your recipes and see how they measure up to your plans to make positive changes in your eating habits.

To reduce sodium

1. Make full use of herbs and spices in place of salt. You may not want to eliminate salt completely, but consider reducing the amount you use.
2. Salt can be eliminated from all recipes except those containing yeast.
3. Avoid recipes that contain substantial amounts of baking powder or baking soda, which may be high in sodium.
4. Use low-sodium or unsalted ingredients during cooking (unsalted margarine, low-sodium canned products, salt-free crackers and cereals, low-sodium stocks).
5. Check processed foods for sodium content and replace with homemade varieties whenever possible, or purchase low-sodium products. Commercial mayonnaise and salad dressings, for example, may contain high levels of sodium.
6. Reduce consumption of luncheon meats (ham, bacon, frankfurters and sausage), smoked, pickled and salted foods. Instead, use fresh meats, poultry and fish. Specially processed low-fat, low-sodium luncheon meats may be acceptable, but check the label for the amount of fat and sodium each contains.
7. Use fresh or frozen fish instead of canned or dried varieties.
8. Water in which salted products are cooked can be poured off and replaced with fresh water.
9. Do not add salt to boiling water when cooking vegetables, pasta and cereals.

You Get Fiber, Too!

Increasing your consumption of certain complex carbohydrates can also help increase dietary fiber. The average American diet is relatively low in fiber.

While fiber will not cure or prevent all of the diseases for which it is recommended by some, it is an essential part of a good diet. Eating more foods high in fiber tends to reduce the symptoms of chronic constipation. There is also some feeling that fiber may help prevent cancer of the colon or lower cholesterol levels. However, more research is needed before these theories can be proven.

What is Fiber?

Grandma called it roughage. It is the tough, fibrous part of plant cell walls. Many different types of fiber are found in a variety of foods. Whole wheat bread, apples, and cabbage contribute different types of fiber to the diet, each of which benefits the body in a different way. For this reason it is important to get fiber from a variety of whole grains, fruits and vegetables.

How Much Fiber?

Too much or too little fiber can cause problems. There is no reason to add fiber to foods that do not already contain it. To make sure you get enough fiber in your diet, eat some whole grains and a variety of fruits and vegetables daily.

What Are Whole Grains?

Whole grains are products that contain the entire grain, or all the grain that is edible. They include the *bran* and *germ* portions which contain most of the fiber, vitamins, and minerals, as well as the starchy *endosperm*.

Some examples are whole wheat, cracked wheat, bulgur, oatmeal, whole cornmeal, popcorn, brown rice, whole rye, and scotch barley.

Whole grain doesn't have to mean bread or cereal. Try these:

Brown rice
Scotch barley - in soups
Corn tortillas
Tabbouleh - a bulgur wheat salad
Popcorn, unbuttered
Whole-wheat pasta

Recognizing the Real Whole Wheat

All whole-wheat bread is brown, but not all brown bread is whole-wheat...

By law, bread that is labeled "whole wheat" must be made from 100 percent whole-wheat flour. "Wheat bread" may be made from varying proportions of enriched white flour and whole-wheat flour. The type of flour present in the largest amount is listed first on the ingredient label. Sometimes a dark color is provided by "caramel coloring," also listed on the label.

The milling of wheat to produce white flour results in the loss of nutrients as the bran and germ are removed. Enrichment replaces four important nutrients: iron, thiamin, riboflavin, and niacin. But flours made from the whole grain contain more of other nutrients, such as folic acid, vitamin B6, vitamin E, phosphorus, magnesium, and zinc, than enriched white flour.

You don't have to switch to whole-wheat bread to increase your intake of whole grains...

Many products on the market are made of a mixture of whole-grain flours and enriched flour. Try those listed below for variety in taste and texture, as well as a bonus of fiber and nutrients. Or, try substituting whole-grain flour for half the amount of white flour when you bake quick breads or cookies.

Bran muffins
Cornbread, from whole, ground cornmeal
Cracked wheat bread
Graham crackers
Oatmeal bread
Pumpernickel bread
Rye bread

Table of Contents

APPETIZERS & BEVERAGES

Beverages

BANANA CRUSH

4 c. sugar (I use 2 c.)
6 c. water
1/2 c. lemon juice
4 c. (or lg. can) pineapple
 juice

1 lg. can orange juice
 (not frozen)
5 bananas, crushed or mashed
3 bottles ginger ale

Make a syrup of water and sugar by heating until sugar is dissolved. Combine with remaining ingredients, except ginger ale. Pour into trays or containers and freeze. (Best to divide into 3 containers.) After frozen, take out of freezer one hour before serving. Mix with ginger ale. Variation: Use lemon-lime soda instead of ginger ale.

Charolette Loncar, Collin County
Brenda Gunn, Oldham County

GOLDEN FRUIT PUNCH

2 pkgs. Kool-Aid (any flavor
 for color)
1 6-oz. can frozen orange
 juice concentrate
1 1/2 pts. pineapple juice,
 unsweetened

2 qts. water
2/3 c. sugar
1 c. pineapple, grated (opt.)
1 lg. bottle ginger ale

Mix all ingredients, except ginger ale. Chill and serve from punch bowl containing large chunk of ice. Add ginger ale just before serving. Makes 30 cups or 18 glasses.

Mary Agnes Jaster
Falls County

HOT TOMATO JUICE COCKTAIL

1 tall can of V-8 juice
1 T. ketchup
1 T. salt

Juice of 1 lemon
Shot of Tabasco sauce

Mix together and serve with sandwiches, salad or before meal.

Murl Mayfield
Floyd County

PARTY PINK PUNCH

1 gal. cranberry cocktail juice
1 46-oz. can pineapple juice

1 qt. ginger ale

Combine all ingredients. Just before serving, pour over ice. Yield: 50 servings.

Virginia Boatright
Coke County

PASSION PURPLE PUNCH

1 6-oz. can frozen lemonade
  concentrate, thawed
1 6-oz. can frozen orange juice
  concentrate, thawed

1 6-oz. can frozen grape juice
  concentrate, thawed
2 c. water
2 67.6-oz. liters ginger ale

Combine first 3 ingredients and water in a large non-metal pitcher or punch bowl. Add ginger ale and ice or ice mold just before serving; stir to blend. Yield: 25 4-oz. servings.

Saunna Blacksher
Collingsworth County

STRAWBERRY PUNCH

1 46-oz. can unsweetened
  pineapple juice
2 bananas
1 1/2 c. sugar

2 sm. pkgs. unsweetened
  strawberry Kool-Aid
1 pkg. frozen sliced
  strawberries
1/2 gal. water

Blend bananas with 1/4 c. pineapple juice. Mix all ingredients. Add red food coloring to make a deeper color and enough water to make one gallon. Freeze to a frozen mush. Pour in punch bowl and add 1 quart ginger ale. Serve.

Isabel Giles
Collin County

TEXAS BRIDES' PUNCH BOWL

3 c. sugar
3 c. boiling water
1 sm. pkg. peach jello
1 sm. pkg. apricot jello
1 12-oz. can frozen lemonade

1 46-oz. can pineapple
  juice or concentrate
1 1-oz. bottle almond extract
3 qts. ginger ale, chilled

Bring sugar and water to boil and stir until dissolved. Remove from heat and add jellos. Stir until dissolved. Add lemonade, pineapple juice and almond extract. Mix well and refrigerate to cool. Just before serving, pour into punch bowl and pour ginger ale on top. Float a ginger ale ice ring on top, if desired. Variation: Use lemon and orange flavored jellos and add 1 6-ounce can frozen orange juice.

Florence McDaniel, Gillespie County
Pat Goerlitz, Victoria County

May I never miss a rainbow or a sunset
because I'm looking down.

HOLIDAY WASSAIL

2-3 qts. sweet apple cider　　　　1 stick cinnamon
3 c. or 1 can frozen orange juice　Whole cloves
1 c. fresh lemon juice　　　　　　Raw honey to taste
1 c. pineapple juice
　　Simmer together 2 minutes and serve hot.

Lyons E. H. Club
Burleson County

PEACH TEA

1 lg. pkg. peach jello　　　　1/2 c. lemonade
1/2 c. instant tea　　　　　　3/4-1 c. sugar
1/2 c. Tang
　　Mix together. Use 2 tablespoonfuls to a cup of hot water.

Velma Tate
Tarrant County

"NOT TOO SWEET" PUNCH

Tea (6 tea bags to 10 c. water)　1 lg. bottle ginger ale
Sweeten to taste　　　　　　　　1 40-oz. bottle cranberry
1 lg. bottle club soda　　　　　　　juice cocktail
　　Pour cooled tea over ice or ice cubes and add cranberry juice. Add ginger ale and club soda just before serving.

FROZEN SLUSH PUNCH

2 sm. or 1 lg. pkg. lemon jello　2 c. sugar
2 c. hot water　　　　　　　　　2 46-oz. cans pineapple juice
6 c. cold water　　　　　　　　　2 lg. bottles ginger ale
　　Dissolve jello in hot water; add sugar and cold water. Freeze until slush or freeze hard. Take out 2 hours before serving. Add ginger ale at serving time (1/2 and 1/2). Serves 35-40.

Fern Maxwell
Wichita County

Give no more to every guest,
than he is able to digest.
Give him always of the prime,
and but little at a time.

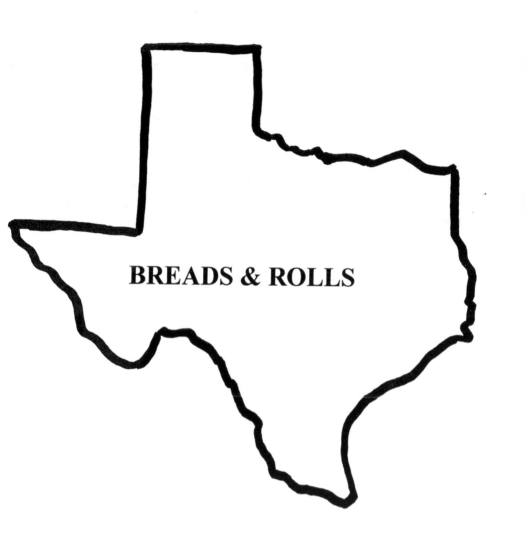

BREADS & ROLLS

Breads and Rolls

Breads

ALABAMA-COUSHATTA INDIAN FRY BREAD

The Indian Fry Bread recipe has been passed down from mother to daughter for several generations at the Alabama-Coushatta Indian Reservation near Livingston in East Texas. It is available during summer months at the Indian Sundown Theatre.

3 c. flour, sifted   1/2 tsp. salt
4 tsp. baking powder

Mix ingredients with enough water to form a stiff dough, about the consistency of biscuits or rolls, working to smooth. Cover and set aside at room temperature 4 to 5 hours. Punch down dough; knead about 5 times. Pinch off small bits of dough; stretch and pat into 5-inch flat circle. Fry in deep oil until golden brown, turning once. Drain on paper.

Note: Warm water or sweet milk can be used instead of water. The dough can "develop" overnight in covered bowl. Serve while hot with butter, syrup, jelly or powdered sugar.

Sandy Dennis
Polk County

APPLESAUCE LOAF

1/2 c. shortening   1/2 tsp. nutmeg
1 1/2 c. sugar   1 tsp. cloves
2 eggs, well beaten   1 c. applesauce
2 c. sifted flour   1 c. golden seedless raisins,
1 tsp. baking powder   chopped
1/2 tsp. soda   1 T. flour
1/4 tsp. salt   1 c. pecans, chopped
1 tsp. cinnamon   1 tsp. butter flavoring

Cream butter and sugar until light and fluffy. Add eggs beating well; sift the flour with baking powder, salt, soda, cinnamon, nutmeg and cloves; add to butter mixture alternately with applesauce. Dredge raisins and pecans with 1 tablespoonful flour and stir into batter. Pour into well greased and floured 9 1/4 x 5 1/4-inch loaf pan. Bake at 350 degrees for about 1 hour. Remove from pan and cool. Serve plain or glaze. Makes 1 loaf.

Thelma Langhoff
Gonzales County

Patience is the ability to idle your motor
when you feel like stripping your gears.

FRESH APPLE NUT BREAD

3 c. sugar
1 1/2 c. cooking oil
3 c. flour
1 tsp. baking soda
1 tsp. salt
1 tsp. cinnamon

3 eggs
1 tsp. vanilla
3 c. raw apples, chopped
1 c. pecans
1 tsp. allspice

Cream sugar and oil. Sift together other dry ingredients and add to creamed mixture alternately with well beaten eggs. Mix in vanilla, apples and pecans. Pour into greased and floured loaf pan. Bake at 325 degrees for 45-60 minutes.

Bonnie Harkey
San Saba County

APRICOT BREAD

1 c. dried apricots
3/4 c. hot water
2 T. butter, softened
1 c. sugar
1 egg, slightly beaten

2 c. flour
1 tsp. baking powder
1/4 tsp. baking soda
1/2 c. orange juice
1/2 c. pecans, chopped

Cut apricots into pieces in small bowl; pour hot water over all. Let soften for 30 minutes. Set aside apricot pieces. Combine butter, sugar and egg in mixing bowl; cream well. In another bowl, combine flour, baking powder and soda. Add dry ingredients to creamed mixture, alternately with "apricot water" and orange juice. Stir in apricots and pecans. Spoon into greased and floured 9 x 5-inch loaf pan. Bake at 350 degrees for 55-65 minutes or until bread test is done with wooden toothpick. Serve with apricot spread. Serves 10.

APRICOT SPREAD

3 oz. cream cheese
2 T. dried apricots, softened
  and chopped

2 pkgs. Equal

Combine ingredients and mix well. Refrigerate until serving time.

Carolyn Botkin
Lynn County

WORDS
A cruel word may wreck a life;
A bitter word may hate instill
A joyous word may light the way;
A loving word may heal and bless.

BANANA NUT BREAD

2 sticks margarine, softened
3 c. sugar
4 eggs
5 ripe bananas, mashed
1 tsp. vanilla

3 c. flour
1 tsp. soda
1/2 tsp. salt
1/2 c. buttermilk
1 c. pecans, finely ground (opt.)

Cream together margarine and sugar. Add one egg at a time to creamed mixture using all four eggs. Add mashed bananas and vanilla. Sift together flour, soda and salt. Blend the flour mixture and buttermilk to the creamed sugar mixture. Blend well and add ground pecans (optional). Bake in two large or three medium size greased bread pans. Begin baking at 375 degrees for 10 minutes. Bake at 350 degrees until done (approximately 45 minutes, depending on pan size). Test for doneness by inserting a straw or toothpick to make sure the loaf is done.

Celestine Matocha
Bastrop County

MAM-MAW'S HAWAIIAN BANANA NUT BREAD

3 c. flour
2 c. sugar
1 tsp. soda
1 tsp. salt
1 tsp. cinnamon
1 c. pecans, chopped

1 16-oz. can crushed pineapple, drained
3 eggs, beaten
1 1/2 c. vegetable oil
2 c. bananas, mashed
2 tsp. vanilla

Combine dry ingredients. Stir in nuts and set aside. Combine remaining ingredients and add to dry ingredients, stirring just until batter is moistened. Spoon batter into 2 greased and floured 9 x 5 x 3-inch loaf pans. Bake in preheated oven at 350 degrees for 1 hour and 15 minutes or until done. Cool 10 minutes before removing from pans.

Kellye Reed
Armstrong County

BREAD STICKS

1 pkg. day-old hot dog buns
1 1/2 sticks oleo/butter

1 1/2 T. Worcestershire sauce

Slice each bun into at least 6 slices. Put on a cookie sheet. Melt oleo/butter. Add Worcestershire sauce. Brush over bread slices. May sprinkle over bread garlic powder, onion powder, seasoning salt, Mrs. Dash or oregano and Parmesan cheese, or you may just use oleo and sesame seeds. Bake in 200 degree oven for one hour. Turn oven off and let bread remain in oven for another hour. Store in Tupperware.

Alma Thomas
Collin County

GLAZED TRIPLE CHOCOLATE BREAD

2/3 c. brown sugar, firmly packed	1 1/2 c. applesauce
1/2 c. butter, softened	1 tsp. baking powder
1 c. mini semi-sweet chocolate chips	1 tsp. baking soda
2 eggs	2 tsp. vanilla
2 1/2 c. all-purpose flour	1/2 c. mini chocolate chips

Heat oven to 350 degrees. Cream together brown sugar and butter. Add melted chocolate chips and eggs. On low speed mix in applesauce, flour, baking powder, soda and vanilla and beat until creamy. By hand, stir in 1/2 cup chocolate chips. Spoon batter into greased mini loaf or foil pans. Bake 35-42 minutes or until crack in center is dry to touch. Cool 10 minutes before glazing. Yield: 5 mini loaves (5 1/2 x 3-inches).

GLAZE

1/2 c. mini chocolate chips	1/2 c. powdered sugar
5 tsp. water	1/4 tsp. vanilla
1 T. butter	Dash of salt

In 2 quart saucepan, combine chocolate chips, water and butter. Cook over low heat, stirring constantly until melted and smooth. Remove from heat and stir in powdered sugar, vanilla and salt. Frost with glaze. If freezing: freeze unfrosted; bring to room temperature before frosting.

Fern Maxwell, Director
District 3, Wichita County

FAY'S CHRISTMAS BREAD

2 c. flour	1 tsp. salt
1 c. milk	1 tsp. baking powder
3 T. oleo	1 tsp. baking soda

Combine all ingredients, mixing well. Roll out 1/2-inch thick on a floured board. Cut with a biscuit cutter. Bake at 500 degrees for 7 minutes. Remove biscuits from oven and cool.

ICING

3/4 c. walnuts, chopped	1/2 c. candied red cherries,
1/2 c. confectioners' sugar	chopped
1/4 c. raisins	1/2 c. milk
	1/2 tsp. lemon extract

Combine icing ingredients and mix well. Ice biscuits when they are sufficiently cool.

Fay McCollum
Scurry County

A good memory is fine -
but the ability to forget is the true test of greatness.

COFFEE CAKE

1/2 c. butter
1 c. boiling water
1/4 c. sugar
1 tsp. salt

2 pkgs. granulated yeast
1 egg, well beaten
3 1/3 c. flour

Pour water over butter, add sugar and salt. When lukewarm, add yeast and let stand until softened. Add egg and stir. Add flour and beat well. Put in large jelly roll pan. Spread evenly. Cut through dough, brush with butter and top with topping.

TOPPING

1/2 c. brown sugar
2 T. flour
1/2 c. pecans

1/2 c. white sugar
2 T. butter

Let rise for about 1 hour. Bake for 20 minutes at 375 degrees.

Evelyn Schelling
Shiner County

DATE NUT BREAD

2 c. boiling water
1 c. sugar
1 c. chopped dates
1 tsp. salt
2 T. shortening
2 tsp. soda

1 egg, beaten
2 tsp. baking powder
1 c. chopped nuts
3 c. all-purpose flour
2 tsp. vanilla extract

Pour boiling water over sugar, dates, salt, shortening and soda in a medium mixing bowl. Stir; let cool. Add remaining ingredients. Mix well. Pour batter into 2 greased and floured 8 1/2 x 4 1/2 x 3-inch loaf pans. Bake at 350 degrees for 45 minutes. Yield: 2 loaves.

Mildred Presley
Waller County

Every morning you are handed 24 golden hours. They are one of the few things in this world that you get for free of charge.

If you had all the money in the world, you couldn't buy an extra hour. What will you do with this priceless treasure?

Remember, you must use it, as it is given only once. Once wasted, you cannot get it back.

DILLY BREAD

1 pkg. dry yeast
1/4 c. warm water
1 c. cottage cheese
2 T. sugar
2 T. onion powder

1 T. margarine, softened
2 tsp. dill weed
1 tsp. salt
1/4 tsp. soda
1 egg, unbeaten
2 1/2 c. flour

Combine yeast and warm water. Heat cottage cheese to luke warm and add to yeast mixture; stir well. Mix in remaining ingredients. Mix in flour or enough to make a stiff dough. Add flour gradually, beating well after each addition. Cover and let rise until double in bulk. Stir down and put in well greased loaf pan. Let rise again. Bake at 350 degrees for 40-50 minutes or until nice and brown. Brush with melted margarine. (I used the rapid yeast and it took about 30 minutes to rise each time.)

Hidalgo County

DUTCH LETTERS

Dough:
3/4 lb. butter or oleo
3 c. flour
3/4 c. water or milk

Filling:
1 lb. almond paste (1 2/3 cup)
2 c. sugar
3 eggs
1 T. vanilla

Mix dough ingredients together well, as it will be soupy. Refrigerate overnight. When ready to bake, divide dough and filling into 8 parts. Roll pieces into 8 oblong shapes and put 1 part of filling on each piece. Lap dough over each side and end. Pinch shut. Brush tops with **1 beaten egg** and **1 tablespoonful sugar** mixed. Punch holes on top with toothpick. Put on greased cookie sheet and bake at 375 degrees for 30 minutes. (I double the dough, not filling, and divide everything into 16 parts.)

Thressa Van Rees
Hidalgo County

HUNDRED YEAR OLD GINGERBREAD

1 c. sorghum molasses
1/2 c. shortening (butter or lard)
2 eggs
2 tsp. baking soda
2 tsp. cinnamon
1/2 tsp. ground cloves

1 c. sugar
1 c. buttermilk
3 c. flour
2 tsp. ginger
1 tsp. allspice
1/2 tsp. nutmeg

Cream shortening and sugar together; add molasses and well-beaten eggs. Sift flour with soda and spices. Add to first mixture alternately with milk. Beat hard until batter is thoroughly mixed. Warm and grease large (10-inch) iron skillet, pour in batter. Bake in moderate (350 degree) oven 50 minutes or until done. (Very good...I made this in an oblong cake pan and it was very good. This is my mother's recipe.)

Marie Harris
Hamilton County

IRISH SODA BREAD

1 1/2 c. buttermilk
2 T. butter, melted
1 lg. egg, lightly beaten
1 1/3 c. raisins
1 tsp. caraway seed (opt.)

3 c. flour
2/3 c. sugar
1 tsp. baking powder
1 tsp. soda
1 tsp. salt

Place first 5 ingredients in bowl. Toss dry ingredients together. Add buttermilk mix and stir to combine. Will be thick. Spoon into round pan. Cut cross in top 1/2-inch deep. Bake 50-55 minutes in 350 degree oven.

Geraldine Dalton
Jasper County

LEMON BREAD

1/2 c. butter
1 c. sugar
2 eggs
1 2/3 c. all-purpose flour
3/4 c. buttermilk

1 1/2 tsp. lemon peel, finely
    shredded or 1 tsp. lemon
    extract
1/2 tsp. soda
1/4 tsp. salt
1/3 c. nuts, chopped

Mix sugar and butter. Add eggs one at a time. Add flour, buttermilk, lemon peel, soda and salt. Beat just until moistened. Add nuts; mix. Bake in a greased loaf pan at 350 degrees for about 40-45 minutes. Cool in pan on wire rack for 10 minutes. Remove from pan and pour glaze over it.

GLAZE

3 T. lemon juice   1 T. sugar

Waliska Couch
Johnson County

MOZZARELLA CHEESE BREAD

1 loaf French Bread, sliced lengthwise
1/2 c. butter or margarine, softened
1/2 c. mayonnaise or salad dressing

2 c. Mozzarella cheese, grated
1 c. black olives, chopped
Garlic powder to taste

Spread both sides of bread with mixture of butter and mayonnaise. Top with Mozzarella cheese, olives and garlic powder. Bake at 400 degrees for 10-15 minutes or until cheese melts.

Cara Wilkens
Ochiltree County

*We are never more discontented with others
than we are discontented with ourselves.*

PORK 'N BEAN BREAD

2 c. granulated sugar	1 tsp. ground cinnamon
1 c. vegetable oil	1/2 tsp. baking powder
3 eggs	1/2 tsp. baking soda
1 16-oz. can pork and beans, drained	1 c. raisins
and mashed	1 tsp. vanilla extract
2 c. all-purpose flour	

Preheat oven to 325 degrees. In a large bowl, mix sugar, oil, eggs, and beans, beating until smooth. In a separate bowl, combine next four ingredients. Add to bean mixture, stirring just until combines. Stir in raisins and vanilla. Fill 5 greased and floured 16-ounce cans 2/3 full with batter.* Place cans on baking sheet and bake 45-50 minutes, testing for doneness with a toothpick. Cool completely on a wire rack before removing bread from cans.

Bread may also be baked in two 8 1/2 x 4 1/2 x 2 3/4-inch loaf pans at 325 degrees for 50-55 minutes. Yield: 5 cans or two loaves of bread.

*NOTE: If desired, open each can, leaving lid attached at point. Bend each lid away from can opening to allow bread to rise while baking.

Marie Denton
Collin County

PUMPKIN BREAD

1 1/2 c. white sugar	1 1/2 c. brown sugar
4 eggs	4 tsp. cinnamon
1 c. oil	1/4 tsp. ginger
2 tsp. nutmeg	1/2 tsp. cloves
1/2 tsp. mace	1/2 tsp. salt
2 tsp. soda	2/3 c. water
3 1/2 c. flour	2 c. (#303 can) pumpkin

Mix as cake. Pour into 4 1-pound greased and floured coffee cans and bake at 350 degrees for about one hour. Pecans may be added. HINT: Fill cans or pans only half full.

Oleta Raper

We may live without poetry,
music and art,
We may live without con-
science and live without heart,
We may live without friends,
we may live without books,
But civilized men may not live
without cooks.

PUMPKIN CHOCOLATE CHIP BREAD

1/2 c. butter or margarine, softened
1 c. sugar
2 eggs
1 1/4 c. canned pumpkin
2 c. flour
1 tsp. baking soda
1 tsp. ground cinnamon

1/2 tsp. ground nutmeg
1/2 tsp. pumpkin pie spice
1/4 tsp. ground cloves
1/4 tsp. ground ginger
1/4 c. chocolate chips
1/4 c. walnuts, chopped

In a large mixing bowl, cream butter. Gradually add sugar, eggs and pumpkin. Combine dry ingredients; stir into creamed mixture and blend well. Stir in chocolate chips and nuts. Pour into a greased and floured 9 x 5 x 3-inch loaf pan. Bake at 350 degrees for 45-50 minutes or until loaf tests done. Cool on a wire rack.

GLAZE

1 T. heavy cream   1/2 c. confectioners' sugar

Combine glaze ingredients and drizzle over cooled bread. YIELD: 1 loaf.

Eulus Damron
Dawson County

STRAWBERRY BREAD WITH CREAM CHEESE SPREAD

3 c. flour
2 c. sugar
1 tsp. soda
1 tsp. salt
1 tsp. cinnamon

4 eggs, well beaten
2 10-oz. pkgs. frozen strawberries, thawed (reserve 1/2 c.
juice)
1 c. oil

Combine all dry ingredients and mix well. Make a well in the center of mixture and pour all liquid ingredients into it. Mix by hand. Grease and flour two 8 x 4-inch loaf pans. Pour mixture into pans and bake at 350 degrees for 1 hour or until tester inserted in center comes out clean. Can be frozen. Slice thinly before completely thawed.

CREAM CHEESE SPREAD

Combine 1 8-ounce package softened cream cheese with enough reserved strawberry juice to make a spreadable mixture. Cut bread very thin and spread with cream cheese mixture to make sandwiches. Refrigerate until served.

Ann Stickney
Harris County

A kitchen is a friendly place,
Full of livings daily grace,
And rich in dignity is she
Who shares its hospitality.

STRAWBERRY NUT BREAD

3 c. flour	4 eggs
1 tsp. soda	1 1/4 c. oil
1 tsp. salt	2 c. strawberries, thawed and
1 tsp. cinnamon	sliced
2 c. sugar	1/2 - 1 c. pecans

Combine dry ingredients. Add oil, eggs, strawberries and pecans. Stir until batter is moist. Spoon into 2 well greased 9 1/2 x 3-inch loaf pans. Bake at 300 degrees for 60-70 minutes. Do not overcook. This recipe is also good for bananas, sweet potato and pumpkin. Freezes well.

Margaret Jordan
Tyler County

CREOLE TOMATO BREAD
(For Bread Making Machine)

1 pkg. yeast	2 T. diced canned pimentos,
2 3/4 c. Better for Bread flour	drained
2 T. gluten	1 T. dried minced onion
1 1/4 tsp. garlic salt	1/2 of 1 10 3/4-oz. can con-
1 tsp. chili powder	densed Tomato soup (1/2 c.
1 tsp. paprika	+ 1 T.)
1/8 tsp. bakng soda	1 egg
1/8 tsp. cayenne pepper	1 T. vegetable oil
1/2 c. fresh mushrooms, sliced	2 tsp. molasses
1/4 c. fresh celery, finely chopped	2/3 c. V-8 vegetable juice,
1/4 c. fresh red bell pepper,	heated
finely chopped	

Add all ingredients into the pan in the order listed. Select white bread and push "Start."

Kohler Krafters
Brown County

A Mother's Prayer

Give me patience when little hands tug at me with ceaseless small demands.
Give me gentle words and smiling eyes, and keep my lips from hasty replies.
Let me not in weariness, confusion or noise obscure my vision from life's fleeting joys.
That when in years to come, my house is still beautiful memories, its rooms may fill.

QUICK AND EASY NUT BREAD

4 c. flour	1 egg
1 c. sugar	1 1/2 c. milk
4 tsp. baking powder	1 c. nuts, chopped
1/2 tsp. salt	No shortening
1/2 tsp. cinnamon or nutmeg (opt.)	

Sift dry ingredients together. Use about 1 teaspoonful flour to coat nuts. Beat egg, add milk and beat together. Add dry ingredients. Mix well with spoon. Stir in nuts. Pour into 2 greased and floured medium loaf pans (about 8 1/2 x 4 1/2 x 2-inch). Batter will be very stiff. Let stand for 20 minutes. Bake in slow oven 275-300 degrees for 1 hour or until toothpick inserted in center comes out clean.

This is an old recipe-probably at least 75 years old. My aunt baked this in the 20's. I remember eating it when I was small. She usually sliced the bread, buttered it and toasted it in the oven for a delicious treat.

Mickey Gibbins
Montague County

WHOLE WHEAT SHORTBREAD

1/2 c. butter, softened	6 T. all-purpose flour
1/3 c. confectioners sugar	1/4 c. cornstarch
1 T. light brown sugar	1/4 tsp. salt
6 T. whole wheat flour	

Heat oven to 350 degrees. Grease 2 large baking sheets. Using large bowl, with electric mixer, beat butter and sugars until fluffy. Add flours, cornstarch and salt. Beat at low speed, scraping sides of bowl occasionally until well mixed. Divide dough into 4 balls. Place 2 balls on each cookie sheet - leaving 4 inches between. Role or pat each ball until a 1/4-inch thick round. With a fork, pierce center of rounds several times, then using tines of fork - crimp around edges. Bake rounds 10-12 minutes or until edges are golden. Remove baking sheets from oven to wire racks, immediately cut each round into 8 wedges. Cool cookies on baking sheets or wire racks. Store in air-tight container.

Betty Fay
Winkler County

Make peace with what has happened,
don't foolishly regret it.
A blunder has no power,
as soon as you forget it.

ZUCCHINI BREAD

2 c. flour	2 c. sugar
2 tsp. soda	1 c. oil
1 T. cinnamon	1 T. vanilla
1/4 tsp. baking powder	2 c. grated zucchini squash
1 tsp. salt	(about 1 lb.)
3 eggs	1 c. pecans, chopped

Sift together flour, soda, cinnamon, baking powder and salt. Set aside. Peel and grate zucchini squash. Set aside. Chop pecans. Set aside. In large mixing bowl, beat eggs until frothy; add sugar, oil and vanilla; beat until thick and lemon colored. Stir in grated zucchini squash. Blend in flour mixture. Fold in pecans. Pour into 4 greased and floured loaf pans (7 1/2 x 3 3/4 x 2 1/3-inches). Bake at 350 degrees for 45 minutes to 1 hour. Cool on rack before removing from pans.

Bettye Jane Dodds
Wise County

Biscuits

BISCUITS

2 c. unbleached flour	2 tsp. sugar
4 tsp. baking powder	1/4 c. butter or oil
1/2 tsp. salt	3/4 c. milk
1/2 tsp. cream of tartar	

Stir together the dry ingredients and cut in the butter until crumbly. Add milk all at once and stir quickly with a fork. Form dough into a ball. Roll out on floured surface to 1/4-inch or 1/2-inch thick and cut with biscuit cutter or glass. Bake on ungreased cookie sheet for 10-12 minutes in 450 degree oven.

Shirley Ashley
Willacy County

SOUR CREAM BISCUITS

2 c. flour	1 c. sour cream
1/2 tsp. salt	1/2 tsp. baking soda
1/4 c. shortening	

Cut shortening into flour and salt mixture. Add baking soda to sour cream and combine with flour mixture to make a soft dough. Pat into 1/2-inch thickness, cut and bake 15 minutes at 425 degrees. Makes 12 biscuits.

Georgia Schmidt
San Patricio/Aransas County

Bran Breads

BRAN BREAD

1 c. boiling water	2 eggs
1 c. shortening	3/4 c. sugar
1 c. All Bran Cereal	1 1/2 tsp. salt
2 pkgs. dry yeast	6 c. flour
1 c. warm water	

Mix first 3 ingredients and set aside until warm. Mix yeast with warm water. Beat eggs in a bowl. Add sugar and salt. Mix in yeast and bran mixtures. Add flour. Let rise 1 hour, then work down and put into greased pans. Let rise for 1-1 1/2 hours. Bake at 325 degrees until done. Makes 3 loaves.

Susan Brady
Wood County

ORANGE-RAISIN BRAN BREAD

1 1/2 c. flour	1/2 c. orange juice
1 c. sugar	3 T. oil
1 T. baking powder	2 T. grated orange peel
1/4 tsp. salt	2 c. bran flakes
2 egg whites	1/4 c. raisins
1 c. skim milk	

Heat oven to 350 degrees. Mix flour, sugar, baking powder and salt in large bowl. Beat egg whites in small bowl; stir in milk, orange juice, oil and orange peel. Add to flour mixture. Stir just until moistened. (Batter will be lumpy.) Stir in cereal and raisins. Pour into greased 9 x 5-inch loaf pan. Bake 1 hour or until toothpick inserted in center comes out clean. Cool 10 minutes. Remove from pan.

Donna Yates
Bosque County

WORDS

DID is a word of achievement.
WON'T is a word of retreat.
MIGHT is a word of bereavement.
CAN'T is a word of defeat.
OUGHT is a word of duty.
TRY is a word of each hour.
WILL is a word of beauty.
CAN is a word of power.

Corn Breads

HUSH PUPPIES

1 c. cornmeal	1 tsp. or 1 T. sugar
1 c. flour	2 eggs
1 tsp. salt	2 T. milk to make real stiff
2 tsp. baking powder	dough

Add:

1 onion, chopped

1 ripe tomato, chopped (use all of tomato and its juice as this is where the liquid is)

Drop by teaspoonfuls in medium to hot oil (doesn't have to be deep oil).

Margaret Lively
Llana County

CORN BREAD FOR BREAD BAKER

1 1/2 c. flour (bread)	1 egg
3/4 c. corn meal	2 T. oil
1 1/2 tsp. yeast (Rapid Rise)	1 T. sugar
2 tsp. cumin	2/3 c. water
2 tsp. chili powder	1/2 c. whole kernel corn
2 T. parsley flakes	

Add all ingredients in bread tub, except corn. Set Baker to notify when corn can be added (according to "addition of fruits, nuts, etc. to dough").

Nacogodoches County

CORN BREAD

1 c. corn meal	1 egg
1 c. flour	1 c. milk
1/4 c. sugar	1/4 c. Crisco
4 tsp. baking powder	1/2 tsp. salt

Mix all ingredients well. Bake at 400 degrees for about 15 or 20 minutes.

Elizabeth Todd
Sabine County

Good judgement comes from experience.
Experience comes from bad judgement.

GREEN CHILI COUNTRY CORN BREAD

2 c. corn meal
1 tsp. soda
1/2 tsp. salt
1 10 3/4-oz. can condensed golden
  corn soup
4 eggs, beaten

1 1/2 c. milk or buttermilk
1/3 c. vegetable oil
1 or 2 4-oz. cans green chilies,
  chopped
2 c. shredded cheddar cheese
  (divided)

Mix corn meal, soda and salt; set aside. Mix corn soup, beaten eggs, milk and vegetable oil. Combine 2 mixes together just until dry ingredients are moistened. Stir in chopped green chilies and 1 cup shredded cheddar cheese. Pour into greased 9 x 13-inch pan and sprinkle with 1 cup shredded cheddar cheese. Bake at 350 degrees for 35-40 minutes or until toothpick inserted in center comes out clean. Serves 12.

Bernice Wells
Pecos County

JALAPENO CORN BREAD

2 c. yellow cornmeal
3 tsp. baking powder
3 T. sugar
2 1/2 c. milk
1 c. sharp cheddar cheese, grated

1 c. jalapenos, sliced
1 c. flour
1 tsp. salt
3 eggs, beaten
1 can cream style corn

Stir all together. It needs to be cooked in an 11 x 17-inch pan that has a generous amount of bacon grease. Oven should be at 450 degrees and it should be cooked until it is done.

Georgia Langford
Stephens County

JALAPENO CORN BREAD

1 c. cornmeal
2/3 c. buttermilk
1/2 tsp. soda
1/2 tsp. salt
1/3 c. shortening, melted

2 eggs
1 c. cheese, grated
3 jalapenos, mashed
1 c. whole kernel corn

Mix and pour into hot greased pan. Bake at 375 degrees until done and brown.

Betty Wilson
San Augustine County

A friend is a present you give yourself.

MEXICAN CORN BREAD

1/2 c. flour	1/2 c. oil
1 c. meal*	1/2 tsp. salt
2/3 c. buttermilk	1/2 tsp. soda
1 c. corn	2 eggs
1 c. cheese, grated	1/2 c. onions, chopped
Hot pepper to taste	

Mix and bake at 400 degrees for 25-30 minutes or until brown. *I use stone ground meal.

Violet Bass
Harrison County

NO FAIL CORN BREAD

1 c. Buttermilk Pancake Mix	1 tsp. baking powder
1 1/2 c. white cornmeal	1 c. water

Pour into greased, preheated 8 x 12-inch baking pan or dish. Bake at 375 degrees for 25-30 minutes.

Roadrunners E. H. Club
Caldwell County

SPICEY CORN BREAD

1 can Campbell's Corn Soup	2 6-oz. pkgs. Corn Bread Mix
2 eggs	1/4 lb. hot sausage
1/4 c. milk	

Brown sausage, drain off fat. Set aside. Combine eggs, soup, corn bread mix and milk. Mix well, fold in sausage. Bake in 9-inch greased pan for 20 minutes or until done in 400 degree oven.

Helen May
Brown County

BROCCOLI CORN BREAD

1 10-oz. pkg. frozen chopped broccoli, thawed	1 tsp. salt
1 med. onion, chopped	3 eggs, beaten
6-oz. chottage cheese (3/4 c.)	1 box Jiffy Corn Bread Muffin Mix
1/2 c. oleo (1 stick), melted	

Mix broccoli, onion, cottage cheese, oleo and salt. Add beaten eggs. Add dry corn bread mix last. Grease 9 x 13-inch pan. Bake at 400 degrees for 30 minutes or until slightly brown. Good hot or cold. Freezes well.

Nettie Freeling
Wilbarger County

Alice Beth Lee from Williamson County uses 4 beaten eggs, 1 large onion, 8-ounces cottage cheese and 1 cup shredded cheddar cheese on top.
Cecelia Schueler from Parmer County uses 1/2 cup chopped onion, 12-ounces cottage cheese, 4 eggs and 1 cup grated cheese on top.

BROCCOLI CORN BREAD

2 boxes Jiffy Corn Bread Mix
4 eggs
1 c. cottage cheese
1 pkg. frozen broccoli, chopped
   and thawed

1 c. onion, diced
2 sticks oleo (or 1 c. vegetable
   oil)

   Bake at 350 degrees for 45 minutes.

Bert Hancock
Hays County

Minnie Lee Wells from Martin County adds 1/4 cup water and bakes for 35 minutes or until done.
Nancy Higgins and **Virginia Humphrey** from Scurry County use 1 small onion and bake in 9 x 13-inch pan for 1 hour.

BROCCOLI CORN BREAD

2 pkgs. corn bread mix
1 med. onion, chopped
1 stick oleo
4 eggs

1 8-oz. carton sour cream
1 box chopped broccoli
1 tsp. baking powder

   Mix all ingredients and pour into a 9 x 13-inch greased pan. Bake at 350 degrees for 45 minutes.

LaVerne Charbula
Wharton County

BROCCOLI CORN BREAD

1 10-oz. box broccoli, thawed
1 c. onion, chopped
1 stick margarine, melted
4 eggs, slightly beaten

2 pkgs. corn bread mix
1 8-oz. cottage cheese (small
   curd)

   Mix in order given. Bake in 9 x 13-inch pan for 20-25 minutes at 400 degrees.

Linda Kinter
Tarrant County

BROCCOLI CORN BREAD

2 pkgs. Jiffy corn bread mix
1 10-oz. pkg. frozen chopped broccoli,
   drained
10 oz. cottage cheese (low fat)

4 eggs (1 carton Egg Beaters)
1 med. onion, chopped
1 1/2 sticks oleo (soft-low fat)

   Heat oleo and mix with corn bread mix and then pour back into hot skillet and bake until good and brown at 375 degrees.

Bettie Roberson
Nederland County

BROCCOLI CORN BREAD

1 box chopped broccoli, thawed	2 c. cottage cheese
1 med. onion, chopped	2 boxes corn bread mix
1 stick margarine, melted	4 large eggs

Mix onion, margarine and cottage cheese in a large bowl. Add and mix, 1 at a time, the boxes of corn bread mix. Beat eggs in 1 at a time. Add and stir in broccoli with all its juice. Bake at 400 degrees for 40 minutes in a well-greased 9 x 13-inch pan.

Linda Cook & Laurene White
Kleberg County

BROCCOLI CORN BREAD

1 stick margarine, melted	1 12-oz. carton small curd
4 eggs, beaten	cottage cheese
2 boxes Jiffy Corn Bread Mix	1 pkg. (10-oz.) chopped broccoli

Mix and bake in 9 x 13-inch pan at 425 degrees for 40 minutes. Can half recipe and bake in 8-inch square pan.

Sabra Patterson
Jones County

BROCCOLI CORN BREAD

2 pkgs. Jiffy Corn Bread Mix	4 eggs, beaten
1 c. small curd cottage cheese	1/2 stick margarine, melted
1 pkg. chopped broccoli	1/2 tsp. salt
1 c. chopped onion	

Mix together and bake in an oblong pan at 350 degrees for 45 minutes.

Stella Williams
Leon County

TAKE TIME FOR 10 THINGS

1. *Take time to work -- it is the price of success.*
2. *Take time to think -- it is the source of power.*
3. *Take time to play -- it is the secret of youth.*
4. *Take time to read -- it is the foundation of knowledge.*
5. *Take time to worship -- it is the highway of reverence and washes the dust of earth from our eyes.*
6. *Take time to help and enjoy friends -- it is the source of happiness.*
7. *Take time to love -- it is the one sacrament of life.*
8. *Take time to dream -- it hitches the soul to the stars.*
9. *Take time to laugh -- it is the singing that helps with life's loads.*
10. *Take time to plan -- it is the secret of being able to have time to take time for the first nine things.*

Muffins

FRESH APPLE MUFFINS

3 baking apples (Granny Smith   1/4 c. whole wheat flour
   or Rome Beauty)   3/4 tsp. baking soda
1 c. vegetable oil   1 tsp. baking powder
1 1/2 c. sugar   1/2 tsp. salt
3 eggs   1/8 tsp. nutmeg
1 tsp. vanilla   1/8 tsp. cinnamon
2 c. all-purpose flour

Preheat oven to 350 degrees. Lightly grease 18 muffin pans. Peel, core and grate apples, set aside. In large bowl, combine vegetable oil, sugar and eggs; beat until creamy. Mix in vanilla. In separate bowl, combine flours, baking soda, baking powder, salt, nutmeg and cinnamon. Slowly add dry ingredients to creamed mixture, mixing well. Stir in grated apples. Pour batter in greased muffin pan filling each 1/3 full. Sprinkle with streusel topping. Bake 20-25 minutes or until golden and top springs back when touched. Makes 18 muffins.

STREUSEL TOPPING

1/4 c. sugar   1 T. vegetable oil
1 tsp. cinnamon

In a small bowl combine sugar and cinnamon. Drizzle vegetable oil over mixture. Stir with fork until crumbly. Sprinkle on top of muffins.

Maryanne Fleitman
Cooke County

APPLE-DATE-NUT MUFFINS

1/2 c. butter or oleo   1 tsp. cinnamon
1 c. Sugar Twin   1/2 tsp. cloves
1 egg, well beaten   Pinch of salt
1 tsp. vanilla   2 tsp. soda
1 1/2 c. apple sauce (sugar free)   1 c. pecans, chopped
2 c. flour   1 c. dates, chopped

Cream butter and Sugar Twin; add egg, apple sauce and vanilla. Save a little flour to dredge dates and pecans. Add dry ingredients to butter mixture. Mix well. Fold in dates and pecans. Bake in greased loaf pan for 30 minutes in 350 degree oven. For cupcakes or muffins, bake less time. Use toothpick test for doneness. (Safe for diabetics.)

Leta Casey
McCulloch County

Kindness is becoming at any age.

ORANGE MUFFINS

1 c. orange juice
1 T. orange peel
1/2 c. raisins, soaked
1/3 c. sugar replacement
1 T. margarine
1 egg

1/4 tsp. salt
1 tsp. baking soda
1 tsp. baking powder
1/2 tsp. vanilla
2 c. flour

Soak raisins in orange juice and orange peel for 1 hour. Cream sugar replacement, margarine and egg; add salt, baking soda, baking powder and vanilla. Stir in orange juice mixture. Add flour. Bake in muffin tins at 350 degrees for 25 minutes or until done.

Dorothy Kavanaugh
Hamilton County

Rolls

AUSTRIAN TWISTS

3 c. flour, sifted
1 pkg. dry yeast, sprinkled over flour
2 sticks oleo or butter

1 c. sour cream
3 eggs yolks

Cut oleo or butter into flour mixture. Mix in egg yolks and sour cream. Mix well and shape into ball. Refrigerate overnight.

Mix:

1 c. sugar
1 1/2 tsp. cinnamon

1 c. nuts, finely chopped

Divide batter into 4 parts. Place 1/4 of cinnamon, sugar, and nut mixture on dough board and 1/4 dough on top of this. Roll the dough into sugar mixture in shape of circle. Cut into 16 equal parts like a pie. Begin with large end and roll toward point. Bake at 350 degrees for 15 minutes. Dribble with icing if desired.

Mary Lou Kelly
Hays County

She measured out the butter with a very solemn air,
The milk and sugar also, and she took the greatest care,
To count the eggs correctly, and to add a little bit,
Of baking powder, which you know beginners oft omit.
Then she stirred it all together and baked it for an hour,
But she never quite forgave herself for leaving out the flour!

BREAD LOGS, LOAF OR ROLLS

1 pkg. active dry yeast
1 tsp. sugar
1/2 c. very warm water (110-115 degrees)
1 3/4 c. lukewarm water (may use potato water or scalded and cooled milk)

3 T. sugar
2 tsp. salt
4 T. melted shortening
7-7 1/4 c. flour (for whole wheat bread, use 1/2 whole wheat flour)

In a small mixing bowl, dissolve 1 teaspoonful sugar with 1/2 c. very warm water. (Water will feel very warm when dropped on wrist.) Sprinkle in the yeast and set aside. (This starts the yeast acting.) In a large mixing bowl, mix together lukewarm water, sugar, salt and melted shortening. Stir yeast in small bowl. Add to mixture in large bowl. (Be sure mixture in large bowl is not too hot. If either waters are too hot, bread will taste yeasty.) Add flour to liquid mixture 3 cups at a time. Mix well. Mix in enough flour until dough cleans the bowl. Turn dough onto floured board or cloth. Let rest 10-15 minutes. Knead until smooth and blistered, about 10 minutes. Place in greased bowl, turning once to bring greased side up. Cover with a cloth. Let rise in warm place (85 degrees) until double, about 1 hour. Punch down, cover and rise again, 30-45 minutes. Punch down, turn onto floured board or cloth. Make into rolls or loaves as desired.

For rolls: Roll dough to 1/2-inch thick; using biscuit cutter, cut out and place on greased pan making sure edges do not touch. Let rise until doubled and bake at 425 degrees for 20-25 minutes.

For loaves: Divide equally and shape into loaves. Place into 9 x 5 x 3-inch greased pans. Let rise until doubled and bake at 425 degrees for 25-30 minutes.

Whole Wheat Chili Cheese Logs: When mixing, use 1/2 whole wheat flour. After second rising, divide dough in half. Roll thin (less than 1/2-inch thick). Spread with Chili Mix (see below). Sprinkle with 1-1 1/2 cups grated cheddar cheese. Start on shortest end of dough and roll up dough as a jelly roll. Roll as tight as possible. Gently lift onto greased cookie sheet, placing seam side down. Let rise 30-40 minutes. Bake at 425 degrees, 30-35 minutes.

Whole Wheat Cream Cheese Log: When mixing, use 1/2 whole wheat flour. After second rising, divide dough in half. Roll thin (less than 1/2-inch thick). Spread with Cream Cheese Mixture (see below). Sprinkle with 1 cup chopped pecans or walnuts (optional). Start on shortest end and roll dough up as a jelly roll. Roll as tight as possible. Gently lift onto a greased cookie sheet, placing seam side down. Let rise 30-40 minutes. Bake at 425 degrees for 30-35 minutes.

continued on next page

continued from page 42

CHILI MIX

1 large onion   1 4-oz. can green chilies

Saute onion in water. Cool and mix with green chilies

CREAM CHEESE MIXTURE

1 8-oz. pkg. cream cheese, softened   1 tsp. vanilla
1/2 c. sugar

Mix together until well blended. May sprinkle cheese with cinnamon.

Carolyn Cook
Ward County

DILLY CASSEROLE BREAD

1 pkg. active dry yeast   2 T. butter, melted
1/4 c. lukewarm water   1 egg
1 c. creamed cottage cheese, lukewarm 1 tsp. salt
2 T. sugar   1/4 tsp. soda
1 T. minced dry onion   3 c. all-purpose flour
2 tsp. dill seed

Preheat oven to 350 degrees. Dissolve yeast in lukewarm water. Combine cottage cheese, sugar, onion, dill seed, butter, egg, salt and soda. Add yeast. Stir in flour, about 1/2 at a time, mixing well after each addition. Let rise in a warm place until doubled (approximately 50-60 minutes). Work down. Knead lightly on well floured board. Place in a well greased casserole dish. Let rise again until doubled (approximately 30-40 minutes). Bake at 350 degrees 45-50 minutes or until golden brown. Brush with soft butter and sprinkle with coarse salt.

Robbie Wyatt
Kent County

RECIPE FOR A HAPPY DAY

Mix together the following ingredients: One full measure of chirping, trilling, birdsong, four quick sprites of gentle, soft spring mist, the sparkling glow in a loved one's look, the enjoyment of a friend's visit. Add the softness of a cuddly, drowsy kitten, the trust and devotion in a puppy's eyes, the festive twinkling of Christmas lights, the whisper of the leaves in a gentle breeze, the bubbling, gurgling murmur of gently flowing water. Fold in five large white, billowy clouds that have been thoroughly laced with early June sunshine. Sprinkle liberally with joyous children's laughter. Bake in the cozy warmth of a snowy, blowy winter evening's kitchen, surrounded by your dear ones.

BUTTERHORNS

1 pkg. active dry yeast	1/2 c. sugar
4 1/2-4 3/4 c. flour	1/2 c. oleo
1 c. milk	3 eggs

In large mixing bowl, combine yeast and 2 3/4 cups flour. In saucepan, heat milk, sugar and oleo just until warm, stirring to melt oleo. (Do not get too hot.) Add to flour mixture. Add eggs. Beat at low speed for 1/2 minute, scraping bowl. Beat 3 more minutes at high speed. By hand, knead in enough remaining flour to make a soft dough that is smooth and elastic, about 5-8 minutes. Place dough in greased bowl turning once to grease surface. Cover and let rise until double. Divide dough into 3 portions, roll each into a 12-inch circle. Brush with melted butter. Cut into 12 pie shaped wedges. Start at wide end of wedge and roll up toward point. Place on greased baking sheet, point down, and brush with melted oleo. Let rise until double, about 1 hour. Bake at 400 degrees for 10-12 minutes. Makes 3 dozen.

Luling E. H. Club
Caldwell County

CINNAMON ROLLS
(Using Cake Mix)

2 1/2 c. warm water	3 eggs
2 pkgs. yeast	1/3 c. oil
1 tsp. sugar	1 tsp. salt
1 yellow cake mix	1 c. flour

Mix water, yeast and sugar; let stand for 5 minutes. Add remaining ingredients and beat with mixer for 5 minutes. Remove from mixer and add 5 cups flour; mix well. Put out on board and knead well. Let dough rise. Divide into 2 parts and shape into cinnamon rolls or your favorite dinner roll. Let rolls rise until double and bake in 350 degree oven until slightly brown.

Pet Ott
Deaf Smith County

The good old things have passed away in silent sad retreat.
We have lots of high-flutting things but nothing much to eat.
And while I never say a word and always pleasant look--
You bet, I've had dysplasias since my daughters learned to cook!

HOT ROLLS

2 compressed yeast cakes
1/2 c. lukewarm water
4 T. shortening, melted
4 T. sugar
1 1/2 tsp. salt
2 c. sweet milk
5-6 c. flour, sifted

Mix yeast cakes in lukewarm water. Let stand while preparing the following:

Add melted shortening, sugar, and salt to sweet milk. Heat until lukewarm and sugar and salt are dissolved. Add yeast cake mixture to milk mixture and mix well.

Sift flour in large mixing bowl. Make a well, or hole in the flour and mix as you would if you were making biscuits. Mix in enough flour to make a soft dough. Turn dough on floured bowl and knead in flour remaining in bowl.

Slightly grease a deep bowl. Put rolled dough in greased pan and just work around in pan, making sure dough will be slightly oily. Cover with clean cup towel and allow dough to double in bulk. Punch down and turn on floured board. Roll and cut or pinch dough off to make rolls. Place on cookie sheet or in regular biscuit pan and let rise for about 2 hours, or as high as you want them to be.

Bake at 425 degrees until well done and browned good on top and bottom. This dough can be kept in the refrigerator for three days. Grease top of dough and cover. Keep punching the dough down occasionally.

Rusk County

"FOOL PROOF" ICE BOX ROLLS

2 yeast cakes or 2 pkgs. dry yeast
1 T. sugar
1/4 c. lukewarm water
1 c. shortening
1/2 c. sugar (3/4 c. if used for tea ring or sweet rolls)
1 tsp. salt
1 1/4 c. boiling water
1 c. cold water
2 eggs, beaten
7 c. flour

Combine yeast and sugar in lukewarm water and let stand until dissolved. Pour boiling water over shortening, sugar and salt; stir until the shortening is melted. Add cold water. Mix well. Add yeast mixture, then add eggs and beat in 4 cups flour. Beat about 2 minutes with electric mixer, then add 3 cups flour. Mix this with a spoon as the mixer will not mix this stiff dough. Cover and place in refrigerator and punch down every hour or two. If made in the morning, you can have rolls for lunch. Take out the amount of dough needed and store remainder in refrigerator. Make out rolls and let them rise 1 hour or more to double in size. Bake at 350 degrees. The dough may be kept in the refrigerator for 3-4 days or you may make out rolls and bake until barely brown, remove, cool and place in the freezer. DO NOT FREEZE RAW DOUGH.

Mary Allen
Taylor County

HOMEMADE ROLLS

2 pkgs. dry yeast
1 c. warm water
1/2 c. sugar
1 1/2 T. salt

1/2 c. shortening
1 c. warm water
1 c. warm water
1/2 of 5-lb. bag flour

Dissolve dry yeast in 1 cup warm water. Dissolve sugar, salt and shortening in 1 cup warm water. Add another 1 cup warm water to this liquid. Add yeast and water mixtures together. Add flour or enough for firm consistency. Grease pans with shortening. Mix and knead dough together until it forms a ball. Put shortening on top so it doesn't dry out. Let rise until double in size. Make rolls and let rise again. Bake at 350 degrees for approximately 30 minutes.

Melody Walker

HOMEMADE BREAD

3 pkgs. dry yeast
1/2 c. warm water
5 c. water
1/2 c. sugar

1/3 c. shortening, melted
4 tsp. salt (or less)
16 c. flour

Sprinkle yeast over 1/2 cup warm water and set aside. Measure 5 cups water, sugar, shortening and salt into a large bowl or pan; add 5 cups flour and mix. Add yeast and continue to mix. Add remaining flour, a cup or two at a time, until dough is not sticky. Put (or leave) in bowl, cover and let rise until double. Punch down and divide into 4 parts, knead. Shape into loaf size and put into greased bread pan that has been sprinkled lightly with cornmeal. Cover; let rise until double in size. Bake at 350-375 degrees. Tap the top of the golden bread—if sounds hollow, it is done (or about 45 minutes). Brush with butter, cool and eat or freeze. Makes four large loaves.

Lee Nell Boenig
Refugio County

YEAST ROLLS

2 c. milk
3/4 c. white sugar
3/4 c. vegetable shortening
2 tsp. salt

1 c. warm water
2 tsp. or 2 pkgs. dry yeast
6 c. flour

In a good size pan (about 4 quarts), combine milk, sugar, shortening and salt and heat until dissolved. Stir. Set aside and let cool. In a bowl, dissolve yeast in warm water. Add milk mixture to yeast mixture, then add all 6 cups flour. If this is not enough flour, add more. Mix well with hands. Let rise about 2 hours, leaving in the same pan. Make dough into biscuits. Freeze extra dough. To freeze, put in a pie pan (don't let them rise). Cover with foil and put in freezer. When you take them out to bake, let rise about 4 hours. Bake at 350 degrees or until brown on top. Butter tops of rolls when you take them out of the oven.

Willie Featherston
Harris County

NO-KNEAD CRESCENT ROLLS

1/4 c. warm water	1/2 c. sugar
1 T. sugar	1 tsp. salt
1 pkg. dry yeast	5 1/2 c. all-purpose flour
4 eggs	1/2 c. shortening, melted
1 c. warm water	

Mix together 1/4 cup warm water, 1 tablespoonful sugar and dry yeast; let stand. In large mixing bowl, combine eggs, 1 cup warm water, 1/2 cup sugar and salt; beat 2 minutes. Add 3 cups flour. Blend well. Add yeast mixture and then 1 cup flour. Add shortening. Hand mix the rest of the flour. Cover and place in refrigerator overnight.

Next day, place on well-floured board. Divide. Roll each half as pie crust and brush with melted butter. Cut as pie into 16 wedges. Roll each from large end. Place on well-greased baking sheet. Let double in size, about 1 1/2-2 hours. Bake at 400 degrees for 10 minutes, then lower heat to 375 degrees for 5 minutes more. Brush with melted butter and cool on rack. Makes 32 rolls.

Maxine E. Jack
Bee County

RANCH ROLLS OR BISCUIT

2 c. buttermilk	1 pkg. dry yeast
1/2 c. water	5 1/2-6 c. flour (this includes
1/2 c. Crisco	flour for kneading)
1/2 c. sugar	1 tsp. soda
1 1/2 tsp. salt	4 tsp. baking powder

In a 3 quart saucepan, heat buttermilk, water and Crisco. Cool to lukewarm. Add sugar, salt and yeast to milk mixture and stir well. In large bowl, combine 4 3/4 cups flour, soda and baking powder. Add flour mixture to milk mixture a little at a time. Stir well after each addition. Knead well with 3/4 cup flour. Place in large oiled bowl, cover with damp cloth. Let rise 2 hours. Work dough down; make into rolls. Can be baked as biscuits or let rise again and bake at 400 degrees.

Hazel Mathiews
Throckmarton County

The ways then to the heart of men,
Man's not the sinner
Is by a clearly well set board
and by a well-cooked dinner.

RANCH BISCUITS

1 pkg. dry yeast	4 1/2 c. flour
1/2 c. warm water	1/2 c. oil
1/2 tsp. salt	2 T. sugar
1/4 tsp. soda	2 c. buttermilk
4 tsp. baking powder	

Dissolve yeast in warm water. Mix dry ingredients together. Add oil and sugar to yeast mixture. Add half of buttermilk and half of dry ingredients to yeast mixture; mix well. Add remainder of buttermilk and dry ingredients. Let set overnight in refrigerator in air-tight container. Pinch off needed amount and knead in flour. Roll out and make into biscuits. Let set 15-20 minutes before baking at 400 degrees for 20 minutes.

Lockhart E. H. Club
Caldwell County

REFRIGERATOR ROLLS

2 yeast cake compresses or dry yeast	2 tsp. salt
1/2 c. lukewarm water	2 eggs
6 T. shortening	2 c. scalded milk
1/2 c. sugar	8 c. all-purpose flour

Dissolve yeast in water. Mix shortening, sugar and salt in a large bowl. Add eggs and scalded milk; mix together. Add yeast and water mixture; beat thoroughly. Add 3 cups flour and mix completely; mix in remaining flour until dough is easy to handle. Knead until smooth consistency; place in large greased bowl and grease surface of dough. cover and let rise. Punch down and place in refrigerator. Chill 2 hours or overnight. Remove from refrigerator, shape into rolls and place on greased pan. Let rise until doubled, approximately 1-1 1/2 hours. Bake at 400 degrees approximately 12-15 minutes or until golden.

Jessie Lee Hicks
Wharton County

It's a little too little to save,
and a little too much to dump.
And nothing to do but eat it,
that makes the housewife plump.

KOLACHES

1/4 c. sugar	1 tsp. vanilla
2 pkgs. active dry yeast	1 egg
1 tsp. salt	6 c. flour
2 1/2 c. warm milk (110 degrees)	3/4 stick margarine, melted

Dissolve sugar, yeast and salt in 1/2 cup warm milk. Set aside for 5 minutes. Add remaining 2 cups warm milk, vanilla and egg. Mix well. Add flour and mix until dough is soft and elastic. Put in greased bowl and let rise until doubled in size. Mix down and let rise again until double in size again. When risen, roll out on floured surface until about 1/2-inch thick. Using a 3-inch cookie cutter, cut dough and place about 2-inches apart on greased cookie sheet. With 2 fingers, make impression in center of each Kolache; fill with a generous teaspoonful of cottage cheese filling. Brush with melted margarine. Let rise in a warm place for about 1/2 hour. While Kolaches are rising, prepare the following:

CRUMBLE TOPPING

3/4 c. sugar	3/4 stick margarine
1 c. flour	

Mix topping ingredients until crumbly. Sprinkle over Kolaches and bake at 325-350 degrees for about 20 minutes.

COTTAGE CHEESE FILLING

1 16-oz. carton large curd creamy	Sugar to taste
cottage cheese	1 T. butter
2 eggs, beaten	1 T. flour

Mix together ingredients.

Brooke Sikes
Runnels County

MONKEY BREAD

1 c. milk	1 pkg. dry yeast
1/2 c. margarine, quartered	3 1/2 c. flour
1/4 c. sugar	1/2 c. margarine, melted
1 tsp. salt	

Combine milk, 1/2 cup quartered margarine, sugar and salt in saucepan; heat until margarine is melted. Cool to 105-115 degrees; add yeast, stirring until dissolved. Place flour in a large bowl; add milk mixture and stir until well blended. Cover and let rise in a warm place (85 degrees) about 1 hour and 20 minutes or until doubled in bulk. Roll into 1 1/2-inch balls; dip each in melted margarine. Layer balls of dough in a 10-inch, one-piece tube pan or bundt pan. Cover and let rise until doubled in bulk (about 45 minutes). Bake at 375 degrees for 35 minutes. Cool in pan 5 minutes; then invert onto serving plate. Makes 1 10-inch loaf.

Charlotte McNeil
Knox County

MONKEY BREAD

1 pkg. dry yeast
1/2 c. lukewarm water
2 sticks margarine
1/4 c. sugar

1 tsp. salt
1/2 c. evaporated milk
3 1/2 c. flour

Dissolve yeast in warm water. Melt 1 stick margarine. Add sugar, salt and milk to margarine. Stir into yeast mixture. Add flour. Stir until thick. Knead until shiny. Let rise 1 hour. Punch down and roll in rectangular 12 x 18-inch piece. Cut into long strips. Dip each piece into second stick of melted margarine. Arrange in bundt pan. Let rise 1 hour. Bake at 350 degrees for 45 minutes.

Geraldine McIntosh
Wood County

SOUR DOUGH BREAD

1 pkg. dry yeast
1 T. sugar
1/2 c. lukewarm water
1 egg, beaten
2 tsp. salt

1/2 c. cooking oil
1/2 c. sugar
1 c. water
1 c. sour dough
6 c. flour (approx.)

Mix yeast, 1 tablespoonful sugar, and 1/2 cup lukewarm water. Let stand 15 minutes. Add remaining ingredients. Knead until elastic. Put in large bowl, cover with cloth and let rise until double; punch down and let rise again until double. Punch down and make into rolls or bread. Put into greased pans; let rise again. Bake in preheated oven: bread at 240 degrees for 30 minutes; rolls at 350 degrees for 12-15 minutes.

SOUR DOUGH STARTER

3 1/2 c. unsifted, unbleached flour
1 T. sugar

1 pkg. dry yeast
2 c. warm water

Combine flour, sugar and yeast in large bowl. Slowly add warm water and beat until smooth. Cover with transparent wrap and let stand in warm place for 2 days.

HOW TO FEED SOUR DOUGH: Set container of sour dough out at room temperature for 2 or 3 hours (before and after feeding). Feed once a week, but do not wait longer than 7 days to feed. May be fed every other day. Wait 24 hours after feeding before using. Must always have 2 cups starter. **Feed: 1 cup sifted flour, 1 cup milk, 1/3 cup sugar.**

Rosa Gibson
Bowie County

A stranger is just a friend you haven't met yet.

SWEET ROLL DOUGH

4 pkg. yeast	2 sticks margarine
1 c. sugar	1 15-oz. can evaporated milk,
1 tsp. salt	plus enough water for 4 c.
12 c. flour	4 eggs

In a large bowl, mix yeast, sugar, salt and 2 cups flour. In a saucepan, melt margarine; add milk and water. Heat until very warm (110-115 degrees). Stir into dry ingredients until dissolved; add eggs. Stir in enough flour until dough is sticky. Place on floured wax paper and knead for 5 minutes. Placed in greased bowl; cover with a warm wet towel. Let rise until double in size (about 1 1/2 hours). Punch down and let rise again. Shape into rolls and bake 375 degrees for 15-20 minutes. Makes 4 dozen rolls. Suitable for cinnamon rolls or coffee cake.

Laura Teal
Reeves County

SWEET POTATO ROLLS

3 c. whole wheat flour	1 1/4 tsp. salt
3 c. all-purpose flour	1/2 c. oleo or butter, softened
2 pkgs. dry yeast	2 eggs
1 1/2 c. warm water	1 c. sweet potatoes, undrained
1/3 c. brown sugar, firmly packed	

Combine flours, mixing well. Combine yeast and warm water, process to dissolve yeast. Add sugar, salt, butter, eggs, sweet potatoes and 1 cup flour to yeast mixture; blend until smooth. Place remaining flour in large bowl; add yeast mixture, mixing to make a soft dough. Turn dough out on a lightly floured board; knead about 5 minutes or until smooth and elastic. Place in a greased bowl, turning to grease top. Cover with plastic wrap and refrigerate 6 hours or overnight. About 1 hour before baking, divide dough in half. On a lightly floured surface, roll out each half into a 16-inch circle about 1/4-inch thick. Cut each circle into 16 wedges; roll up each wedge, beginning at widest edge. Place wedges on greased baking sheets with point on the bottom. Cover and let rise in warm place about 30 minutes. Bake at 350 degrees for 15 minutes. Yield: 32 rolls.

Linda Blair
Lubbock County

It is always commendable to get in and dig,
but be careful where you throw the dirt.

WHOLE WHEAT BATTER BREAD

1 pkg. dry yeast
1/2 c. warm water
1/8 tsp. ground ginger
3 T. sugar

1 2/3 c. evaporated milk
1 tsp. salt
2 T. salad oil
4-4 1/4 c. whole wheat flour

Dissolve yeast in water in large mixer bowl; blend in ginger and 1 table-spoonful sugar. Let stand in warm place until mixture is bubbly. Stir in remaining sugar, milk, salt and salad oil. With mixer on low speed, beat in flour 1 cup at a time, beating very well after each addition. Add flour until dough is very heavy and stiff, but too sticky to knead. Place dough in a well greased 2-pound coffee can or 2 1-pound coffee cans. Cover with well greased plastic lids. Let covered cans stand in warm place until dough rises and pops off lids. Discard lids and bake in 350 degree oven for 45 minutes for 1-pound cans, or 60 minutes for 2-pound can.

Margaret Caldwell
Panola County

Waffles

YEAST WAFFLES

1/4 c. shortening
1 T. sugar
1 tsp. salt
1 3/4 c. milk, heated to lukewarm

3 eggs
1 pkg. yeast in 1/4 c. warm
water
2 c. flour

Add shortening, sugar and salt to warm milk; mix well. Add eggs and yeast; stir. Add flour, stirring until smooth. Let rise at room temperature for 1 hour or more. Stir down and put in refrigerator overnight or until ready to use.

Margie Simms
District 10 Director

It's good to have money and
the things that money can buy,
but it's good, too, to check up
once in a while and make sure
you haven't lost the things that
money can't buy.

G. H. Larimer

YEAST WAFFLES

1 pkg. yeast	1 tsp. salt
1/4 c. warm water	2 c. warm milk
1 T. sugar	2 eggs, well beaten
3 c. flour	1/2 c. Wesson Oil

Dissolve yeast in warm water. Add sugar. Combine dry ingredients; add milk and yeast to dry mixture. Add eggs and oil. Beat until batter is smooth. Keep covered in the refrigerator. Stir before using. (This recipe is best when mixed up the night before you plan to use it.)

MAPLE SYRUP

1 c. water	1/2 tsp. maple flavoring
2 c. sugar	

Heat water to a boil; add sugar, stirring continually. When sugar dissolves, add maple flavoring. Serve warm over hot waffles.

Nancy Cruse
Swisher County

STRESS DIET

BREAKFAST
1/2 grapefruit
1 slice whole wheat toast
8-oz. skim milk

LUNCH
4-oz. lean broiled chicken breast
1 c. steamed zucchini
1 Oreo cookie
Herb tea

MID-AFTERNOON SNACK
Rest of the package of Oreos
1 qt. rocky road ice cream
1 jar hot fudge

DINNER
2 loaves garlic bread, cheese
  optional
1 lg. pepperoni and mushroom
  pizza
Large pitchers of beer
3 Milky Way candy bars
Entire frozen Sara Lee cheesecake
  eaten directly from the freezer.

CAKES & DESSERTS

Cakes and Desserts

Cakes

FRESH APPLE CAKE

4 c. apples, peeled and sliced	1 tsp. salt
2 c. sugar	2 eggs
2 c. flour	3/4 c. vegetable oil
1 1/2 tsp. baking soda	2 tsp. vanilla extract
2 tsp. cinnamon	1 c. pecans, chopped

Preheat oven to 350 degrees. In large bowl, stir together apples and sugar. Add dry ingredients; stir well. In seperate bowl, beat eggs, oil and vanilla. Stir egg mixture into apple mixture, blending until thoroughly moistened. Stir in pecans. Pour into greased 13 x 9 x 2-inch pan. Bake 50 minutes or until cake springs back when lightly pressed. Serve with warm Apple Dessert Sauce. It is also delicious served with no icing.

Anne Mae Technik
Lavaca County

FRESH APPLE CAKE

2 c. sugar	3 c. flour
1 1/2 c. vegetable oil	1 1/4 tsp. baking soda
2 T. vanilla	1 tsp. salt
2 eggs, beaten	3 c. apples, chopped
1/2 tsp. lemon juice	1 1/2 c. pecans, chopped

In a mixing bowl, combine sugar, oil, vanilla, eggs and lemon juice. Sift together the flour, soda and salt. Add the dry ingredients to the batter. Fold in the chopped apples and pecans. Pour batter into a greased and floured tube or bundt pan. Bake at 325 degrees (preheated) for 1 hour and 30 minutes. Test for doneness with a toothpick.

GLAZE

1 c. sugar	1 tsp. cinnamon
1 c. brown sugar	1 tsp. cream of tartar
1/4 c. butter	1/2 c. milk
1 tsp. nutmeg	

In the top of a double boiler, combine sugars, butter, spices and cream of tartar. Add the milk. Blend well and place over boiling water to cook. Stir constantly until the mixture is warm and the sugars dissolved. Pour over cooled cake. NOTE: To reduce the fat content in this cake, applesauce can be substituted for the oil, egg beaters for the eggs, butter buds for the butter and raisins for half the pecans.

Janice Cordray
Angelina County

JEWISH APPLE CAKE

First Bowl:

4-5 apples, peeled and thinly sliced	5 T. sugar
	1 T. cinnamon

Mix and let stand until second bowl is mixed.

Second Bowl:

3 1/2 c. flour, lightly spooned	2 c. sugar
1 c. Wesson oil	3 tsp. baking powder
1/2 c. orange juice	1 tsp. salt
4 eggs	1 tsp. vanilla

Mix batter well with electric mixer. Grease bundt or angel food cake pan (no flour). Put in one layer batter, one layer apple mixture. Repeat until bowls are empty. Bake at 350 degrees for 1 hour. Test for doneness. Cool 25 minutes. Invert onto serving plate. This is a good coffee cake.

Rose Gannon
Cameron County

LOUISIANA APPLE CAKE

4 c. apples, peeled and finely chopped	2 tsp. soda
	1/2 tsp. salt
2 c. sugar	3/4 c. vegetable oil
1 c. nuts, chopped	1 tsp. vanilla
3 c. flour, sifted	2 eggs, well-beaten
1 tsp. cinnamon	

Combine apples, sugar and nuts and let stand for 40 minutes. Sift dry ingredients together. Combine dry ingredients and apple mixture. Stir in oil, vanilla and eggs. Beat 20 strokes only. Grease bottom of a tube pan. Bake 1 hour and 5 minutes at 350 degrees. Cool.

ICING

1 c. brown sugar	1 c. powdered sugar
1/4 lb. oleo	1 tsp vanilla
1/2 c. Pet Milk	

Mix brown sugar, oleo and Pet Milk. Bring to a boil and cook 6 minutes. Stir often. Put powdered sugar and vanilla in mixing bowl. Pour hot mixture over it. Beat rapidly with mixer until stiff. Spread on top of cake. Decorate with **pecan halves** and **maraschino cherries**. (I find that one-half of this icing is plenty.)

Esther Chism

Stay is a charming word in a friend's vocabulary.

OLD TIME APPLESAUCE CAKE

1 c. sugar
1/2 c. shortening
1 1/2 c. applesauce
2 T. molasses
2 c. all-purpose flour

1 tsp. soda
1 tsp. ground cinnamon
1 tsp. ground cloves
1/2 tsp. salt
1 c. raisins

Cream sugar and shortening in mixing bowl. Beat in applesauce and molasses. Add dry ingredients to batter and mix well to moisten. Stir in raisins. Pour into greased and floured fluted tube pan. Bake at 350 degrees for 45 minutes or until wooden toothpick comes out clean.

Jo Ellen Ball
Denton County

DIET APPLESAUCE CAKE

1/2 c. margarine
1/2 tsp. cinnamon
1/4 tsp. nutmeg or cloves
2 tsp. Sweet 'N Low (8 pkgs.)
1 c. dates or raisins, chopped

1 1/2 c. unsweetened applesauce
1 c. pecans, chopped
1 tsp. vanilla
2 c. flour
2 tsp. baking soda

Soften margarine and mix all ingredients together. Pour into oiled bundt pan and bake at 350 degrees for 30-45 minutes. Let set for about 5 minutes after removing cake from the oven, then remove from pan and let cool on a wire rack.

Wynette Russell
Coryell County

SUGARLESS APPLESAUCE CAKE

1 stick oleo
1 c. dates, chopped
3 T. Sugar Twin
1 egg
1 1/2 c. applesauce
1 c. pecans, chopped

1 tsp. cinnamon
1/2 tsp. nutmeg
1/2 tsp. cloves
1 tsp. vanilla
2 tsp. soda
2 c. flour

Melt oleo and pour over dates. Add other ingredients; mix well. Bake at 350 degrees for 45 minutes in a greased and floured bundt pan. You can use whole can of applesauce and whole package of dates. Cake is more moist after setting 24 hours.

Covington E. H. Club
Hill County

Faults are thick when love is thin.

AUNT MARY'S CAKE

First Layer:

1 stick butter   1 egg
1 box yellow butter cake mix (18 1/4-oz.)

Second Layer:

1 1-lb. box confectioners' sugar   2 eggs
1 stick butter   2 tsp. almond flavoring
1 8-oz. pkg. cream cheese

Soften 1 stick butter; then mix butter, butter cake mix and 1 egg. This will be a very thick batter. Pour into Pyrex baking dish (at least 10 x 6 x 2-inches) and pat down evenly; set aside. Mix the confectioners' sugar, the second stick of butter, cream cheese (softened), 2 eggs, and almond flavoring. Pour this mixture on top of set aside batter. Bake at 350 degrees for about 30 minutes. (This cake looks like it flops as it cools but it is rich and really good.

Susan Richards
Cooke County

HOLIDAY BANANA CAKE

3 c. flour   2 eggs
2 c. sugar   1 tsp. vanilla
1 tsp. soda   1 tsp. cinnamon
1 tsp. salt   1 c. pecans, chopped
1 1/4 c. Wesson oil   3 c. bananas, mashed (about 12)

Put all ingredients in mixing bowl. Mix **by hand** until well mixed. Pour into well greased and floured tube or bundt pan. Bake in preheated 350 degree oven for 1 hour or until cake springs back when touched. When cool, ice with Creamy Nut Icing.

CREAMY NUT ICING

1/4 c. shortening   1/2 c. brown sugar
1/4 c. butter (or margarine) 2 c. powdered sugar
2 1/2 T. flour   1/2 tsp. vanilla
1/4 tsp. salt   1/2 c. pecans, broken
1/2 c. milk

Melt shortening and butter in saucepan; remove from heat. Blend in flour and salt. Stir in slowly milk. Bring to a boil, stirring constantly. Boil for 1 minute (if mixture curdles do not be alarmed). Stir in brown sugar. Remove from heat and stir in powdered sugar. Set pan in cold water. Beat until thick enough to spread. Stir in vanilla and pecans. Pour over cake and dribble down the sides.

Christine Wade
Runnels County

BANANA SPLIT CAKE

3/4 c. margarine, melted
1 1/2 c. flour
1 1/2 c. pecans, chopped
1 c. confectioners' sugar
1 8-oz. pkg. cream cheese, softened
1 env. whipped topping mix
1/2 c. milk
1 tsp. vanilla

3-4 bananas, sliced
1/2 c. pineapple juice
1/4 c. lemon juice
1 20-oz. can crushed pineapple, drained
1 8-oz. carton whipped topping
1/2 c. pecans, chopped
1/4 c. maraschino cherries, chopped

Combine first three ingredients in bowl, mixing well. Pat into 9 x 13-inch baking dish. Bake at 350 degrees until light brown. Cool.

Cream confectioners' sugar and cream cheese in bowl until light and fluffy. Combine topping mix, milk and vanilla. Beat at high speed for 4 minutes. Fold into cream cheese mixture. Spread on cooled crust. Chill for 20 minutes.

Coat bananas with mixture of pineapple juice and lemon juice; drain. Layer bananas, pineapple and whipped topping over creamed mixture. Sprinkle chopped pecans and cherries over top. Chill until set. Can be made a day ahead.

Maudie Bell
Gregg County

LIZ'S BLACKBERRY WINE CAKE

1 pkg. Duncan Hines White Cake Mix
1 pkg. (3-oz.) Blackberry Jello
  (can use Black Cherry)

4 eggs
1/2 c. salad oil
1 c. Mogen David Blackberry Wine

In large bowl, mix all ingredients together. Beat on low speed until moist, then beat on medium speed for 2 minutes. Grease and flour (I just spray Pam, no flour) bundt or tube pan. Sprinkle 1/2 c. finely chopped nuts in bottom of pan. Pour cake batter over nuts and bake at 325 degrees for 1 hour. Glaze while hot.

GLAZE

1 c. powdered sugar
1/2 c. Blackberry Wine

1/2 c. margarine

Bring all ingredients to a rolling boil. When cake is brought from the oven and leaving it in the pan, pour 1/2 of glaze over cake. Let stand 30 minutes. Turn cake onto a cake plate and pour rest of glaze over the top of cake. I usually reheat glaze before pouring it on cake.

Liz Pierce
Henderson County

No sword bites so fiercely as an evil tongue.

MELT IN YOUR MOUTH BLUEBERRY CAKE

2 eggs, separated
1 c. sugar
1/2 c. shortening
1/4 tsp. salt
1 tsp. vanilla

1 1/2 c. flour
1 tsp. baking powder
1/3 c. milk
1 1/2 c. fresh blueberries

Beat egg whites until stiff, adding 1/4 c. sugar. Cream shortening, adding rest of sugar, salt and vanilla. Add egg yolks and beat until creamy. Sift flour and baking powder together; add to creamed mixture with milk. Fold in egg whites. Coat berries with 1 tablespoonful flour and fold into batter. Turn into well greased 8 x 8-inch pan. Sprinkle top with **1 tablespoonful sugar**. Bake 50 minutes in 350 degree oven. Serves 8.

Jean Fomby
Marion County

CARMEL PECAN CAKE

2 c. flour, sifted
3/4 tsp. salt
3 tsp. baking powder
1/3 c. butter or Crisco

3/4 c. milk
1 egg
1 tsp. vanilla

Mix first 3 ingredients; set aside. In mixing bowl, stir shortening just to soften. Sift in dry ingredients. Add milk and mix until flour is dampened. Then beat 2 minutes; add egg and vanilla and beat 1 minute longer. Heat oven to 300 degrees. Line 2 pans with paper; grease well.

QUICK CARAMEL FROSTING

1/2 c. margarine
1 c. light brown sugar

1/4 c. milk

Melt butter and sugar over low heat. Heat 2 minutes, stirring constantly. Add milk stirring until it comes to a boil; remove from heat. Cool. Add enough **powdered sugar** until at right consistency to spread on cake. Put **pecans** between layers and on top of cake.

Myrtle Whitener
Navarro County

Life is hard by the yard;
but by the inch,
life's a cinch!

CARROT CAKE

2 c. all-purpose flour, sifted	3 c. carrots, grated
2 c. sugar	4 eggs
2 tsp. baking soda	1 1/2 c. salad oil
2 tsp. salt	1 c. nuts
1 T. cinnamon	

Preheat oven to 350 degrees. Sift dry ingredients into large bowl and set aside. In blender container, blend 1 cup carrots with 1 egg and 1/2 cup salad oil. Repeat twice, adding nuts and extra egg during last blending. Combine with dry ingredients, mixing well. Pour into a greased 10-inch tube or oblong pan. Bake at 350 degrees for 1 hour. Cool and frost.

CREAM CHEESE FROSTING

1/2 c. butter or margarine	1 1-lb. box confectioners' sugar
1 8-oz. pkg. cream cheese, softened	1 tsp. vanilla extract

Cream butter and cream cheese together. Blend in confectioners' sugar and vanilla until smooth. Spread on cake.

Johnnie Messer
District 1 Director, Deaf Smith County

Loretta "Bill" Mahan, District 13 Director, from Bexar County uses 1 teaspoonful salt and bakes this cake in 3 greased and floured layer cake pans at 325 degrees for 45 minutes.

CARROT CAKE

2 c. sugar	2 tsp. cinnamon
1 1/4 c. corn oil	2 c. raw carrots, grated
3 eggs	1 sm. can crushed pineapple
1 tsp. soda	2 tsp. vanilla
1 1/2 tsp. salt	1 c. pecans
3 c. all-purpose flour	

Cream sugar and corn oil; add eggs 1 at a time, beating well after each addition. Sift dry ingredients together; mix into batter. Add carrots, pineapple, vanilla and nuts. Pour into 10-inch tube pan. Bake at 275 degrees for 1 1/2 hours. Yield: 20 servings

GLAZE

1 c. sugar	1 T. grated orange peel
1/2 c. fresh orange juice	

Warm juice and sugar to melt sugar; add orange peel. Pour on warm cake.

Bonnie Crumpler
Titus County

It takes courage to stand alone,
but that's the way we learn to walk.

CARROT CAKE WITH ORANGE GLAZE

2 c. sugar	2 tsp. soda
4 eggs	1/2 c. buttermilk
1 1/3 c. vegetable oil	1 tsp. lemon extract
3 c. flour	3 c. carrots, shredded
1 tsp. cinnamon	

Bake cake in tube pan (not a bundt pan) for 2 hours at 250 degrees, or 2 loaf pans at 350 degrees for 1 1/2 hours.

ORANGE GLAZE

2 c. sugar	1 c. orange juice

Near end of baking time, bring to a boil sugar and orange juice. Remove cake from oven. While still in pan, pour boiling orange mixture slowly over cake. Leave in pan until cool.

Rejenia Anderson
Williamson County

CHOCOLATE CAKE

2 c. flour	3 1/2 T. cocoa
2 c. sugar	1 c. water
Pinch of salt	2 eggs
1 stick margarine	1/2 c. buttermilk
1/2 c. Crisco	1 tsp. soda
1 tsp. vanilla	

Sift flour, salt and sugar together. Put Crisco, margarine, cocoa and water into pan and bring to rapid boil. Pour over flour and sugar and mix well. Add eggs, buttermilk, vanilla and soda. Mix well. Pour into a greased and floured 9 x 13-inch pan. Bake at 400 degrees for 25 minutes.

ICING

1 stick margarine	1 box powdered sugar
3 1/2 T. cocoa	1 c. pecans
1/3 c. milk	1/2 c. coconut
1 c. small marshmallows	1 tsp. vanilla

Bring margarine, cocoa and milk to boil. Remove from heat and add marshmallows and pour over powdered sugar, pecans, coconut and vanilla. Mix. Put on cake about 5 minutes after removing from oven.

Charlsta Smith
Parker County

Before you flare up at anyone's faults,
take time to count to ten --
ten of your own.

MO' CHOCOLATE CAKE AND FROSTING

1/2 c. margarine, softened	1/2 c. cocoa
2 c. sugar	1 1/2 tsp. baking soda
1 tsp. vanilla	1 tsp. baking powder
1 tsp. chocolate extract	3/4 c. buttermilk
2 eggs	1 c. boiling water
2 c. flour	

Cream margarine and sugar well. Add flavorings and eggs, 1 at a time. Beat to mix well. Combine dry ingredients and add to fat mixture alternately with buttermilk beginning and ending with flour mixture. Add boiling water and stir just to mix well. Bake at 350 degrees in greased and floured 9 x 13-inch pan or 2 9-inch layers, approximately 30 minutes or until it tests done.

MO' CHOCOLATE FROSTING

2 c. sugar	6 T. cocoa
1/2 c. shortening	1 1/2 tsp. vanilla
1/2 c. milk	1 tsp. chocolate extract
1/4 c. white corn syrup	

Mix in saucepan everything except flavorings. Bring to boil over low heat and boil vigorously for 1 1/2 minutes. Cool, add flavorings, then cool to spreading consistency.

Linda B. Sullivan
Kleberg County

EASY CHERRY CHOCOLATE CAKE

3 eggs	1 pkg. (4 serving size) chocolate
1 pkg. Supermoist Devil's Food	pudding & pie filling
Cake Mix	Maraschino cherries
1 21-oz. can cherry pie filling	Whipped cream
1/3 c. vegetable oil	

Heat oven to 350 degrees. Grease and flour 9 x 13-inch pan. Beat eggs in large bowl, stir in cake mix, cherry pie filling and oil until blended. Spread in pan. Bake 35-40 minutes or until a toothpick inserted in center comes out clean. (Surface of cake will be bumpy.) Cool completely. Prepare pie/pudding filling as directed on package. Let stand about 5 minutes or until thickened. Spread over cake. Store covered in refrigerator. When ready to serve, add dollops of whipped cream and a maraschino cherry with stem on top.

Alma Barreza
Sherman County

Taste makes waist.

BRIDGIE'S CHOCOLATE ICE CREAM CAKE

1 6-oz. pkg. semi-sweet chocolate

1 13-oz. can milk

1 10 1/2-oz. pkg. miniature marshmallows (5 c.)

1 1/2 c. flaked coconut

6 T. margarine

2 c. Rice Krispies

1 c. nuts, chopped (walnuts or pecans

1/2 gal. brick vanilla ice cream

Mix chocolate and milk together. Bring to a boil and cook 4 minutes. Add marshmallows and keep on heat until all marshmallows are melted. Chill mixture while you are browning coconut in margarine. After browning, add Rice Krispies and nuts. Cut ice cream lengthwise in half, each one-half section to be cut in 12 even squares. Spread 3 cups of cereal and coconut mix in bottom of 13 x 9 x 2-inch pan. Then arrange 12 squares of ice cream over cereal mixture. Add a layer of chocolate. Next, add remaining 12 squares of ice cream, remaining chocolate and on top the rest of cereal mixture. Put in freezer until ready to serve. Yield: 12 servings.

Ruth Taylor
Jefferson County

DIRT CAKE

1 1/4 lbs. Oreo Cookies, crushed

1 8-oz. pkg. cream cheese

1/2 stick butter or margarine

1 c. sugar

1 16-oz. carton Cool Whip

Line an 8-inch flower pot with foil. Crush Oreo cookies; set aside. Cream butter, cream cheese, and sugar. Add Cool Whip; beating to blend. Layer beginning with cookie crumbs. Add cream filling and another layer of cookie crumbs followed by rest of cream filling. Last, add cookie crumbs. Wrap a flower stem with seran wrap and place in middle of flower pot. Add a big bow around pot. You may add chopped nuts or cherries for color.
NOTE: A wonderful idea for children's birthdays, picnic in the park. Dish up in small dishes to serve. Yield: 15 servings.

Iva Mae Heath
Brown County

A happy home is not one
without problems,
but one that handles them
with understanding and love.

65

FUDGE RIBBON CAKE

1 18 1/4 or 18 1/2-oz. pkg.
  chocolate cake mix
1 8-oz. pkg. cream cheese,
  softened
2 T. margarine or butter
1 T. cornstarch

1 14-oz. can sweetened
  condensed milk
1 egg
1 tsp. vanilla
Confectioners' sugar or
  Chocolate Glaze

Preheat oven to 350 degrees. Prepare cake mix as package directs. Pour batter into well-greased and floured 10-inch bundt pan. In small mixer bowl, beat cream cheese, margarine and cornstarch until fluffy. Gradually beat in sweetened condensed milk, then egg and vanilla until smooth. Pour evenly over cake batter. Bake 50-55 minutes or until wooden toothpick inserted near center comes out clean. Cool 15 minutes; remove from pan. Cool. Sprinkle with confectioners' sugar or drizzle with Chocolate Glaze.

CHOCOLATE GLAZE

1-oz. (1 square) unsweetened or
  semi-sweet chocolate
1 T. margarine or butter

2 T. water
3/4 c. confectioners' sugar
1/2 tsp. vanilla

In small saucepan, over low heat, melt chocolate, margarine, and water. Remove from heat. Stir in confectioners' sugar and vanilla. Stir until smooth and well blended. (Makes about 1/3 cup.)

Karmen McCulloch
Hockley County

FUDGE UPSIDE-DOWN CAKE

Batter:
2 T. butter
3/4 c. sugar
4 T. cocoa
1 c. flour
2 tsp. baking powder
1/4 tsp. salt
1/2 c. milk
1 tsp. vanilla
1/2 c. nuts

Sauce:
1/2 c. sugar
1/2 c. brown sugar
3 T. cocoa
1 square chocolate
1 c. milk
1 T. butter
1/2 tsp. almond flavoring
1/2 c. nuts

Batter: Melt butter and add sugar and cocoa. Mix well. Add dry ingredients alternately with milk. Add vanilla and chopped nuts. Pour into greased pan 1 x 8 x 12-inches. Do flour or grease pan. Sauce: Heat ingredients for sauce stirring until smooth. Pour over batter (this will be very thin). Bake at 350 degrees for about 35 minutes. The sauce will be very thin and will go to bottom of pan during baking. This sauce makes a creamy, rich topping. Serve this cake with ice cream or whipped cream. THIS IS A VERY RICH CAKE AND A SMALL SERVING IS ADEQUATE.

Wilma Richardson
Cooke County

EASY RED DEVIL'S FOOD CAKE

3/4 c. butter
2 c. sugar
2 eggs
1 tsp. vanilla
1 c. sour milk

2 1/2 c. flour
1 tsp. soda
1 tsp. salt
1/2 c. cocoa
1 c. boiling water

Cream butter and sugar. Add eggs 1 at a time. Beat well after each addition. Add vanilla to milk; sift flour, soda, salt and cocoa together and add with milk to mixture. Pour in boiling water (all at once) and stir until well combined. Bake in three layers at 350 degrees for 30 minutes or if baked in sheet cake for 45 minutes. Cool. Frost with "Magic Chocolate Frosting".

MAGIC CHOCOLATE FROSTING

1 can Eagle Brand milk
1 T. water
2 squares unsweetened chocolate

1/8 tsp. salt
1/2 tsp. vanilla

Put milk, water and salt in top of double broiler. Mix well. Add chocolate. Cook over rapidly boiling water, stirring often until thick, about 10 minutes. Remove from heat and cool. Stir in vanilla and spread on cooled cake. Sprinkle with chopped nuts if desired or leave plain.

Doris Chamness
Hood County

CHOCOLATE PINEAPPLE UPSIDE DOWN CAKE

1/4 c. shortening
2/3 c. granulated sugar
1 egg, well beaten
1 c. flour
1/2 tsp. baking soda
1/4 tsp. salt
6 T. milk

1/2 tsp. vanilla
1-oz. square unsweetened
   chocolate, melted
3 T. butter
1/2 c. granulated sugar
7 or 8 slices pineapple

Preheat oven to 350 degrees. In a large mixing bowl, cream the shortening and 2/3 cup sugar together until creamy. Add the egg and mix well. Stir together the dry ingredients and add alternately with the milk. Stir in vanilla and melted chocolate. Beat 1 minute. Melt the butter in an 8 x 8 x 2-inch baking pan. Add the 1/2 cup sugar and mix together. Place the pineapple slices on top of the butter mixture and pour the batter over the pineapple. Bake in a 350 degree oven for 50 minutes. Loosen cake from sides of pan and turn out onto a serving platter. Yield: 8-10 servings.

Eulaine Phillips
Bailey County

TEXAS SHEET CAKE

1/2 lb. butter or margarine	1/2 tsp. salt
1 c. water	2 eggs
1/4 c. cocoa powder	1 c. sour cream
2 c. flour	1 tsp. baking soda
2 c. sugar	2 tsp. cinnamon (opt.)

Combine butter, water and cocoa in medium saucepan; bring to boiling and cook at a simmer for two minutes. Add flour sugar and salt; blend well. Remove pan from heat and beat in eggs, sour cream and baking soda until smooth. Pour batter into a greased and floured 10 x 15-inch pan and bake in a preheated 375 degree oven for 20-22 minutes, or until cake tests done. When done, remove from oven and let stand, in pan, on rack to cool.

FROSTING

1/4 lb. butter or margarine	1 lb. powdered sugar
1/4 c. cocoa powder	1 tsp. vanilla extract
6 T. milk	1 c. pecans, chopped

Using same saucepan as for cake (it doesn't have to be washed), combine butter, cocoa and milk. Bring just to boiling and let simmer one minute. Remove from heat, add sugar, vanilla and chopped nuts, and mix well. Spread frosting over cake while it is still in the pan and while it is still warm. Cut cake into squares like brownies or in larger pieces. Remove pieces with spatula. Do not attempt to turn the entire cake out of the pan.

Joyce Harris
Henderson County

COCONUT CAKE

2 sticks margarine	1 tsp. baking powder
1 1/2 c. sugar	1/2 tsp. salt
4 egg yolks	1 c. buttermilk
1 1/2 c. flour	1 tsp. vanilla extract
1/2 tsp. soda	

Cream margarine and sugar, add egg yolks, beating after each addition. Sift dry ingredients. Add dry ingredients and buttermilk alternately to first ingredients. Bake in 2 greased and floured 9-inch pans at 350 degrees for approximately 40 minutes. Cool for 10 minutes. Turn out of pans, cool and ice.

FROSTING

1 1/2 c. sugar	2 T. sugar
1/2 c. water	1 tsp. vanilla extract
4 egg whites	

Boil 1 1/2 c. sugar and water until thread spins from spoon. Beat egg whites until stiff. Add 2 tablespoonfuls sugar; beat again until smooth. Pour hot syrup into egg whites, beating constantly. Add vanilla. Stack layers of cake with angel flake coconut.

Elma McIntosh
Wood County

PEGGY'S RED VELVET CAKE

1 1/2 c. sugar	1 tsp. salt
2 c. oil	2 T. cocoa
2 eggs	1 tsp. soda
1 tsp. vinegar	1 c. buttermilk
2 oz. red food coloring	1 tsp. vanilla
2 1/2 c. flour	

Beat well sugar, oil and eggs. Add vinegar and food coloring. Sift flour, salt, cocoa and soda and alternate with buttermilk and vanilla. Can be made in 2 layers, but I always make 3 9-inch pans. Bake at 350 degrees for 25 minutes. Frost with Cream Cheese Icing or Fluffy White Icing.

CREAM CHEESE ICING

1 8-oz. pkg. cream cheese	1 tsp. vanilla
4 T. margarine	1 c. pecans, chopped
1 box powdered sugar	

If frosting is too thick, add a little milk to make thinner.

FLUFFY WHITE ICING

1 c. milk	1 c. butter or Crisco
1/4 c. flour	2 tsp. vanilla
1 c. sugar	

Combine milk and flour and boil until thickened. Cover while cooling. Combine sugar, butter or Crisco and vanilla and beat until fluffy. Add milk mixture and continue beating until very fluffy. Ice cake and add **coconut**. Very good!

Bernadette Bludau, Golden Circle
Lavaca County

ICEBOX COCONUT CAKE

1 box white cake mix	1 lg. carton Cool Whip
1 tsp. vanilla	1/2 c. sugar
1 1/2 c. angel flake coconut	8-oz. sour cream

Bake cake as directed, adding vanilla; then cut layers in half to make four layers. Mix Cool Whip and sugar until sugar dissolves; add sour cream and 1 cup coconut. Spread layers and top with mixture; then sprinkle with remaining coconut. Cover and refrigerate for 24 hours before serving.

Evelyn Sherrill
Cheerful E. H. C. T.

The happiest times we ever spend
are those we share with a special friend.

RAVING REVIEW COCONUT CAKE

1 pkg. yellow cake mix	1/2 c. oil
1 pkg. vanilla instant pudding	2 c. coconut
1 1/3 c. water	1 c. nuts, chopped
4 eggs	

Blend cake mix, instant pudding, water, eggs and oil in large mixing bowl. Beat for 4 minutes. Stir in coconut and nuts. Pour into 3 greased and floured 9-inch layer pans. Bake at 350 degrees for 35 minutes. Cool in pans for 15 minutes and remove.

COCONUT CREAM CHEESE FROSTING

4 T. butter or margarine	2 tsp. milk
2 c. coconut	3 1/2 c. powdered sugar
1 8-oz. pkg. cream cheese	1/2 tsp. vanilla

Melt 2 tablespoonfuls margarine in skillet and add coconut. Stir until golden brown; spread on paper towel to cool. Cream 2 tablespoonfuls margarine with cream cheese. Add milk, beat in sugar. Blend in vanilla. Stir in 1 3/4 cups of coconut. Spread on tops of cake layers. Stack and sprinkle with the remaining coconut.

Bessie Zeitler
Pecos County

RAVING COCONUT CHOCOLATE CAKE

1 pkg. yellow cake mix	1/4 c. oil
1 pkg. (small) Jello chocolate instant pudding mix	1 1/3 c. Baker's angel flake coconut
1 1/3 c. water	1 c. nuts
4 eggs	

Combine cake mix, pudding mix, water, eggs and oil in large mixer bowl. Blend by beating at medium speed for 4 minutes. Stir in coconut and nuts. Pour into greased and floured 10-inch tube pan or 2 round pans. Bake at 325 degrees for 60 minutes or 30-35 minutes if you use the 2 round pans. Cool 15 minutes. Remove from pan.

COCONUT CREAM CHEESE FROSTING

1/3 c. butter	4 tsp. milk
2 pkgs. (3-oz. each) cream cheese	1/2 tsp. vanilla
1 16-oz. box confectioners' sugar	

Cream butter and cream cheese. Add confectioners' sugar alternately with milk; beating well after each addition. Add vanilla. Spread frosting over top of cake and sides.

Lee Nell Boenig
Refugio County

A pint of good example is worth a gallon of advise.

DELUXE WHITE COCONUT CAKE

3 egg whites
1 box Duncan Hines
 white cake mix
1 evn. plain gelatin
1 c. sour cream
1 1/4 c. water
1/3 c. oil

1 tsp. almond flavoring
1 tsp. white vanilla
1/2 can Coco Lopez cream of
 coconut**
Frozen fresh grated coconut or
 angel flake coconut

Beat egg whites until stiff. In another bowl, mix the cake mix, gelatin, sour cream, water, oil and flavorings on low speed with electric mixer. Fold in egg whites. Grease two cake pans, line with wax paper and dust with flour. Spread batter into pans. Bake at 350 degrees until "just" done. Do not overbake or cake will be dry. Cool on cake racks.

Split each layer. Spread approximately 3 tablespoonfuls cream of coconut on each (you can punch some holes in top of layer with toothpick) so cake will absorb the cream of coconut. Spread icing on each layer, and secure with two or three toothpicks. After last layer is put on, spread icing over sides and top of cake. Cover cake with loose coconut, packing lightly as you go with coconut in your fingers. Keep in cool place. After completely cool and icing is set, store in large cake carrier or cover. **Can use 1 can (8-oz.) crushed pineapple. Spread about 2 tablespoonfuls pineapple juice over cake layer, and a fourth of the crushed pineapple.

SEVEN MINUTE ICING

2 egg whites
1 1/2 c. sugar
1/4 tsp. cream of tartar

Pinch of salt
1/3 c. water
1/2 t. vanilla or coconut
 flavoring

Put all ingredients (except flavoring) in top of double boiler. Beat with electric beater until thick, and whites make peaks. Remove from heat. Beat a few minutes with large spoon. Add flavoring and beat about 1/2 minute.

Frances Rosette
Gregg County

*You are richer today than you were yesterday -
if you have laughed often, given something,
forgiven even more, made a new friend,
or made stepping-stones of stumbling blocks.*

CORNMEAL SOUR CREAM CAKE

1 c. butter or margarine
3 c. granulated sugar
1 tsp. vanilla
1 tsp. lemon extract
1 tsp. almond extract
Pinch of salt
6 egg yolks

1 1/2 c. plain flour
1 1/2 c. plain cornmeal
1/4 tsp. baking soda
1/2 tsp. baking powder
1 c. sour cream
6 egg whites
1/4 tsp. salt

Grease and flour 10-inch bundt pan; set aside. Cream butter; add sugar and beat until light. Add extracts and pinch of salt. Then add egg yolks, one at a time, beating after each addition. Sift flour, cornmeal, soda and baking powder together 3 times; add alternately with south cream to creamed mixture. Add salt to egg whites and beat until peaks form. Fold into creamed mixture. Pour into pan and bake at 350 degrees for 1 hour or until done. Cool 10 minutes and turn onto rack.

Murri Mills
McCulloch County

SUGAR-FREE DATE CAKE

1/2 c. margarine (can use calorie-
    reduced)
1 T. Sweet-10 (liquid sugar
    substitute)
2 c. flour
1 c. dates, chopped

1 1/2 c. applesauce
    (unsweetened)
2 eggs
2 tsp. baking soda
1/4 tsp. ground cloves
1 1/2 tsp. ground cinnamon
1 c. pecans, chopped

Mix all ingredients in a large mixing bowl. Pour into a greased 10-inch tube pan or two 9 x 5 x 2-inch loaf pans. Bake at 350 degrees for about 50 minutes or until done. Do not overbake. This cake freezes well.

Joyce Cabe, Health & Safety Committee Chairman
District 2, Terry County

EARTHQUAKE CAKE

1 c. pecans
1 c. coconut
1 box German Chocolate
    Cake Mix

1 8-oz. cream cheese
1/2 c. margarine
1 tsp. vanilla
1 lb. powdered sugar (4 c.)

Grease bottom only of 9 x 13-inch baking dish. Mix pecans and coconut and spread into bottom of pan. Prepare cake mix as per box directions and pour over pecans and coconut. Combine cream cheese, margarine, vanilla and powdered sugar and spread over cake mix. Bake at 350 degrees for 50-55 minutes.

Vera Evans
Montgomery County

EGGNOG CAKE

1 lg. angel food cake
1/2 lb. sweet butter
1 3/4 c. powdered sugar
5 egg yolks, beaten
1 c. almonds, chopped and
  lightly toasted
1/2-1/3 c. bourbon
2-3 T. rum

1/2 tsp. almond extract
1 doz. almond macaroons,
  toasted and ground
1 c. heavy cream, whipped
2 T. powdered sugar
1 T. bourbon
1 T. rum

Slice cake horizontally 3 times, yielding 4 layers. Cream butter and powdered sugar thoroughly; add egg yolks. Stir in 3/4 cup of the almonds, 1/2 to 1/3 cup bourbon, 2-3 tablespoonfuls rum, almond extract and ground macaroons. Spread filling between layers of cake; cover with plastic wrap and store overnight in refrigerator. Next morning whip cream, add 2 tablespoonfuls rum. Frost cake with cream mixture and garnish with remaining 1/2 cup almonds. Return to refrigerator until serving time. Leftovers freeze beautifully.

Rusk County

CHRISTMAS PLUM CAKE

2 c. flour
1/2 tsp. soda
1/2 tsp. salt
1 tsp. cloves
1 tsp. cinnamon
2 c. sugar

3 eggs, beaten
1 c. cooking oil
2 sm. jars plum baby food
2 T. red food coloring
1 c. pecans, chopped

Mix first 9 ingredients well; add food coloring and nuts. Bake in greased and floured tube pan at 350 degrees for 1 hour. Let cool 10 minutes and remove from pan.

GLAZE

1 c. powdered sugar
2 1/2 T. lemon juice

1 T. red food coloring

Mix well and spread on top of cake and let run down sides.

Trellis Sue Harrington
Baylor County

A kind word is never lost.
It keeps going on and on,
from one person to another,
until at last it comes back to you again.

FRIENDSHIP CAKE (30 days)

Abut 20 years ago, while visiting relatives in the Seven Devils area of Northern Idaho, I first tasted this cake and immediately begged for the recipe. It lists using starter from a friend, which makes the cake taste better. However, one can follow the recipe, obtain starter from drained juice and gradually with time the full flavor will develop. The drained juice can be used over ice cream, fruit, cakes, pancakes or simply sipped.

1 glass gallon jar
1 1/2 c. starter from a friend

1 qt. sliced peaches with juice
   (canned)
2 1/2 c. sugar

Combine and lightly stir daily for 10 days. On the 10th day add:

2 1/2 c. sugar

20-oz. chunk pineapple and juice

Combine and lightly stir daily for 10 days. On the 20th day add:

2 1/2 c. sugar

27-oz. maraschino cherries (no juice)

Combine and lightly stir daily for 10 days. On the 30th day the cakes can be baked. Separate juice from fruit. There is enough starter for 4 new batches. Save some for yourself. For each cake you need:

1 1/2 c. brandied fruit, well drained
2/3 c. oil (Crisco or Wesson)
1 c. nuts, chopped
Raisins, dates, etc.

1 box cake mix
4 eggs
1 sm. box instant pudding to correspond with cake mix flavor

Mix all cake ingredients and pour into greased and floured Bundt pan or loaf pan. Bake for 50-60 minutes.

GLAZE FOR 4 CAKES

1 8-oz. cream cheese
1 tsp. vanilla

1 box powdered sugar
1 stick margarine

Blend glaze ingredients.

NOTE: Do not refrigerate because starter won't ferment. May use coconut, raisins, and nuts.

Maxine Shannahan
Hays County

Love, love, love and be richer
for the giving.
Grow each day in some good way,
and life will be worth living.

BOURBON LACED FRUIT & NUT CAKE

8 egg whites (room temp.)
3 1/2 c. cake flour, sifted
3 1/2 tsp. baking powder
3/4 tsp. salt

1 c. lightly salted butter
2 c. sugar
1 tsp. vanilla
1 c. milk

Preheat oven to 375 degrees. Line bottoms of 4 buttered 9-inch round cake pans with waxed paper. Beat egg whites with an electric mixer at high speed until stiff peaks form; set aside. Sift flour with baking powder and salt. In large bowl, beat butter until smooth. Gradually add sugar to butter, beating well after each addition; add vanilla. Add dry ingredients alternately with milk, blending until smooth. Gently fold in egg whites; pour batter into prepared pans and bake for 20 minutes. Let layers cool completely before removing from pans.

CAKE FILLING

3/4 c. butter
1 3/4 c. sugar
1/2 tsp. salt
12 egg yolks
1/2 c. bourbon whiskey
1 1/2 c. pecans, coarsely chopped

1 1/2 c. dark raisins (soaked in
hot water for 5 min. and
drained)
1 1/2 c. shredded coconut
1 1/2 c. candied red cherries,
quartered

Beat butter, sugar, salt and egg yolks in top of a double boiler. Cook over simmering water until slightly thickened. Remove from heat; add bourbon and beat 1 minute. Transfer to large bowl. Add nuts and fruit; let cool at room temperature.

FROSTING

1 1/2 c. sugar
1/2 tsp. cream of tartar
1/2 c. water

1/2 c. egg whites (room temp.)
1/2 tsp. vanilla

Combine sugar, cream of tartar and water in a medium size saucepan. Cook over medium heat until sugar is dissolved and syrup is clear. Continue cooking without stirring until syrup registers 240 on a candy thermometer. Meanwhile, with mixer at medium speed, beat egg whites until soft peaks form. At high speed, slowly pour hot syrup in thin stream over egg whites, beating constantly. Add vanilla and beat until stiff peaks form. Spread cooled filling between cooled layers and over top. Spread sides with frosting.

Kathy Kyrish
Wilson County

*When you sneer and point
your finger of scorn,
three fingers are pointing at you.*

GRANDMA'S FRUIT SPICE CAKE

4 c. flour
3 tsp. baking powder
1 tsp. soda
1/2 tsp. salt
2 T. cocoa
1 tsp. allspice
1 tsp. cloves
1 tsp. nutmeg

1 tsp. cinnamon
1 1/2 c. white sugar
1 c. brown sugar
1 c. butter
4 eggs
1 c. buttermilk
1/2 c. water
1 1/2 c. raisins

Sift flour, baking powder, soda, salt, cocoa and spices together 3 times; set aside. Cream sugars and butter until fluffy. Add eggs and beat well. Fold in flour mixture, alternating with the buttermilk and water. Beat well. Add raisins last. Pour into floured and greased loaf or tube pan. Bake in 350 degree oven for 1 hour or until cake is done. Serve with or without an icing. Chocolate icing is very good for a special occasion.

Mary Frances Smith
Coleman County

MEXICAN FRUIT CAKE

2 c. flour
1 c. pecans, chopped
2 c. sugar
2 eggs, beaten

2 tsp. baking soda
1 20-oz. can unsweetened
    crushed pineapple

Combine all cake ingredients in mixer bowl and blend well. Spread in greased and floured 9 x 13-inch cake pan. Bake at 350 degrees for 30-35 minutes.

CREAM CHEESE FROSTING

1 8-oz. pkg. cream cheese
2 c. powdered sugar

1 tsp. vanilla
3/4 c. pecans, chopped

Combine cream cheese, powdered sugar and vanilla with mixer. Spread over hot cake and sprinkle with pecans.

Frances Cook
Knox County

If you meet someone too tired to smile,
leave one of yours --
nobody needs a smile as much
as those who have none to give.

PEAR PRESERVE CAKE

3/4 c. butter
2 1/2 c. sugar
4 eggs
3 c. flour
1/2 tsp. soda
Dash of salt (opt.)

1 8-oz. jar cherries with
   juice, diced
1 c. coconut
1 c. pecans, chopped
1 c. raisins
1 c. pear preserves
1 tsp. vanilla

Combine butter and sugar together, cream well. Add eggs, mix well. Combine flour and soda and sift. Add flour to mixture. Add cherries, juice, coconut, pecans, raisins, pear preserves and vanilla. Mix well. Grease and flour a tube pan. Bake at 325 degrees for 2 hours or until done.

NOTE: This cake can be frozen by the slice or whole. The pear preserves keep it moist.

Corine Safford
Limestone County

BOILED RAISIN CAKE

1 sm. box mincemeat
1 box raisins
1 tsp. cinnamon
1 tsp. nutmeg
2 sticks margarine

2 1/2 c. boiling water
1 1/2 c. sugar
4 c. flour
2 tsp. soda
1 c. pecans

Boil mixture of mincemeat, raisins, spices, margarine and sugar in water for 15 minutes; cool. Add flour, soda and pecans. Pour into a greased and floured bundt pan. Bake at 300 degrees for 1 1/2 -2 hours. Cool. Drizzle a mixture of **1 cup powdered sugar** and **2 tablespoonfuls pineapple juice** on top of cake.

Dimple Enge
Limestone County

WHITE FRUIT CAKE

1 lb. candied cherries, chopped
1 lb. candied pineapple, chopped
3 pt. pecans, chopped
2 c. flour, sifted

1 c. sugar
5 egg whites
1 tsp. baking powder

Combine cherries, pineapple and pecans in a large bowl. Mix flour and sugar. Pour over fruit mixture and mix well until all fruit is coated. Beat egg whites and baking powder until stiff. Pour egg white mixture over fruit mixture and mix well. Line tube or loaf pan with wax paper and pour in cake mixture. Bake 1 hour and 40 minutes at 300 degrees. Check cake after 1 hour and 30 minutes.

Earline Mitchell
Grimes County

WHITE CHRISTMAS FRUIT CAKE

1 white cake mix
4 c. candied fruit
1 c. coconut

3 1/2 c. nuts, chopped
1 can vanilla frosting

Cook cake as directed. Crumble cake. Add fruit, coconut and nuts. Mix in frosting. Line a loaf pan with wax paper. Pour mixture into pan. Refrigerate. Do not cook.

Lou Vincent
Howard County

THE "HAGGARD CAKE"

NOTE: This recipe is correct - it does not call for eggs or shortening!

2 c. flour
1 1/2 c. sugar

2 tsp. soda
1 (No. 2) can crushed pineapple
and juice

Mix all cake ingredients together with a spoon and pour into a greased and floured pan or Pyrex dish about 9 x 12-inches. Bake at 350 degrees in a pre-heated oven for 34 minutes. Leave in pan.

ICING

1 1/2 c. sugar
1 sm. can evaporated milk
(1/2 c.)
1 stick margarine

1 c. coconut
1 c. pecans, cut in small pieces
1 tsp. vanilla
Dash of salt

While cake is baking, mix sugar, milk and margarine in saucepan; boil 2 minutes. Add coconut, pecans, vanilla and salt. Pour over the cake while both are warm. When cake is cold, cover with foil. When ready to serve, cut into squares.

Lue Ann Huckaby
Comanche County

EXTRA MOIST LEMONADE CAKE

1 pkg. lemon cake mix or pudding
included cake mix
1 pkg. lemon flavor instant pudding

4 eggs
1 c. water
1/4 c. oil

Combine cake mix, pudding mix, eggs, water and oil. Beat for 4 minutes. Pour into greased and floured tube pan. Bake at 350 degrees for 50 minutes. Do not underbake. Cool in pan 5 minutes. Then prick cake with wooden pick completely through to bottom of cake. Gradually spoon glaze over cake until completely absorbed. Cool 15 minutes and remove from pan. Sprinkle with **confectioners' sugar**.

GLAZE

1 can (6-oz.) frozen lemonade,
thawed

2 c. confectioners' sugar

Blend well.

Sharon Sarandos
Leon County

LEMON PIE-CAKE

Crust:

1 pkg. Lemon Cake Mix   1/2 c. margarine, softened
1 egg

Grease bottom and sides of 13 x 9-inch pan. In large bowl, combine ingredients and press in greased pan.

Filling:

1 1/3 c. sugar   2 T. margarine
1/2 c. cornstarch   1/2 c. lemon juice (3 sm. lemons)
1 3/4 c. water   1/4 tsp. salt
4 eggs, separated

In heavy saucepan, combine sugar, cornstarch, salt and water. Cook over medium heat stirring constantly until mixture comes to a boil. Remove from heat and beat egg yolks slightly and stir in part of cornstarch mix from saucepan. Continue cooking until mixture thickens. Stir in oleo and lemon juice. Pour over cake mix in pan.

Meringue:

4 egg whites   1/2 c. sugar
1/2 tsp. cream of tartar

Beat egg whites with cream of tartar until frothy. Gradually add sugar and beat until stiff peaks form. Spread over cake filling in pan. Leave 1/2-inch from sides of pan. Bake 25-30 minutes at 350 degrees or until meringue is golden brown. Cool 1 hour before cutting into squares. Grate lemon rind in filling and meringue.

Molly Heine-Gillmore
McLennan County

OATMEAL CAKE

1 c. quick oatmeal   1 1/3 c. flour
1 1/3 c. boiling water   1 tsp. soda
1 c. granulated sugar   1 tsp. baking powder
1 c. brown sugar   1/2 tsp. salt
1 c. shortening   1 tsp. cinnamon
2 eggs   1 tsp. vanilla

Soak oatmeal in boiling water for 20 minutes. Cream together sugars and shortening. Add eggs and beat. Add soaked oatmeal and mix well. Sift together all dry ingredients. Add flour mix to sugar mix plus vanilla and stir. Bake at 350 degrees in a greased and floured 9 x 13-inch pan about 35 minutes.

TOPPING

1 c. brown sugar   1/3 c. cream or milk
4 T. margarine   1 c. coconut

Mix ingredients and spread on cake. Cook under broiler until topping bubbles and runs together.

Naomi Woolam
Cameron County

PRETTY PEA-RIFFIC CAKE

2 c. flour
2 tsp. soda
1/2 tsp. baking powder
1/2 tsp. salt
1 tsp. cinnamon
1 tsp. allspice
3 eggs
2 c. sugar
3/4 c. vegetable oil

3 c. black-eyed peas, cooked
(puree in blender and
measure out 2 c.)
1 sm. 4-oz. jar carrots baby
food
1/2 c. crushed pineapple,
drained
1/2 c. cherries, chopped
1/2 c. almonds, chopped

Combine flour, soda, baking powder, salt and spices. Beat eggs, add sugar, oil and **vanilla**. Beat until smooth. Stir in pureed peas and remaining ingredients. Pour into 2 round cake pans. Bake at 350 degrees for 35-40 minutes.

ORANGE CREAM CHEESE FROSTING

1 c. butter or margarine
1 8-oz. cream cheese, softened
1 tsp. vanilla

2 c. powdered sugar, sifted
1 tsp. orange juice

Germaine Meyer
Dallam County

PECAN ITALIAN CREAM CAKE

2 c. sugar
1/2 c. Crisco
1/2 c. margarine (1 stick)
5 eggs, separated
2 c. flour
1 tsp. baking soda

1/2 tsp. salt
1 c. buttermilk
1 tsp. vanilla
2 c. coconut
1 c. pecans, chopped

Cream sugar, Crisco and margarine until smooth. Add beaten egg yolks. Combine flour, baking soda and salt and add to creamed mixture alternately with the buttermilk. Stir in vanilla, coconut and pecans. Fold in stiffly beaten egg whites. Pour into 3 greased and floured cake pans and bake at 350 degrees for 30 minutes or until done.

CREAM CHEESE FROSTING

1 8-oz. pkg. cream cheese
1 box powdered sugar
Pecans, chopped

1/4 c. (1/2 stick) margarine
1 tsp. vanilla

Mix all ingredients until smooth. Spread between each layer, on top and sides, sprinkling with pecans as you go.

Alta Lewis
San Saba County

PECAN PIE CAKE

1 box yellow cake mix   1/2 stick margarine
1 egg
Pie Filling:
1/2 c. margarine, melted   1 1/2 c. white Karo syrup
2/3 c. of cake mix   2 tsp. vanilla
1/2 c. brown sugar   2 c. pecans, chopped
4 eggs

Combine all but 2/3 cup of cake mix with beaten egg and margarine. Grease 9 x 13-inch pan. Spread in pan and bake for 15 minutes at 350 degrees. Pour pie filling over the cooked crust and bake 35-50 minutes at 350 degrees. Cool, cut into bars.

Virginia Flournoy
Wichita County

PINEAPPLE CAKE

1 box Lemon Supreme Cake Mix   1/3 c. oil (Crisco preferred)
1 1/3 c. crushed pineapple   3 eggs

Preheat oven to 350 degrees. Grease sides and bottom of pans (2-round or 1-9 x 13-inch) with shortening and flour. Blend together cake mix, pineapple, oil and eggs in large bowl. Beat at medium speed for 2 minutes. Pour batter into pans immediately and bake at 350 degrees for 30-35 minutes. Cake is done when checked with toothpick and it comes out clean. Use icing of your choice.

Lud Hughs
La Vaca County

PINEAPPLE PUDDING CAKE

1 1/2 c. sugar   1 No. 2 can crushed pineapple
2 c. flour   1 egg
2 tsp. soda   2 T. margarine, melted
1 tsp. salt

Sift together dry ingredients. Make hole in center. Mix together pineapple, egg, and margarine. Pour into center of dry ingredients. Mix well. Bake in 13 x 9-inch greased and floured pan at 325 degrees for 30 minutes.

FROSTING

3/4 c. sugar   3/4 c. Milnot canned milk
1 stick margarine

Bring to a boil. Cook 7 minutes. Add 1/2 cup chopped nuts and 1/2 cup coconut. Spread on top of cake.

Opal Talley
Gaines County

SWEDISH PINEAPPLE CAKE

2 c. sugar
1 20-oz. can crushed pineapple
  with liquid
1 tsp. soda

1 tsp. vanilla
2 c. flour
1/2 - 1 c. pecans, chopped

Mix ingredients by hand in order given. Pour into ungreased, unfloured 13 x 9 x 2-inch pan. Bake at 350 degrees for 30 minutes or until toothpick inserted in center comes out clean.

CREAM CHEESE TOPPING

1 8-oz. pkg. cream cheese,
  softened
1 stick margarine or butter, melted

1 c. confectioners' sugar
1/2 - 1 c. pecans, chopped

Combine and mix well. Ice cake while still warm.

Eleanora Talley
Wilson County

POPPY SEED CAKE

1 Duncan Hines Butter Cake Mix
1/2 c. sugar
1/4 c. poppy seed

3/4 c. Crisco oil
8 oz. sour cream
4 eggs

Mix all ingredients together except eggs. Mix well. Then add eggs, 1 at a time, mixing well after each egg. Oil bundt pan and pour in cake mixture. Bake at 350 degrees for 45-50 minutes. Cool for 20-25 minutes and then sprinkle with sugar.

Earline Mitchell
Grimes County

POPPY SEED CAKE

1/4 c. sweet milk
1 T. poppy seed
6 eggs
3 c. sugar
1 c. butter (or 1/2 c. butter and
  1/2 c. Crisco)

1 c. buttermilk
1 tsp. almond extract
1 tsp. lemon extract
1/4 tsp. soda
3 c. regular flour

Soak milk and poppy seed for 2 hours. (I use canned poppy seed.) Separate eggs. Beat whites until stiff, but not dry. Set aside. Combine sugar, butter and egg yolks, cream well. Add poppy seed and milk to buttermilk. Add flavorings. Add soda to flour and add to creamed mixture, alternating milk with flour. Mix well. Add the egg whites to cake batter. Bake in a prepared angel food cake pan. Bake at 325 degrees for 1 hour.

Maude Schwierzke
Bee County

EASY AND DELICIOUS POUND CAKE

1 1/2 c. shortening	1 c. milk
3 c. sugar	3 tsp. vanilla
3 1/2 c. flour	6 eggs
1 tsp. baking powder	

Cream shortening and sugar well. Sift dry ingredients; add alternately with milk. Add flour and eggs; mix well. Bake at 325 degrees for 1 hour and 15 minutes. YIELD: 23 servings.

Rita Harris
Marion County

FRESH APPLE POUND CAKE

1 c. shortening or margarine	1/2 tsp. nutmeg
2 c. sugar	1/2 tsp. salt
4 large eggs (or 5 med.)	1 1/2 tsp. soda
2 tsp. vanilla	3/4 c. buttermilk
1 tsp. butter flavoring	1 c. fresh apples, finely
3 c. flour, sifted	chopped or grated
1 tsp. allspice	1/2 c. pecans, chopped
1 1/2 tsp. cinnamon	

Cream shortening and sugar. Add eggs 1 at a time. Add vanilla and butter flavoring. Mix well. Sift flour, allspice, cinnamon, nutmeg, salt and soda, then add alternately with buttermilk. Fold in apples and pecans, blend well. Pour into a 10-inch bundt pan that is greased and floured. Bake at 325 degrees for 1 hour and 20 minutes or until done. Do not overbake. Remove cake from pan while hot and brush on icing with pastry brush covering top and sides.

ICING

1 c. sugar	1/2 tsp. vanilla
1/2 c. water	1/2 tsp. butter flavoring
1 T. margarine	1/2 tsp. cinnamon
1/4 c. fresh apples, crushed or grated	

Combine all ingredients. Bring slowly to a boil, stirring constantly. Let boil 1 1/2 minutes, let sit for 2 minutes, then apply to cake while still hot.

Oneida Hutto

Apple, apple dumplings: my first choice
Cry all the husbands with one voice,
Apple for the filling; sugar and spice
Wrap it up in pastry and count me twice!

BROWN SUGAR POUND CAKE

1 c. shortening	1/2 tsp. salt
1 stick margarine	1/2 tsp. baking powder
2 1/3 c. light brown sugar	1 c. milk
5 eggs	2 tsp. vanilla
3 c. flour	Brown Sugar Frosting

Cream shortening, margarine and brown sugar. Add eggs 1 at a time, beating well after each addition. Sift dry ingredients and add them alternately with milk. Add vanilla. Pour mixture into greased and floured tube pan. Bake at 350 degrees for 1 hour and 10 minutes. Cool in pan for 10 minutes.

BROWN SUGAR FROSTING

1 stick margarine	3 c. powdered sugar
1 c. brown sugar	1 tsp. vanilla
1/4 c. milk	

Melt margarine on medium heat. Add brown sugar and boil for 1 minute, stirring constantly. Add milk, powdered sugar and vanilla. Blend until creamy.

Krick Youngblood
Kermit, Texas

LEMON-BUTTERMILK POUND CAKE

1 c. shortening	1/2 tsp. salt
1/2 c. butter, softened	1 tsp. lemon extract
2 1/2 c. sugar	3 1/2 c. all-purpose flour
4 eggs	1 c. buttermilk
1/2 tsp. soda	Lemon Sauce
1 T. hot water	

Cream shortening, butter and sugar until light and fluffy; add eggs 1 at a time, beating well after each addition. Dissolve soda in hot water, add salt and lemon extract and stir into creamed mixture. Add flour to creamed mixture alternately with buttermilk, beginning and ending with flour; beat well after each addition. Pour batter into a well-greased and floured 10-inch tube pan or bundt pan. Bake at 325 degrees for 1 hour and 15 minutes. While still warm, punch holes in cake with a toothpick; spoon lemon sauce over cake.

LEMON SAUCE

1 c. sugar	1/2 c. hot water
2 lemons, juice and grated rind	

Combine all ingredients in a small saucepan; bring to a boil. Reduce heat and simmer 10-12 minutes.

Bonnie Daugherty McGee

It's better to be a has been,
than to never have been at all.

BUTTERMILK POUND CAKE

1 c. butter
3 c. sugar
6 egg yolks
3 c. flour
1/4 tsp. soda
1/2 tsp. salt

1 c. buttermilk
1 tsp. vanilla
1 tsp. butter extract
2 tsp. lemon extract
6 egg whites, beaten

Cream butter with sugar. Add egg yolks, 1 at a time, beating after each yolk. Sift dry ingredients together. Add buttermilk and dry ingredients alternately. Add flavorings. Fold in beaten egg whites. Bake 1 hour and 15 minutes at 350 degrees in bundt pan sprayed with Pam.

Marguerite McLeod
Cherokee County

COCONUT POUND CAKE

1 1/2 c. shortening
2 1/4 c. sugar
5 whole eggs
3 c. cake flour, sifted

1/4 tsp. salt
1 c. milk
1 7-oz. pkg. flaked coconut

Beat shortening at medium speed with electric mixer. Gradually add sugar, beating well. Add whole eggs, 1 at a time. Combine flour and salt and add to creamed mixture alternately with milk, beginning and ending with flour mixture. Stir in coconut. Pour batter into greased and floured 10-inch pan. Bake at 325 degrees for 1 hour and 25 minutes or until a wooden pick inserted in center comes out clean. Cool on wire rack.

Catherine Porter
Navarro County

COCONUT POUND CAKE

2 sticks margarine
2/3 c. solid vegetable shortening
3 c. sugar
5 eggs
3 c. all-purpose flour
1/2 tsp. baking powder

1 tsp. salt
1/2 tsp. baking soda
1 c. buttermilk
1 tsp. vanilla
1 c. coconut

Preheat oven to 325 degrees. Cream margarine, shortening and sugar; add eggs, 1 at a time, beating well after each addition. Combine dry ingredients and add alternately with buttermilk and vanilla, ending with flour. Fold in coconut. Bake in large (10-inch) well greased tube pan or use a bundt pan and bake remaining batter in a small pan for the family. Bake 1 hour in a bundt pan or about 1 hour and 15 minutes to 1 hour and 30 minutes in a tube pan. Cool in pan 10 minutes before turning out.

Houston County

CORNSTARCH POUND CAKE

3 c. sugar
6 eggs, separated
1 c. Crisco vegetable shortening
1/2 tsp. salt
1 c. buttermilk

1/4 tsp. soda
3 c. flour minus 6 T.
6 T. cornstarch
1 tsp. butter flavoring

Cream sugar, egg yolks, Crisco and salt. Mix soda with buttermilk. Add alternately with flour and cornstarch to sugar mixture. Add butter flavoring. Beat. Beat egg whites until stiff. Fold into cake batter. Bake in greased and floured tube pan for approximately 1 hour at 350 degrees.

Joan Warren
Upshur County

CREAM CHEESE POUND CAKE

3 sticks butter
1 8-oz. pkg. cream cheese
3 c. sugar

6 eggs
3 c. cake flour
1 T. almond extract

Cream butter, cream cheese and sugar. Add eggs alternately with flour, beating well after each addition. Add flavoring. Bake in stem pan 1 hour at 350 degrees or until tester comes out clean.

Blake Sparks
Concho County

CREAM CHEESE POUND CAKE

1 1/2 c. pecans, chopped and
  and divided
1 1/2 c. real butter, softened
1 8-oz. pkg. cream cheese
3 c. sugar

6 eggs
3 c. cake flour, sifted
Dash of salt
1 1/2 tsp. vanilla

Sprinkle 1/2 cup of pecans in a greased and floured pan. Set aside. Cream butter and cream cheese; gradually add sugar, beating until light and fluffy. Add eggs 1 at a time, beating well. After each addition, add flour and salt, stirring until combined. Stir in vanilla and remaining pecans. Bake at 325 degrees for 1 hour and 30 minutes. Cool in pan 10 minutes. Do not overbake. Start checking with a toothpick after baking 1 hour and 15 minutes. This is a very moist cake.

Joyce Wells
Martin County

Laughter is the shock absorber that eases the blow of life.

COCONUT CREAM CHEESE POUND CAKE

3 c. sugar
1/2 c. Crisco shortening
1 c. butter
1 8-oz. pkg. cream cheese
3 c. flour, sifted
6 eggs

1 tsp. vanilla
1 tsp. coconut extract
1/4 tsp. salt
1/2 tsp. baking powder
1 6-oz. pkg. frozen coconut
(thawed)

Preheat oven to 350 degrees. Cream sugar, shortening and butter. Add cream cheese and beat well. Add flour and eggs alternately, beat well. Add extracts, salt, baking powder and coconut. Pour into well-greased tube pan. Bake 1 hour and 15 to 20 minutes. When done, cool for 15 minutes and invert on rack.

Aline Barnett
Panola County

CHARLOTTE 5 FLAVOR CAKE

2 sticks butter or margarine
1/2 c. vegetable shortening
3 c. sugar
5 eggs, well beaten
3 c. all-purpose flour
1/2 tsp. baking powder

1 c. milk
1 tsp. coconut flavoring
1 tsp. rum extract
1 tsp. butter flavoring
1 tsp. lemon extract
1 tsp. vanilla extract

Cream butter, shortening and sugar until light and fluffy. Add well beaten eggs. Combine flour and baking powder and add to creamed mixture alternately with milk. Stir in flavorings. Spoon into prepared 10-inch tube pan (or loaf pans). Bake at 325 degrees for 1 hour and 30 minutes (loaf pan approximately 45 minutes or until light brown). Cool in pan about 10 minutes before turning. Cool on wire racks. Freezes well.

GLAZE

1/2 c. sugar
1/4 c. water
1/2 tsp. coconut flavoring
1/2 tsp. rum extract

1/2 tsp. butter flavoring
1/2 tsp. lemon extract
1/2 tsp. vanilla extract
1/2 tsp. almond extract

Combine ingredients in sauce pan. Bring to boil, stirring until sugar is melted. Pour glaze over cool cake.

Charlotte M. Wymore
Willacy County

A gossiper is like an old shoe -
its tongue never stays in place.

FIVE FLAVOR POUND CAKE

2 sticks margarine
1/2 c. shortening
3 c. sugar
5 eggs, well beaten
3 c. flour
1/2 tsp. baking powder

1 c. milk
1 tsp. vanilla extract
1 tsp. coconut extract
1 tsp. rum extract
1 tsp. lemon extract
1 tsp. almond extract

Cream shortening, margarine and sugar until light. Add well-beaten eggs, flour and baking powder alternately with milk. Add flavorings. Bake at 325 degrees in greased and floured tube or loaf pans for 1 hour and 30 minutes. Cover with glaze while hot.

GLAZE

1 c. sugar
1/2 c. water

1 tsp. coconut extract
1 tsp. almond extract

Bring sugar and water to boil; add flavorings. Put on cake while hot.

Voncille Driver
Fisher County

JO ANN'S BLUE RIBBON SOUR CREAM POUND CAKE

1/2 lb. butter or margarine
3 c. sugar
6 eggs
3 c. cake flour

1/2 pt. sour cream
1/4 tsp. baking soda
2 tsp. vanilla extract
2 tsp. almond extract

Cream butter and sugar; add eggs, 1 at a time, and beat well. Add flour, reserving 2 tablespoonfuls; add sour cream and mix. Add reserved flour with baking soda, and add flavorings. Bake in a greased and floured 10-inch tube pan at 325 degrees for 1 1/2 hours. This makes a very large cake which stays moist longer than other pound cakes. Also freezes well. This recipe won a blue ribbon at the Victoria "Kounty Fair" in March 1982. Delicious served with fresh strawberries and whipped cream or ice cream. This is one of my favorite cake recipes.

Jo Ann Swanson
Victoria County

How do you sleep at night?
Do you count "sheep" or
do you talk to the "Shepherd"?

SOUR CREAM CHOCOLATE POUND CAKE

1 c. butter or margarine
2 c. sugar
2 eggs
2 sq. unsweetened chocolate or
    4 T. cocoa
2 tsp. vanilla
1 c. sour cream
2 tsp. soda
2 1/2 c. flour
1/4 tsp. salt
1 c. boiling water

Cream butter and sugar; add eggs, 1 at a time, beating well after each addition. Stir in chocolate and vanilla. Mix sour cream and soda; add to mixture. Sift together flour and salt; add to mixture. Add boiling water. Pour into tube pan, greased and dusted with cocoa. Bake 1 hour and 30 minutes at 325 degrees.

Pearlie Love
Grimes County

SOUR CREAM LEMON POUND CAKE

1 stick margarine
1/2 c. shortening
3 c. sugar
5 large eggs
1 c. sour cream
1/4 c. sweet milk
3 c. flour
1/2 tsp. baking powder
1/4 tsp. salt
1 T. vanilla
1 T. lemon extract

Cream margarine, shortening and sugar. Add eggs, 1 at a time, beating well after each. Add sour cream, milk and flour, baking powder and salt mixture. Mix well. Add vanilla and lemon extracts. Bake in a well-floured tube pan in a preheated 325 degree oven for 1 hour and 45 minutes.

Nadine Weatherford
Smith County

PUDDIN' CAKE

1 stick margarine
1 c. flour
1 c. pecans, chopped
1 8-oz. pkg. cream cheese,
    softened
1 c. powdered sugar
1 lg. carton Cool Whip
1 (4 1/2-oz.) pkg. Instant
    chocolate pudding
1 (3 1/2-oz.) pkg. Instant
    vanilla pudding
3 c. cold milk
1 plain chocolate bar, grated

Combine margarine, flour and pecans for crust and press into bottom of 9 x 13-inch pan. Bake at 350 degrees for 20 minutes and cool. Blend cream cheese, powdered sugar and 1 cup Cool Whip. Spread over cool crust. Prepare instant puddings using 1 1/2 cups milk each. Pour vanilla pudding, then chocolate pudding over cream cheese filling. Top with remaining Cool Whip and grated chocolate. Chill.

Wanza Graham
Mitchell County

PUMPKIN CAKE

3 c. sugar	4 eggs
1 c. cooking oil	2 c. pumpkin
2 c. nuts	1 lb. raisins
2 tsp. soda	1 1/4 tsp. salt
1 tsp. nutmeg	1 tsp. cinnamon
1/2 c. water	3 1/2 c. flour

Mix dry ingredients, make a well. Add water, oil and eggs, mix until well blended with electric mixer. Add nuts and raisins. Bake in floured and greased bundt or loaf pans at 325 degrees for about 45 minutes to 1 hour.

Mrs. J. L. Rochelle
Young County

PUMPKIN PIE CAKE

1 can pumpkin (29 oz. or 2 scant cups)	1 tsp. ginger
	1/2 tsp. nutmeg
4 eggs	1 box yellow cake mix
1 13-oz. can evaporated milk	1 c. (2 sticks) butter or
1 1/2 c. granulated sugar	margarine, melted
2 tsp. cinnamon	1 c. nuts, chopped

Preheat oven to 350 degrees. Beat first 7 ingredients together and pour into ungreased 9 x 13-inch cake pan. Sprinkle dry cake mix over the batter. Pour melted butter over the cake mix and sprinkle with chopped nuts. Bake 1 hour, no longer. (I think 3/4 c. sugar is sweet enough for this cake.)

Lispcomb County

PUMPKIN PIE CAKE

1 30-oz. can pumpkin pie mix	2 sticks butter
1 yellow or white cake mix	1 c. pecans, chopped

Follow instructions on pumpkin pie mix. Pour into a 9 x 12-inch pan sprayed with Pam. Evenly spread dry cake mix on top. Melt butter and evenly pour over top of cake mix, then put chopped pecans on top. Bake at 350 degrees for 1 hour.

Sondra Yancey
Newton County

The toughest part of dieting
isn't watching what you eat --
it's watching what your friends eat.

PUNCH BOWL "CAKE"

1 yellow cake mix
1 lg. can cherry pie filling or
  other fruit as desired
1 lg. can (#2) crushed pineapple,
  drained.

1 sm. box dry vanilla instant
  pudding mix
1 lg. Cool Whip
1 c. pecans, chopped

Mix and bake cake mix in 9 x 13-inch pan according to directions. In small punch bowl layer in four layers or as many as desired. Divide in fourths and layer in the following order: Cake layer (pinched or crumbled), pie filling, pineapple, vanilla pudding, Cool Whip. Then sprinkle pecans on top of Cool Whip as a garnish. For larger layers, double pie filling, pineapple, and pudding mix.

Mary Agnes Jaster
Falls County

PUNCH BOWL CAKE

1 box yellow cake mix
1 lg. box vanilla instant pie
  filling
3 c. milk
1 can cherry pie filling
1 can strawberry pie filling

1 lg. can crushed pineapple,
  undrained
1 lg. container Cool Whip
2 c. coconut
Maraschino cherries
Pecans

Bake cake as directed on box in 9 x 13-inch pan. Cool. Crumble cake in bottom of punch bowl. Mix pie filling with milk and chill. Mix cherry and strawberry pie fillings with vanilla mix. Pour over cake. Layer pineapple over this. Spread Cool Whip over pineapple and sprinkle with coconut. Drain cherries, place on top. Sprinkle with pecans. Chill.

Hoy Belle Duffey
Upshur County

PUNCH BOWL CAKE

1 pineapple or yellow cake mix
1 lg. instant vanilla pudding
2 c. cherry pie filling
2 c. crushed pineapple, drained

2 sm. cartons Cool Whip
2-4 bananas
1 c. nuts, chopped
4 c. milk

Bake cake as directed on box. Cool. Crumble 1/2 cake in small glass punch bowl. Mix instant pudding with 4 cups milk. Spread 1/2 of pudding on top of cake. Spread 1 can pie filling on pudding. Spread 1 can pineapple on top of this. Chop 1 banana on top of this. Spread 1 carton Cool Whip on next and sprinkle 1/2 cup nuts on top; continue layering. Can decorate with maraschino cherries, if desired. Can substitute ready baked angel food cake. Refrigerate.

Vera McCaffety
Polk County

RUM CAKE

1 box yellow cake mix
1 box instant vanilla pudding
1/4 c. rum
1/4 c. vegetable oil

1/4 c. margarine
1 c. nuts, chopped
4 eggs

Mix all cake ingredients. Pour into bundt pan and bake at 350 degrees for 50-60 minutes. While cake is still hot in pan, pour glaze over top and allow to soak in.

GLAZE

1/4 lb. margarine
1/4 c. water

1 c. sugar
1/4 c. rum

Mix margarine, water and sugar together in sauce pan and bring to boil. Add rum. Pour over hot cake. Allow cake to cool, then remove from pan.

Barbria Rich
Wise County

SAD CAKE

4 eggs
2 c. Bisquick mix
1 box brown sugar

1 tsp. vanilla
Coconut
Pecans

Mix ingredients together and bake at 375 degrees for 30 minutes. This cake rises up and then falls.

Jaunice Richards
Winkler County

7-UP CAKE

1 1/2 c. butter
1 3/4 c. sugar
5 eggs

3 c. flour, sifted
2 tsp. lemon flavoring
3/4 c. 7-Up

Combine butter and sugar until fluffy. Add and blend eggs, 1 at a time. Mix in flour, lemon flavoring and 7-Up. Mix for 2 minutes. Bake in floured tube pan at 325 degrees for 1 hour and 15 minutes.

Wanda King and Sharon Miles
Wheeler County

*A good memory is fine --
but the ability to forget is the
true test of greatness.*

SILVER CAKE

3 c. cake flour
3 tsp. baking powder
1/2 c. butter
1 1/2 c. sugar
1 c. milk
1/2 tsp. lemon extract
4 egg whites, stiffly beaten

Sift flour once, measure, add baking powder; sift together 3 times. Cream butter and add sugar gradually; cream together until light and fluffy. Add flour alternately with milk, a small amount at a time. Beat after each addition until smooth. Add flavoring. Fold in egg whites and bake in 3 greased cake pans in moderate oven (375 degrees) about 20 or 30 minutes.

Elizabeth Davis
Gonzales County

SOUR CREAM COFFEE CAKE

1 c. (2 sticks) butter or
    margarine, softened
1 1/4 c. sugar
2 eggs
1 c. (8-oz. carton) sour cream
2 c. flour, sifted
1/2 tsp. baking soda
1 1/2 tsp. baking powder
1 tsp. vanilla extract

Filling and Topping:
1 pkg. pecan pieces
1 tsp. cinnamon
1/4 c. light brown sugar
2 T. sugar

Combine butter or margarine, sugar and eggs; beat until light and fluffy. Blend in sour cream. Sift flour, baking soda and baking powder into the cream mixture and blend well. Add vanilla and blend well. Grease and flour a 9-inch tube pan, spoon half of batter into pan. Combine filling and topping ingredients and sprinkle half of this mixture over batter. Spoon in remaining batter and top with rest of topping mixture. Place in cold oven; set oven temperature to 350 degrees and bake about 55 minutes.

Shelby County

SOUR CREAM SNACK CAKE

1 Duncan Hines Butter Recipe
    Cake mix
4 eggs
1 8-oz. carton sour cream
1/2 c. sugar
1 1/2 tsp. vanilla
1/2 c. vegetable oil

Mix all ingredients together and pour into greased and floured bundt pan. Bake at 350 degrees or 35-40 minutes. Check cake for doneness. Do not over bake.

Betty Moreland
Panola County

LOU LOU'S SPECIAL CAKE

2 2/3 c. flour, sifted
1 tsp. salt
2 1/2 tsp. Calumet baking powder
4 eggs, separated
1/2 c. butter flavor Crisco
  shortening

1 stick margarine
2 c. sugar
1 c. milk
1 tsp. vanilla and almond
  extract
1 tsp. butter flavoring

Sift flour, salt and baking powder 2 times. Beat egg whites until stiff and dry. Beat egg yolks for 5 minutes. Cream shortening and margarine; gradually add sugar. Beat in egg yolks. Add flavorings; mix well. Add flour and milk alternately. Fold in egg whites. Pour into 3 9-inch greased pans. Bake at 350 degrees for 30-35 minutes. Cool. Yield: 18 servings.

Louise Melancon
Meatra Harrison

SUGARLESS SPICE CAKE

2 c. raisins
2 c. water
1 c. unsweetened applesauce
2 eggs, beaten
2 T. liquid artificial sweetener
3/4 c. vegetable oil

1 tsp. baking soda
2 c. all-purpose flour
1 1/2 tsp. ground cinnamon
1/2 tsp. ground nutmeg
1 tsp. vanilla extract
Whipped cream, opt.

In a saucepan, cook raisins in water until water evaporates. Add applesauce, eggs, sweetener and oil; mix well. Blend in baking soda and flour. Stir in cinnamon, nutmeg and vanilla. Pour into a greased 8 x 8-inch baking pan. Bake at 350 degrees for 25 minutes or until cake tests done. Serve with a dollop of whipped cream, if desired. Yield: 20 servings. Diabetic Exchanges: One serving (without whipped cream topping) equals 1 starch, 1/2 fruit, 2 fat; also 181 calories 18 mg sodium, 10 mg. cholesterol, 24 gm carbohydrate, 3 gm protein, 9 gm fat.

Luella Ledwig, Matagorda County
Eulus Damron, Dawson County

Happy are the merciful --
those who know how to forgive --
which is another way of saying,
"Happy are they who can take the first step."

SWEET POTATO CAKE

2 c. sugar	1 tsp. vanilla flavoring
1 1/2 c. Wesson oil	1 tsp. soda
2 c. flour, sifted	1 tsp. baking powder
3 eggs	1 1/2 c. mashed sweet potatoes
1 tsp. butter flavoring	1 1/2 tsp. cinnamon
1 tsp. salt	

Beat sugar and oil until mixed Add eggs, beating well. Add remaining ingredients and beat well. This makes 2 9-inch layers. Bake in greased and floured pans at 350 degrees for 30 minutes or until tests done.

ICING

1 box powdered sugar	1 stick margarine
1 8-oz pkg. cream cheese	1 c. pecans, chopped

Mary Casey
Van Zandt County

LEE'S TWINKIE CAKE

1 10 1/2-oz. pkg. sweetened	1 3-oz. box instant French
frozen strawberries, thawed	vanilla pudding
2 bananas, sliced	1 sm. container Cool Whip
1 box Twinkies	

In 8 or 9-inch glass dish, line with thawed strawberries. Slice bananas on top, lay Twinkies on top side by side (takes approximately 10). Mix pudding according to package. Pour over twinkies. Put in refrigerator until set. Top with Cool Whip. Can be garnished with chopped nuts or sprinkles. Recipe can be doubled to 9 x 13-inch container.

Lee Baker
Collin County

WATERMELON CAKE

1 box white cake mix	1 1/3 c. seedless watermelon
1 3-oz. pkg. mixed fruit jello	cubes
	3 egg whites

Mix all ingredients. Pour into greased and floured bundt pan. Bake about 35 minutes. When cool, can ice with the following:

ICING

2 3-oz. pkgs. cream cheese	1/4 c. watermelon juice
1/4 c. butter	2 c. confectioners' sugar

Mix cream cheese and butter until fluffy. Add sugar and juice. Stir until blended. Spread on cooled cake.

Lillie B. Morse
Brooks County

SWIRLED HONEY COFFEE CAKE

4 1/2- 4 3/4 c. all-purpose flour	1 c. apples, cooked
2 pkgs. dry yeast	1/2 c. raisins
1 c. milk	1 c. pecans, chopped
1/2 c. sugar	1/2 c. honey
1/2 c. butter or margarine	1/3 c. brown sugar
1 tsp. salt	1 tsp ground cinnamon
2 eggs	1 recipe Powdered Sugar Icing

In large mixing bowl, stir together 2 cups of the flour and the yeast. Heat milk, sugar, butter or margarine and salt just until warm (115 to 120 degrees), stirring until butter almost melts. Add to dry ingredients in mixer bowl; add eggs. Beat at low speed of mixer 1/2 minute, scraping sides constantly. Beat 3 minutes at high speed. By hand, sir in enough remaining flour to make a moderately soft dough. Turn out onto lightly floured surface; knead 5-8 minutes or until smooth and elastic. Place in greased bowl; turn once. Cover; let rise 1 1/4 to 1 1/2 hours or until double.

Punch down. Divide dough in half. Cover; let rest 10 minutes. On lightly floured surface roll half the dough to a 14 x 8-inch rectangle. Stir together remaining ingredients except icing; spread half the filling mixture over rectangle to within 1/2-inch of edges. Starting from long side, roll up jelly-roll fashion. Pinch edge to seal. Cut in 1-inch slices. Arrange in layers in greased 10-inch tube pan. Repeat with remaining dough and filling. Cover and let rise 45-50 minutes or until double. Bake in 350 degree oven 40-50 minutes. After half the time, cover with foil to prevent burning.

POWDERED SUGAR ICING

2 T. margarine	1/2 tsp. vanilla
1 c. powdered sugar	Milk

Melt margarine; add powdered sugar, vanilla and enough milk to make a drizzling consistency.

Doris Saathoff
Madina County

FUDGE ICING

1/2 c. margarine	1 lb. powdered sugar
1/3 c. milk	1 tsp. vanilla
1/4 c. cocoa	1/4 tsp. salt

Microwave margarine, milk and cocoa in a glass bowl on high for 2 minutes. Stir in sugar, vanilla and salt. Spread icing over both cakes in the pan they are cooked in. Cut like brownies.

Ruth Redmon
District 9

A heart full of love always has something to give.

BURNT SUGAR ICING

2 1/2 c. granulated sugar
1 c. whole milk
3 T. butter or margarine
1/2 tsp. vanilla

Place 2 cups of the sugar and the milk in a sauce pan and begin cooking on low heat. Burn 1/2 cup of sugar in a heavy skillet until golden brown. Stir in the burnt sugar to the cooking mixture of milk and sugar. Continue stirring and cooking until the syrup will form a soft ball in cold water. Allow to cook for about 10 minutes and beat until about consistency of batter. Add the butter and vanilla and continue beating until the right consistency to spread. This is a good icing for white or yellow cake mix cakes.

Mildred Reynolds, Stanton E. H. Club
Martin County

Desserts

NO BAKE CHEESECAKE

Crust:
1 1/2 c. graham cracker crumbs
3 T. sugar
1/3 c. margarine, melted

Combine crust ingredients and press in spring form pan. Bake in 350 degree oven for 7-10 minutes.

Filling:
3 oz. box lemon jello
1 c. boiling water
16-oz. cream cheese
3/4 c. sugar
1 T. lemon juice
1 9-oz. container whipped topping

Dissolve jello in boiling water, set aside until syrupy. Cream cheese and sugar, add lemon juice. Stir in syrupy jello. Fold in whipped topping. Put in cooled pie shell. Refrigerate.

Billie Horn
Potter County

MIRACLE CHEESECAKE

1 1/4 c. graham cracker
1/4 c. sugar
6 T. butter or margarine, melted
1 pkg. lemon jello
1 c. boiling water
3 T. lemon juice
1 8-oz. pkg. cream cheese
1 c. sugar
1 lg. can Milnot, chilled
1 tsp. vanilla

Crush graham crackers, add sugar and butter. Line three pie plates or large baking dish with crust. Save a little to sprinkle on top. Dissolve jello in water; add lemon juice. Cool, but do not let jell. Add a little at a time to cheese and sugar mixture. Whip Milnot until it forms a peak. Gently fold cheese jello mixture into Milnot. Put into crust and sprinkle topping on top. Refrigerate but do not freeze. Let set 6 hours before serving.

Lipscomb County

CREAM CHEESECAKE

3 sticks butter
3 c. sugar
1 8-oz. pkg. cream cheese

3 c. Softasilk enriched cake flour
2 tsp. lemon extract
6 eggs (at room temperature)

Mix butter and eggs until creamy. Add cream cheese and mix until smooth and fluffy. Mix 1 cup of enriched cake flour with 2 eggs with hand mixer until smooth. Continue until all eggs and flour are used. Add lemon extract. Beat with mixing spoon until all lumps are out. Oil baking pan with **Mazola Corn Oil**. Dust with a dash of enriched cake flour. Place cream cheese mixture in pan and bake at 320 degree oven for 1 hour and 30 minutes or until brown. Do not force the cake to come out of pan. Turn on cake pan and leave for 30 minutes. It will automatically leave the pan.

District 9, Shelby County

CHERRY-ALMOND CHEESECAKE

24 chocolate wafer cookies
1/2 c. slivered almonds, blanched
3/4 c. + 2 T. sugar, divided
4 T. butter, melted
1 tsp. almond extract, divided
2 env. unflavored gelatin
1 c. boiling water

2 16-oz. containers cottage cheese
1 8-oz. pkg. cream cheese (at room temperature)
1 c. heavy cream
1 T. vanilla extract
1 21-oz. can cherry pie filling

In food processor, process cookies, almonds, and 2 tablespoonfuls sugar for 1 minute or until fine crumbs; place into 9-inch spring form pan. Toss in butter and 1/2 teaspoonful almond extract until well combined. Press crumbs onto bottom and halfway up sides of pan. Freeze 15 minutes.

In large bowl of mixer, stir gelatin and 1/4 cup sugar. Add water; stir until gelatin is completely dissolved. Beat in 1/2 cup sugar, 1/2 teaspoonful almond extract, cheeses, heavy cream and vanilla. Beat 5 minutes longer; pour into prepared crust. Chill 4 1/2 hours until mixture is firm. To serve, spoon cherry pie filling over top.

Martha Schueler
Parmer County

Love doesn't just sit there,
like a stone;
it has to be made,
like bread,
remade all the time,
made new.

CHOCOLATE RIBBON CHEESECAKE

2 c. chocolate wafer crumbs
1/2 c. Parkay margarine, melted
1 env. unflavored gelatin
1/4 c. cold water
2 8-oz. pkgs. Philadelphia Brand
   cream cheese, softened
1/4 c. sugar
1 tsp. vanilla
1 7-oz. jar Kraft marshmallow
   creme
1 c. whipping cream, whipped
1/2 c. semi-sweet chocolate
   pieces, melted

Combine crumbs and margarine; press onto bottom of 9-inch spring form pan. Chill. Soften gelatin in water; stir over low heat until dissolved. Combine cream cheese, sugar and vanilla, mixing until well blended. Beat in marshmallow creme; fold in whipped cream. Fold chocolate into 2 cups gelatin mixture. Pour remaining gelatin mixture over crust; carefully spoon on chocolate mixture. Chill until firm. Yield: 10-12 servings.

District 9, Rusk County

PECAN PRALINE CHEESECAKE

1 1/4 c. graham crackers, crushed
1/4 c. granulated sugar
1/4 c. margarine
3 8-oz. pkgs. cream cheese
1 c. light brown sugar
1 5-oz. can evaporated milk
2 T. flour
2 1/2 tsp. vanilla, divided
3 large eggs
1 c. pecans, chopped
1 c. dark corn syrup
1/2 tsp. corn starch
2 T. brown sugar

Crust:

Place margarine in pie plate and microwave on high 30 seconds. Combine graham crackers and sugar with margarine and press on bottom and sides of pie plate. Microwave on 70% medium high power for 3 minutes. Let cool.

Cheesecake:

Place unwrapped cream cheese in large glass mixer bowl. Microwave on 50% medium power for 3- 3 1/2 minutes or until softened. Using mixer, beat cream cheese with brown sugar, milk, flour and 1 1/2 teaspoonful vanilla. Add eggs and beat just until blended. Pour into baked crust. Microwave on 70% power 12-15 minutes or until set, rotating once. Cool at least 30 minutes before serving.

Topping:

Sprinkle pecan pieces over top of cheesecake. In a 4 cup glass measure, pour in dark corn syrup. Add corn starch, brown sugar and 1 teaspoonful vanilla. Microwave on high for 3 minutes. Spoon warm sauce over top of cheesecake.

NOTE: This cheesecake can be baked either in a 10-inch glass pie plate or in a 2-quart rectangular dish. If using the rectangular dish, press crust on bottom only.

Kathy Schwegmann
Williamson County

DOUBLE STRAWBERRY CHEESECAKE

1 pkg. Deluxe Strawberry Supreme Cake Mix	4 eggs
1 T. Crisco oil	1 1/2 c. milk
2 8-oz. pkgs. cream cheese	1 T. lemon juice
1/2 c. sugar	4 drops red food coloring
	2-2 1/2 c. whipped topping

Preheat oven to 350 degrees. Reserve 1 cup dry cake mix. In a large mixing bowl, combine remaining cake mix, 1 egg and oil. Mixture will be crumbly. Press crushed mixture evenly into bottom and 3/4 ways up side of a greased 9 x 13-inch pan. In the same bowl, blend cream cheese and sugar. Add 3 eggs and reserved cake mix. Beat for 1 minute at medium speed. At low speed, slowly add milk, lemon juice and food coloring. Mix until smooth. Pour into crust. Bake at 300 degrees for 50-60 minutes until center is firm. When cool, spread whipped topping. Refrigerate before serving. To freeze, cover with foil.

Joan Frost, State TEHA Treasurer
Swisher County

A GOOD DESSERT

1 c. flour, unsifted	2 pkgs. instant chocolate pudding
1 stick margarine	
1 c. pecans, chopped	3 c. cold milk
1 8-oz. pkg. cream cheese	Sliced almonds for garnish
1 c. powdered sugar, unsifted	(opt.)
2 c. frozen whipped topping, thawed	

Put margarine, flour, and pecans in food processor and blend well. Press into 13 x 9-inch baking pan. Bake in a preheated 350 degree oven for 15-20 minutes. Cool completely before proceeding.

Blend cream cheese and powdered sugar in processor until smooth. Fold in 1 cup whipped topping. Spread over cooled crust. Mix instant pudding with milk until well blended. Chill mixture 5 minutes in refrigerator. Carefully spoon onto cream cheese mixture, spreading carefully to make a smooth layer. Do not stir. Spoon remaining 1 cup whipped topping on top of chocolate layer. Garnish with almond slices. Cover with plastic wrap and refrigerate until serving time.

Betty Katcsmorak
Atascosa County

And whatever you do,
do it with kindness and love.

APPLE STRUDEL

3/4 c. butter	2 egg yolks
1/ c. warm milk	3 1/4 c. flour

Combine milk, butter and egg yolks. Mix well. Work it into the flour a little at a time. Work this together by hand until dough is formed. Divide into three parts; place in plastic bags in refrigerator over night or for at least 3 hours. Take out one bag at a time and roll on floured cloth until extremely thin.

FILLING (For one Strudel)

3 apples	1 c. sugar
1/4 c. raisins	1/2 c. coconut
1 c. pecans, chopped	1 c. corn flakes, crushed
Sprinkle of cinnamon	1/4 c. butter, melted

Combine all ingredients, except melted butter Brush melted butter on dough, place filling on dough and roll up and seal ends. Place on aluminum foil on cookie sheet. Bake at 350 degrees for about 35-40 minutes or until crust is flaky and brown.

Annie Mae Hubnik
Ector County

BLUEBERRY CRUNCH

1 8-oz. can crushed pineapple, juice and all	1 box yellow cake mix, right out of the box
3 c. fresh or frozen blueberries	1 stick margarine, melted
3/4 c. sugar	1 c. sugar
	1/2 c. pecans, chopped

In 9 x 13-inch baking dish, layer the ingredients in order listed. Bake in 350 degree oven for 1 hour.

Dottie Johnson
Tyler County

OLD-FASHIONED BREAD PUDDING

2 c. milk	2 eggs, slightly beaten
4 c. bread crumbs (small chunks)	1/4 tsp. salt
1/4 c. butter, melted	1 tsp. cinnamon
1/2 c. sugar	1/2 c. raisins, (opt.)

Heat milk to scalding. Pour over bread crumbs. Cool and add butter, sugar, eggs, salt, cinnamon and raisins. Pour into buttered 1 1/2 quart casserole. Bake at 350 degrees for 40-45 minutes or until silver knife inserted in pudding comes out clean.

Jean McIntyre
Collin County

CAPIROTADA (MEXICAN BREAD PUDDING)

2 c. water
1 cone piloncillo or 1 1/2 c.
  dark brown sugar
2 sticks cinnamon
1 tsp. anise seed
3 T. butter
6-8 slices french bread, toasted

1/4-1/2 lb. cheddar cheese,
  grated
1/2 c. raisins
1/2 c. nuts, chopped
2 apples, peeled and sliced
2 bananas, (opt.)

Boil piloncillo or sugar in water with cinnamon and anise seed. Simmer until sugar or piloncillo is dissolved; add butter and set aside. In 2-quart baking dish, layer bread, cheese, raisins, nuts, apples and bananas alternately, end with bread on top. Pour the sugar-water mixture over the bread-cheese mixture. Bake in preheated 400 degree oven for 20-30 minutes. Yield: 4-6 servings.

Connie Escobedo
Cameron County

CHERRY DREAM SQUARES

1 pkg. Pillsbury white cake mix
1 1/4 c. rolled oats
1/2 c. margarine or butter,
  softened
1 egg

1 21-oz. can cherry pie filling
1/2 c. nuts, chopped
1/4 c. brown sugar, firmly
  packed

Heat oven to 350 degrees. Grease 13 x 9-inch pan. In large bowl, combine cake mix, 6 tablespoonfuls margarine and 1 cup rolled oats. Mix until crumbly. Reserve 1 cup crumbs for topping. To remaining crumbs, add egg, mix until well blended. Press into prepared pan. Pour cherry pie filling over crust, spread to cover. To reserved crumbs, in large bowl, add remaining 1/4 cup rolled oats, 2 tablespoonfuls margarine, nuts and brown sugar. Beat until thoroughly mixed. Sprinkle over cherry mixture. Bake at 350 degrees for 30-40 minutes or until golden brown. Cool completely. If desired, serve with a dollop of whipped cream. Makes 12 servings.

Lillian Winston
Terry County

"STALL" CINNAMON ROLL PUDDING

16 cinnamon rolls
3 eggs
1 c. sugar
1 tsp. cinnamon

3 c. milk
1 stick margarine or butter,
  melted

Place cinnamon rolls in baking dish. Mix all ingredients and pour over cinnamon rolls. Mash until the rolls soak up liquid. May need to add more milk - approximately 1 cup. Sprinkle with **pecan halves**. Place baking pan in pan of water. Bake at 350 degrees approximately 45 minutes to 1 hour.

Ed Wilson
Anderson County

CHERRY COBBLER

1 can cherries
1 1/2 c. sugar
1/2 stick margarine
1/2 tsp. almond flavoring

Cook cherries, sugar and margarine until hot and margarine is melted. Add flavoring. Put in baking dish and cover with crust. Poke holes all over dough and sprinkle liberally with sugar. Add small pats of butter all over. Bake.

Bertha Hunter
Jones County

CRESCENT ROLL FRUIT COBBLER

1 pkg. dairy case Crescent
  Rolls (8)
2 c. fruit, cut up into pieces
  (any kind canned or fresh
  apples, peaches, blueberries,
  etc.)
1/2 c. fruit juice (orange, pear
  nectar, peach, whatever you
  want)
1 c. sugar
1 stick butter or margarine
Spices of choice

Melt butter, sugar and juice in microwave or on top of stove. Pat 4 rolls into bottom of 8 x 8-inch buttered pan. Pour in fruit, spread evenly on top of rolls. Place remainder 4 rolls on top of fruit. Pour warm mixture over fruit. You can add spices of your choice to fruit before putting on top crust. Bake at 350 degrees for 40 minutes. *This is an original recipe - a Blue Ribbon winner!

Patricia K. Tully
Kaufman County

PEACH COBBLER

6-8 lg. ripe peaches, peeled
  and sliced
Crust:
1 c. flour
2 egg yolks
1/4 c. butter or margarine, melted
2 1/2 T. cornstarch
3/4-1 c. sugar

1 tsp. baking powder
1 c. sugar
2 egg whites, stiffly beaten

Combine peaches, cornstarch and sugar. Pour into a greased 13 x 9 x 2-inch baking pan. For crust, combine all ingredients except egg whites in a mixing bowl. Gently fold egg whites into batter. Spread over peaches. Bake at 375 degrees or about 45 minutes or until the fruit is bubbling around edges and top is golden. Yield: 12 servings.

Eulus Damron
Dawson County

Courtesy is a jewel which needs constant polishing.

DEATH BY CHOCOLATE

1 family size Fudge Brownie Mix
3 tsp. almond extract
3 3 1/2-oz. boxes Jello Chocolate
  Mousse

8 Skor or Heath candy bars,
  crushed
1 16-oz. carton Cool Whip

Bake brownies, punch with a fork and pour almond extract over them. Break into chunks and put into a large glass bowl. Make mousse according to package directions. Layer half the mousse. Add half of candy bars and half of the Cool Whip. Repeat each layer in order, beginning with the brownie chunks and ending with crushed candy bars on top. You'll think you've died and gone to heaven when you see and taste this dessert. It is truly "Death by Chocolate."

Geraldine McIntosh
Wood County

CHOCOLATE RICE CREAM

1 c. flour
1/4 c. rice bran (replace with
  other bran if you can't find
  rice bran)
1 c. pecans, finely chopped
1/2 c. margarine, softened
1 c. cooked rice, creamed

1 8-oz. pkg. cream cheese,
  softened
1 c. powdered sugar
1 12-oz. carton Cool Whip Lite
1 lg. jello instant chocolate
  pudding
3 c. milk

Make crust by combining flour, bran, pecans and margarine. Mix well and press into bottom of 9 x 13 x 2-inch pan. Bake 20 minutes at 350 degrees. Cool. Blend cooked rice until creamy. Beat cheese and powdered sugar until fluffy. Fold in 1 cup Cool Whip and creamed rice. Pour in cooled crust. Chill. Combine pudding mix with 3 cups milk. Mix until thick. Pour over cream cheese layer. Chill again. Top with rest of Cool Whip. Chill until ready to serve.

Judy Johnson
Jackson County

CRANBERRY SURPRISE

2 pkgs. raw cranberries
1 c. sugar
3 bananas, sliced
1 c. pecans, chopped

1 1/2 sm. cans pineapple
  tidbits, drained well
2 T. lemon juice
1 lg. container Cool Whip

Coarsely chop cranberries in food processor. Add sugar and refrigerate overnight. Just before serving add bananas, pecans, pineapple and lemon juice. Fold in Cool Whip. Good with turkey at Thanksgiving or Christmas. Refrigerate any left overs.

Meynell Geers
Ector County

DATE TORTE

1 c. sugar	1 c. dates, pitted
1 c. flour	1 tsp. vanilla
1 tsp. baking powder	3 eggs, beaten
1 c. walnuts	

Mix sugar, flour, baking powder, and walnuts in order. Add dates, vanilla, and beaten eggs. Preheat oven to 350 degrees. Grease and dust pan with flour. Brush egg on top. Bake for 25-45 minutes. Sprinkle powdered sugar on top. Slice.

S. DeLeon
Hidalgo County

ECLAIRS

2 sm. pkgs. vanilla instant pudding	3 T. butter
	3 T. milk
1 12-oz. graham crackers	1/2 c. powdered sugar
1 bar German chocolate	Cool Whip

Prepare pudding as directed on package. Fold in Cool Whip. In 9 x 13-inch dish, place layer of graham crackers, then one-half of pudding mixture, and repeat with graham crackers and pudding. Top with layer of graham crackers. Melt German chocolate with butter and milk, add powdered sugar. Spread over last layer of graham crackers. The flavor is better if this is made a day or two ahead of time.

Karen Kohler
Wichita County

FRUIT FAJITAS

8 lg. tortillas	1 1/2 c. water
1 can fruit pie mix	1 c. sugar
1/2 stick margarine	

In a saucepan, mix sugar, water and margarine. Bring to a boil and remove from heat. Place 2 heaping tablespoonfuls of pie mix on tortilla and roll up. Place in an 8 x 8-inch pan. Continue this procedure for all 8 tortillas. Pour sauce over rolled tortillas and allow to stand 30 minutes, basting with sauce occasionally. Bake in a 350 degree oven for 20 minutes.

Joan Adams
Nueces County

*It is good to have the things that money can buy,
but better to have things that money can't buy.*

FRUIT PIZZA

Crust:

1 roll refrigerated sugar cookies   1/4 c. sugar
1 8-oz. cream cheese, softened

Slice cookie dough and arrange on pizza pan, just touching. Bake in 350 degree oven until light brown. Cool. Mix cream cheese and sugar. Spread on cooled cookie crust.

Glaze:

1 c. orange juice   1 c. sugar
1/8 c. lemon juice   3 T. cornstarch
3/4 c. water (or pineapple juice,   Few drops of red food coloring,
  etc.)   if desired

Mix cornstarch and sugar and combine with liquid ingredients. Cook on stove or in microwave until thickened (about 2 minutes). Cool.

Fruit:

Slice assorted colorful fruits (**bananas, strawberries, kiwi, grapes, pineapple, cherries, etc.**). Arrange over cream cheese on cookie crust. Pour cooled glaze over fruit and chill. Slice in 12 or more pizza wedges to serve.

Earlene Morris
Wilbarger County

KANUKI

1 half gallon ice cream or   1 pkg. frozen sliced
  frozen yogurt, softened   strawberries
1 sm. pkg. Oreo cookies   1 sm. container Cool Whip
1 c. pecans, chopped

Add to softened ice cream or yogurt crumbled Oreo cookies, chopped pecans, thawed strawberries and Cool Whip. Mix all ingredients together and place in a 9 x 13-inch baking dish and place in freezer until frozen solid. Cut into cake size pieces and serve. (This is a very rich dessert so you may want to cut in smaller servings and let your guests ask for seconds.)

Lee Ann James
Parker County

Flatter me -- and I may not believe you.
Criticize me -- and I may not like you.
Ignore me -- and I may not forgive you.
Encourage me -- and I will never forget you.

LEMON LUSH

1 stick margarine
1 c. flour
1/2 c. nuts
1 8-oz. pkg. Philadelphia Cream
  Cheese

2 pkgs. lemon instant pudding
3 c. milk
1 c. powdered sugar
1/4 c. nuts

Mix margarine, flour and 1/2 cup nuts and place in 9 x 13-inch pan and bake in 350 degrees for 15 minutes. Let cool. Put cream cheese on top of crust. Put 2 packages of lemon instant pudding in 3 cups milk on top of cheese. Mix powdered sugar and Cool Whip. Spread on top. Sprinkle with nuts. Yield: 18 servings.

Imogene Kostiha
Palo Pinto County

LEMON SPONGE PUDDING

2 c. sugar
2/3 c. flour
4 T. shortening, melted
8-10 T. lemon juice

2 tsp. grated lemon peel
4 eggs, separated
2 c. milk, scalded

Combine sugar, flour and shortening. Add lemon juice and grated peel. Stir in egg yolks and milk; mix. Beat egg whites until stiff; fold into mixture. Pour into greased shallow casserole dish. Bake in pan with 1-inch hot water surrounding. Bake at 325 degrees for 1 hour. Sponge cake goes to top; custard to bottom.

Sidney Murphey
Yoakum County

NUT ROLL

1 c. sugar
2 pkgs. dry yeast
1/2 c. warm water
2 c. milk

1 tsp. salt
2 eggs
2/3 c. Crisco
7 1/2 c. flour

Mix sugar and yeast in large bowl. Add water; stir until dissolved. Add rest of ingredients, then flour. Let rise 1 hour. Roll out. Makes 8. Brush tops with beaten egg whites and bake at 375 degrees until brown.

NUT FILLING

2 eggs
1 c. sugar
1/2 c. margarine

1/2 c. milk
1/2 c. honey
4 c. pecans, crushed

Mix together all ingredients and spread on dough. Roll as for a cinnamon roll. Put filling on rolled out dough before baking.

Melodye Franks

ORANGE SALAD DESSERT

2 sm. or 1 lg. orange jello
2 c. boiling water
1 sm. can frozen orange juice
2 sm. cans mandarin oranges, drained
1 lg. can crushed pineapple and juice
1 pkg. instant lemon pudding mix
1 c. milk
1 2-oz. pkg. whipped topping, prepared according to pkg. directions
Finely ground nutmeats

Dissolve jello in boiling water. Cool and add orange juice, oranges and pineapple. Pour into 13 x 9-inch pan. Let set until solid. Beat together instant pudding and milk. Let set. Fold whipped topping into the pudding. Spread over jello mixture. Let set in refrigerator. Before serving, top with ground nutmeats. This is best made a day before serving. Makes 8-10 servings.

Sunnyside Club
Lavaca County

PEACH YUMMY

2 can sliced peaches
1 c. brown sugar
1 box yellow cake mix
1 stick margarine

Spread peaches in 9 x 13-inch pan. Reserve juice from 1 can of peaches. Spread brown sugar over peaches and top with cake mix. Melt margarine and mix with peach juice. Pour over top. Bake at 350 degrees for 35 minutes. Top with whipped cream if desired.

Willie McGee
Denton County

PEANUT ORANGE BALLS

1 c. roasted peanuts, chopped
1 12-oz. pkg. orange candy slices, diced
1 14-oz. pkg. flaked coconut
1 14-oz. can sweetened condensed milk
2/3 c. confectioners' sugar

Combine peanuts, orange slices and coconut in large mixing bowl. Add sweetened condensed milk; mix well. Shape into 1-inch balls, roll in confectioners' sugar. Yields about 6 dozen.

Erma Lee Lowrie
Collingsworth County

Some of what I cooked was a burnt offering.
And other things I cooked were a sacrifice.

POPPY SEED LOAF

3 c. flour	2 1/4 c. sugar
1 tsp. salt	1 1/2 tsp. baking powder
3 eggs	1 1/2 c. milk
1 1/2 T. vanilla	1 1/2 c. oil
1 1/2 T. butter extract	1 1/2 T. almonds
1 1/2 T. poppy seed	

Mix all ingredients for 1 or 2 minutes. Pour into greased and floured loaf pans (2 large or 6 small pans). Bake 1 hour at 350 degrees (small pans about 30-40 minutes).

Dorothy Fisher
Cooke County

PUMPKIN LAYERED DELIGHT

First Layer:

1 stick butter or margarine	1 c. flour
1 c. nuts, ground	

Mix and spread on bottom of 9 x 13-inch pan. Bake 20 minutes at 350 degrees. Cool.

Second Layer:

1 8-oz. pkg. cream cheese	1 c. Cool Whip
1 c. powdered sugar	

Blend ingredients well and spread on top of first cooled layer.

Third Layer:

1 c. milk or half & half	1 tsp. ground cinnamon
2 sm. pkgs. of Jello Instant	1/2 tsp. ground ginger
Pudding & Pie Filling	1/4 tsp. ground cloves
1 16-oz. can pumpkin	

Pour milk into bowl. Add pudding mix. Mix until well blended (mixture will be thick). Stir in pumpkin and spices; mix well. Spread over cream cheese layer. Garnish with additional whipped topping and nuts, if desired. Refrigerate several hours before serving.

Jo Johnson
Tom Green County

Brows may wrinkle,
hair grow gray,
but friendship never
knows decay.

PUMPKIN PUDDING DESSERT

1 stick butter
1 c. flour
1 c. pecans
1 pkg. dry vanilla pudding
1 c. pumpkin
1 can Eagle Brand Milk
1 c. Cool Whip

1 tsp. pumpkin spice
1 c. sour cream
1 8-oz. pkg. cream cheese, softened
1/2 c. sugar
1 tsp. vanilla

Mix well butter, flour and pecans. Bake at 350 degrees for 20-25 minutes. Cool and put in bowl as bottom layer. Mix well pudding, pumpkin, milk, Cool Whip and pumpkin spice and place in bowl for middle layer. Mix well sour cream, cream cheese, sugar and vanilla and use as topping.

Amy Adrian, Chairman
Young Family Issues Committee, Hale County

PUMPKIN ROLL

3 eggs
1 tsp. lemon juice
2/3 c. pumpkin
1 c. sugar
3/4 c. flour

1 tsp. baking powder
1/2 tsp. salt
2 tsp. cinnamon
1 tsp. ginger
1/2 tsp. nutmeg

Beat eggs on high for 5 minutes. Gradually add lemon juice and sugar. Fold in pumpkin. Stir in dry ingredients. Spread over a well-greased and floured 10 x 15-inch cookie sheet. Bake at 375 degrees for 15 minutes. Turn out immediately on a kitchen towel sprinkled with powdered sugar. Roll towel and let cool. Unroll for filling.

FILLING

1 8-oz. pkg. cream cheese, softened
4 T. margarine, softened

1 c. powdered sugar
1/2 tsp. vanilla
1 c. pecans, chopped

Combine all ingredients except pecans and beat until smooth. Add pecans and mix well. Spread filling over cake roll and re-roll. Wrap in foil or plastic wrap and refrigerate several hours before slicing. Excellent for freezing and can be served directly from the freezer.

Winnie Sitton

QUICK DELIGHT

1 1-lb. 5-oz. can cherry pie filling
1 8-oz. can crushed pineapple, drained

1 c. small marshmallows
1 c. pecans, broken
1 14-oz. can Eagle Brand Milk
1 8-oz. container Cool Whip

Mix ingredients in large mixing bowl. Chill and serve.

Frances Lannom
Pecos County

RHUBARB CRUNCH

First Layer:

4 c. rhubarb	1/4 tsp. salt
1 c. sugar	

Mix and place in bottom of 8 x 11-inch baking dish.

Second Layer:

1 c. flour	1 tsp. baking powder
1 c. sugar	1 egg
1/2 tsp. salt	1/3 c. butter, melted

Mix flour, sugar, salt, baking powder and egg until crumbly. Sprinkle over rhubarb. Pour melted butter over top. Bake at 350 degrees for 45 minutes.

Josephine Rodriguez
Concho County

RICE PUDDING

1 1/2 qts. milk (whole or half whole and half 2%)	1/3 c. sugar
	1/3 c. raisins
1/3 c. long grain rice	1 tsp. vanilla
3 eggs	

Bring to boil milk with rice, cook about 20 minutes until rice is softened. In Pyrex 2-quart oven bowl, mix the eggs and sugar. Gradually add to this the rice and milk and return the milk, rice, eggs and sugar mixture to the pot and cook 2 more minutes. Pour the whole thing in the oven proof bowl to which you add raisins and vanilla. Place the bowl in a pan of water in a 300 degree oven for about 1 hour. Test for doneness with a knife. When the consistency of custard, remove and cool.

Phyllis Williams
El Paso County

SLOAN'S CASSEROLE

2 lg. cans crushed pineapple	1 tube (36) crushed Ritz
2 c. shredded cheddar cheese	crackers
1 c. sugar	4 oz. butter, melted
6 T. flour	

Preheat oven to 350 degrees. Mix pineapple and cheese. Mix sugar and flour and add to first mixture. Spread in an 8 x 11-inch or 9 x 12-inch casserole dish. Spread crackers on top. Pour melted butter over all. Bake 35-40 minutes.

Joye Graves
Bowie County

Life can only be understood backward,
but it must be lived forward.

111

SOPAPILLAS

1 c. flour	1/2 T. shortening
1 1/2 tsp. baking powder	Few T. lukewarm water
1/4 tsp. salt	

Sift flour, baking powder and salt. Cut in shortening. Add water to make soft dough. Let dough rest for 10 minutes. Roll very thin as for pie crust. Cut into squares about 1-2-inches wide. Fry in hot oil. While frying, take fork and push the ends down into the oil for even browning. Place on paper towels to drain. Sprinkle with **sugar** and/or **honey**. Enjoy!

Esther Siller
Cameron County

SUNDAY DELIGHT

First Layer:

1 c. flour	1 c. nuts, chopped
1 stick margarine	

Second Layer:

1 8-oz. pkg. cream cheese	1 c. Cool Whip
1 c. powdered sugar	

Third Layer:

1 lg. pkg. vanilla instant pudding	3 c. cold milk

Fourth Layer:

1 c. Cool Whip

Mix first layer and press into 9 x 13-inch pan. Bake 15 minutes at 375 degrees. Mix second layer and spread over first layer. For third layer, mix pudding package with milk and layer over mixture in pan. Put Cool Whip on top. Refrigerate at least four hours before eating. Overnight is best.

Barbara Kopplin
Live Oak County

SQUASH AND APPLE BAKE

2 lbs. butternut or buttercup squash	1 T. flour
	1 tsp. salt
1/2 c. brown sugar	1/2 tsp. mace
1/4 c. margarine, melted	2 apples, cored and sliced

Heat oven to 350 degrees. Cut squash in half, pare and cut into 1/2-inch thick slices. Stir together remaining ingredients, except apples. Arrange squash in ungreased 11 1/2 x 7 1/2-inch glass baking dish. Top with apples. Sprinkle sugar mixture on top. Cover with foil. Bake 1 hour or until tender.

Frances Fischer
Hunt County

It's easier to do it than explain why you didn't.

SUNRISE PINK DESSERT

1 6-oz. pkg. strawberry gelatin	2 10-oz. pkgs. frozen sliced
2 c. boiling water	strawberries
1 med. banana, mashed	2 T. lemon juice
	1 pt. sour cream

Dissolve gelatin in boiling water. Add unthawed berries; stir until thawed. Add banana and lemon juice. Stir sour cream into the berry mixture. Pour into a 2-quart mold. Chill until set.

Katheryn Barjenbruch
Collingsworth County

SWEET POTATO PUDDING

2 eggs	2 c. raw sweet potatoes, grated
1 c. sugar	3/4 c. margarine, melted
Pinch of salt	1/2 tsp. cinnamon
1 1/2 c. canned milk	2 tsp. vanilla

Beat eggs and sugar until light. Add other ingredients. Bake in greased casserole dish at 250 degrees for 45-59 minutes or until firm.

Catherine Deason
Tyler County

PINA COLADA ICE CREAM

10 eggs	1 16-oz. can crushed pineapple
1 c. sugar	1 pt. whipping cream
1 can Eagle Brand Milk	Milk
1 can Cream of Coconut	

Mix ingredients together and put in a gallon ice cream freezer container. Add milk to the "fill line" on freezer container and freeze. Makes 1 gallon. This is one of the club's best sellers at our annual ice cream booth at the Texline Community Days.

Handy Homemakers E. H. Club
Dallam County

SUGAR FREE ICE CREAM

2 sm. pkgs. instant sugar free pudding	2 cans low-fat Pet milk
2 qts. 1/2% milk (or powdered milk mixed to make 2 qts.)	5 bananas, mashed
	1/2 c. pecans, chopped
6 tsp. Sweet 'N Low or 18 pkgs. Equal	1 tsp. vanilla
	1/8 tsp. salt

Mix together and put in freezer can. Add more milk to fill can. Freeze usual way. Yield: 1 gallon.

Waulden McKinney
Lamb County

SUGARLESS & MILKLESS VANILLA ICE CREAM

6 eggs
1 22-oz. jar non-dairy powdered
  creamer
2 qts. liquid non-dairy creamer
12 pkgs. Sweet 'N Low
2 T. vanilla

Beat eggs, 1 at a time, with electric mixer until frothy. Gradually add powdered non-dairy creamer alternately with liquid non-dairy creamer. Add Sweet 'N Low and vanilla. The secret is to beat until all powdered ingredients are dissolved. Freeze.

Rita Snodgrass
Yoakum County

DIET TIPS

1. *If no one sees you eat it, it has no calories.*

2. *If you drink a diet soda with a candy bar, they cancel each other out.*

3. *When eating with someone else, calories don't count if you both eat the same amount.*

4. *Food used for medical purposes never counts such as: hot chocolate, brandy, toast and Sara Lee cheeseake.*

5. *If you fatten up everyone else around you, then you look thinner.*

6. *Movie related foods don't count because they are simply part of the entertainment experiences, and not of one's personal fuel, such as Milk Duds, popcorn with butter, Junior Mints and red licorice.*

7. *Cookie pieces contain no calories. The process of breakage causes caloric leakage.*

COOKIES, CANDIES & BARS

Cookies, Candies and Bars

Cookies

SANDIES

1 c. butter or margarine
1/3 c. granulated sugar
2 tsp. water

2 tsp. vanilla
2 c. all-purpose flour, sifted
1 c. pecans, chopped

Cream butter and sugar; add water and vanilla and mix well. Blend in flour and nuts. Chill 4 hours. Shape in balls or fingers. Bake on ungreased cookie sheet at 325 degrees about 20 minutes. Remove from pan; cool slightly. Roll in confectioners' sugar. Roll second time in confectioners' sugar. Yield: 3 dozen cookies.

Mildred Presley
Waller County

Adell Jordan from Medina County uses 1 tablespoonful water, 2 1/2 cups flour and bakes at 300 degrees for same amount of time.

ICE BOX OATMEAL COOKIES

3 c. oatmeal
1 c. brown sugar
1/4 c. hot water
1/2 tsp. salt
1 tsp. soda

1 c. butter, melted
1 c. flour
1 c. pecans, chopped
1 tsp. vanilla

Mix all ingredients and make into 2 rolls. Chill. Slice thin and bake at 325 degrees for 10-12 minutes.

Louisa Deanda
Menard County

LACE COOKIES

2 1/2 c. oats
1 c. brown sugar
1/2 c. margarine, melted

2 tsp. baking powder
1 egg, beaten

Add margarine to dry ingredients, add egg; mix well. Drop 1-inch apart on greased cookie sheet. Bake 10 minutes at 350 degrees. Let set 10 minutes before removing from pan.

Nacogdoches County

The quickest way to acquire self-confidence
is to do exactly what you are afraid to do.

RANGER COOKIES

1 c. shortening	1 c. granulated sugar
1 c. brown sugar	2 eggs
2 c. corn flakes	2 c. raw oatmeal
2 c. flour	1/2 tsp. salt
1 tsp. baking powder	2 tsp. soda
1 c. coconut	1 c. pecans, chopped
1 tsp. vanilla	

Mix in order given. Roll in small balls. Press out on cookie sheet. Bake at 325 degrees for 10-15 minutes. Yield: about 125 cookies.

Houston County

AUNT RUTH'S COOKIES

1 c. sugar	1 tsp. soda
1 c. brown sugar	3 1/2 c. flour
1 c. butter or margarine	1 1/2 c. crisp rice cereal
1/2 c. vegetable oil	1 1/2 c. flaked coconut
1 egg	1 c. quick cooking oatmeal,
1 tsp. vanilla	uncooked
1 tsp. cream of tartar	1 c. pecans, chopped

Cream first 4 ingredients together. Stir in egg and vanilla. Sift cream of tartar, soda and flour together and add to the creamed mixture. Add remaining ingredients in order listed. Drop by teaspoonfuls onto lightly greased baking sheet. Flatten with a fork. Bake at 350 degrees for 10-12 minutes or until light golden brown. Yield: 12 dozen.

Totsy Hurta
Matagorda County

RANGER COOKIES

1 c. shortening	1/2 tsp. baking powder
1 c. granulated sugar	2 tsp. baking soda
1 c. brown sugar	1/2 tsp. salt
2 eggs	1 c. coconut
2 c. cornflakes	1 c. pecans, chopped
2 c. oatmeal	1 tsp. vanilla
2 c. flour	

Mix shortening, sugars and egg together with a fork. Add cornflakes and oatmeal. Sift together and add flour, baking powder, baking soda and salt. Add coconut, pecans and vanilla. Mix well; place batter in a teaspoon and form into balls. Bake at 325-350 degrees for 8-10 minutes.

Mrs. Tedia Killyon
Limestone County

DROP COOKIES

1 c. shortening	1 c. raisins
1 c. sugar	1/2 c. nuts
2 eggs	1 tsp. baking soda
1 tsp. vanilla	Pinch of salt
1 c. oatmeal	1 tsp. cinnamon
2 c. flour	1/4 c. milk
1 c. coconut	

Cream shortening and sugar. Add eggs and vanilla. Mix together dry ingredients. Add dry ingredients then milk. Drop on greased cookie sheet. Bake at 375 degrees 10 minutes or until done.

Lyons E. H. Club
Burleson County

POWER COOKIES

2 c. dark brown sugar	2 tsp. salt
2 c. granulated sugar	2 tsp. baking soda
3/4 c. butter, softened	3 c. uncooked oats
1 c. vegetable shortening	2 c. coconut
4 eggs	2 c. raisins
2 tsp. vanilla	1 c. chocolate chips
3 c. all-purpose flour	1 c. nuts, chopped

Cream together dark brown sugar, granulated sugar, butter and shortening. Beat in the eggs and vanilla. Combine flour, salt and soda and beat into first mixture. Add remaining ingredients and knead into first mixture. Drop by heaping teaspoonfuls 2-inches apart on greased baking sheet. Bake in preheated 350 degree oven for about 8 minutes or until cookies are nicely browned. Let cookies cool on baking sheet about 1 minute before removing to rack to cool. For best results, shape dough into rolls, wrap and chill several hours; then slice and bake as above. Store in airtight container. Makes 7 dozen irresistible cookies.

Carolyn Manvile
Fort Bend County

CHOCOLATE OATMEAL COOKIES

2 c. sugar	3 c. quick cooking oatmeal
1/2 c. cocoa	1 c. pecans
1 stick margarine	1 c. coconut
1/2 c. milk	1 tsp. vanilla

Bring to a rolling boil the first 4 ingredients. Add next 3 ingredients; mix well. Add vanilla. Mix all ingredients and drop by teaspoonful onto wax paper.

Dorotha Conner
Baylor County

OATMEAL COOKIES
(Helps Cholesterol)

1 1/4 c. low-fat margarine
  (Parkay)
3/4 c. brown sugar
1 egg
1 tsp. vanilla
1 1/2 c. all-purpose flour

1 tsp. baking soda
1 tsp. cinnamon
1/4 tsp. nutmeg
Dash of salt
3 c. uncooked oatmeal
1/2 c. or more nuts

Heat oven to 375 degrees. Beat together margarine and sugar until fluffy. Beat in egg and vanilla. Combine flour, baking soda, salt and spices and add to margarine mixture. Mix well. Stir in oats. Drop by rounded tablespoonfuls onto ungreased cookie sheet. Bake 8-9 minutes for a chewie cookie or 10 minutes or a crisp cookie. Cool 1 minute on wire cooling rack. Store in tightly covered container. Yield: 4 1/2 dozen.

Janice Carter
Gray County

OATMEAL PEANUT BUTTER COOKIES

1 1/2 c. brown sugar, firmly
  packed
1 c. chunky peanut butter
3/4 c. margarine
1/3 c. water
1 egg
1 tsp. vanilla

3 c. quick oats
1 1/2 c. all-purpose flour
1/2 tsp. baking soda
1 12-oz. pkg. semisweet
  chocolate pieces (2 c.)
4 tsp. shortening
2/3 c. pecans, chopped

In large mixer bowl, beat brown sugar, peanut butter and margarine until light and fluffy; blend n water, egg and vanilla. Add oats, flour and soda; mix well. Chill dough until firm (about 30 minutes). Form dough into 1-inch balls; place on ungreased cookie sheet and flatten slightly with the bottom of a glass dipped in sugar. Bake at 350 degrees for 8-10 minutes. Cool. In heavy saucepan, stir together chocolate pieces and shortening over low heat until melted. Spread 1/2 teaspoonful chocolate mixture on each cookie. Sprinkle with pecans. Chill until set. Yield: 5 dozen cookies.

Lorene Ashworth
Wise County

The grand essentials for happiness
in this life are --
something to do,
something to love,
and something to hope for.

OATMEAL PEANUT BUTTER COOKIES

3/4 c. margarine
1 c. brown sugar, packed
1/2 c. sugar
1/2 c. crunchy peanut butter
2 eggs
1 tsp. vanilla

1/4 c. milk
2 c. flour
1 tsp. baking soda
1 tsp. salt
1 1/2 tsp. apple pie spice
1 1/2 c. oatmeal

Cream margarine, sugars and peanut butter together. Add eggs, vanilla and milk; beat well. Stir together remaining ingredients, blend into creamed mixture. Drop by tablespoonfuls onto ungreased baking sheets. Bake at 350 degrees for 15 minutes or until lightly browned.

Margaret Lively
Llano County

CHUCK WAGON OATMEAL COOKIES

1 box Duncan Hines Spice Cake
2 c. oats (3 min.)
1 tsp. soda
1/2 c. brown sugar

2 eggs
1 c. Crisco oil
3 tsp. vanilla
1 c. nuts, chopped

Combine first 4 ingredients; add remaining ingredients and mix well. Drop by teaspoonfuls onto cookie sheet. Bake at 350 degrees for 8-10 minutes. Yield: 7-8 dozen.

Agnes Benedict
Gonzales County

OATMEAL-BANANA-CHERRY COOKIES

1 c. brown sugar
1 c. white sugar
2 sticks margarine
2 eggs
1 tsp. baking soda
1 tsp. baking powder
2 1/4 c. flour

1 c. oatmeal (1 c. corn flakes
   can be substituted
1 tsp. vanilla
1 c. pecans, chopped
1 sm. or 1/2 lg. banana
1/2 c. maraschino cherries,
   chopped

Cream sugars and margarine; add eggs. Stir in remaining ingredients and drop by tablespoonfuls onto ungreased cookie sheet. Bake at 350 degrees for 10-15 minutes. Do not over cook.

Marvel Dyer
Coryell County

How beautiful a day can be when kindness touches it.

120

FOUR-IN-ONE COOKIES

1 c. margarine, softened
1 c. sugar
1 c. brown sugar
2 eggs
1 1/4 c. flour
1 tsp. soda

1/2 tsp. salt
1/2 tsp. vanilla
3 c. rolled oats
1 c. pecans, chopped
1 6-oz. pkg. chocolate chips

Preheat oven to 350 degrees. Place shortening, sugars and eggs in bowl; beat thoroughly. Sift together flour, soda and salt. Add to shortening mixture; mix thoroughly. Sir in vanilla and oats. Add pecans and chocolate chips. Drop onto greased cookie sheet 2-inches apart. Bake 12-15 minutes.

Virginia Rutter
Nolan County

VANILLA NUT COOKIES

1 c. shortening
4 c. flour
2 c. sugar
1/2 c. brown sugar
3 tsp. baking powder

1/4 tsp. salt
1 T. vanilla
3 lg. eggs, well beaten
2 c. pecans, chopped

Cut shortening or oleo into dry ingredients as if for pie crust. Add well beaten eggs and vanilla. Dough is very stiff. Shape into rolls and chill until firm. Bake 8-10 minutes at 375 degrees. Makes a big batch and freezes well baked and unbaked.

Dorothy Fisher
Cooke County

PECAN PUFFS

1/2 c. butter
2 T. sugar
1 tsp. vanilla

1 c. flour, sifted
1 c. pecans, ground (walnuts
or almonds may be used)

Mix all ingredients together. Shape into small balls. Bake at 300 degrees for 40-45 minutes. Roll in powdered sugar.

Zeena Nickerson
Galveston County

Love begins when another person's needs become more important than your own.

PECAN DROP COOKIES

1 c. Crisco	2 c. + 4 T. flour
1 c. granulated sugar	1 tsp. salt
1/2 c. brown sugar	1 tsp. soda
2 eggs	1 c. nuts, chopped
1 tsp. vanilla	1/2 c. chocolate chips, opt.

Cream shortening and sugars; add eggs. Mix well. Add vanilla. Mix flour, salt and soda and add to above mixture. Add chopped nuts last. Drop by teaspoonfuls onto ungreased cookie sheet. Bake at 350 degrees 8-10 minutes. Might as well double recipe as these go fast.

Lamar County

PARTY COOKIES

1 tsp. cinnamon	1/4 tsp. salt
1 1/2 c. sugar	2 c. pecans, chopped
3 egg whites, beaten stiff	

Mix cinnamon and sugar. Add to beaten egg whites gradually and drop by tablespoonfuls onto well-greased cookie sheet. Bake at 250 degrees for 35 minutes. Let cool in pan after removing from oven for 2-3 minutes. Cool on rack or brown paper. Yield: 2 dozen.

Ellen Shumate
Young County

GRANDMA'S TEA CAKES

1 c. butter or margarine	1/2 tsp. salt
3 c. sugar	1 tsp. soda
3 eggs	1/2 c. buttermilk
1 tsp. lemon or vanilla extract	3 c. flour

Cream together butter and sugar. Add eggs, 1 at a time, beating well after each one. Add flavoring and salt. Mix soda with buttermilk and add alternately with flour. Mix well. Take about one-half of mixture and knead with more flour until it reaches a good consistency to roll out. Use desired shape cookie cutters and bake about 12-15 minutes in medium oven.

Wunelle Brown
Eastland County

Those who try to do something and fail
are much better off than those who
try to do nothing and succeed.

PECAN PRALINE COOKIES

1 2/3 c. all-purpose flour, sifted	1 1/2 c. brown sugar, firmly
1 1/2 tsp. baking powder	packed
1/2 tsp. salt	1 egg, unbeaten
1/2 c. butter	1 tsp. vanilla
	1 c. pecan halves

Sift flour with baking powder and salt; set aside. Cream butter. Add brown sugar gradually, creaming well. Blend in egg, vanilla and dry ingredients; mix well. Drop by rounded teaspoonfuls onto ungreased baking sheets. Bake at 350 degrees for 10-12 minutes. Cool. Break pecan halves into 2-4 pieces. Place 4-5 pieces on each cookie. Drizzle a teaspoonful of frosting over top of each cookie. Yield: 3 1/2 dozen.

PRALINE FROSTING

1 c. brown sugar, firmly packed	1 c. confectioners' sugar,
1/2 c. cream	sifted

Combine brown sugar and cream in small saucepan. Bring to boil, stirring constantly; boil 2 minutes. Remove from heat. Blend in confectioners' sugar; beat until smooth. If it thickens, thin with cream.

Patsy Graff
Medina County

PRIZE COOKIES

1 c. shortening	1 tsp. baking soda
1 1/2 c. sugar	1/2 tsp. salt
3 eggs, well beaten	1 9-oz. pkg. condensed
3 1/4 c. flour	mincemeat

In a large bowl, cream shortening. Gradually add sugar, blending well after each addition. Add eggs and beat until smooth. Sift flour, soda and salt. Gradually add to creamed mixture. Crumble and stir in mincemeat. Drop mixture by teaspoonfuls onto greased baking sheets, about 2-inches apart. Bake at 400 degrees for 12 minutes or until lightly brown. Yield: 5 dozen 3-inch cookies.

Seadrift E. H. Club
Calhoun County

DICKENS ON THE STRAND — BROWN SUGAR BISCUITS

1 c. butter or margarine	1 egg yolk
3/4 c. brown sugar	2 c. flour

Mix all ingredients and shape into balls. Bake at 375 degrees or 10 minutes. Makes about 50 cookies about 1 1/2-2-inches across. These are also good to press a pecan half on top before baking.

These cookies are called biscuits typical of English desserts and have been served at the Festival of Dickens Evening on the Strand in Galveston each year.

Virginia Burks
Galveston County

PEANUT BUTTER COOKIES

2 c. sugar
1 c. flour
2 tsp. baking soda
1 c. peanut butter

2 eggs
1 c. butter or shortening
1 tsp. vanilla

Mix dry ingredients. Add peanut butter, eggs, butter and vanilla. Stir well. Shape dough into wanut size balls. Place on greased cookie sheet. Mash with a fork. Bake at 325 degrees until slightly brown. This makes a soft cookie.

Lela Parker, Coke County
Laura Harris, Wise County

EASY PEANUT BUTTER COOKIES

1 14-oz. can sweetened
  condensed milk
1 egg

1 tsp. vanilla extract
3/4 c. peanut butter
2 c. Biscuit Baking Mix

In large mixing bowl, mix milk, egg and vanilla until smooth. Chill 1-hour. Shape into 1-inch balls and roll in sugar. Place on ungreased cookie sheets, flatten with fork. Bake in 350 degree oven for 6-8 minutes. Store at room temperature.

Alice Rahlwes
Colorado County

SPECIAL K COOKIES

1 c. sugar
1 c. corn syrup
1 tsp. vanilla

1 1/2 c. peanut butter
4 c. "Special K" cereal

Bring sugar and corn syrup to boil. Add vanilla and peanut butter. After peanut butter melts, add cereal. Drop by tablespoonfuls onto wax paper.

Charlotte Cragar
Knox County

PUPPY CHOW SNACKS

1 6-oz. pkg. semi-sweet
  chocolate morsels
1/4 c. vegetable oil

1/4 c. creamy peanut butter
6 c. Kellogg's Crispix cereal
2 c. powdered sugar

Melt chocolate morsels and oil. Stir in peanut butter. Pour over cereal. Place powdered sugar in a large plastic bag. Add coated cereal and close bag tightly. Shake to coat cereal with powdered sugar. Refrigerate in an air-tight container.

Alvina Sassman
Travis County

A smile is a crooked line that sets a lot of things straight.

DATE PECAN LOAF

3 c. sugar
1 1/2 c. evaporated milk
1/3 c. Karo syrup
Dash of salt

5 dates, chopped
2 c. pecans, chopped
1 tsp. vanilla
1/2 stick margarine

Cook sugar, milk and Karo syrup in deep heavy skillet to firm ball stage (250 degrees). Add remaining ingredients and cook 5 minutes longer. Beat until creamy and firm. Form a long roll and wrap in a damp towel. Chill and slice.

Bessie Barker
San Saba County

BELLE STARR'S SUGAR COOKIES

1 c. powdered sugar
1 c. sugar
1 c. vegetable oil
1 c. butter or margarine
2 eggs

1 tsp. vanilla
4 1/4 c. flour
1 tsp. soda
1 tsp. salt
1 tsp. cream of tartar

Cream sugars, oil and butter. Add eggs and vanilla. Add dry ingredients and blend. Chill over night. Roll into small balls; place on ungreased cookie sheet and flatten with heel of hand or bottom of water glass (make thin). Bake at 350 degrees for 10 minutes.

Bee Crenshaw, Travis County
Adrene Bracewell, Bastrop County

Lou Gilly from Haskell County uses 4 cups flour and does not use baking soda.

CLÁRA'S SUGAR COOKIES

2 1/2 c. flour
1 c. sugar
2 tsp. cream of tartar
1 tsp. soda
1/2 tsp. salt

1 c. butter or margarine or use
1/2 of each
2 eggs
1 tsp. vanilla

Mix all ingredients and chill dough. Take teaspoonful of dough and place on cookie sheet; mash with glass dipped in sugar. Bake 15 minutes at 350 degrees.

Clara Thompson, Esther Thomas, Jeanne Thompson

*Don't let your mind become so busy
that your heart can't respond.*

125

SOFT BANANA COOKIES

2 lg. bananas
3/4 c. shortening
1 c. sugar
1/4 tsp. salt
2 eggs

2 1/4 c. flour
2 tsp. baking powder
Chocolate chips or nuts,
  if desired

Mix all ingredients well. Drop by teaspoonful onto greased cookie sheet. Bake until slightly brown.

Mrs. W. P. Wright
Brooks County

HAWAIIAN COCONUT COOKIES

1/2 c. granulated sugar
1/2 c. brown sugar
1/2 c. margarine
1 egg
1/2 tsp. almond extract
1 c. flour, sifted

1 tsp. soda
1/2 tsp. salt
1 c. coconut
1 c. raw rolled oats
1 c. nuts

Cream sugars and margarine; add egg, extract, flour, soda, salt, coconut, oats and nuts. Drop onto lightly greased cookie sheet. Bake at 350 degrees until golden brown.

Darlien Kaminski
Austin County

BUTTER SCOTCH COOKIE RECIPE

3 1/2 c. flour
2 1/2 tsp. baking powder
1/2 tsp. salt
1 c. butter or margarine
1 1/2 c. brown sugar

2 eggs, unbeaten
1 1/2 tsp. lemon juice
1 c.pecans
1 1/2 tsp. vanilla

Roll in log and freeze or chill before slicing. Bake at 475 degrees for 8-10 minutes.

Margaret Groseclose
Childress County

Never serve meals on time.
Hungry people enjoy food more,
and the starving eat anything.

BUTTERSCOTCH ROUNDS

3/4 c. butter (1 1/2 sticks)
1 c. light brown sugar, firmly
  packed
1 egg
1 tsp. vanilla
2 c. all-purpose flour, sifted
1 tsp. baking soda
1/4 tsp. ground ginger
1/4 tsp. cinnamon
1/4 tsp. salt
1 c. walnuts or pecans,
  finely chopped
Candied cherries, opt.

In mixing bowl, cream butter; gradually add sugar and beat until light and fluffy. Add egg and vanilla; beat thoroughly. Sift together flour, baking soda, ginger, cinnamon and salt; gradually add to creamed mixture. Stir in nuts. Chill for ease in handling. Shape into balls 1-inch in diameter. Place on baking sheet. Flatten slightly with bottom of glass which has been dipped in flour. Press cherry into top, if desired. Bake in preheated 350 degree oven for 12-15 minutes. Remove to wire rack to cool. Yield: 4-5 dozen.

Shelby County

CREAM CHEESE COOKIES

1 c. butter or margarine
1 8-oz. pkg. cream cheese
2 c. sugar
1 T. vanilla
1 1/2 c. pecans, chopped
2 1/2 c. flour

Blend butter with cream cheese. Add sugar, vanilla and nuts. Blend well. Add flour and mix well. Drop by teaspoonful onto ungreased cookie sheet. Bake at 350 degrees for 10-12 minutes or until edges of cookies are brown. Yield: 4-5 dozen chewy cookies.

Dorothy M. Doehring
Fayette County

JELLY-FILLED COOKIES

1 c. butter or margarine
1 8-oz.pkg. cream cheese at
  room temperature
1 egg yolk, beaten
1 T. sugar
1 T. milk
1/2 tsp. baking powder
1 1/2 c. flour
Jelly or jam

Mix butter and cream cheese. Add egg yolk, sugar and milk; beat well. Mix baking powder and flour; add to cheese mixture. Drop by teaspoonfuls onto cookie sheet; pat into circles 1/2-1/3-inch high. Press thumb-print in center; fill with jellies or jams. Bake at 400 degrees for 10 minutes. Yield: 3-3 1/2 dozen cookies.

Bertha Carnero
Parmer County

DATE NUT COOKIES

3 eggs	1 1/2 c. nuts, chopped
1 c. brown sugar	1 c. dates, chopped
1 c. white sugar	3/4 tsp. soda
1 T. cinnamon	1/4 tsp. cloves
2 T. butter	3 c. flour (about)

Mix first 3 ingredients, add to this the floured nuts, spices, dates and enough flour for drop cookies. Use greased cookie sheet and bake about 10 minutes at 350 degrees.

Elizabeth Thurman
Menard County

LEMON BALLS

3 c. powdered sugar	1 stick margarine
1 12-oz. pkg. vanilla wafers, crushed	1 6-oz. can lemonade
	Pecans, crushed

Mix the above ingredients. Form into balls about the size of a walnut. Roll in crushed pecans. Good frozen.

Roadrunner E. H. Club
Hill County

MELTING MOMENTS

1 c. butter or margarine, softened	1 1/4 c. all-purpose flour
1/3 c. powdered sugar, sifted	1/2 c. cornstarch

Cream butter; add sugar and beat well. Gradually add flour and cornstarch, beating until smooth. Drop by teaspoonfuls onto ungreased cookie sheets. Bake at 350 degrees for 10-12 minutes (cookies do not brown on top). Cool slightly on cookie sheet; remove cookies to wire racks to cool completely. Frost cookies with Lemon Frosting. Yield: 7 dozen.

LEMON FROSTING

1/4 c. butter or margarine, softened	2 T. fresh lemon juice
1 1/2 c. powdered sugar, sifted	1 T. grated lemon rind

Cream butter; gradually add powdered sugar and lemon juice, beat until smooth. Stir in lemon rind. Yield: 2 cups frosting.

Dorothy Van Arman
McLennan County

*He who is wrapped up in himself
makes a small package.*

GRAHAM CRACKER COOKIES

1 c. brown sugar
1 1/2 sticks margarine

1 c. nuts, chopped or
    flaked coconut
Graham crackers

Bring sugar, margarine and nuts to a boil and boil for 2 minutes stirring constantly. Line a cookie sheet which has sides with whole graham crackers. Pour boiled mixture over the crackers spreading close to the edge. Bake at 300 degrees for 10-12 minutes. Run a spatula or knife around edges when you take cookies from the oven. Let cool in pan, then break or cut into pieces. (Mrs. McQueen credits Mrs. Lola Dodson of Coleman, Texas for this recipe.)

Winnie McQueen
Coleman County

ORANGE ICEBOX COOKIES

1 c. Crisco
1 c. brown sugar
1 egg

2 T. orange juice
2 3/4 c. flour
1/4 tsp. soda

Cream shortening, sugar and egg together. Add orange juice. Add flour and soda mixed together. Divide dough into 3 parts. Work each part into long squares, about 6 or 7-inches long. If you put in refrigerator, wrap in Saran Wrap. Will keep for several days. Slice into slices about 5 or 6 to an inch. Bake at 375 degrees for 8-10 minutes. Yield: 50 or more cookies.

Nannie Pearl Woods

ORANGE COOKIES

1/2 c. butter
1/2 c. sugar
1 c. flour

1/2 tsp. salt
1 tsp. vanilla
1/2 tsp. orange peel

Preheat oven to 425 degrees. Grease cookie sheets. Cream butter and sugar together. Sift flour and salt together. Mix all ingredients together with a wooden spoon. Grate orange peel. Add. Place on cookie sheet 1/2-inch apart. Bake 10-12 minutes. Let cool before removing from cookie sheet.

Maggie Lee Freeman

The greatness of a man can nearly always be
measured by his willingness to be kind.

ORANGE SLICE COOKIES

2 c. sugar
1 c. brown sugar
2 c. shortening
3 eggs
1 1/2 tsp. soda in 3 T. water
3 c. flour

1 1/2 tsp. baking powder
3 c. oatmeal
30 orange slices, chopped
1 sm. can flaked coconut
1 1/2 c. pecans, chopped

Cream sugars and shortening in large mixing bowl. Add eggs, soda and flour with baking powder mixed in. With your hands, mix in the oatmeal, orange slice bits, coconut and pecans. Chill several hours after rolling tube fashion (4) in plastic wrap. Slice and bake at 325 degrees for 10-15 minutes. Yield: 4 dozen cookies

Jessie Shumate
Young County

CINNAMON WAFERS

2 c. flour
2 tsp. cinnamon
1 c. sugar
1 c. butter (only butter)

1 tsp. vanilla
1 egg, separated
1 c. nuts, chopped

Heat oven to 350 degrees. Sift flour and cinnamon together. Separate egg. Cream sugar and butter, mix in vanilla and egg yolk, stir in flour and cinnamon. Mix well. Spread evenly and thin into a 10 x 15-inch ungreased jelly roll pan. Spread the unbeaten egg white over the dough with your hand. Sprinkle nuts over dough and press down with palm of hand. Bake at 350 degrees for 25 minutes. Cut into squares or fingers as soon as taken from oven. Cool in pan. Secret: Use butter and spread thin.

Mabel Helton
Montgomery County

"PUTTIN" ON THE RITZ

1 14-oz. can sweetened condensed
  milk
1 c. dates, chopped

1 c. pecans, chopped
70-80 Ritz crackers

Boil sweetened condensed milk and dates until thickened. Add nuts and spread on crackers. Bake at 325 degrees for 8 minutes. Frost.

FROSTING

1 1/2 c. powdered sugar
1/2 c. margarine, softened

1 3-oz. pkg. cream cheese
1 tsp. vanilla

Mix all ingredients and spread over cooled cookies. Refrigerate or keep covered. Yields: 5 1/2 dozen cookies.

Gerry Zummer, Director
District 8, Eastland County

Agnes Benedict from Gonzales County uses 2 cups powdered sugar and 2 teaspoonfuls vanilla.

130

SUGARLESS COOKIES

1 c. raisins
3/4 c. apples, chopped
1/2 c. shortening

3/4 c. dates, chopped
1 c. water

Mix first 4 ingredients, bring to a boil, and cook for 3 minutes. Add shortening to mixture and stir, then set mixture aside to cool.

Mix together:

1 c. flour
1 tsp. soda

1/2 tsp. cinnamon
1/4 tsp. salt

Add to cooled fruit mixture:

2 eggs, beaten
1 tsp. vanilla

4 pkgs. Equal (or 3 tsp.
liquid sweetener)

Add flour mixture to fruit mixture. Mix well. Refrigerate until well chilled. Drop by teaspoonfuls onto cookie sheet. Bake at 350 degrees for 10-12 minutes.

Jane Bingaman
Hamilton County

NUTMEG SUGAR COOKIES

2 c. all-purpose flour
1 tsp. baking powder
1/2 tsp. soda
1 tsp. ground nutmeg
1/2 tsp. salt

1 c. sugar
1/2 c. shortening
2 eggs, beaten
2 tsp. milk
Additional sugar

Sift together first 5 ingredients in a bowl; set aside. Combine 1 cup sugar and shortening in a large bowl, creaming well. Add eggs and milk; beat well. Add dry ingredients, and mix well. Drop dough by teaspoonfuls onto lightly greased cookie sheets. Slightly flatten each with a spoon; sprinkle with sugar. Bake at 375 degrees for 10-12 minutes. Place on rack to cool. Yield: about 5 1/2 dozen.

Winnie Bartley
Swisher County

THE COOKIE JAR
Like the love of a mother
It shines through the years
It has soothed all our cares
And dried away tears
It has paid up for toiling
In sorrow and joy
It has always brought kindness
To each girl and boy
And I'm sorry for people
whoever they are
Who live in a house
Where there's no cookie jar.

OLD FASHIONED MOLASSES DROP COOKIES

2 1/2 c. all-purpose flour,
  unsifted
1 tsp. baking soda
1/4 tsp. salt
1/4 tsp. cloves
1 tsp. cinnamon
1 tsp. ginger

1/2 c. shortening
1/2 c. sugar
1 egg
3/4 c. molasses
1/2 c. buttermilk
1/2 c. dark raisins, opt.
Confectioners' sugar

Heat oven to 350 degrees. Lightly grease cookie sheet. Sift flour, baking soda, salt, cloves, cinnamon and ginger. In large bowl, with electric mixer at medium speed or with a wooden spoon, beat shortening, sugar, egg and molasses until light and fluffy. Add flour mixture and buttermilk. Beat with wooden spoon until well blended. Stir in raisins. Drop dough onto prepared cookie sheets 1/3 cup at a time. Spread each into a 5-inch round. Bake 10-12 minutes or until tops feel firm when gently touched. Let cookies stand about 1 minute. Then remove to wire rack, let cool completely. Sift confectioners' sugar over tops. Yield: 9 cookies.

Betty Stallard
Reeves County

FROSTED PINTO BEAN COOKIES

2 c. pinto beans, cooked and
  drained
3/4 c. butter or margarine,
  melted
2 c. sugar
2 eggs
1 1/4 c. all-purpose flour

1 tsp. baking soda
1/2 tsp. baking powder
1 1/2 tsp. ground cinnamon
1/2 tsp. ground cloves
1/2 tsp. ground allspice
1/2 c. pecans, chopped

In a large bowl, beat beans with electric mixer until fluffy. Add butter and sugar and beat until blended. Beat in eggs. Mix all dry ingredients and gradually add to bean mixture. Beat until well blended. Pour into a 13 x 9 x 2-inch greased pan and bake at 350 degrees for 50-60 minutes or until done. Cool completely and spread frosting on top. Sprinkle with pecans. Cut into 1 x 3 1/4-inch bars. Yield: approximately 3 dozen.

CREAMY FROSTING

1 3-oz. pkg. cream cheese,
  softened
1/3 c. butter or margarine,
  softened

1 lb. confectioners' sugar
2 tsp. clear vanilla
2-3 T. milk
1/2 c. pecans, toasted

In a medium mixing bowl, beat cream cheese and butter until creamy. Add sugar and vanilla and beat. Add enough milk to make a creamy frosting.

Bobbie Elmore
District IV Director

132

POTATO CHIP COOKIES

1 lb. butter, softened
1 c. sugar
3 1/4 c. flour

1 tsp. vanilla
1 1/2 c. potato chips,
finely crushed

Mix butter and sugar together well. Add flour and vanilla. Fold in crushed potato chips. Drop by teaspoonfuls onto ungreased cookie sheet. Take a fork and lightly press to make thinner. Bake in a 300 degree oven for about 20 minutes. After taking from oven, sprinkle with **powdered sugar.**

Marianne Hayes
Matagorda County

SOUR CREAM COOKIES

1/2 c. shortening
1 1/2 c. sugar
2 eggs, well beaten
3 1/2 c. flour
1/2 tsp. soda

1/2 tsp. baking powder
1/2 tsp. salt
1 c. thick sour cream
1 tsp. vanilla

Cream shortening and sugar; add well beaten eggs and blend well. Sift together flour, soda, baking powder and salt. Add to first mixture, alternately with sour cream, mixing well after each addition. Mix in vanilla. Drop by teaspoonfuls onto a greased cookie sheet. Bake at 400 degrees for 12-15 minutes or until browned to desire. One-half cup pecans or 1/2 cup chocolate chips may be added, if desired. For Christmas cookie, add 1/2 to 3/4 cup chopped candied fruits, dredged in flour.

Carolyn Hunter Cook
Crane County

VANILLA COOKIES

1 c. butter
1 1/2 c. sugar (or 1 1/4 c. if
 desired)
2 eggs

3 c. flour
1/2 tsp. soda
1 tsp. baking powder
1 tsp. vanilla

Cream sugar and butter; beat in eggs. Mix together flour, soda and baking powder. Add to butter, sugar and egg mixture. Will be a stiff dough. Drop by small teaspoonfuls onto oiled cookie sheet. Bake at 375 degrees for about 10 minutes.

Louise Wood
Newton County

Happiness is a conscious choice,
not an automatic response.

MEXICAN WEDDING COOKIES

1 c. butter or margarine,
  softened
1 c. confectioners' sugar
1 tsp. vanilla

1 3/4 c. all-purpose flour
1/4 tsp. salt
3/4 c. pecans, finely chopped

Heat oven to 400 degrees. Mix thoroughly butter and sugar. Work in flour, salt and pecans until dough holds together. Shape dough into 1-inch balls. Place on ungreased baking sheet. Bake 10-12 minutes or until set, not brown.

Margaret Lindley
Loving County

MEXICAN WEDDING COOKIES
(PAN DE POLVO)

1/2 c. cinnamon tea (approx.)
2 lbs. or 7 c. all-purpose flour
3/4 c. sugar
1 tsp. baking powder

1 lb. lard or shortening, softened
1/4 c. sugar
1 tsp. cinnamon

Prepare tea by boiling **1 1/2 cups water with 3 or 4 pieces of stick cinnamon** for about 5 minutes. Remove sticks and add 3/4 cup sugar, stir until dissolved. Set aside. Mix flour with baking powder, blend in lard or shortening. When it's well blended, gradually add the tea, just enough to hold the dough together. Roll out dough like thick pie crust. Cut with cookie cutters and place onto ungreased cookie sheets. Bake at 350 degrees for 12-15 minutes. Mix 1/4 cup sugar and cinnamon and roll cookies in while still hot. Handle carefully or they will crumble. These may be prepared ahead of time and frozen. Yield: 6-8 dozen.

Connie Escobedo
Cameron County

Candies

CANDY CARMELS

2 c. sugar
3/4 c. light corn syrup
1/8 tsp. salt
1/4 c butter

2 c. heavy cream
1 tsp. vanilla
1/2 c. pecans, chopped
  (opt.)

Combine sugar, syrup, salt, butter and 1 cup cream in large saucepan. Stir constantly until mixture comes to a full boil. Gradually add remaining cream so boiling does not stop. Continue stirring to hard ball stage (250 degrees). Remove from heat. Stir in vanilla and nuts. Pour into buttered 8-inch square pan. When cold turn out onto cutting board and cut in 3/4-inch squares. Put each square in petit-four baking cups or wrap individually in aluminum foil.

Deanna Campbell
Armstrong County

GRAND PRIZE DIVINITY CANDY

3 c. sugar
1 c. white Karo syrup
2/3 c. water
1 c. sugar

1/3 c. water
3 egg whites
2 c. pecans, chopped
1 tsp. vanilla

Place first 3 ingredients in large boiler and boil until it hardens when dropped in cold water and tingles on side of cup. Place 1 cup sugar and 1/3 cup water in small boiler and let boil until it ropes when dropped from spoon. Beat egg whites stiff and pour contents of small boiler over this. When contents of large boiler are ready, pour into egg whites and beat. Add nuts and vanilla; drop by spoonfuls onto wax paper. Yield: 125 pieces.

Margaret Smith
Bastrop County

Lillie Klaus from San Patricio/Aransas County uses 1/2 cup Karo syrup, 1/2 cup hot water, 2 beaten egg whites and 1/8 teaspoonful salt.

CAN'T FAIL DIVINITY

2 c. sugar
1/2 c. water
Pinch of salt

1 pt. marshmallow creme
1/2 c. nuts or fruit
1 tsp. vanilla

Boil sugar, water and salt until mixture forms a hard ball in cold water. Place marshmallow creme in mixing bowl and stir in hot syrup. Continue stirring until slightly stiff. Fold in nuts or fruit and vanilla. Drop from spoon onto waxed paper. Yield: 24 pieces.

Jan Bennett
Hardin County

DIVINITY FUDGE

3 c. sugar
1/2 c. light corn syrup
1/2 c. cold water

2 egg whites
1 tsp. vanilla

Place sugar, syrup and water in a pan over low heat. Stir only until sugar is dissolved. Cook until a little dropped in cold water forms a soft ball. Beat egg whites at high speed until stiff. Continue beating and pour one half of mixture slowly over egg whites. Cook the rest of the syrup until it forms a hard ball when dropped in a cup of cold water (should crack when hit against cup). Add the syrup gradually to egg mixture beating constantly. Add vanilla and continue beating until a spoonful dropped onto a buttered plate will hold its shape. Nut meats may be added if desired just before candy is ready to spoon.

Mildred Davis
Wichita County

CREAMY BLUEBERRY CLUSTERS

3 c. fresh blueberries   4 blocks white almond bark
1/2 c. almonds, crushed

Wash, drain and dry blueberries. Shred or chop almond bark and melt in microwave or double boiler. Spoon blueberries in melted almond bark, 4 or 5 at a time. Remove in clusters of 3 or 4 berries. Dip in crushed almonds and lay on plate lined with paper. Refrigerate to harden. Yield: 100 clusters.

Ellazine Tanton
Jasper County

DUTCH OVEN CANDY

1 lb. real butter   3/4 c. dark Karo syrup
1 lg. can evaporated milk   1 tsp. vanilla
7 c. white sugar   3 c. pecans, chopped

Stir together butter, milk, syrup and sugar. Cook in dutch oven at 275 degrees for 3 hours. Stir occasionally until soft ball stage. Remove and add vanilla. Let cool for 1 hour. Then beat with electric mixer for exactly 10 minutes. Add pecans. Stir and pour into buttered dish. Cut into squares to serve.

Elizabeth Rogers
Cherokee County

GOODY BALLS

1/2 c. margarine   2 eggs, well beaten
1 c. sugar   1/2 c. marshmallows
1 c. nuts, chopped   3 c. rice cereal (your choice)

Melt margarine. Add sugar, nuts, eggs and marshmallows and stir over medium heat for 5 minutes. Remove from heat and add rice cereal. Cool and shape into balls. Roll in 1/2 cup coconut. Enjoy!

Silena Pace
Newton County

LECHE QUEMADA

2 c. sugar   1 c. pecans, chopped
1 c. buttermilk   2 T. butter
1 tsp. baking soda   1 tsp. vanilla

Bring sugar, buttermilk and soda to a boil. Boil until it reaches a soft ball stage and turns golden brown. Remove from heat. Add pecans, butter and vanilla. Beat with a spoon until mixture loses its gloss. Drop by teaspoonfuls onto waxed paper.

Jeanette Walsh
Gillespie County

It's not how you fall, but how you get up that counts.

MEXICAN PECAN CANDY

1 1/2 c. sugar	1/3 c. margarine
3 T. white syrup	8 lg. marshmallows
1/2 c. milk	1 tsp. vanilla
Dash of salt	2 c. nuts, chopped

Mix sugar, syrup, milk, salt and margarine. Cook to soft ball stage. Add marshmallows that have been cut in half. Cool. Add vanilla and beat until smooth and begins to harden. Add chopped pecans and drop onto waxed paper.

Ardell Floyd
Fisher County

WILSON COUNTY PEANUT BRITTLE

3 c. white sugar	1 T. margarine
1 c. white Karo syrup	1 1/4 tsp. soda
1/2 c. water	1 tsp. salt

Using a heavy-duty 3-quart saucepan, bring to boil the sugar, syrup and water until a thread spins. Then add **raw peanuts** and stir frequently with a wooden spoon. Cook this mixture until it turns amber. Remove from heat and add margarine, salt and soda. Continue stirring vigorously until it is very well-blended and the color is once again a lovely gold. Pour at once onto a well-buttered heavy-duty foil paper (18 x 24-inches) in a large oval platter shape. Edges should be crimped up so mixture won't run off paper. Do not spread with your spoon as that will tend to flatten the natural air bubbles which make it such a lovely brittle candy. It's advisable to prepare the foil paper before you start cooking as one has to work quickly once you take it off the burner. Break into pieces when cool and enjoy! Store in a sealed jar or zip-lock bag to keep fresh.

Bulk ingredients for 25 pounds of peanuts:

25 lbs. peanuts	1 box soda
40 lbs. sugar	1 box salt
2 gal. light corn syrup	Extra heavy duty foil
2 lbs. margarine	95 qt. size heavy duty zip-lock bags

Acknowledgement: In 1938 Miss Fannie Sue Brasuel, the Home Demonstration Agent, introduced the above brittle recipe to the Wilson County clubs. At this time, it was made for exhibit only by the members. In 1940, clubs started making it for the annual Peanut Festival as a finance project, which became a tradition. Mrs. Fannie Sue (Brasuel) Carnes is now an active member in the Labatt Extension Homemakers Club.

Love can come from surprising places.

PEANUT BRITTLE

3 c. sugar
3/4 c. corn syrup
2/3 c. water
3-4 c. raw, shelled peanuts

2 T. butter or margarine
2 tsp. vanilla
1 T. soda
1/2 tsp. salt

In heavy 4-quart saucepan, boil sugar, syrup and water until syrup spins a thread when dropped from a spoon. Add peanuts and cook, stirring occasionally until syrup is light golden brown and peanuts smell done. Add butter and vanilla and stir to blend. Add soda, stirring fast to mix well. When it is pulling away from the pan and foaming is about to spill over, pour onto 2 buttered cookie tins. Do not spread. When cool, break into pieces and store in air-tight containers.

Nell Watson
District 11

PEANUT PATTIES

4 c. sugar
1 c. white syrup
1 c. sweet milk

1/2 c. water
5 c. raw peanuts
Few drops red food coloring

Bring first 4 ingredients to full boil; add half of raw peanuts. Boil for a few minutes and add rest of nuts. Let boil stirring constantly to soft ball stage (238 degrees on candy thermometer). Remove from heat; add food coloring. Stir candy (not constantly) until it starts getting sugary around edges and stays fairly firm when spooned onto counter that has been greased with margarine. Use 2 spoons to drop as it will be hot. It takes about 30 minutes to be ready. You don't have much time when it's ready before it gets too hard.

Freeda Ives
Hood County

PEANUT PATTIE CANDY

3 c. sugar
1 c. water
1 c white Karo syrup
1 lb. raw peanuts

Margarine
Salt
1 can angel flake coconut
Red food coloring

Bring sugar, water and Karo syrup to a boil. Add peanuts. Cook until candy hardens when dropped in cold water. Turn off burner and add margarine, a sprinkle of salt and the coconut. Beat until too thick to beat. Pour onto greased cookie sheet. Add food coloring if desired, before beating. Break into pieces when cool.

Burnelle Knight
Stephens County

Plant a little gossip and you will reap a harvest of regret.

PEANUT PATTIES

2 1/2 c. sugar
2/3 c. white corn syrup
1 c. milk
2 1/2 c. raw Spanish peanuts

4 tsp. butter or margarine
4 drops red food coloring
1 c. powdered sugar

Pour sugar, corn syrup, milk and peanuts in large heavy saucepan. Cook slowly until mixture forms a soft ball (240 degrees on candy thermometer). This takes approximately 45 minutes after mixture starts to boil. Remove from heat and add butter, food coloring and powdered sugar. Stir mixture constantly until thick. Drop by spoonfuls on buttered cookie sheet. Allow room to spread.

Pearlie Hall
Bowie County

CREAMY PRALINES

1 c. white Karo syrup
1 c. whipping cream
2 c. sugar
1 tsp. vanilla

4 T. butter
Few grains of salt
2 or 3 c. pecan halves

Blend all ingredients except pecans; cook to soft ball stage when tested in cool water. Add pecans and beat immediately until creamy. Drop by spoonfuls onto wax paper. Yield: 2 dozen.

Floy Ray Tonne
Concho County

CHEWY PRALINES

2 c. sugar
2 c. white corn syrup
1 lb. sweet cream butter

2 c. whipping cream
2 tsp. vanilla
8 c. pecans, chopped

Cook sugar and corn syrup over medium-low heat until candy thermometer reaches 250 degrees. Remove from heat, add butter and stir until dissolved. Add whipping cream (not whipped) slowly. Return to heat stirring constantly and cook until thermometer reaches 242 degrees. Remove from heat and add vanilla and pecans. Drop onto foil sprayed with Pam. When cool, wrap pralines in Saran wrap. Yield: 42 pralines.

Helen Hamilton
Guadalupe County

*One of the most important trips a person can make
is that involved in meeting the other person halfway.*

TEXAS PRALINES FAST

1 c. sugar
1/2 c. brown sugar
1/4 c. milk
1 T. butter or margarine

1 c. pecans pieces (some
   whole for looks)
1 tsp. vanilla

Mix sugar, brown sugar, milk, butter and pecan pieces and bring to a boil. Boil by the clock for 1 1/2 minutes only. Remove from stove; add vanilla, then beat until creamy, very short time. Drop by spoonfuls onto waxed paper. Work fast. It gets sugary fast, but looks liquid. Start pouring.

Joyce Etheridge
Polk County

POPCORN CARAMEL CRUNCH

4 c. popped corn
1 c. dry roasted peanuts
1 c. chow mein noodles
1/2 c. raisins
1 c. sugar

3/4 c. butter
1/2 c. light corn syrup
2 T. water
1 tsp. ground cinnamon

In a large greased bowl, combine first 4 ingredients. Set aside. In a large saucepan, combine sugar, butter, corn syrup and water. Cook over medium heat, stirring occasionally, until mixture reaches soft crack stage (280-290 degrees) with a candy thermometer. Remove from heat. Stir in cinnamon. Pour over popcorn mixture; stir until all ingredients are evenly coated. Immediately pour onto a greased 15 x 10-inch pan. When cool enough to handle, break into pieces. Store in covered containers to enjoy later or to give as gifts. Yield: about 8 cups.

Eulus Damron
Dawson County

TIGER BUTTER

1 lb. white chocolate
1 12-oz. jar chunky peanut butter

1 lb. semi-sweet chocolate
   pieces, melted

Combine white chocolate and peanut butter in top of a double boiler. Bring water to a boil. Reduce heat to low, cook until chocolate and peanut butter melt, stirring constantly. Spread mixture onto a 15 x 10 x 1-inch jelly roll pan lined with waxed paper. Pour semi-sweet chocolate over peanut butter mixture, and swirl through with knife. Chill until firm. Cut into 1 1/2 x 1-inch pieces. Store in refrigerator. Yield: 6 dozen pieces.

Jean Wulf
Smith County

Procrastination is the thief of time.

PEANUT BUTTER PINWHEEL

1/2 c. margarine
1 1-lb. box confectioners' sugar
1 tsp. vanilla

Canned milk
Peanut butter

Cream margarine and add sugar a little at a time. Also also vanilla. Add some canned milk. Roll in ball and divide into thirds. Chill. Put confectioners' sugar on three pieces of waxed paper. Roll out dough and spread with peanut butter all over. Roll as for jelly roll. Refrigerate, then slice.

Charlotte Watson, State TEHA President
Williamson County

PEANUT BUTTER CHOCOLATE BALLS

1 c. margarine, melted
1 c. graham cracker crumbs
1 c. rice cereal, crushed fine
1 1/2 c. flaked coconut
1 1/2 c. peanuts or pecans, chopped
1 16-oz. pkg. powdered sugar, sifted

1 12-oz. jar chunky peanut butter
1 tsp. vanilla extract
1 12-oz. pkg. semi-sweet chocolate morsels
3 T. shortening

Combine first 8 ingredients, stirring well. Shape mixture into 1-inch balls. Combine chocolate morsels and shortening in top of double boiler; bring water to boil. Reduce heat to low. Cook until chocolate melts. Dip balls into chocolate mixture; place on wax paper to cool. Store in refrigerator.

Judy Johnson
Jackson County

PINTO BEAN FUDGE

1/2 c. pinto beans, cooked and mashed
1 lb. confectioners' sugar, sifted

1/8 tsp. salt
1 1/2 c. chocolate chips
1/4 tsp. vanilla flavoring
1/2 c. nuts, chopped

Mix beans, confectioners' sugar and salt. Melt chocolate chips and mix well. Add vanilla and nuts. Spread into greased pan. Chill; then cut.

Linda Lewis
Brown County

It's not what you've got,
but what you give;
that measures the worth
of the life you live.

ROCKY ROAD CANDY

1 12-oz. pkg. chocolate chips
2 T. margarine
1/8 tsp. salt
1 tsp. vanilla

1 can sweetened condensed milk
1 10 1/2-oz. pkg. miniature
 marshmallows
1 c. pecans, chopped

Melt chocolate chips and margarine over low heat or in microwave oven. Remove from heat and add remaining ingredients, blending well. Pour into buttered 9 x 13-inch pan. Chill several hours or overnight before cutting into squares.

Mary White
Hunt County

WALNUT CANDY

1/2 lb. butter
2 c. sugar
1 1/2 c. white corn syrup

2 c. whipping cream
(not whipped)
1 tsp. vanilla
5 c. walnuts

Mix butter, sugar, syrup and 1 cup of the cream and cook until it boils. Then add the remaining 1 cup cream. Boil in a hard boil until a small amount in water forms a soft ball. Add vanilla and walnuts. Pour into buttered pan and when cool, cut into squares. Makes a large amount.

Lelah Beyer
McLennan County

Bars

LUSCIOUS APRICOT BARS

2/3 c. dried apricots
1/2 c. butter, softened
1/4 c. sugar
1 1/3 c. flour, divided
1/2 tsp. baking powder
1/4 tsp. salt

1 c. brown sugar, firmly
 packed
2 eggs, beaten
1/2 tsp. vanilla
1/2 c. nuts, chopped
1/2 c. confectioners' sugar

Cover apricots with water, boil 10 minutes. Drain, cool and chop. Preheat oven to 350 degrees, grease an 8-inch square pan. In medium bowl, mix butter, sugar and 1 cup flour until crumbly. Press into pan. Bake 25 minutes or until lightly browned. Combine 1/3 c. flour with baking powder and salt. In large mixer bowl, beat brown sugar and eggs until light and fluffy. Mix in flour mixture, vanilla, nuts and apricots. Spread over baked crust. Bake 40 minutes more. Cool in pan on wire rack. Sift confectioners' sugar over bars. Cut in squares. Yield: 32 cookies.

Lucille Lutkenhaus
Cooke County

BEST BROWNIES

1/2 c. oil	1/3 c. cocoa
1 c. sugar	1/4 tsp. baking powder
2 eggs	1/4 tsp. salt
1 tsp. vanilla	1/2 c. nuts, chopped
1/2 c. flour	

Blend oil, sugar, beaten eggs and vanilla in mixing bowl. Combine dry ingredients; add to egg mixture and stir in nuts. Spread into greased 9-inch square pan. Bake at 350 degrees for 20 minutes. Cool in pan.

Nacogdoches County

BEST BROWNIES

1/2 c. Crisco	1/2 tsp. salt
1 c. sugar	3/4 c. flour
2 eggs	1 T. water
2 tsp. chocolate	1 tsp. vanilla
1/2 tsp. baking powder	1 c. nuts

Cream Crisco and sugar. Add eggs and chocolate. Put dry ingredients in flour. Add water and vanilla. Add nuts. Bake at 350 degrees for 25 minutes in greased and floured sheath pan. Ice while still at warm temperature.

ICING

3 c. confectioners' sugar	3 T. condensed milk
1 tsp. vanilla	2 T. chocolate
1/4 stick margarine	

Shelby County

CANDY BAR BROWNIES

4 lg. eggs	1/4 tsp. salt
2 c. sugar	1/3 c. cocoa
3/4 c. butter or margarine, melted	4 (2.07-oz.) chocolate-coated caramel peanut nougat bars, coarsely chopped
2 tsp. vanilla extract	3 (1.55-oz.) milk chocolate bars, finely chopped
1 1/2 c. all-purpose flour	
1/2 tsp. baking powder	

Combine first 4 ingredients in a large bowl. Combine flour and next 3 ingredients; stir into sugar mixture. Fold in chopped nougat bars. Spoon into greased and floured 13 x 9 x 2-inch pan; sprinkle with chopped milk chocolate bars. Bake at 350 degrees for 30 minutes. Cool and cut into squares. Yield: 2 1/2 dozen.

Barbara Oden
Fayette County

To add to your joy, count your blessings.

BROWNIES

2 c. sugar	1 tsp. salt
4 eggs	2 sticks margarine, melted
1 1/2 c. flour	2 tsp. vanilla
1/4 c. cocoa	1-1 1/2 c. pecans, chopped

Preheat oven. While oven is heating, melt margarine in a 15 x 10 1/2 x 2-inch baking pan. Combine sugar and eggs. Add flour, cocoa and salt, mixing lightly. Add melted margarine and vanilla; mix well. Add chopped pecans. Pour into pan and spread evenly. Bake at 350 for 30 minutes. When brownies have been baking 15 minutes, prepare frosting and pour on warm brownies (optional).

FROSTING

1 c. sugar	1/2 c. milk
1/4 c. cocoa	2 T. white Karo syrup
1/4 c. margarine (1/2 stick),	1/8 tsp. salt
melted	1/2 box powdered sugar

In a 2-quart saucepan, mix sugar, cocoa, margarine, milk, syrup and salt; cook to soft ball stage. Cool to lukewarm. Add about 1/2 box powdered sugar until proper consistency to spread. Spread on warm brownies.

Margaret Womack
Castro County

QUICK BROWNIES

1 box butter recipe fudge	1/4 c. cooking oil
cake mix	1 c. chocolate chips
2 eggs	1 c. nuts, chopped

Make sure the cake mix is smooth (no lumps). Mix eggs and oil together. Pour over cake mix; stir well. Add chocolate chips and nuts. Batter will be very stiff. Press into greased 9 x 13-inch pan. Bake 25 minutes in a 350 degree oven. Do not over bake. Note: Other chocolate cake mixes may be used.

Llano County 4-H

BROWNIE TRIFLE

1 (19.8-oz.) pkg. fudge brownie	8 (1.4-oz.) toffee-flavored
mix	candy bars, crushed
1/4 c. praline or coffee-flavored	1 (12-oz.) container frozen
liqueur, opt.	whipped topping, thawed
1 (3.5-oz.) pkg. instant chocolate mousse mix	

Prepare brownie mix and bake according to package directions in a 13 x 9 x 2-inch pan. Prick top of warm brownies at 1-inch intervals using a meat fork and brush with liqueur, if desired. Let cool and crumble. Prepare chocolate mousse according to package directions, omitting chilling. Place half of crumbled brownies in bottom of a 3-quart trifle dish. Top with half of mousse, crushed candy bars and whipped topping. Repeat layers with remaining ingredients, ending with whipped topping. Garnish with chocolate curls if desired. Chill 8 hours. Yield: 16-18 servings.

Maxcine Guffey, Director
District 5, Bowie County

CARMEL CHEWS

2 sticks or 1/2-lb. butter or
  margarine, melted
2 c. or 1-lb. box brown sugar
2 c. pecans, chopped
1 1/2 tsp. baking powder

1 1/2 c. flour
2 tsp. vanilla extract
1 tsp. butter flavoring
2 eggs

Melt butter or margarine, add brown sugar, stir well until sugar is dissolved. Let cool. Add eggs, 1 at a time, and beat well. Add butter and vanilla flavorings, flour, baking powder and pecans. Mix well, pour into well greased and floured 10 x 15-inch sheet pan and bake at 325 degrees or about 40-45 minutes. Cool and cut into squares.

Myrtle Huebinger
Guadalupe County

NELLIE'S CHRISTMAS BARS

1/2 c. margarine
2/3 c. brown sugar
2 T. water
1 c. candied fruit (pineapple,
  red, and green cherries)
1 egg, slightly beaten
1/2 tsp. vanilla flavoring

1/2 tsp. lemon flavoring
1/2 c. nuts, chopped
1 c. flour
1 1/4 tsp. baking powder
1/2 tsp. nutmeg
1/4 tsp. cinnamon

Melt margarine in saucepan. Remove from heat. Add brown sugar and water, blend well. Stir in egg, fruit, flavorings and nuts. Combine flour, baking powder and spices. Sir into mixture. Pour into buttered 9-inch square pan. Bake 30 minutes at 350 degrees. Glaze while warm.

GLAZE

1 c. powdered sugar
1 c. oil

2 T. water
1/2 tsp. vanilla

Mix and drizzle over bars. Cool before cutting. Freezes well.

Nellie Williams
Willacy County

CINNAMON STICKS

1/2-lb. butter or margarine
1 c. sugar
1 egg, separated

2 c. flour
2 tsp. cinnamon

Cream together butter, sugar and egg yolk. Add flour and cinnamon. Spread in 12 x 15-inch cookie sheet with sides.

TOPPING

1 egg white
1 c. nuts, finely chopped

Beat egg white until frothy. Spread over dough. Spread and press nuts over top. Bake at 250 degrees for 1 1/2 hours. Cut into 1 1/2 x 2-inch bars while still hot.

Pat Miller
Dallas County

DATE NUT SQUARES

3/4 c. flour, sifted	1 c. pitted dates, chopped
1 c. sugar	1 c. nuts, chopped
1/4 tsp. salt	3 eggs, well beaten

Sift together dry ingredients. Stir in remaining ingredients. Pour into greased 8 x 8 x 2-inch pan. Bake in a slow oven (325 degrees) about 40 minutes. Cut into 2 x 2-inch squares.

Pat Kliebert
McLennan County

GRAHAM CRACKER TOFFEE BARS

1 c. brown sugar, firmly packed	1 1/2 sticks margarine
1 c. nuts, chopped	Graham crackers to cover bottom of pan

Combine sugar, nuts and margarine. Bring to boil and cook 3 minutes. Place graham crackers on a large cookie sheet. Spread the sugar mixture over the crackers and bake 10 minutes at 350 degrees. Cut between crackers when they are still warm.

Sue Maxey
Garza County

MAGIC DELIGHT

40 saltine crackers	1 6-oz. pkg. chocolate chips
1 c. butter (real butter, no	(real chips, no chocolate-
substitutions	flavored chips)
1 c. brown sugar, packed	1/2 c. nuts, chopped

Place layer of crackers side by side in a 10 x 15-inch foil lined jelly roll pan. Boil sugar and butter 3 minutes. Pour over crackers. Bake at 350 degrees for 5 minutes or until crackers float. Sprinkle chips over crackers. When melted, spread and top with nuts. Cool and cut into bars (a pizza cutter works great for cutting).

Elizabeth Urbanek
Runnels County

CHOCO-MALLO LOGS

1 6-oz. pkg. semi-sweet	3 c. miniature marshmallows
chocolate pieces	(white, colored or mixed)
2 T. Parkay margarine	1 c. nuts, chopped
1 egg, beaten	Confectioners' sugar

Melt chocolate and margarine over low heat or in microwave. Remove from heat, add egg and mix well. Cool slightly. Mix marshmallows and nuts in large bowl. Pour chocolate mixture over marshmallows and nuts; mix well. Divide mixture in half into a roll approximately 8-inches long. Sprinkle confectioners' sugar on large piece of waxed paper. (Use more as needed, lifting sides of paper mold until mixture sticks together.) Wrap in wax paper. Chill until firm and slice.

Gladys Reeves
Blanco County

TEA CAKES

2 sticks butter, softened
2 c. sugar
3 eggs
4 c. flour
1 tsp. soda

2 tsp. baking powder
Dash of salt
1 tsp. lemon extract
1 tsp. vanilla

Mix butter, sugar and eggs in a large mixing bowl. In sifter add flour, soda, baking powder and salt. Sift one-half dry ingredients into liquid mixture; mix well. Then add the other half. Mix dough with large spoon. Cut dough into 4 parts. Roll out until about 1/4-inch thick on floured board. Bake at 375 degrees until brown.

Jewell Carruthers
Navarro County

PEANUT BUTTER BARS

1 c. sugar
1 c. white syrup
1 tsp. vanilla

2 c. peanut butter
3 c. Cheerios
1 c. roasted peanuts

Cook sugar and syrup until sugar is dissolved but not boiling. Remove from heat. Add vanilla and peanut butter; mix well. Add Cheerios and peanuts; mix well. Press into a greased 9 x 13-inch pan. Pat down and cut into bars.

Betty Bourne
Johnson County

LEMON BARS

1 c. flour
1/2 c. butter or margarine
1/4 c. powdered sugar
2 eggs
3 /4 c. granulated sugar

1/2 tsp. lemon peel
3 T. lemon juice
2 T. flour
1/4 tsp. baking powder

Cut in flour, butter and powdered sugar until mixture clings together. Pat into an 8 x 8 x 2-inch pan. Bake at 350 degrees 10-12 minutes. Beat eggs; add sugar, lemon peel, juice, flour and baking powder. Blend well and pour over crust. Bake at 350 degrees for 20-25 minutes.

Top of Texas Club
Potter County

Help me to remember that faith never was meant to be an escalator to carry me in comfort up the steep hill of life. Help me to understand it is but a staff on which I lean while I do the climbing.

LEMON BARS

Crust:

1 yellow cake mix   1/3 c. oil
1 egg

Lemon filling:

1 8-oz. pkg. cream cheese, softened   1/3 c. sugar
1 egg   1-2 tsp. lemon juice

Preheat oven to 350 degrees. Mix cake mix, 1 egg and oil until crumbly. Pat into an ungreased 9 x 13-inch cake pan. Bake for 10 minutes. While crust is baking, prepare lemon filling. Beat cream cheese, sugar, lemon juice and 1 egg until light and smooth. Spread filling over slightly cooled crust and bake for 15 minutes. Cool and cut into bars. Can sprinkle powdered sugar over top if desired.

Linda Hendrick
Angelina County

WAXY PECAN SQUARES

4 eggs, slightly beaten   2 c. pecans, chopped
1 box brown sugar   1 T. cream or milk
2 c. biscuit mix   1 tsp. vanilla

Mix eggs and brown sugar in double boiler, cook 15 minutes, stirring occasionally. Remove from heat and add biscuit mix and other ingredients; mix well. Place in greased 9 x 13-inch pan and bake for 20-25 minutes at 350 degrees.

Jo Ann Bone, Director
District 14, Victoria County

PECAN PIE BARS

4 eggs   3 T. margarine, melted
1 1/2 c. light or dark corn syrup   1 1/2 tsp. vanilla
1 1/2 c. sugar   2 1/2 c. pecan halves or
                                             coarsely chopped

Preheat oven to 350 degrees. Prepare and bake cookie crust. Meanwhile, in large bowl, beat eggs, corn syrup, sugar, margarine and vanilla until well blended. Stir in pecans. Immediately pour over hot crust; spread evenly. Bake 25 minutes or until filling is firm around edges and slightly firm in center. Cool completely. Cut into 2 x 1 1/2-inch bars. Yield: 48 bars.

COOKIE CRUST

2 1/2 c. flour   1/2 c. sugar
1 c. cold butter or margarine,   1/2 tsp. salt
  cut in pieces

Spray 15 x 10 x 1-inch baking pan with corn oil cooking spray. In large bowl at medium speed, beat flour, butter, sugar and salt until mixture resembles fine crumbs. Press firmly into prepared pan. Bake 20-23 minutes or until brown. Top with filling and finish baking as mentioned above.

Lucille Faulkenberry
Gaines County

PECAN DREAM BARS

1/2 c. butter

3 c. flour

1/2 tsp. baking soda

2 c. sugar

3 eggs

Mix all ingredients by hand. Mixture will be very thick. Grease and flour large (12 x 22-inch) cookie sheet with sides. Spread in pan and set aside.

1 8-oz. pkg. cream cheese, softened

2 eggs

1-lb. box powdered sugar

1 T. vanilla

2 c. pecans, finely chopped

Mix first 4 ingredients together and beat 2 minutes. Pour over mixture on cookie sheet. Top with pecans. Bake at 350 degrees for 35 minutes. Yield: 24 2-inch bars.

Sarah Lambert
San Saba County

PECAN BARS

3/4 c. butter

3/4 c. sugar

2 eggs

Rind of 1 lemon, grated

3 c. flour, sifted

1/2 tsp. baking powder

Pecan Topping

Preheat oven to 375 degrees 10 minutes before dough is ready to bake. Grease and flour two 9 x 9 x 2-inch baking pans. Cream butter and sugar; add eggs and lemon rind. Beat well. Chill until you can handle well. Press dough into pan, 1/8-inch thick. Prick all over with fork. Bake until it looks half done, 12-15 minutes. Remove; lower temperature to 350 degrees.

PECAN TOPPING

1 c. butter

1 c. light brown sugar, packed

1 c. honey

1/4 c. whipping cream

3 c. pecans, chopped

Combine butter, sugar and honey in heavy saucepan. Boil, stirring 5 minutes. Remove from heat. Cool slightly and add cream and chopped nuts. Mix well. Spread topping evenly with a buttered, wooden spoon or a flexible spatula on crust. Bake at 350 degrees for 30-35 minutes. Cool. Cut into 1 x 2-inch bars. Yield: approximately 54.

Helen Ruth Louder
Martin County

The best preparation for tomorrow
is the proper use of today.

PEANUT BUTTER PIECES

2 sticks butter

1-lb. powdered sugar

1 c. graham cracker crumbs

1 c. peanut butter

1 12-oz. pkg. chocolate chips

Place butter in large bowl. Microwave for 2-3 minutes. When butter is melted, add sugar, crumbs and peanut butter. Mix together until smooth; press into an 8 x 8-inch dish. Microwave on high 2 minutes. Put chocolate chips into large bowl and microwave for 3-4 minutes. Stir several times while cooking, then spread on mixture and chill in refrigerator. Cut in squares and store in air-tight container.

Grace Rodgers
Wichita County

JUST A LINE

Just a line to say I'm living
That I'm not among the dead.
Though I'm getting more forget-
ful,
And more mixed up in the
head.
For sometimes I can't remember,
When I stand at foot of stairs,
If I must go up for something,
Or if I've just come down from
there.
And before the frig', so often
My poor mind is filled with doubt,
Have I just put food away, or
Have I come to take some out.
So, if it's my turn to write you,
There's no need in getting sore,
I may think that I have written
And don't want to be a bore.
So, remember--I do love you,
And I wish that you were here,
But now, it's nearly mail time
So, I must say "Good-bye" dear.
There I stood beside the mail
box,
With a face so very red,
Instead of mailing you my letter,
I had opened it instead.

MEATS & MAIN DISHES

Meats and Main Dishes

CHICKEN POT PIE

Crust:

1 1/2 c. flour	3 T. shortening
3 tsp. baking powder	1/2 c. milk
1/2 tsp. salt	3/4 c. cheddar cheese, grated
1/2 tsp. black pepper	1 7-oz. jar pimentos, finely chopped

Mix first 6 ingredients as for a pie crust (makes 2 crusts). Roll each crust very thin and sprinkle each with one-half the amount of grated cheese and one-half the amount of chopped pimentos. Roll each crust as if making a jelly roll, place in wax paper, and chill overnight.

Chicken Mixture:

l lg. chicken, cooked and boned	1 T. lemon juice
3 c. stock	1/4 c. green bell pepper, chopped
2 c. milk	1/2 c. onion, chopped
3 T. margarine	3 T. flour

Cook all together in saucepan until flour has thickened the sauce. Pour into a large baking dish. Slice chilled crust rolls and place on top of chicken mixture. Bake in 350 degree oven for 45 minutes.

Blanche Keith
Young County

CHICKEN POT PIE

2 c. chicken broth	4 c. cooked chicken, chopped
1 16-oz. pkg. frozen mixed vegetables, thawed	1/4 tsp. pepper
1 10 3/4-oz. can cream of chicken soup	1 c. self-rising flour
1 10 3/4-oz. can cream of mushroom soup	1 c. milk
	1/2 c. margarine, melted

Combine chicken broth and thawed vegetables in a large saucepan. Bring to a boil. Cover, reduce heat and simmer 10 minutes or until vegetables are tender. Stir in soups, chicken and pepper. Spoon into a 13 x 9 x 2-inch baking dish. Combine flour, milk, margarine; spoon over chicken mixture. Bake at 350 degrees for 55 minutes or until golden brown. Yield: 8 servings.

Annie Bell Reavis
Burnet County

CHICKEN PIE

1 can cream of chicken soup
1 can mixed vegetables, drained

2 c. chicken, cooked and chopped
Pie crust dough

Mix all ingredients together and pour into an 8-inch square pan lined with pie dough. Top with another pie crust. Bake 30 minutes at 400 degrees or until done.

Edith Stevens
Rains County

CHICKEN POT PIE

2 c. chicken, cooked and cubed
1 can cream of chicken soup
2 c. chicken broth
1 lg. potato, cubed
1/2 c. onion, diced
1 can English peas, drained
1 stick celery, diced
1 bell pepper, diced
2 carrots, diced
1 1/2 c. self-rising flour
1 1/2 c. milk
Tony Chachere's Creole seasoning

Preheat oven to 450 degrees. Spread vegetables and meat in 9 x 13-inch pan. Mix cream of chicken soup and broth. Pour over vegetables. Sprinkle Tony's seasoning liberally over mix. Mix flour and milk with whisk or shake well in a jar. Pour over vegetables. Optional—dot well with butter. Bake 30-35 minutes or until golden brown. Let stand about 10 minutes before serving.

Jane Cheatham
Marion County

CHICKEN-SPAGHETTI CASSEROLE

1 lg. hen, cooked and cut to bite-size pieces, broth reserved
1 12-oz. pkg. spaghetti
2 T. butter
1 c. onion, chopped
3 c. celery, diced
2-3 garlic buds, chopped
1 17-oz. can English peas
1 4-oz. can pimentos
1 can mushrooms
1 12-oz. can tomatoes
1 4-oz. can tomato sauce
1 hot pepper, opt.
1 lb. cheese, grated

Cook spaghetti in reserved chicken broth. Saute onions, celery and garlic in butter. Combine chicken, spaghetti and remaining ingredients. Cook over very low heat until taste is well mingled. Put in casserole dish and cover with grated cheese. Bake in 350 degree oven until bubbly, about 10-15 minutes.

Houston County

Trial is the school of trust.

153

CHICKEN FETTUCINE

1/2 c. onion, chopped
1/4 c. bell pepper, chopped
1 1/2 c. celery, chopped
Chicken fat or butter
1 can whole Hunts tomatoes, chopped
1 sm. can mushrooms (stems and pieces)
1/4 c. pimentos, chopped
1 10-oz. pkg. fettucine, broken 3 times
1/2 lb. Velveeta cheese, diced
3 or 4 chicken breasts, cooked and diced
1 c. chicken both (reserve)

Saute onions, peppers, celery in chicken fat; add tomatoes, mushrooms and pimentos. Cook sauce 5 minutes. Cook fettucine in chicken broth and water, drain. Mix with sauce and pour in large casserole. Stir in diced cheese, chicken and 1 cup chicken broth. Bake at 350 degrees for 30 minutes uncovered, or put in microwave until bubbly and cheese melts. Yield: 8-12 servings.

Janie Little Marzuez
Leon County

CHICKEN TETRAZZINI

1 chicken
1 8-oz. pkg. macaroni
1/4 lb. margarine
1 onion, diced
1 green pepper, diced
1 1/2 lb.Velveeta cheese
1 can mushroom soup
Salt to taste

Cook chicken in salted water, remove from bones and cut into chunks. Cook the macaroni in chicken stock. Melt margarine in pan, add onions and green pepper. Cook until tender. Add cheese and stir until melted. Add mushroom soup and pour over combined chicken and drained macaroni in buttered pan. Bake for 30 minutes at 350 degrees.

Esther Stacy
Coleman County

CHICKEN SQUIGGLERONI

1 lg. fryer, boiled, skinned and deboned
1 jar spaghetti sauce with meat
1 can cream of mushroom soup
1 can tomatoes
1 can water chestnuts, sliced
1 pkg. spiral spaghetti, cooked according to pkg. directions, drained
1 c. cheddar cheese

Cut chicken into bite size pieces. Mix with spaghetti and sauce mixture. Salt and pepper to taste. Pour into lightly greased 9 x 13-inch casserole. Sprinkle with cheddar cheese and bake at 350 degrees until cheese is melted.

Marcelle McKenzie
Kleberg County

TURKEY TETRAZZINI

1 12-oz. pkg. narrow egg noodles
1/2 c. onion, chopped
1/2 c. celery, chopped
1/2. c. green bell pepper, chopped
3 c. baked turkey, chopped
  (chicken or tuna may be used)
1 lg. can pimentos
1 lg. can mushrooms

1 or 2 cans cream of mushroom
  soup (1 for dry, 2 for moist)
1 pkg. frozen or canned Italian
  cut green beans
1 12-oz. pkg. cheddar cheese,
  grated (mild, med. or strong)
1 6-oz. pkg. slivered almonds
Seasoning salt

Cook noodles according to directions on the package. Saute chopped onion, celery and bell peppers into a dish. Alternate noodles layered with all other ingredients in a large Pyrex casserole dish. Save enough cheese to sprinkle on top layer. Sprinkle each layer with a small amount of seasoning salt. (Add a small amount of milk, by the tablespoonful, if mixture seems to be too dry.) Bake for 1 hour at 350 degrees.

Mary Harter
Erath County

CHICKEN TETRAZZINI

1 whole chicken
1 c. celery
1 c. onion
1 bell pepper, cut up
1 c. fresh or canned mushrooms

Grated cheese
2 8-oz. cans cream of
  mushroom soup
1 8-oz. box spaghetti

Boil cut up chicken in enough water where you will have enough broth. When tender, take skin off, bone it and cut into bite size pieces. Set aside one day. The next day, cut or dice celery, onion, bell pepper and mushrooms and saute in skillet with butter or margarine. Add cream of mushroom soup. Put chicken back into it and set aside. Boil spaghetti in broth. When done, put grated cheese over casserole. Bake in oven until cheese is melted.

Helen Mathews
Falls County

*Self-preservation is the first law of nature,
but self-sacrifice is the highest rule of grace.*

CHICKEN SPAGHETTI CASSEROLE

1 8-oz. pkg. spaghetti
1 green bell pepper
1 onion
1/4 c. butter
1 4-oz. can mushrooms
1 can mushroom soup
1 can cream of chicken soup
1/2 c. Monterey Jack Cheese, shredded
1/2 c. mild cheddar cheese, shredded
1 4-oz. can chicken
1 sm. can onion rings

Cook spaghetti by package directions. Saute onion and bell pepper in butter until soft. Pour in drained mushrooms. Stir in chicken and the soups. Mix spaghetti with soup mixture. In an oblong casserole dish, put half of spaghetti mixture; top with half of cheese. Add remaining spaghetti and top with rest of cheese and onion rings. Bake at 350 degrees until cheese melts.

Betty Myers
Nolan County

CHICKEN SPAGHETTI

1 chicken
1 stalk celery, chopped
1 lg. jar pimentos, chopped
1 lg. bell pepper, chopped
1/2 onion, chopped
1 stick margarine
1 can cream of chicken soup
1 can cream of celery soup
1 can cream of mushroom soup
1 sm. jar Cheez Whiz
Spaghetti

Boil chicken; de-bone. Cook spaghetti in chicken broth; drain and rinse in hot water. In skillet, melt margarine and saute celery, pimentos, bell pepper and onion. Cook slow until tender, then add soups and Cheez Whiz. Do not add water to soups. Combine chicken and all other ingredients (add some broth if dry). Bake just until hot at 350 degrees for about 20 minutes. Serves 10-12. (I put a little hot sauce in mine.)

Eugenia Bennett
Washington County

SOY SAUCE CHICKEN

3-4 lbs. chicken breasts or
  1 whole fryer
2 10-oz. cans cream of
  mushroom soup
1 pkg. mushroom/onion dry
  soup mix
10 T. soy sauce
2 T. white vinegar
1/4 tsp. garlic powder

Mix all sauce ingredients. Add no other liquid. Add chicken. Cook 9-10 hours in slow cooker. May be served over rice or noodles.

Ava Oats
Coryell County

GOLDEN CHICKEN ROLLS

6 chicken breasts, skinned,
  boned and split
12 thin slices boiled or
  baked ham
12 thin slices Swiss cheese

1/2 c. butter, melted
2 1/3 c. soft bread crumbs
1/4 c. grated Parmesan cheese
Velvety Mushroom Sauce

The day before: Flatten chicken to about 7 1/2 x 6-inch pieces using flat side of a meat mallet or rolling pin. Place 1 slice of ham and 1 slice of Swiss cheese on each. Roll up like a jelly roll, folding in sides to hold in ham and cheese. Dip each roll in melted butter, then in combined bread crumbs and Parmesan cheese. Cover and refrigerate. Forty-five minutes before serving: Arrange chicken in 15 1/2 x 10 1/2 x 1-inch jelly roll pan or shallow roasting pan. Bake at 350 degrees for 40 minutes or until golden brown. Meanwhile, prepare Velvety Mushroom Sauce. Serve with sauce. Makes 12 servings.

VELVETY MUSHROOM SAUCE

1 10 3/4-oz. can condensed
  cream of chicken soup
1 4-oz. can sliced mushrooms,
  undrained
1/2 c. milk

2 T. fresh or freeze-dried
  chives
1 c. dairy sour cream
1/4 c. fresh parsley, chopped

Mix soup, mushrooms, milk and chives in saucepan. Cook over medium heat, stirring occasionally, until mixture comes to a boil. Remove from heat. Stir some of the hot mixture into sour cream. Then stir sour cream mixture back into hot mixture. Warm over low heat. Just before serving, stir in parsley.

Pauline Kettler
Washington County

FANCY FEAST CHICKEN

3 chicken breasts; split,
  boned, skinned
1 can sliced mushrooms
1 can cream of chicken soup
1/2 c. white cooking wine

6 slices Swiss cheese
2 c. Pepperidge Farm Herb
  Stuffing Mix
1 stick butter, melted

Place chicken breasts in lightly greased 9 x 13-inch baking dish. Top each piece with a slice of Swiss cheese. Cover with mushroom pieces. Mix soup and wine and pour over chicken. Sprinkle stuffing mix over top and drizzle with melted butter. Bake at 350 degrees for 1 hour.

Evelyn Fuchs
Washington County

Specialize in doing what you can't.

CHICKEN AND STUFFING

1 pkg. chicken breasts
1 can cream of chicken
  soup, undiluted

1 pkg. Stove Top Stuffing
  Mix
Monterey Jack Cheese

Mix stuffing according to microwave directions and set aside. Spread soup in large casserole dish. Arrange chicken breasts in single layer in dish. Lay one slice of cheese on top of each piece of chicken. Place a heaping serving of stuffing mix on top of each piece of chicken. Bake at 350 degrees until chicken is done. Time will vary according to type of chicken used (boneless, frozen breasts take about 1 hour and 45 minutes).

Carolyn Botkin
Lynn County

CHICKEN AND DRESSING CASSEROLE

1 whole fryer, without giblets
1 c. sour cream
2 cans cream of mushroom soup

1 bag seasoned bread stuffing
  mix
Shredded cheddar cheese,
  to taste

Mix together soup and sour cream. Set aside. Boil chicken until meat comes easily off the bone. De-bone chicken and place on bottom of a 9 x 13-inch pan. Layer cheese, soup and sour cream mixture. Mix stuffing with enough broth from chicken to moisten it and spread on top of casserole. Bake at 375 degrees for 30-45 minutes until hot and bubbly.

Jan Smith
Lampasas County

CHICKEN ENCHILADA PIE

1 3-lb. chicken
1 can condensed cream of
  mushroom soup
1 can condensed cream of
  chicken soup
1 4-oz. can green chilies,
  chopped
1 tsp. chili powder

4 tsp. minced onion
1/8 tsp. garlic powder
1/4 tsp. black pepper
1/4 tsp. Tabasco sauce
1 c. chicken broth
4 c. corn chips
8-oz. sharp cheddar cheese,
  grated

Cook and bone chicken. Reserve 1 cup of the chicken broth. Combine soups, green chilies, spices, Tabasco sauce and chicken broth. Blend well. Preheat oven to 350 degrees. Cover the bottom of a 2 1/2 or 3-quart casserole with 2 cups corn chips. Spread half the chicken over this layer; then half the sauce; then half the grated cheese. Repeat, ending with cheese. Bake at 350 degrees for 25-30 minutes.

Agatha Lilley
Lampasas County

MEXICAN CHICKEN

1 3-lb. fryer, cut up	1 med. green pepper, chopped
Salt and pepper	1 clove garlic, chopped
1/2 c. all-purpose flour	1 c. regular rice, uncooked
1 tsp. chili powder	1 14 1/2-oz. can stewed
1/3 c. vegetable oil	tomatoes
1 med. onion, chopped	2 c. water

Sprinkle chicken with salt and pepper. Combine flour and chili powder. Dredge chicken in flour mixture and brown in hot oil in electric skillet. Add onion, green pepper and garlic to skillet and saute until tender. Stir in rice, tomatoes and water. Arrange chicken over rice and vegetables. Cover and simmer for 35-45 minutes. Yield: 4-6 servings.

Louise Denson
San Augustine County

CHICKEN SPAGHETTI

1 3-lb. chicken	2 tsp. salt
2 bay leaves	1/2 tsp. black pepper
1 clove garlic, chopped	1 can cream of mushroom soup
2 onions, chopped	1 8-oz. can tomato sauce
1 green pepper, chopped	2 7-oz. boxes spaghetti
4 sticks celery, chopped	1 c. cheese, grated

Cook the chicken, bay leaves, garlic, onion, green pepper, celery, salt and pepper in enough water to cover meat. Cook until chicken de-bones easily. De-bone chicken and cube. Cook spaghetti in 6-7 cups of broth (add water if needed). When spaghetti is cooked, add the cheese and stir until cheese is melted. Then add cubed chicken, tomato sauce and cream of mushroom soup. Pour into casserole and sprinkle with some grated cheese. Bake at 350 degrees until cheese is melted and lightly browned.

Evelyn Schelling
Shiner County

MEXICAN CHICKEN

1 cooked chicken, cut into	1 pkg. corn tortillas
bite size pieces	1 tsp. garlic salt
1 onion, chopped	1 can Rotel tomatoes/chilies
1 tsp. chili powder	2 cans chicken soup
1/2-lb. cheese, grated	Reserved chicken stock

Mix all ingredients together. Mash tomatoes first. Boil 1 package soft tortillas in chicken stock. Place in bottom of casserole dish. Then add mixture. Pour chicken soup on top. Bake at 350 degrees for 35 minutes.

Patricia K. Tully
Kaufman County

SOUTH OF THE BORDER CHICKEN

4 chicken breast halves,
   skinned and boned
1 11-oz. can Cheddar cheese
   soup, undiluted

1 10 3/4-oz. can cream of
   chicken soup, undiluted
1 14-oz. can Mexican stewed
   tomatoes

Cut chicken into bite size pieces. Brown chicken in 1 tablespoonful oil in a non-stick skillet and cook until done. Combine chicken soup, cheese soup, and tomatoes. Layer half of **chips** and all of chicken in lightly greased oblong dish; pour soup mixture over chicken. Bake in 350 degree oven for 20 minutes; top with remaining chips and bake an additional 5 minutes. Yield: 6 servings.

Helen Klepac
Williamson County

TURKEY MEAT LOAF

3 slices light whole-wheat or
   white bread
1 12-oz. pkg. mushrooms
2 med. carrots
1 lg. onion
1 lg. celery stalk
1 sm. red pepper
2 T. salad oil

Salt
2-lbs. ground turkey
1 8-oz. container nonfat
   plain yogurt
1/2 c. chili sauce
1/4 c. parsley, chopped
1 1/2 tsp. chili powder

Finely chop bread; set aside. Finely chop mushrooms, carrots, onion, celery and red pepper. In 12-inch skillet over medium-high heat, in hot salad oil, cook vegetables and 1/2 teaspoonful salt until vegetables are tender and well browned, about 20 minutes. Remove skillet from heat; cool slightly. Preheat oven to 375 degrees. In large bowl, mix ground turkey, yogurt, chili sauce, chopped parsley, chili powder and 1 teaspoonful salt until well blended. Stir in vegetable mixture and bread. Pat turkey mixture into 12 x 5-inch oval loaf. Bake 50 minutes. Makes 8 main-dish servings.

Mildred Leatherman
Ochiltree County

FIT FOR A KING

1 fryer, cooked and diced
1 pkg. Uncle Ben's Wild Rice,
   cooked as directed
1 can French style green beans
1 sm. jar pimentos

1 can water chestnuts
1/2 c. celery
1/2 c. onion
1 c. chicken broth
1 c. mushroom soup

Cook celery and onion in chicken broth for 5 minutes. Mix remaining ingredients and place in greased casserole dish. Bake at 350 degrees for 30 minutes. Serves 10.

Nacogdoches County

TURKEY TORTILLA CASSEROLE

1/2 c. onion, chopped
1/2 c. chicken broth
1/4 c. celery, chopped
3 c. turkey, chopped
10-12 6-inch tortillas, cut
  into bite size pieces
1 10-oz. can cream of chicken
  soup
1 tsp. pepper
1 c. cheddar cheese, shredded
1 c. Monterey Jack cheese,
  shredded
1 c. salsa

Simmer onion, chicken broth and celery for 5-6 minutes. Add turkey, tortillas, chicken soup and pepper. Mix in 1/2 cup of shredded cheddar cheese and 1/2 cup of shredded Monterey Jack cheese. Place mixture in a lightly oiled 12 x 9 x 2-inch baking dish. Top with salsa and the remaining cheese. Bake for 30 minutes in a 350 degree oven or until heated through. Let stand 5 minutes before serving.

Allegra Hackett
Angelina County

MEXICAN SPAGHETTI

1-lb. ground chuck
1 sm. onion, chopped
1 T. garlic powder
3 T. chili powder
Salt and pepper to taste
1 lg. can tomato sauce
1 12-oz. pkg. spaghetti,
  cooked and drained
1 c. sour cream
1 c. cottage cheese
1 bunch green onion tops,
  chopped
2 c. cheddar cheese, grated

Preheat oven to 350 degrees. Saute beef and onion until done. Add spices and sauce. Simmer for 10 minutes. While sauce is simmering, mix spaghetti, sour cream, cottage cheese and onion tops. Pour into greased casserole. Pour sauce over the spaghetti and top with cheese. Bake for 25 minutes or until cheese begins to brown.

JoAnn Stiffler
Tarrant County

Wife's Delight
Ingredients -- One husband.
Directions -- Take one husband
and dine out...Anywhere!

CHICKEN CASSEROLE

2 c. cooked turkey or chicken,
cut into bite size pieces
2 c. celery, thinly sliced
1/2 c. sliced almonds
1/3 c. green pepper, chopped
2 T. pimentos, chopped

2 T. onion or scallions, minced
1/2 c. mayonnaise or salad
dressing
1/2 c. lemon juice
1/2 c. cheddar cheese, shredded
2 1/2 c. potato chips, crushed

Mix together turkey or chicken, celery, almonds, green pepper, pimentos, onion, mayonnaise, lemon juice and cheese. Place in a greased casserole dish; top with chips. Bake in 350 degree oven or microwave until heated through. Note: This recipe makes a very light, crunchy dish that could be considered a hot chicken salad. Serve with guacomole salad and hot bread or rolls.

Birdie Girawunder
Austin County

CHICKEN CASSEROLE

1 chicken, boiled
2 10 3/4-oz. cans cream of
chicken soup, undiluted

1 8-oz. carton sour cream
1 box stuffing mix

Preheat oven to 350 degrees. Cool chicken, de-bone and cut into bite size pieces. Place chicken in bottom of 9 x 13-inch casserole dish. Mix cream of chicken soup and sour cream together. Pour over chicken. Prepare stuffing according to directions on box. Spread stuffing over soup mixture and bake in 350 degree oven for 40 minutes

Pat Carter
Mitchell County

VAL'S CHICKEN AND DRESSING CASSEROLE

1 chicken, stewed and boned
2 boxes Stove Top stuffing
(1 corn bread and 1 chicken
flavored)
1/2 c. milk

1 can cream of chicken soup
1/2 c. onion, chopped
1/2 c. celery, chopped
Paprika and pimento

After cooking chicken, save broth for dressing. Prepare dressing according to package directions, using broth for part of liquid. Add onion, celery and cut up chicken giblets along with seasoning packets from dressing mixes and simmer according to package directions. Mix dressing fairly moist - not too dry. Place dressing in 9 x 13-inch casserole dish. Place boned chicken (small pieces) on top of dressing in center of dish. Mix cream of chicken soup with 1/2 cup milk until smooth and pour over chicken. Garnish with paprika and pieces of pimento. Bake at 350 degrees for 35-40 minutes.

Darlene Terrel
Wichita County

CHICKEN SPAGHETTI

1/2 stick margarine	1 1-oz. jar pimento
1/2 c. celery, chopped	1/2 c. bell pepper, chopped
1/2 c. onion, chopped	1/2 clove garlic
1/4 c. stuffed olives, chopped	1 7-oz. pkg. spaghetti
1/2 lb. Velveeta cheese	1 chicken

Boil chicken until done; remove bones when cool. Place margarine in skillet over burner and melt. Add celery, onion, olives, cheese, pimentos, bell pepper, garlic; mix until cheese melts. Stir about 10 minutes. Add **salt and pepper** as desired. Add chicken pieces. Cook spaghetti in chicken broth and add to sauce.

Bobbie McKinney
Fisher County

ORIENTAL CHICKEN CASSEROLE

1 3-lb. fryer	1 can pimentos, diced
1 box white and wild rice mix	2 cans water chestnuts
1 can French style green	1 can cream of celery soup
beans, drained	1/2 c. Hellman's mayonnaise

Cook chicken until tender and cut into small pieces. Prepare rice according to package directions using chicken broth. Mix all ingredients together. Pour into greased casserole and bake at 350 degrees for 30-45 minutes or until it bubbles.

Elaine Fieldhouse
Wilbarger County

WONDERFUL TURKEY CASSEROLE

1 lb. ground turkey	1 tsp. Italian seasoning
2 cloves garlic, chopped	Salt and pepper to taste
1 c. red onion, chopped	2 c. zucchini, sliced
1 c. bell pepper, thinly sliced	2 c. elbow macaroni, cooked
1 c. fresh mushroom, sliced	
4 c. canned Italian tomatoes, crushed	

Cook turkey in skillet sprayed with Pam along with garlic, onion and pepper until turkey is brown. Stir in mushrooms, tomatoes and seasonings. Cover and simmer over low heat for 20 minutes. Add zucchini and macaroni. Spoon into a casserole dish (sprayed with Pam) and bake at 350 degrees for 30 minutes. Serves 6.

Mrs. Vickie Orsak
Lavaca County

Dieting: The triumph of mind over platter!

RITZY CHICKEN CASSEROLE

4 chicken breasts or 1 chicken
1 can cream of chicken soup
1 sm. carton sour cream

1 stick or less, margarine,
 melted
35 Ritz crackers, crushed
Poppy seed

Boil, de-bone and cut up chicken. Mix cream of chicken soup and sour cream and combine with chicken in casserole dish. Combine margarine with crackers and sprinkle with poppy seed on top of chicken mixture. Bake 30 minutes at 325 degrees.

Kathleen Dyer
Wood County

THREE CHEESE CHICKEN BAKE

1 chicken, boiled and de-boned
1 pkg. lasagna noodles, cooked
1 16-oz. carton cottage cheese
Parmesan cheese to taste
1-lb. Velveeta cheese, grated
1 med. can green chilies, chopped

1 onion, chopped
1 c. milk
1 can cream of mushroom soup
2 T. margarine
1 T. flour
Salt and pepper to taste

Saute onions in margarine, add green chilies. Thicken with flour. Add salt, pepper and milk; stir until smooth. Add cream of mushroom soup. Stir over low heat for 5 minutes. Grease a 13 x 9 x 2-inch baking dish. Place chicken pieces in casserole dish and then layer with noodles, cottage cheese, sprinkle with Parmesan cheese, Velveeta cheese and 1/2 of the sauce. Repeat layers. Top with more Velveeta. Cook in 350 degree oven for 45 minutes.

Leta Richardson
Midland County

Consider how hard it is
to change yourself,
and you will understand
what little chance you
have trying to change others.

CREAMY HAM-AND-CHICKEN MEDLEY

1 T. butter or margarine
1/2 c. fresh mushrooms, sliced
1/3 c. butter or margarine
1/3 c. all-purpose flour
2 1/2-3 c. milk, divided
1 c. whipping cream
1 c. Parmesan cheese, freshly
  grated
1/2 tsp. salt

1/4 tsp. black pepper, freshly
  ground
1/4 tsp. ground nutmeg
Dash of ground red pepper
2 c. cooked chicken, chopped
2 c. cooked ham, chopped
2 10-oz. pkgs. frozen puff
  pastry shells, baked OR
  cooked angel hair pasta
Paprika

Melt 1 tablespoonful butter in a large saucepan over medium heat; add mushrooms and cook until tender, stirring constantly. Remove from saucepan; set aside. Melt 1/3 cup butter in saucepan over low heat; add flour, stirring until smooth. Cook 1 minute, stirring constantly. Gradually add 2 1/2 cups milk; cook over medium heat, stirring constantly, until thickened and bubbly. Stir in whipping cream and next 5 ingredients. Cook, stirring constantly, until cheese melts and mixture is smooth; stir in chicken and ham. Add enough of remaining 1/2 cup milk for thinner consistency, if desired. To serve, spoon into shells or over hot cooked angel hair and sprinkle with paprika. May sprinkle with freshly grated Parmesan cheese, if desired. Yield: 12 servings. *This was served at the District 1 1993 planning meeting at Dalhart, Dallam County.

Bunkerhill
Dallam County

DIANNA'S CHICKEN CASSEROLE

8 lg. chicken breasts
1 16-oz. pkg. egg noodes
1 lg. onion, chopped
1 lg. green bell pepper, chopped

1 6-oz. jar diced pimento
  peppers
2 cans chicken soup
Salt and pepper to taste
3 c. Velveeta cheese, shredded

Put chicken breasts in large pan. Cover with water; cook until tender. Cool chicken and cube meat; save the broth. Cook noodles until tender in broth and add more water if needed. Noodles need to be covered with broth when they are fully cooked. Mix the chicken cubes into the noodles. Brown onion and green pepper in skillet with small amount of butter. Add onions, peppers, pimentos, and chicken soup to the chicken and noodles mixture. Add salt and pepper to taste. Mix 2 cups of Velveeta cheese into the chicken mixture and put into a large casserole dish that has been sprayed with Pam. Spread 1 cup of the Velveeta cheese on top. Cook casserole about 30 minutes at 350 degrees or until hot and bubbly. Casserole can be divided for smaller portion and freezes very well. Serves 12-14 people. Serve with salad and hot rolls.

Darlene Hayes
Hale County

CREAMY CHICKEN ENCHILADAS

2 c. cooked chicken/turkey,
  chopped
1 c. green pepper, chopped
1 8-oz. jar Pace Picante sauce,
  divided

1 8-oz. pkg. Philadelphia
  cream cheese, softened
8 flour tortillas (6-inches)
1/2 lb. Velveeta Cheese,
  or more if desired
1/4 c. milk

Stir chicken, green pepper, 1/2 cup Picante sauce and cream cheese in saucepan over low heat until smooth (or in microwave until smooth). Warm tortillas in microwave for 1 minute or until soft. Spoon approximately 1/3 cup chicken mixture in each tortilla; roll. Place seam side down in lightly greased 12 x 8-inch pan. Stir cheese spread (cubed) and milk in saucepan over low heat until smooth. Pour sauce over tortillas; cover with foil. Bake at 350 degrees for 20 minutes or until thoroughly heated. Pour remaining Picante sauce over tortillas. Good served with sour cream. Yield: 4-6 servings.

Ollie Ann Baker
Burnet County

TEX MEX TURKEY ENCHILADAS

1 1/2 c. turkey, chopped
1 c. Picante sauce
1 3-oz. pkg. cream cheese
1 c. green onions, sliced
3/4 tsp. ground cumin

1/4 tsp. oregano
1 1/2 c. Monterey Jack or
  Colby cheese, shredded
8 flour tortillas

Combine turkey, 1/4 cup Picante sauce, cream cheese (cubed), onions, cumin and oregano in skillet. Place over low heat until cheese is melted. Stir in 1/2 cup of Monterey Jack or Colby cheese. Spoon scant 1/3 cup turkey mixture down the center of each tortilla; roll and place seam side down in a lightly greased 12 x 7-inch baking dish. Spoon 3/4 cup Picante sauce evenly over the enchiladas; cover with 1 cup additional cheese. Bake in 350 degree oven for 15 minutes or until heated thoroughly. Makes 4 servings.

Elaine Beeson, Director
District 7, Tom Green County

Do not resent growing old.
Think how much you'd resent
being denied the privilege.

GREEN ENCHILADA CASSEROLE

1 chicken, cooked and cut up	1 can cream of mushroom soup
1 8-oz. pkg. cream cheese	1 can cream of celery soup
1 8-oz. carton sour cream	1 can cream of chicken soup
1 onion, minced	1 pkg. corn tortillas (12)
1 can green chilies, chopped and seeds removed	Cheddar cheese, grated

Cook chicken (saving broth), de-bone and dice. Mix cream cheese and sour cream; add onion and green chilies. Blend with soups and then add the diced chicken. Heat broth and dip tortillas until limp. Line large casserole with tortillas. Cover with chicken mixture, alternating layers or tortillas and chicken, ending with tortillas. Cover with grated cheese. Bake at 350 degrees for about 40 minutes or until heated through. Serves about 10. For a larger amount, this recipe is easily doubled.

Evelyn Killough
Lavaca County

M-M-M-GOOD MEXICAN CASSEROLE

1-lb. ground lean beef	1 pkg. tortilla chips
1 can cream of chicken soup	1 sm. onion
1 can Rotel tomatoes	1 c. cheese, grated

Brown meat; drain off fat. Spray a glass casserole dish with Pam, then line it with tortilla chips. Pour the can of cream of chicken soup, Rotel tomatoes and small onion into the blender and puree. Layer meat, then chips into casserole and pour soup/tomato/onion puree over all of this. Sprinkle grated cheese over the top and put into the microwave for 20 minutes or until cheese is melted.

Helen Parker
Hill County

CHICKEN ENCHILADA CASSEROLE

2 c. chicken, cooked and cut
   into bite-size pieces
	1/4-lb. Longhorn cheese,
	   grated

1 med. onion, chopped	1 sm. can green chilies
1/2 can cream of chicken soup	3-4 c. Doritos

Saute onion in 2 tablespoonfuls cooking oil until tender. Add chicken and chilies that have been cut into small pieces. Then add canned soup. Layer this mixture in casserole with Doritos and cheese. Bake at 325 degrees for about 1 hour.

Burleson County

ENCHILADA PIE

1 5-oz. can boned chicken
1 can cream of chicken or
  mushroom soup
1 soup can of milk
1 sm. can green chilies, chopped

1/3 c. jalapeno relish, opt.
1/2 of 15.5-oz. pkg. corn chips,
  crushed
1/4-lb. Cheddar cheese, grated

Combine chicken, soup, milk, chilies and relish. Spread crushed corn chips in 8 x 12-inch casserole dish. Pour chicken mixture over chips. Sprinkle grated cheese on top. Bake at 350 degrees until brown. Serves 6.

Dorothy Tiemann
Ector County

GREEN ENCHILADA CASSEROLE

1-lb. ground meat
1 c. onion, chopped
1/2-lb. cheese, shredded
1 12-oz. pkg. corn tortillas
1/4 c. butter

1/2 c. flour
2 c. milk
1 6-oz. can green chilies,
  chopped
1/2-lb. processed cheese

Cook ground meat in large skillet until brown. Add chopped onion and shredded cheese. Heat corn tortillas just until soft in **hot oil**. Fill with meat/cheese mixture. Roll and place in baking pan. Melt butter in sauce pan; stir in flour until smooth. Add milk; heat to boiling, stirring constantly. Stir in chopped green chilies and processed cheese (cubed). Cook sauce over low heat until cheese melts. Pour sauce over enchiladas and bake 20-30 minutes at 350 degrees.

Ethel Houdmann
Live Oak County

SWISS ENCHILADAS

1 onion, chopped
1 T. cooking oil
1 clove garlic, minced
1 15-oz. can tomato puree
2 canned green chilies,
  seeded and chopped
2 c. cooked chicken, chopped

1/2 tsp. salt
10-12 cooked crepes
1/2-lb. cheese, grated
3 chicken bouillon cubes,
  crumbled
1 c. light cream

In large saucepan, saute onion in oil until soft. Add garlic, tomato puree, chilies, chicken and salt. Simmer about 10 minutes. In large shallow pan, spoon tomato/chicken mixture onto center of each cooked crepe. Fold over. Combine cheese with bouillon cubes and cream; pour over filled crepes. Bake at 350 degrees for 20-25 minutes. Serve hot.

Ethel Houdmann
Live Oak County

CHEESE ENCHILADAS WITH SAUCE

12-14 dried red chili pods
1 tsp. garlic salt
1/2 tsp. salt
2 T. flour
2 T. oil
1 onion, diced
1 lb. American or cheddar
   cheese
1 lb. ground beef (opt.)
12-18 corn tortillas

Remove tops of chili pods, shake out as many seeds as possible. Wash pods well, put in pan with enough water to cover them. Bring to a boil; after pods are soft, remove from water and put in blender. Use enough water to fill the blender 3/4 full or just a little above the pods. Add garlic salt and salt, blend for 5 minutes or until most of the pods are liquified. Put a bit of oil into a saucepan, add enough flour to make a paste. Add slowly the chili blend to make sauce. Add more garlic and salt if needed. When sauce has simmered for about 5 minutes, begin frying tortillas. Cook tortillas only long enough to soften them. Dip tortillas in sauce, place on a plate or casserole dish, sprinkle with onion and cheese (meat is optional). Repeat until you have used all the tortillas. Pour remaining sauce over the stack. Serve or reheat for later.

Lupe Olivas
Sherman County

CHICKEN ENCHILADA PIE

1 3-lb. chicken
1 can cream of mushroom soup
1 can cream of chicken soup
1 4-oz. can green chilies,
   chopped
1 tsp. chili powder
4 tsp. onion, minced
1/8 tsp. garlic powder
1/4 tsp. black pepper
1/4 tsp. Tabasco sauce
1 c. chicken broth
4 c. corn chips
8-oz. sharp Cheddar cheese,
   grated

Cook and de-bone chicken. Reserve 1 cup of the chicken broth. Combine soups, green chilies, spices, Tabasco sauce and chicken broth. Blend well. Cover the bottom of a 2 1/2-3 quart casserole dish with 2 cups of corn chips. Spread half the chicken over the chips, then layer half of sauce mixture, then layer half of cheese. Repeat layers ending with cheese. Preheat oven to 350 degrees. Bake for 25-30 minutes.

Alberta Minor
Grimes County

The longest period in a woman's
life is the 10 years between
the time she is 39 and 40.

YUMMY ENCHILADA CASSEROLE

1 1/2 lb. hamburger meat
1 med. onion, chopped
Salt and pepper to taste
1 can refried beans
10 (Ground Honey Wheat)
  flour tortillas
1 can cream of mushroom soup
1 can cream of chicken soup
1 can Rotel tomatoes, diced
1 can Enchilada sauce
1 lb. Cheddar cheese, grated
1 lb. Monterey Jack cheese,
  grated
1 can mild green chilies,
  chopped
1 pkg. flour tortillas

Preheat oven to 375 degrees. Brown hamburger meat; drain grease. Add about 1/4 of onions to meat, add 1/4 can green chilies, add 1 can refried beans and a little water to moisten mixture. Simmer meat mixture. In a large saucepan, mix together both soups, Rotel tomatoes, milk, 1/4 of onion, 1/4 can green chilies. Simmer and set aside. In baking pan of your choice, layer flour tortillas, spoon soup mixture to cover bottom, meat mixture to cover, tablespoonful of onions, sprinkle of green chilies and cheese. Then repeat layers, ending with heated enchilada sauce and top with cheese. Bake for approximately 30 minutes. Cool for 10 minutes and serve.

Joy Gilbert
Armstrong County

PAULA'S ENCHILADAS

1/2 c. oil
1 c. flour
2 T. chili powder
2 tsp. salt
5 c. water
1 lb. ground beef
1 tsp. salt
1/4 tsp. pepper
20 tortillas
12-16-oz. cheese, grated
1/4 c. onion, chopped (opt.)

Make sauce by heating oil in large saucepan. Add flour and cook until brown, stirring constantly. Add chili powder, salt and water, cooking and stirring until boiling. Brown ground beef in skillet, seasoning with salt and pepper. Chopped onion may be added. Heat **1 cup oil** in skillet; dip tortillas in until soft. Drain and dip in sauce. Place spoonful of meat, sprinkle with cheese, and roll. Place in a 9 x 13-inch baking pan. Pour sauce over, making sure it covers over and between enchiladas. Sprinkle with cheese. Cover and heat thoroughly at 325 degrees for 15-20 minutes.

Paula Sosa
Randall County

The person who forgives ends the quarrel.

GREEN CHILI-CHICKEN ENCHILADAS

1 lg. pkg. chicken breasts,
  skinless and boneless
3 10-oz. cans Old El Paso Green
  Chili Enchilada Sauce (may
  use more sauce as needed)

20-40 corn tortillas
Cooking oil

Wash chicken breasts and then boil until done. Shred the meat by hand or with a paring knife. Quick fry the tortillas in cooking oil and blot off oil. Pour enchilada sauce in pan and heat (being careful not to scorch). Dip each tortilla in the sauce, put on a plate and add some shredded chicken; roll and put into a large shallow pan. Pour remaining sauce over rolled enchiladas. Heat at 375 degrees for 20 minutes or until bubbling hot. (Good for people who are allergic to wheat and milk-cheese products). Contains no eggs, wheat, or milk products. **Ingredient amounts may vary due to personal taste. Be sure to use ample amount of enchilada sauce.

Rose Budd Stambaugh
Hale County

ENCHILADA CASSEROLE

3 c. boiling water
1 can El Monterey Sauce mix
1 c. cold water
1 8-oz. can tomato sauce
3 lb. ground beef

1 med. onion, chopped
Tortillas
1 1/2 lbs. American or
  Longhorn cheese, grated

To prepare sauce: bring 3 cups water to a boil. Next blend sauce mix with 1 cup cold water and stir slowly into the boiling water. When thick, add tomato sauce. Set aside. Brown the onion and beef just enough to heat through. Place a layer of tortillas into a large oiled baking dish. Add a layer of meat, then sauce, then cheese. Repeat layers. Bake at 350 degrees for 35 minutes or until the casserole is bubbly and cheese is melted. If cheese on top is getting over-brown, cover with foil and finish baking.

Patsy Zachary
Parmer County

CHICKEN ENCHILADAS

1 chicken, boiled and de-boned
1 6-oz. can de-boned chicken
1 lg. onion, chopped
1/2 c. margarine
1 can cream of chicken soup

1 sm. can chili (no beans)
1 c. chicken broth
1/4 tsp. pepper
8 corn tortillas
1/2 lb. cheese, grated

Layer tortillas, chicken mixture and grated cheese. Bake 20 minutes in 350 degree oven.

Refa Nelson
Gaines County

CHICKEN BREASTS FLORENTINE

2 10-oz. pkgs. frozen chopped
  spinach (can use 2 16-oz. bags)
3 lg. whole chicken breasts,
  skinned, boned and halved
1 rib celery, chopped
1/2 med. onion, chopped
1/4 c. butter or margarine
Dash of white pepper

1/4 c. Parmesan cheese,
  grated
1/2 tsp. salt
1/4 c. all-purpose flour
1 c. light cream (can use
  Half & Half)
Dash of ground nutmeg

Cook spinach according to package directions; drain well. Place chicken in saucepan with celery, onion, salt and **1 cup water**. Bring to boil; reduce heat and simmer until meat is tender, about 20 minutes. Remove chicken from broth. Strain broth; reserve 1 cup. Discard vegetables. In saucepan, melt butter; blend in flour and pepper. Stir in reserved broth and cream. Cook and stir until thickened and bubbly. Remove from heat; stir 1/2 cup of the sauce in drained spinach along with half the cheese and nutmeg; spread into a 10 x 6 x 2-inch baking dish. Arrange chicken on top. Pour remaining sauce over all. Bake, uncovered, at 375 degrees for 25-30 minutes or until lightly browned. Serves 6.

Nancy R. Pappenfuss
Atascosa County

HONEY ORANGE CHICKEN

2 T. cornstarch
1/2 tsp. salt
1/8 tsp. pepper
4 chicken breasts, skinless and
  boneless (about 1 1/4 lbs.)
2 T. butter
2 T. parsley, chopped (opt.)

1/2 c. chicken broth
2 T. frozen orange juice
  concentrate
1 tsp. Dijon mustard
1/2 tsp. honey
Orange slices (opt.)

In a bag, combine cornstarch, salt and pepper and shake to mix. Add the chicken and shake to coat lightly. Remove the chicken and reserve the excess cornstarch mix. In a large skillet, melt 1 tablespoonful butter over medium heat until hot. Add chicken and brown (about 5 minutes). Add remaining butter, turn chicken and brown second side. Remove chicken from pan, set aside. Dissolve the cornstarch mix in the chicken broth. Whisk the broth, orange juice, mustard, and honey in juices in skillet. Bring mixture to a boil, stirring constantly. Add chicken. Cover and cook on low heat until tender. 244 calories per serving, 8 gm. fat, 98 gm. cholesterol.

Jeanette Bergstrom
Potter County

CHICKEN CASSEROLE

2 c. chicken, cooked
1 can cream of chicken soup
3/4 c. mayonnaise
1 T. lemon juice
1 c. celery, diced
1 1/2 c. rice, cooked
1/2 tsp. salt
1 T. onion, grated
Corn flake crumbs
Almonds, sliced
Paprika

Mix chicken, soup, mayonnaise, lemon juice, celery, rice, salt and onion; refrigerate 24 hours. Take out of refrigerator 2 hours before baking and top with corn flake crumbs, sliced almonds and paprika. Bake at 375 degrees for 30-40 minutes. Approximately 8 servings.

Jennie Kitching
TX A & M

BERON OF PHEASANT

1-2 pheasants
2-3 T. butter
2-4 slices salt pork, thinly sliced
1 c. chicken broth
1/2 tsp. salt
1/4 tsp. pepper
Pinch each of nutmeg, cloves
    and thyme
1 bay leaf
1/2 c. celery, chopped
2 T. onion, grated
1 T. parsley, chopped
2 T. flour
1 10 1/2-oz. can chicken
    broth

Split pheasants. Place the halved birds in heavy pan or dutch oven. Add butter and brown on both sides. Cover with slices of salt pork. Add chicken broth, spices, celery, onion and parsley. Cover the pan and roast in 350 degree oven for 1 1/2 hours. Remove birds to hot platter. Strain pan juices. Remove fat. Thicken with flour mixed with the canned chicken broth to make gravy. Serves 5.

District 12

RITZY CHICKEN CASSEROLE

4 chicken breasts or 1 chicken
1 can cream of chicken soup
1 sm. carton sour cream
1 stick or less margarine,
    melted
35 Ritz crackers, crushed
Poppy seed

Boil, de-bone and cut up chicken. Mix cream of chicken soup and sour cream and combine with chicken in casserole dish. Combine margarine with crackers and sprinkle with poppy seed on top of chicken mixture. Bake 30 minutes at 325 degrees.

Kathleen Dyer
Wood County

CHILIES RELLENO CASSEROLE

1 c. milk	1/2 lb. Monterey Jack cheese,
1/3 c. flour	grated
2 eggs	1/2 lb. sharp Cheddar cheese,
3 4-oz. cans green chilies,	grated
chopped	1 8-oz. can tomato sauce

Mix milk and flour, add eggs and beat until smooth. Put 1/2 of cheeses and chilies in greased dish, then pour in 1/2 of milk/egg mixture. Repeat until all is used. Pour tomato sauce over all and bake at 350 degrees for 1 1/4 hours. NOTE: Use food processor to grate the cheeses. Can microwave this dish 20 minutes at high power if desired.

Lola Pearl Gough

BEAN CHALUPAS

1 lb. pinto beans	1 T. cumin
3 lbs. pork roast (approx.)	1 tsp. oregano
7 c. water	1 4-oz. can green chilies,
1/2 c. onion, chopped	chopped
2 cloves garlic, minced	1 2-oz. jar pimentos, diced
1 T. salt	Corn chips or tortillas
2 T. chili powder	

Place beans, roast and water in heavy kettle. Add remaining ingredients, except chips. Cover and simmer on top of range about 5 hours or until roast is fork tender. Remove roast and break up with fork. Return meat to pot. Cook uncovered until thick, stirring often. Cook about 1/2 hour. Serve over corn chips or on tortillas.

Vi Bilbro
Upshur County

IMPOSSIBLE TACO PIE

1 lb. ground meat	3 eggs
1/2 c. onion, chopped	2 tomatoes, diced
1 env. Taco Seasoning Mix	1 c. Cheddar cheese,
1 4-oz. can chopped green	shredded
chilies, drained	Lettuce
1 1/4 c. milk	Sour Cream
3/4 c. Bisquick	

Heat oven to 400 degrees. Grease 10 x 1 1/2-inch pie plate. Cook and stir beef and onion until brown. Stir in seasoning mix. Spread in plate; top with chilies. Beat milk, baking mix and eggs smooth. Pour into plate. Bake 25 minutes. Top with cheese. Bake until knife inserted in center comes out clean (8-10 minutes). Cool 5 minutes. Serve with sour cream, diced tomatoes, shredded lettuce and shredded cheese, if desired.

Mary Ann Hueske
Kent County

ENCHILADA CASSEROLE

2 lbs. ground beef
1 lg. onion, chopped
2 T. chili powder
2 tsp. ground cumin
1 tsp. salt
1 15-oz. can Ranch Style
  Beans
6 corn tortillas
1 1/4 c. Cheddar cheese,
  grated
1 1/4 c. Monterey Jack cheese
1 can diced tomatoes and green
  chilies, undrained
1 can cream of mushroom soup

Cook ground beef and onion. Drain. Add chili powder, cumin and salt. Cook over low heat for 10 minutes. Spoon meat mixture into 9 x 13-inch pan. Layer beans, tortillas and cheeses over meat. Spread tomatos and green chilies over cheeses. Pour soup over tomatoes and chilies. Cover and refrigerate overnight. Bake uncovered at 350 degrees for 1 hour.

Margaret Lively
Llano County

MEXICAN CASSEROLE

10-oz. ground turkey, cooked
1/2 c. bell pepper, diced
1 med. onion, chopped
2 c. canned tomatoes, chopped
Salt and pepper to taste
8-oz. jalapeno cheese
1 tsp. garlic, minced
1 pkg. chili seasoning mix
2 c. rice, cooked

Brown meat in skillet. Add onion and bell pepper. Simmer 5 minutes. Add tomatoes, chili seasoning, salt and pepper. Simmer until liquid is gone. Stir in rice. Add cheese, saving some for top. Stir until cheese is melted. Place in 9 x 13-inch pan and bake at 350 degrees for 15 minutes. (4 1/2 lbs. - 2 1/2 lbs. turkey and 2 lbs. cheese). Serves 6-8.

Vickie Orsak
Lavaca County

KING RANCH CHICKEN

1 3-lb. chicken
1 can mushroom soup
1 can cream of chicken soup
1 can Rotel tomatoes
Green chilies
8-12 flour tortillas
1 1/2 c. cheese, grated
1 c. chicken broth

Boil chicken until tender. Cool and de-bone. Cut into bite size pieces. In 9 x 13-inch baking dish, tear 4-6 tortillas to line bottom of dish. Spread chicken over tortillas. Cover chicken with other 4-6 tortillas. Combine the 2 soups, tomatoes, chilies and chicken broth. Heat until all is smooth. Spoon over tortillas and chicken. Cover with foil and bake at 325 degrees for 30-45 minutes. Remove foil and top with cheese. Return to oven until cheese is melted.

Georgie Myers

DINNER IN FOIL

1 round steak, cut into serving
   pieces
1/2 pkg. dried onion soup

1 can mushroom soup
3/4 can water
Potatoes and carrots

   Place carrots and potatoes around meat. Mix soups and water and pour over meat. Fold up foil and cook for 1 to 1 1/4 hours at 375 degrees.

Georgie Myers

SLOPPY JOES

2 lbs. ground meat, browned
   and drained
3 T. brown sugar
3 T. Worcestershire sauce
1 onion, chopped
1/2 c. prepared mustard

2 T. vinegar
4 T. lemon juice
1/3 c. water
1 c. catsup
Salt, pepper, garlic powder
   to taste

   Combine all ingredients. Cook 1 hour. Serve on buns.

Margaret Lively
Llano County

BOUNTY RICE

1 lb. ground beef
2 cans Rotel tomatoes with
   diced green chilies
1 T. salt
1-2 tsp. each oregano and
   basil leaves
1/2 tsp. garlic powder

3 c. rice, cooked
4 c. cabbage, coarsely
   chopped (small head)
1 c. sour cream
1 c. each onion and green
   pepper, chopped
1 c. mozzarella cheese, grated

   Saute beef with onion and pepper. Stir in Rotel tomatoes, rice and cabbage. Cover and cook 10-15 minutes or until cabbage is tender and crisp. Stir in sour cream. Put into serving dish. Sprinkle with cheese. Let stand, allowing cheese to melt.

Betty Houser
Jackson County

__Add__ to the pleasure of others;
__Subtract__ from another's unhappiness;
__Multiply__ the pleasure of others;
__Divide__ the good things that come your way.

WESTERN SPAGHETTI

1 1/2 lbs. ground beef	1/8 tsp. pepper
1/2 c. onion, chopped	1 tsp. salt
1/2 c. ripe olives, sliced	1 can Cheddar cheese soup,
4 c. tomato juice	undiluted
1/2 c. stuffed olives, sliced	1 can nacho cheese soup,
1 7-oz. pkg. spaghetti (broken	undiluted
in half)	

Brown ground beef. Add tomato juice to beef. Cover and simmer 30 minutes. Add onions, olives, spaghetti and seasonings to above mixture. Simmer until spaghetti is cooked. Remove from heat; add cheese soups. Stir until blended. Makes 6 servings.

Geraldine Tomanek
Knox County

CHILI RICE CASSEROLE

3 c. rice, cooked	1 19-oz. can chili
1/2 c. onion, chopped	1 c. corn chips, crushed
4-oz. Cheddar cheese, shredded	

Place rice in buttered baking dish. Spread half the onions and cheese over the rice. Heat chili and pour over rice. Top with remaining cheese, onions and crushed corn chips. Heat in 375 degree oven for about 25 minutes.

Wynema Wheeler
Oldham County

BEROX

2 lbs. ground beef	1 head cabbage
1 onion	Canned biscuits
Salt, pepper, garlic powder and	
red pepper flakes to taste	

Brown meat and onion; drain if necessary. Grate cabbage and steam for a few minutes. Mix meat and cabbage together and add salt, pepper, garlic powder and red pepper flakes to taste. Roll canned biscuits thin as possible. Put filling on one side, fold over as for turnovers and seal edges. Bake at 350 degrees for 20-25 minutes. Makes at least 65-76 Berox. To freeze: Bake 10-15 minutes; cool. Put into containers and freeze. Alternate: roll meat/cabbage mixture in soft flour or corn tortillas. Bake or freeze as above. I use flour tortillas.

Gretchen Stiles
Cooke County

A ready accuser may be a self-excuser.

BAR-B-QUE SLOPPY JOES

1 lg. ground beef	1/4 c. onion, chopped
1 c. Kraft Bar-B-Que sauce	8 hamburger buns, split
1/4 c. green pepper, chopped	Velveeta cheese slices

Brown meat. Stir in Bar-B-Que sauce, green pepper and onion. Cover and cook for 15 minutes. Cover top halves of buns with cheese slices; broil until cheese melts. Spoon meat mixture on bottom halves of buns. Serve with cheese top of buns. Serves 8.

Jan Bennett
Hardin County

BARBECUPS

3/4 lb. ground beef	1 8-oz. can Pillsbury
1/2 c. barbecue sauce	Tenderflake biscuits
1 T. onion or more, minced	3/4 c. cheese, shredded
2 T. brown sugar (opt.)	

In large skillet, brown meat; drain. Add barbecue sauce, onions and brown sugar. Set aside. Separate biscuit dough into 12 biscuits. Place 1 in each of 12 muffin cups pressing dough up sides to edge of cup. Spoon meat mixture into cups. Sprinkle each with cheese. Bake at 400 degrees for 10-12 minutes or until golden brown.

Peggy Henderson
Denton County

TOLULENE (tol' u lene)

1 1/2 lbs. ground meat	1 med. pkg. medium noodles
4 or 5 bell peppers	2 c. Cheddar cheese, grated
4 lg. onions	2 T. chili powder
2 8-oz. cans tomato sauce	1 15-oz. can tomatoes
1 can whole kernel corn, undrained	1 clove garlic
1 can pitted ripe olives, undrained	Salt and pepper to taste

Brown meat with the onions, bell peppers and garlic. Add chili powder, tomatoes, tomato sauce and entire contents of corn and olives. Cook noodles lightly and add to mixture. Place in a large baking dish. Sprinkle grated cheese on top. Bake at 350 degrees for 45 minutes. (Tolulene is best when served the day after it is cooked.)

Rosa Gibson
Bowie County

Good friends are like diamonds --
precious and rare.

MEATBALLS IN MUSHROOM GRAVY

1 lb. ground beef
1 egg
1/4 c. instant potatoes (dry) or
　bread crumbs ground up
1/2 tsp. pepper
1/4 tsp. salt
1 onion

Slice onion and brown in small amount of oil in skillet. Remove onion. Mix all other ingredients; shape into meatballs and brown in skillet. Add **1 can cream of mushroom soup** and **1/2 can water** along with onions and simmer until done.

Marcella Hightower
Childress County

CRANBERRY MEATBALLS

2 lbs. ground chuck
2 eggs
1/3 c. parsley, chopped
1/4 tsp. pepper
1 tsp. garlic salt
2 T. instant onion
1 c. corn flakes, crushed
1/3 c. ketchup

Mix and form into walnut sized balls. (Can use ready-made meatballs.) Place in a single layer in a 9 x 13-inch pan.

SAUCE

1 can cranberry sauce
1 12-oz. chili sauce
2 T. brown sugar
1 T. lemon juice

Mix sauce and pour over meatballs. Bake 45-60 minutes 350 degree oven. Makes 6-8 servings.

Gwen Behringer
Tom Green County

MEXICAN CASSEROLE

1 1/2 lbs. ground meat
1 lg. onion, chopped
Salt and pepper to taste
1 tsp. chili powder
1 can cream of mushroom soup
1 can cream of chicken soup
1 can tomatoes and chilies
9-12 corn tortillas
1 1/2-2 c. cheese, grated

Brown meat with chopped onion. Season with salt, pepper and chili powder. Mix the 2 cans of soup with the can of tomatoes and chilies. Add this to your meat mixture and blend well. Tear tortillas into strips. Layer meat mixture, tortillas and cheese. Top with cheese. Bake about 30 minutes at 350 degrees. Yield: 10-12 servings.
NOTE: This can be prepared a day ahead and refrigerated.

LaVerne Roach
Burnet County

HAMBURGER ROLL-UPS

2 c. Bisquick	3 T. catsup
1/2 c. cold water (approx.)	1 T. prepared mustard
3 T. butter or margarine (not Soft or Light)	1 lb. hamburger meat

Mix Bisquick and enough cold water to make a stiff dough (or use your own biscuit dough). Roll out onto a floured board about 1/2-inch thick in a rectangle about 16 x 10-inches. Melt butter to soften, add catsup and mustard. Spread on rectangle of dough. Spread hamburger on dough over catsup mixture. Pat down firmly. Starting on long side, roll up like a jelly roll with seam side down. This is easier to do using a long spatula. Cut into 1-inch slices. Place in greased, shallow pan or cookie sheet, cut side down, about 1 1/2-inches apart. Bake at 350 degrees for about 30 minutes or until lightly browned. Serve hot with sauce or gravy.

BROCCOLI CHEESE SAUCE

1 can broccoli cheese soup   1/3 can milk

Mix and heat. Serve hot over Hamburger Roll-ups.

NOTE: Use other cream soup flavors or make your own cheese sauce or serve with roast beef gravy. Yield: 15 slices or 7 servings.

Betty Alexander
Burnet County

MOCK FILET MIGNON

2 c. soft bread crumbs	1 tsp. salt
2 lbs. ground meat	1/4 tsp. garlic powder
1/4 tsp. pepper	Bacon slices
1 c. sweet milk	

Mix first 6 ingredients together well. Form into patties. Wrap a slice of bacon around each patty. Make it secure. Brown filet on both sides, slowly. Pour off fat. Pour sauce over patties. Cover and simmer 45 minutes. Turn once.

SAUCE

1 c. tomato catsup	1/4 c. vinegar
1 c. water	1/4 c. Worcestershire sauce
1 T. prepared mustard	

Mix well and pour over filets. Very economical and easy. Can be prepared without the bacon.

Mary Beckner
Hamilton County

Running people down is a bad habit,
whether you are a gossip or a motorist.

SPANISH RICE PRONTO

1/2 c. onion, thinly sliced
1/3 c. green pepper, diced
2 c. instant rice
1/4 c. bacon drippings or butter

2 c. hot water
2 8-oz. can tomato sauce
1 tsp. salt
Dash of pepper

Saute onion, green pepper and minute rice (right from the box) in the bacon drippings. Add remaining ingredients; mix well. Bring to a boil. Then reduce heat and simmer, uncovered, for 5 minutes. Makes 6 servings.
NOTE: Can use 4 c. tomatoes (canned-2 cans, 1 lb. each) and omit the water.

Jowili Etchison
Howard County

YUM-A-SETTA

2 lbs. hamburger
Salt and pepper to taste
1 T. brown sugar or to
    taste
1/4 onion, chopped
1 can tomato soup, undiluted

1 16-oz. pkg. egg noodles
1 can cream of chicken
    soup, undiluted
1 8-oz. pkg. processed
    cheese

Brown hamburger with salt, pepper, brown sugar and onion. Add tomato soup. Cook egg noodles; drain. Add cream of chicken soup to noodles. Layer hamburger mixture and noodle mixture in casserole dish with processed cheese between layers. Bake at 350 degrees for 30 minutes. Serve with a salad.

Carrie H. Smith
Runnels County

TEXAS UNSTUFFED CABBAGE

12-oz. lean ground beef
1 onion, chopped
1/2 med. size head green cabbage
    (about 1 1/2 lbs. or 8 c.)
1 c. carrots, shredded

2 15-oz. cans Mexican style
    tomatoes
1 T. brown sugar, packed
1 T. distilled white vinegar
1/2 tsp. salt

Brown meat in a 4-5 quart dutch oven. Add onions and cook over medium heat 5-6 minutes stirring often. Core and quarter cabbage. Cut crosswise into inch-wide strips. Add to meat mixture with carrots. Cover and cook 5-7 minutes or until cabbage wilts and carrots are tender. Stir in tomatoes, sugar, vinegar and salt. Bring to boil, reduce heat, cover and simmer, stirring once in a while, for 10 minutes or until cabbage is tender. Serve over rice or noodles.

Nell Habiger
Coleman County

One loving spirit sets another on fire.

LOW FAT CHICKEN BURGERS

8-oz. ground chicken
1/2 c. brown rice, cooked
1/2 lg. onion, chopped
2 tsp. Dijon mustard
2 T. celery stalks
2 T. parsley
Salt and pepper to taste

Handle carefully when turning. Serve on wheat buns.

Barbara Creagor
Loving County

DIRTY RICE

2 or 3 chicken gizzards
2 or 3 chicken livers
1/4 c. butter or margarine
1 bunch green onions, finely
  chopped
3 med. onions, finely chopped
1 c. celery, chopped
1/2 c. green pepper, chopped
1/4 c. parsley flakes
3 buds garlic, crushed
1/2 lb. ground beef
Pinch of thyme
Salt to taste
Red pepper to taste
4 c. cooked rice

Cook gizzards in enough water to cover until almost done. Add livers; cook until tender. Chop. Heat butter in large skillet. Add green onions, onions, celery and green pepper. Cook over low heat until vegetables are soft. Add parsley flakes, garlic, giblets and ground beef. Cook over low heat for about 20 minutes; stirring until well blended. Add thyme, salt, pepper and red pepper. Add rice; mix well. Spoon into casserole. Bake in 325 degree preheated oven for about 20 minutes or until bubbly.

Emma Mae Johnson
Navarro County

EASY CRANBERRY CHICKEN

2 chickens, cut into pieces
1 8-oz. bottle any brand vinegar
  and oil dressing
1 16-oz. can whole cranberry
  sauce
1 16-oz. can jellied cranberry
  sauce
1 pkg. Lipton's dry onion soup
  mix

Arrange chicken in baking dish. Mix balance of ingredients and pour over chicken. Marinate at least 2 hours or overnight. Bake at 350 degrees for 1 1/2 hours. Mixture develops into a delicious sauce.

Vera Good
Gillespie County

Age is a quality of the mind.

182

JUDY'S HONOLULU CHICKEN

1 fryer, cut into
  serving pieces
Salt and pepper
Cooking oil
1 10-oz. jar peach preserves
1/2 c. barbecue sauce

1/2 c. green onion, sliced
2 T. soy sauce
1 can water chestnuts, sliced
1 green pepper, cut into
  strips
Hot cooked rice

Salt and pepper chicken pieces and brown in oil in skillet. Drain oil. Combine preserves, barbecue sauce, green onions and soy sauce; pour over chicken. Cover and simmer 40 minutes or until chicken is done and tender. Add water chestnuts and green pepper strips during the last 10 minutes of cooking time. Serve over hot cooked rice. Serves 4.

Sue Lowery
Matagorda County

SPANISH RICE

1/2 lb. ground beef
1 green pepper, chopped
1 c. onion, chopped
1 c. celery, chopped
3 c. canned tomatoes, chopped

2 tsp. salt
1/4 tsp. pepper
Dash of hot sauce
1 c. rice, uncooked

Brown beef in skillet. Pour off excess fat. Add vegetables and tomatoes with juice. Add and blend remaining ingredients. Cover and cook on high until mixture boils. Reduce heat and simmer 30-35 minutes.

Jean Gray
Montgomery County

TATER TOT CASSEROLE

1 lb. hamburger meat
1 16-oz. can Veg-all
1 can Cheddar cheese soup

1/2 soup can of milk
1 2-lb. pkg. tater tots
Salt and pepper to taste

Brown meat and drain. Add drained Veg-all, soup and milk. Season to taste with salt and pepper. Pour into a 9 x 13-inch casserole dish. Top with tater tots. Bake at 375 degrees for 30-40 minutes or until tots are golden brown and crisp. Serves 6-8.

Soundra Christy
Childress County

*People will take your example
far more seriously
than they will your advice.*

WEST OF THE PECAS CASSEROLE

1 stick (1/2 c.) butter or
  margarine
2 lbs. lean ground meat
1 lg. onion, chopped
1 lg. green pepper, chopped
1 6-oz. can mushrooms, sliced
2 tsp. chili powder
Salt and pepper to taste

1/4 c. Worcestershire sauce
1 #1 can cream style corn
1 #1 can green tomatoes and
  chilies
1 can tomato soup
1 12-oz. pkg. noodles, cooked
1 c. Cheddar cheese, grated

Melt butter or margarine in heavy skillet (use less if watching diet); add meat, onions, green pepper, mushrooms, chili powder, Worcestershire sauce, salt and pepper. When meat is browned, add soup, corn, tomatoes; simmer 30 minutes. Add cooked noodles. Pour into casserole. Bake 1 hour at 325 degrees. After 30 minutes, sprinkle top with grated Cheddar cheese. Serves 10-12.

Jennie Gourley
Dallas County

VEGETABLE PIZZA

2 pkgs. pastry, biscuit or
  crescent rolls
2 lg. pkgs. cream cheese
Cauliflower
Olives (black or green)
Carrots, sheared

Broccoli
Mushrooms, fresh or
  canned
Other desired vegetables
  in season

Open biscuit packages; spread onto cookie sheet. Work with fingers until smooth and 1 big crust. Bake 15 minutes at 425 degrees or just until golden brown. When cool, soften cream cheese; add small amount of **Miracle Whip or salad dressing**. When spreadable, smooth it on top of crust. Top with your choice of vegetables. Cover with clear wrap until ready to serve. (Can also use 1 package hot roll mix; follow directions on box for pizza crust. Bake for about 15 minutes at 425 degrees.)

Jo Burdette
Hays County

Just about the time you think
you can make both ends meet,
somebody moves the ends.

CHEDDAR VEGETABLE SQUARES

1 onion, chopped
1/4 c. oil
1 lb. mixed frozen vegetables
  (4 cups)
1/2 tsp. dried marjoram
Salt and pepper
1 1/2 c. Cheddar cheese,
  grated
4 eggs
1 c. Bisquick

Heat oven to 350 degrees. Butter 1 1/2 quart baking dish. In large frypan, heat oil; add onion, cover and cook about 5 minutes. Add frozen vegetables, marjoram, 3/4 teaspoonful salt and 1/2 teaspoonful pepper. Cook until tender or about 5 minutes. Meanwhile, grate cheese. Beat eggs with 1/2 teaspoonful salt. Transfer vegetable mixture to a bowl. Stir in Bisquick, 1 cup of cheese and egg mixture until well combined. Transfer to the prepared baking dish. Sprinkle with remaining cheese. Bake until puffed and set, 25 minutes. Serves 6.

Shirley Koestler
El Paso County

CHEESY HOT QUICHE

8 eggs
1/2 c. flour
1 tsp. baking powder
3/4 tsp. salt
4 c. (1-lb.) Monterey Jack
  cheese, shredded
1 1/2 c. cottage cheese
1/4 c. jalapeno peppers,
  chopped

Beat eggs for 3 minutes. In another container, combine flour, baking powder and salt. Add to eggs and mix well. Stir in cheese, cottage cheese and peppers. Pour into a greased 13 x 9 x 2-inch baking pan. Bake at 350 degrees for 30-35 minutes. Let cook for 10 minutes. Cut into squares.

Alma Faye Carter
Lamb County

BAKED MACARONI & CHEESE

1 12-oz. pkg. macaroni
1 can Cheddar cheese soup
1 1/2 c. Cheddar cheese, grated
1 c. evaporated milk
1 egg
1/4 c. butter or margarine
Salt and pepper to taste

Boil macaroni (according to package directions); stir in soup, evaporated milk, egg, butter or margarine and salt and pepper and then stir in 1 cup of grated cheese in pot of macaroni. Pour into baking dish; sprinkle 1/2 cup of grated cheese over top of macaroni mixture. Bake in oblong baking dish at 350 degrees for about 45 minutes. Serves 8.

Louise Barton
Demorette

MOM'S SPECIAL MACARONI AND CHEESE

2 c. raw macaroni
1/4 c. margarine
1/2 c. celery, chopped
1/2 c. ripe olives, chopped
2 T. chili sauce
1 T. water
1 tsp. seasoned salt

1/4 tsp. Worcestershire sauce
1 c. smoked cheese, grated
1 1/2 c. American cheese,
  grated
1/4 c. cream
1 c. dry bread crumbs
1 T. margarine, melted

Cook macaroni as directed on box. Melt margarine in saucepan. Add celery, olives, chili sauce and water; simmer until tender. Add seasoned salt and Worcestershire sauce. Mix cooked macaroni, cheeses and cooked seasonings together. Pour into an 8 x 8-inch greased Pyrex dish. Pour cream over top. Mix bread crumbs with margarine or butter and place on top. Bake for 30 minutes at 350 degrees. Freezes well. Serves 8.

Thelma Elm
Blanco County

PAESOLE

4 slices bacon, diced
1 lg. red onion, chopped
1 clove garlic, diced
1 med. red bell pepper, diced
3 green chilies, chopped
1/4 tsp. cumin

1/8 tsp. oregano
1 tsp. chili powder
2 cans white hominy, drained
2 cans yellow hominy, drained
2 cans tomatoes
Salt

Fry bacon. Add red onion, garlic, bell pepper and green chilies. Saute until tender. Add cumin, oregano, chili powder, white hominy, yellow hominy, tomatoes and salt to taste. Let simmer 15 minutes. Serves 8.

Carolynda Thames
Ward County

CANNELONI ROMA

1/2 lb. ground beef
1/4 c. onion, chopped
1/2 c. Parmesan cheese, grated
1 egg, beaten
1/2 tsp. oregano leaves
1/2 tsp. garlic salt

8 manicotti shells
1 16-oz. can tomatoes
1 8-oz. can tomato sauce
1/4 c. water
1 4-oz. pkg. mozzarella cheese

Brown meat; drain. Add onion; cook until tender. Stir in 1/4 cup Parmesan cheese, egg and seasoning. Fill manicotti shells, place in 10 x 6-inch baking dish. Pour combined tomatoes, chopped into smaller pieces, tomato sauce and water over manicotti. Sprinkle with remaining Parmesan cheese. Cover with aluminum foil and bake at 350 degrees for 1 hour. Top with mozzarella cheese, continue baking until melted. Makes 4 servings.

Janet Garbutt
Cherokee County

SPAGHETTI ON A PLATE

1 lb. ground beef
3 8-oz. cans tomato sauce
1 T. onion powder
1 T. garlic powder

1/2 tsp. oregano
1/4-1/2 tsp. seasoned salt
1/4 c. soy sauce
1/2 T. chili powder

Separate ground beef and cook thoroughly; then drain the grease off. Stir in tomato sauce and soy sauce. Sprinkle onion powder, garlic powder, seasoned salt, oregano and chili powder in and stir until thoroughly mixed. Simmer for 10 minutes. Boil desired amount of spaghetti noodles until thoroughly cooked. (Egg noodles may be substituted for the spaghetti noodles.) Serve with spaghetti sauce over noodles on a dinner plate.

Jill Brown
Coryell County

VEGETABLE SPAGHETTI

Sauce:
4 sm. cans tomato sauce
1 clove garlic, crushed and chopped
1 tsp. Italian Seasonings

1/2 tsp. oregano
1 T. dried pepper flakes
Salt and pepper to taste

Simmer sauce over low heat for 30 minutes.

5 or 6 zucchini or yellow
   squash (or both)
3 or 4 green onions
1 carrot (opt.)

1 clove garlic, crushed and
   chopped
Olive oil or nonstick spray

Use vegetable peeler to slice squash into thin slices, then stack 3 or 4 slices and cut into thin strips. Shred carrots and slice onion lengthwise in thin strips. Heat skillet, add olive oil to thin coat bottom or spray non-stick. Saute garlic and carrots. Then add squash and onion. Cook until limp. Drain and place in casserole dish. Pour sauce over top and sprinkle Parmesan cheese on top. Serve while hot. This is a good diet dish and a way to get your children to eat vegetables.

Marian Clark
Loving County

*Remember not only to say the right
thing in the right place,
but far more difficult still,
to leave unsaid the wrong thing
at the tempting moment.*

QUICK SPAGHETTI

1 1/2 lb. ground steak
1 sm. onion, chopped
1 sm. green pepper, chopped
1/2 c. olives, sliced
1/2 c. mushrooms, sliced
1 c. tomato sauce
2 1/2 c. canned tomatoes

2 c. water
1 tsp. salt
1/4 tsp. pepper
1 tsp. Worcestershire sauce
6 drops Tabasco sauce
6-oz. spaghetti, cooked

Brown meat in large pan. Add onion and green pepper; cook 5 minutes. Add olives, mushrooms and tomato sauce. To tomatoes, add water, salt, pepper, Worcestershire sauce and Tabasco sauce; stir all into meat mixture. Add uncooked spaghetti and bring to boiling point. Cover, reduce heat to low and simmer 30-40 minutes stirring occasionally. Serves 12.

Glenda Gibson
Swisher County

HAM SPAGHETTI SKILLET

4 slices bacon, cooked and
  diced
1/2 c. onion, chopped
1/4 c. green pepper, chopped
2 c. cooked ham, chopped
1 clove garlic, minced

1 28-oz. can whole tomatoes,
  undrained and chopped
1 7-oz. pkg. spaghetti, cooked
  and drained
1 c. (4-oz.) cheddar cheese,
  shredded

Cook diced bacon. Reserve 2 tablespoonfuls drippings for sauteing onion, pepper and garlic. Add tomatoes and juice and ham. Cook liquid down. Stir in cheese.

Nell Davis
Reeves County

We live in the present,
we dream of the future,
but we learn eternal truths
from the past.

LASAGNA

3 lbs. ground beef
1 lg. onion, diced
4 cloves garlic
Salt and pepper to taste
1 tsp. chili powder
1 tsp. oregano
1 tsp. basil
1 1/2 tsp. Worcestershire sauce

3 whole bay leaves
1 12-oz. can tomato paste
1 8-oz. can tomato sauce
32 oz. water
1 1/2 lbs. mozzarella cheese, grated
1 c. Parmesan cheese, grated
1 8-oz. box lasagna noodles
1 24-oz. carton cottage cheese

Brown meat and drain. Saute onion and garlic. Over medium heat, stir in everything but cheeses and lasagna noodles. Reduce heat, let simmer until water has evaporated and sauce is "thick" (stir often). Remove bay leaves. Cook lasagna noodles until they get limp. In 1 large or 2 small chafing dishes make layers of sauce mix, lasagna noodles, cottage cheese, mozzarella cheese, Parmesan cheese and top with extra mozzarella cheese. Makes 12-15 servings.

Sharon Fitch
Fort Bend County

SPINACH LASAGNA

1 8-oz. pkg. lasagna noodles, cooked and drained
3 10-oz. pkgs. frozen chopped spinach
1 36-oz. carton cottage cheese
4 eggs
1/4 c. parsley, chopped
1/2 c. soft margarine or butter

1 lb. Monterey Jack cheese, grated
1 c. Parmesan cheese, grated
1/2 tsp. garlic powder
1/2 tsp. salt
1/4 tsp. pepper

Cook noodles; drain. Cook spinach according to package directions; drain. Mix cottage cheese, eggs, parsley, margarine and spices in mixing bowl. Grease 13 x 9 x 2-inch pan. Layer twice! Place half of the noodles, followed by layers of cottage cheese mixture, Monterey Jack cheese, spinach and Parmesan cheese. Repeat layers. Bake in 350 degree oven for 45-50 minutes. "Great" reheated second day! Great for pot-luck supper!

Margie Kalinec
Kleberg County

Happiness may be thought,
sought and caught,
but not bought.

EASY LASAGNA

1 lb. lean ground meat
2 15-oz. jars Ragu or Prego
   spaghetti sauce (add 1 sm.
   can tomato sauce if sauce
   seems too thick)
8-10 uncooked lasagna
   noodles
1 lb. mozzarella cheese
1 lb. carton cottage cheese

Brown meat, add sauce and heat thoroughly. Oil lightly a 9 x 13-inch dish, and layer 1/2 meat mixture, 1/2 uncooked noodles, 1/2 pound grated mozzarella cheese and 1/2 carton cottage cheese. Repeat the layers. Cover and bake 1 hour at 350 degrees. Put baking dish on cookie sheet since it might drip. This freezes well.

Bernice Taylor
Gaines County

EASY LASAGNA

1 box lasagna
1 lb. ground beef, cooked
3 1/2 c. Prego sauce
3 c. mozzarella cheese, grated
2 c. cottage cheese
1/2 c. Parmesan cheese, grated
2 eggs
1/4 c. parsley, chopped
1 tsp. salt
1/2 tsp. pepper

Brown beef for 10 minutes or until brown; drain and set aside. In large bowl, mix all cheeses and egg together. Add parsley, salt and pepper. In lasagna pan, pour 1/2 cup Prego sauce in bottom of pan. Pour sauce and beef together. Layer lasagna, sauce and cheese until all is used. Cover and bake 1 hour at 350 degrees. Uncover and cook 10 minutes more.

Jo Helen White
Gregg County

QUICK CASSEROLE

4 c. egg noodles, cooked
2 c. canned pork or any meat
1 can cream of chicken soup
1 can cream of mushroom soup
1 med. onion, chopped
1/4 tsp. black pepper
1/2 tsp. Accent

Mix together, put into a casserole dish. Cover with slices of **Velveeta cheese.** Bake at 350 degrees for about 30-40 minutes. Serves 6-8.

Juanita Anderson
Lubbock County

Enjoyed the trip with you to Waco
Hope you try the recipe.
1993
Juanita Andes

It's not that I spend more than I earn,
it's just that I spend it quicker than I earn it.

190

COMIDA MEXICANA

1 lb. seasoned sausage	2 T. chili powder
1 c. onion, chopped	1 tsp. comino
1 c. green pepper, diced	1/2 tsp. salt (if needed)
2 c. canned tomatoes	2 or 3 c. vermicelli,
2 c. buttermilk	uncooked

Partially brown sausage in large skillet; add onion and pepper and finish browning. Add tomatoes and seasoning. Bring to a boil, add buttermilk, stirring constantly. Mixture should be bubbling when vermicelli is added. Cover and simmer until vermicelli is tender; do not overcook. The buttermilk gives a cheesy taste. Variations: Can use ground beef and pork, ground turkey or venison. May add more seasoning to your taste.

Margaret Laws
Travis County

BUSY DAY LASAGNA

1 1/2 lbs. ground chuck or ground turkey	1 lg. can tomatoes, chopped fine
2 12-oz. cans V-8 juice	1 8-oz. can tomato sauce
2 pkgs. McCormick Spaghetti Seasoning	Dash of garlic powder

Brown ground chuck, add rest of ingredients and simmer for 10 minutes. Put thin layer of meat on bottom of 9 x 13 x 3-inch deep pan. Lay uncooked lasagna noodles. Then spread 1/2 carton of **12-ounce small curd cottage cheese** and 1/2 package of **8-ounce shredded mozzarella cheese**, and 1/2 of meat. Add another layer of noodles, rest of cottage cheese and mozzarella cheese. Finish with rest of meat. Seal tightly with foil.* Place on cookie sheet and bake for 1 hour at 350 degrees. Remove foil and sprinkle top with Parmesan cheese. Return to oven and bake 15 more minutes. Let set for 15 minutes before serving. *May be frozen and baked later.

Jo Lee
Deaf Smith County

A habit is like a soft bed --
easy to get into,
but hard to get out of.

CHICKEN AND VEGETABLE CASSEROLE

1/4 c. onion, chopped
1/4 c. sweet butter
1 1/2 c. chicken stock
3 c. chicken, cooked and
  diced
2 c. fine bread crumbs
1 16-oz. can corn, drained

1 10-oz. pkg. frozen peas,
  cooked and drained
2 eggs, well beaten
1 tsp. salt
1/4 tsp. pepper, freshly
  ground

Preheat oven to 350 degrees. Lightly butter 2-quart casserole. Saute onion in butter; stir in stock; heat to simmer. Combine chicken, bread crumbs, corn, peas, eggs, salt and pepper in prepared casserole. Stir in onion-stock mixture. Bake 30-35 minutes or until bubbly. Let set 10 minutes.

Lisa Herrandez

JALAPENO CHEESE RICE

4 c. water
2 c. Minute Rice
3 chicken bouillon cubes
1/2 stick margarine

1/2 c. cooking oil
1/2 lb. Velveeta cheese
2-3 jalapeno peppers

In iron skillet, bring water, rice and bouillon cubes to boil. Reduce heat and add cheese, margarine and oil and let thicken. Add jalapenos to taste. Serve.

Wanda Finke
Calhoun County

SPANISH CHICKEN

1 chicken, cut up
Shortening, melted
Salt and pepper
1 c. onion, chopped
1/2 c. celery, chopped
1/2 c. green pepper, chopped
2 cloves garlic, minced
2 T. butter, melted
1 1/2 tsp. salt

1 tsp. black pepper
1 T. flour
4 c. tomato sauce
1 1/2 tsp. sugar
1 tsp. margarine
1/2 tsp. lemon rind, grated
1/2 tsp. thyme
Hot cooked rice

Season chicken and brown in hot shortening. Remove and place in 13 x 9-inch baking dish. Saute onion, celery, green pepper and garlic in butter. Spoon over chicken. Combine remaining ingredients, except rice, and simmer over low heat 10-12 minutes. Pour over chicken. Bake uncovered at 350 degrees for 1 hour. Serve over rice.

Lucille Snider
Refugio County

KING RANCH CHICKEN

3/4 c. chicken, cooked and diced	1 c. green pepper, chopped
12 corn tortillas	1 c. onion, chopped
1 can cream of mushroom soup	1 tsp. chili powder
1 can cream of celery soup	1 lb. Cheddar cheese, grated
1/2 c. chicken stock	1 can Rotel tomatoes with green chilies

Line bottom and sides of greased casserole with 6 tortillas, cut into 1-inch strips. Sprinkle with 2 or more tablespoonfuls chicken stock. Combine soups, peppers, onion, chili powder and chicken in saucepan and heat. Pour 1/2 over tortillas and sprinkle with half of cheese. Repeat layers ending with cheese. Top with Rotel tomatoes. Bake in 350 degree oven for 1 hour or until hot and bubbly.

Doris Davis
Tyler County

KING RANCH CHICKEN

1 chicken, boiled and diced	1 lg. onion, diced
2 cans cream of mushroom soup	Tostados
1 green pepper, diced	Sharp Cheddar cheese, grated
2 cans cream of chicken soup	
1 can Rotel brand tomatoes and peppers	

Mix chicken, mushroom soup, green pepper, cream of chicken soup, tomatoes and onion. Using a large casserole dish, arrange in layer, 1 layer of tostados, 1 layer of grated sharp Cheddar cheese and 1 layer of chicken mixture. Top with grated cheese. Bake 40 minutes at 300 degrees.

Louise McWilliams
Menard County

CHICKEN IN RICE

1 stick margarine	1 can cream of celery soup
3 c. Minute Rice	1 can water
1 can cream of mushroom soup	Chicken, cut in parts
1 can mushroom pieces	

Mix all together. Remove 1 1/2 cups of mixture and put the rest in a baking dish. Lay raw chicken parts (salted to taste) over the mixture. Pour the remaining 1 1/2 cups of mixture over chicken. Bake 2 1/2 hours at 350 degrees.

Mary Mizell
Guadalupe County

*Better to suffer for the truth
than be rewarded for a lie.*

ROLLED FLAT DUMPLINGS

1 egg   1 c. milk
1 egg yolk   3 T. shortening, melted
1 tsp. salt   Flour

Beat eggs and salt until lemon colored. Add milk; beat well. Add enough flour to make a stiff dough. Roll into thin strips; pinch off 1-inch pieces and drop into boiling liquid after chicken or other meat has been removed. Return meat to mixture and cook 15 minutes with lid on the pot.

Helen Phillips
Eastland County

CHICKEN AND VEGETABLE STIR-FRY

1 lb. chicken breast, skinned   1 1/2 c. broccoli, cut into
3 med. carrots, peeled and   1-inch pieces
  biased sliced   1 tsp. salt
1 tsp. cornstarch   2 T. soy sauce
1/2 tsp. sugar   2 c. rice, cooked
2 T. cooking oil

Partially freeze chicken; slice very thin across the grain into bite-size pieces. Cook broccoli and carrots 2 minutes. Mix cornstarch, salt and sugar; blend into soy sauce. Set aside. Preheat wok or large skillet over high heat; add oil. Add chicken; stir-fry until all pink has disappeared and juice has been absorbed. Stir soy mixture; add to wok. Cook and stir until mixture has thickened and bubbly. Add vegetables; cover and cook 1 minute more. Serve over pre-cooked rice. *Any vegetable may be added to suit your taste.

Patsy McCurdy
Bell County

HAWAIIAN CHICKEN

2 pkgs. chicken wing sections   Salt and pepper (red and black)
1 16-oz. can pineapple chunks,   to taste
  including juice   1/2 c. picante sauce or more
1/2 c. brown sugar, packed   to taste
2 T. flour or cornstarch
  dissolved in 2 T. milk

Season chicken wing pieces with salt and peppers and place in shallow baking pan. Bake at 350 degrees until chicken is browned on all sides. Mix together pineapple juice, brown sugar and flour (or cornstarch); add pineapple chunks. Pour over browned chicken and bake until slightly thickened, approximately 10-15 minutes. Pour picante sauce over chicken, cover with foil and bake until sauce is heated through and chicken is tender.

Gertrude Craft
Wharton County

HAWAIIAN CHICKEN

1 c. chicken, chopped
1 c. celery, chopped
1/4 c. onion, chopped
1 sm. container or can of
   Chinese noodles

1 c. cashew nuts
2 cans cream of chicken soup,
   undiluted
1 soup can milk

Mix the above ingredients and pour to a 9 x 13-inch pan sprayed with Pam. Bake 1 hour. If metal pan is used, bake at 300 degrees; if glass pan is used, bake at 275 degrees.

Tommie Moulder

CHICKEN ORIENT

1 chicken, cooked and boned
   (or 4 thighs and 3 breasts)
1 pkg. Uncle Ben's Wild
   Rice, cooked
1 can french style green
   beans, drained
1/4 c. onion, chopped

1/2 jar of pimentos
1 can cream of celery soup
3/4 c. mayonnaise
1 c. water chestnuts
1 pkg. slivered almonds
   (or pecans)

Mix all ingredients together. Put into casserole and bake 30 minutes at 350 degrees.

Marie Kell
Dallas County

CHILI

3 lbs. diced lean beef
   (never veal)
1/4 c. olive oil
1 qt. water
3 or 4 T. chili powder (more
   if desired)
3 tsp. salt
3 or 4 cloves garlic, finely
   chopped (more if desired)

1 tsp. ground cumin
1 tsp. oregano or marjoram
1/2 tsp. red pepper
1 T. sugar
3 T. paprika (for color)
3 T. flour
6 T. meal

When olive oil is hot in a 6-quart pot, add the meat and sear over high heat, stirring constantly until meat is gray, not brown. Add water. Cover and cook at bubbling simmer for 1 1/2 to 2 hours. Add all remaining ingredients, except flour and meal, which is saved until last for thickening. Cook 30 minutes longer. Next mix flour and meal with 1 cup water. Add thickening to chili and cook for 5 minutes. (I use Crock Pot, sear meat, add all ingredients, except thickening, and add 1 8-ounce can tomato sauce. Can simmer all day, then add thickening.)

Lorene Jo Smith
Anderson County

CHILI VERDI

1 lb. ground turkey	1 tsp. garlic powder
1 lb. fresh lean pork, cubed	1/2 tsp. cumin powder
1/2 tsp. salt	2 4-oz. cans green chilies,
1 T. oil	chopped
2 16-oz. cans tomato sauce	1 lg. onion, chopped
2 16-oz. cans tomatoes, chopped	12 flour or corn tortillas

In large kettle, brown turkey and pork in oil. Cover with water, add salt, cover and simmer until tender, about 2 hours. Add tomato sauce, chopped tomatoes, green chilies, onion, garlic powder and cumin. Simmer for 30 minutes or more. Serve in bowls with warmed tortillas. Serves 8-10.

Virginia Helton
Parker County

WHITE CHILI

1 lb. Great Northern beans	1/2 tsp. marjoram
6 c. chicken broth	3-4 c. chicken, cooked
1 clove garlic, minced	and diced
1 onion, chopped	1 flat can green chilies,
1/8 tsp. white pepper	chopped
1 tsp. cumin	Tortilla chips
1/2 tsp. oregano	

Presoak beans in water overnight or at least 4 hours; drain. Simmer beans in chicken broth with garlic, onion and seasonings for 1 hour. Add chicken and chilies. Simmer 1 hour. To serve, spoon into bowls over tortilla chips or a flour tortilla. Sliced jalapeno peppers, Monterey Jack cheese, ripe olives, salsa and sour cream can finish off this dish.

Helen Roach
Tom Green County

LAREDO CHILI

1 lb. ground beef	1 16-oz. can Ranch Style beans
1/2 c. onion, chopped	1 16-oz. can tomatoes
1/2 c. green pepper, chopped	1 8-oz. jar Cheez Whiz
2 tsp. chili powder	Crackers or corn chips

Brown meat and drain. Add onion and green pepper. Cool until tender. Stir in rest of ingredients. Simmer 15 minutes. Serve with crackers or corn chips.

Mary Singer
Hood County

The greatest undeveloped territory
in the world lies under your hat.

CHILI

1 T. shortening	2 tsp. ground cumin seeds
2 lbs. ground beef	2 T. flour
4 T. garlic, finely chopped	3 c. water
1 sm. bottle of Gebhart's Eagle	1 T. salt
Chili powder	1/4 tsp. red pepper

Place shortening in frying pan until hot. Add ground beef and garlic and cover with lid. Turn fire low; let cook for 15 minutes. Then add chili powder mixed with cumin and flour. Stir well and add water. Season with salt and red pepper. Cook for 35 minutes. This recipe is a State Fair winner of the fifties. It is also good using venison for 1/2 the meat.

Burnelle Knight
Stephens County

FESTIVE CHILI

1 1/2- 2 lbs. ground beef	1 10 3/4-oz. can cream of
1 onion, chopped	mushroom soup
1 10-oz. can tomatoes and	1 12-oz. pkg. corn chips,
chilies (diced Rotel)	crushed
2 15 1/2-oz. cans Ranch Style	1 tsp. chili powder (opt.)
beans	

Place colander in 3-quart casserole. Place beef and onion inside and cook in microwave for 7-9 minutes, uncovered at 100% power. Add tomatoes, soup and beans and simmer for 3-5 minutes at 100% power, uncovered. In 3-quart casserole, layer bean/soup mixture, cheese and chips. Repeat, ending with chips. Cook uncovered for 8-10 minutes at 50% power. Can be used as an appetizer (dip with nacho chips) or main dish topped with sour cream, guacamole, lettuce, tomatos, onions or any other topping you desire.

Janet Gary
Collin County

TALLERINA

3 lbs. ground beef	1 lg. can tomatoes
1 lb. Cheddar cheese, grated	1 can Rotel tomatoes with
1 lg. onion, chopped	chilies
1 T. margarine	1 can ripe olives, sliced
1 can whole kernel corn	1 lb. narrow egg noodles
	1 c. mushrooms, sliced (opt.)

Saute onion in margarine; set aside. Cook noodles as per package directions; drain and blanch. Saute meat while noodles cook; drain. Mix all ingredients except 1/2 of grated cheese (save to sprinkle on top). Bake at 350 degrees until cheese melts on top. Good with toss salad and garlic bread. Serves 16-20.

Katie Wilson
Anderson County

CORN BREAD CASSEROLE

2 pkgs. jalapeno corn bread mix
1 c. cheese or desired amount
1 can whole kernel corn, drained

1 c. Pace picante sauce
(desired hotness)
1 lb. hamburger meat
(cooked and drained)

Mix corn bread mix according to directions and add drained corn. Pour half in pan and put 1/2 of cheese, picante sauce and hamburger meat on top evenly. Pour other half of corn bread mix on top, then add other half of cheese. Bake at 375 degrees for 30 minutes or until done. (May also mix up your own corn bread and add chopped jalapeno to taste.)

Sondra Yancey
Newton County

HAMBURGER-CORN PIE

1 lb. hamburger
1/4 lb. bulk pork sausage
1 sm. onion, chopped (1/4 c.)
1 clove garlic, finely chopped
1 16-oz. can whole kernel corn,
   drained
20-24 pitted ripe olives, chopped
1 1/2-3 tsp. chili powder

1 1/2 tsp. salt
1 c. cornmeal
1 c. milk
2 eggs, well beaten
1 c. Cheddar cheese, shredded
(about 4 oz.)
1 16-oz. can tomatoes, whole

Cook and stir hamburger, pork sausage, onion and garlic until meat is brown; drain. Stir in tomatoes (with liquid), corn, olives, chili powder and salt. Heat to boiling. Pour into ungreased 9 x 9 x 2-inch or 12 x 7 1/2 x 2-inch baking dish or 2-quart casserole. Mix cornmeal, milk and eggs; pour over meat mixture. Sprinkle with cheese. Cook in 350 degree oven until golden brown, 40-50 minutes. Garnish with parsley sprigs and black olives, if desired. Yield: 8 servings.

Georgia Wade
Kaufman County

MACARONI DELIGHT

2 T. oil
1 med. onion, chopped
1 clove garlic
1 green pepper
2 lbs. ground meat
1 box macaroni, cooked

1 c. cheese, grated
1 can tomato soup
1 can mushroom soup
1 can whole kernel soup
2 T. Worcestershire sauce
Salt and pepper to taste

Combine first 5 ingredients and cook until done. Cook macaroni in boiling salted water until fairly tender. Drain and add grated cheese while still hot. Mix well and add last four ingredients. Mix all together, add salt and pepper to taste. Sprinkle with grated cheese and bake in slow oven for a few minutes.

Annetta Simmons
Jones County

MEXICAN CASSEROLE

1 1/2 lbs. ground beef	1 can cream of mushroom soup
1 med. onion, chopped	1 lg. can taco sauce
1 tsp. salt	1/2 lb. Cheddar cheese, grated
1/4 tsp. pepper	1 pkg. corn tortillas, torn into
1 sm. can green chilies	pieces
1 can cream of chicken soup	

Brown meat with onion, salt and pepper. Drain off any grease. Add chilies, soups and taco sauce. Simmer 5 minutes. In a large casserole dish, layer the torn tortillas and meat mixture. Alternate until all of mixture is used. Top with cheese. Bake for 30 minutes in a 350 degree oven.

Lucile Ratliff
Llano County

MEXICAN CORN BREAD CASSEROLE

1 lb. ground beef	1 can cream-style corn
1/4 c. onion, chopped	2/3 c. milk
2 T. fresh jalapeno, chopped	1 6 1/2-oz. pkg. corn bread mix
2 eggs, beaten	4-6 slices American cheese

Preheat oven to 425 degrees. Brown ground beef, onion and jalapeno in skillet. Season ground beef as desired. Drain well. Combine eggs, 1 cup of corn and milk; add corn bread mix. Stir until well moistened. Pour 1/2 corn bread mixture into greased 9-inch square cake pan. Top with beef mixture, cheese slices and remaining corn. Pour other 1/2 of corn bread mixture over top. Bake 25-30 minutes or until corn bread is golden brown. Cut into squares and serve with a mixed salad.

Sylvia Pearce
Midland County

BLACK-EYED PEA CASSEROLE

1 lb. ground beef	1 can tomatoes
1 lg. green pepper, diced	1 can tomatos with green chilies
1 lg. onion, diced	1 pkg. jalapeno pepper corn
1 can black-eyed peas	bread mix

Brown ground beef with green pepper and onion. Add black-eyed peas, tomatoes and tomatos with green chilies. Mix and bring to a boil. Put in large casserole dish. Make corn bread mix according to package directions. Pour over casserole mixture. Bake at 375 degrees until bread is done.

Eulabel Sheldon
Lampasas County

Don't pray for rain if you are going to complain about the mud.

MEXICAN CHICKEN

1 chicken, cooked and cut
  into bite size pieces
1 onion, chopped
1 tsp. chili powder
1/2 lb. cheese, grated
1 pkg. corn tortillas

1 tsp. garlic salt
1 can tomatoes with chilies,
  mashed
2 cans chicken soup
Reserved chicken stock
  (do not add to mixture)

Mix all ingredients together except tortillas and stock. Boil soft tortillas in chicken stock. Place in bottom of greased casserole dish. Add mixture, then pour 2 cans chicken soup on top. Gently stir just to mix a little. Bake at 350 degrees for 35 minutes.

Patricia K. Tully
Kaufman County

CHICKEN DIVAN

1 1/2 10-oz. pkgs. frozen
  broccoli, thawed
3 c. chicken, cooked (can bake)
1 c. English peas, thawed
1 10 1/2 oz. can cream of chicken
  soup

1/4 c. Miracle Whip salad
  dressing
1/4 c. milk
1 tsp. lemon juice
6 slices American cheese
1 T. fine dry bread crumbs

Combine the first 3 ingredients; set aside. Combine soup, salad dressing, milk and lemon juice. Pour over broccoli mixture, stirring to coat. Spoon into greased 12 x 8 x 2-inch baking dish. Bake at 350 degrees for 25 minutes. Arrange cheese slices on top, sprinkle with bread crumbs and bake 5 minutes longer. Serves 6-8. *Grand Champion - Colorado County Fair.

Bernice Heinsohn
Colorado County

OVEN FRIED CHICKEN

3 lbs. frying chicken pieces,
  rinsed and drained
Salt and pepper
1 egg

1/2 c. milk
1 3/4 c. corn flakes crumbs
3 T. butter or margarine,
  melted

In small mixing bowl, beat egg and milk. Salt and pepper chicken. Dip chicken into egg and milk wash. Coat chicken with corn flakes crumbs. Place in single layer, skin side down, in greased or foil-lined shallow baking pan. Drizzle with melted butter. Bake at 350 degrees for about 1 hour or until chicken is tender. Turn chicken about halfway through baking. Serves 6. *Best of Section - Colorado County Fair

Rita H. Addicks
Colorado County

CRISPY ITALIAN CHICKEN

3 lbs. chicken pieces or cut-up fryer
1/3 c. Italian salad dressing (oil and vinegar type)
3/4 c. Corn Flakes crumbs
1/4 c. Romano or Parmesan cheese, grated
1 tsp. Italian seasoning
1/4 tsp. red pepper, crushed (opt.)

Skin chicken if desired. Marinate chicken in salad dressing 30 minutes (longer if you have time). Combine crumbs, cheese and seasoning. Roll chicken in mixture. Arrange on microwave meat rack. Place the thickest or meaty pieces toward the outside. Thin or bony pieces should be in the center (such as wings and drumstick ends). Cross tip of wing behind large joint to make a compact shape. Microwave on High 7-8 minutes per pound, rotating rack once. Let stand 5-10 minutes before serving. Serves 4-6. Freezes well.

Taylor County

CABBAGE ROLLS

2 lbs. ground beef
1 med. onion, finely chopped
1 1/2 tsp. salt
1/4 tsp. pepper
3 eggs
1/2 c. catsup
1/4 c. sugar
3/4 c. instant rice
1 head cabbage
1 sm. can tomato sauce

Mix ground beef, onion, salt, pepper, eggs, catsup and sugar thoroughly. Prepare instant rice according to package directions. Set aside. In a large pot, heat water enough to cover a head of cabbage. Core cabbage center out and place in hot water to wilt leaves. Remove leaves as they soften. Mix together rice and meat mixtures. Place about 1/4 cup meat into each cabbage leaf and roll up; place in greased electric skillet. Sprinkle a small amount of salt and sugar over the top of the rolls.* Pour tomato sauce over the top. Cover and cook for 1 hour at 250 degrees (temperature may need adjusting).
*NOTE: The remaining cabbage may be quartered and placed on top of the rolls to steam as it cooks.

Maurine Gilmore
Titus County

*Learn from the mistakes of others,
you can't live long enough to make them all yourself.*

201

CABBAGE TAMALE

1 1/2 lbs. ground chuck	1 tsp. Worcestershire sauce
1 med. onion	1 c. tomatoes with green chilies
2 1/2 T. chili powder	1 c. tomato sauce
2/3 c. cornmeal	1/2 tsp. pepper
1 tsp. salt	Dash of garlic powder

Mix all the above ingredients and leave overnight if possible. Take an **extra large loose-leaf cabbage.** Cut out core and put in large kettle of hot water. As the leaves wilt, remove about 12 or 15. Take a handful of the meat mixture and roll in the cabbage leaves. Place in a large heavy bottom pan. Cover with a cup of water and let steam and cook slowly for 2 or more hours. Great with potato salad. Freezes well for a later day. *This is an old time favorite recipe in family for many years.

Alda Beth Garrison
Childress County

RICE BALLS

Rice:

3 c. short-grain rice	1 stick margarine
7 c. salted water	

Add rice to salted water and bring to a boil; cover and simmer until cooked, but mushy. Add margarine and let cool.

Filling:

1 1/2 lbs. ground meat	1 8-oz. can tomato sauce
3/4 c. onion, chopped	1/2 c. water
1 c. celery, chopped	Salt and pepper to taste
2 T. chili powder	

Fry meat until meat loses redness. Add onions and celery; cook slowly for about 10 minutes. Add chili powder, tomato sauce and water; simmer 1 hour. Remove from heat and add seasoning. Set aside to cool.

Outside Covering:

3 eggs, beaten	4-5 c. seasoned bread
1/2 c. water	crumbs (or make your own in blender with your seasoning)

To Make Balls: With wet hands, place 1/3 cup rice into palm and press out. Add a little meat in the center (1 tablespoonful maybe). Roll rice around meat, making ball. Chill on cookie sheet in freezer. Dip in egg and water mixture. Roll in bread crumbs. Refreeze. Place in bags for later use or fry in deep fat until brown. Makes 4 dozen small balls.

Nona Broussard

MEATBALLS

1 lb. hamburger meat	1 egg
1/2 c. bread crumbs	1 T. parsley
1/3 c. onions, chopped	1/2 T. Worcestershire sauce
1/4 c. milk	Salt and pepper

Combine ingredients and make into meatballs. They may be cooked in a skillet or in the oven. When done, put into sauce made of **12-ounces chili sauce** and **10-ounces of grape jelly**. Beat sauce and jelly together until smooth and hot.

Joy Payne
Galveston County

MEATBALL STROGANOFF

2-3 lbs. ground lean beef	Garlic salt
1 can chicken gumbo soup	1/4 tsp. dill weed
2 eggs	Onion flakes or chopped onion
1 tsp. poultry seasoning	1/2-1 c. fine bread crumbs

Mix together all ingredients and make balls about 1-inch in diameter. Place close together in a baking pan. Bake at 350 degrees for about 20 minutes or until done. Remove from pan. Pour grease from drippings in pan. Make gravy by adding **1/2-1 cup wine** and **1/2-1 cup sour cream** mixed together to drippings. Pour over meat balls and keep hot. A chafing dish is good for serving this, or may be served over rice. Season with salt and pepper.

Doris Thomas
Gonzales County

MAKE-AHEAD MEXICAN CASSEROLE

1 1/2 lbs. ground beef	1 10 3/4-oz. can cream of
1 lg. onion, chopped	chicken soup, undiluted
1 10-oz. can tomatoes with green	1 10-oz. can enchilada sauce
chilies	2 doz. corn tortillas, cut
1 10 3/4-oz. can cream of	into eighths
mushroom soup, undiluted	2 c. Cheddar cheese, shredded

Saute ground beef and onion until lightly browned, stirring to crumble meat. Stir in remaining ingredients, except tortillas and cheese. Alternately layer meat mixture and tortillas, beginning and ending with meat mixture, into a greased 13 x 9 x 2-inch pan. Sprinkle with cheese, cover with foil and refrigerate if not baking immediately. To serve, remove from refrigerator and let stand about 30 minutes. Remove foil and bake at 350 degrees for 35 minutes or until bubbly. Yield: 8 ample servings.

Billie Woods
Mitchell County

CELERY STEAK

1 round steak, cut into serving   3 T. oil
   size pieces   1 tsp. salt
1 can cream of celery soup   1 tsp. pepper
5 T. flour   1 sm. onion, sliced

Dredge steak in flour, salt and pepper. Brown in oil. Drain and place steak in slow cooker. Top with onion and celery soup. Cook 6-8 hours on low heat.

June Ellen Domino
Titus County

MEAT CASSEROLE

3 med. potatoes, sliced (as   1 1/2 tsp. salt
   for scalloped potatoes)   1/4 tsp. black pepper
1 lb. cabbage, shredded by   1/4 c. flour
   hand with knife   1 can cream of celery soup
1/2 c. onion, chopped and   (or cream of chicken soup)
   browned lightly   1/2 c. sweet milk
Pork chops or pork steaks

Mix together salt, pepper and flour; set aside. Mix together soup and milk; set aside. Brown onions in **2 tablespoonfuls of oil**, remove from skillet, add more oil, then brown the pork chops or pork steak. (If using pork steak, cut into strips as for fingering.) Butter casserole dish and put in a layer of potatoes, sprinkle lightly with some of flour mixture, layer of onions, flour mixture again, sprinkle cabbage and add flour mixture again. (If you put the flour mixture into a salt shaker, it is easier to use.) Continue to layer until all vegetables are used. Pour soup and milk mixture over the vegetables. Place pork or other meat on top. Cover and bake for about 1 hour at 350 degrees to cook the vegetables and blend the flavors.

Helen Hogan
Gray County

PEPPER STEAK

2 or 3 lbs. round steak   1 4-oz. can green chilies,
1 can cream of mushroom soup   chopped
Garlic salt   1 can cream of celery soup
                                  Salt and pepper to taste

Cut steak into serving size pieces; salt and pepper. Roll in **flour** and brown in **hot grease**. Does not have to cook, just brown. Place in a baking dish. Sprinkle with garlic salt to taste. Cover with soups and green chilies. Cover and bake for 3 hours at 350 degrees. Serve with salad and garlic toast. You can use tough cuts of steak or venison.

Nell Finney
Swisher County

HOMEMADE BEEF SALAMI

2 lbs. ground chuck	1 c. water
2 T. Morton's Quick salt	1 1/2 T. liquid smoke
1/4 tsp. garlic powder	1/2 tsp. onion powder
1 tsp. mustard seed	1 tsp. cracked black pepper

Mix all ingredients together well with hands. Shape into 6 rolls about 6-inches long each. Wrap each roll in Saran Wrap, twist ends closed. Refrigerate 24 hours. Remove wrap, place on rack with drip pan, and bake 1 1/2 hours at 300 degrees. Cook on rack. Wrap in clean Saran Wrap and refrigerate. Ideal for slicing for party crackers. Great eatable gift idea to package. Keeps up to a month in refrigerator. Make ahead for the holidays.

Kay Chastain, "Messenger" Editor
Rains County

Geneva J. Mc Afee from Ward County uses 1/2 teaspoonful garlic salt, 2 teaspoonfuls mustard seed, 1 tablespoonful liquid smoke, 1 tablespoonful brown sugar, 2 tablespoonfuls cracked black pepper and no onion powder.

CARNE GUISADA

3 lbs. chuck steak or shoulder round	1 or 2 T. Worcestershire sauce
3-4 T. fat	Salt to taste
2 or 3 cloves garlic, finely chopped (may substitute 1 T. garlic powder)	1/2 tsp. cumin seed powder
1 env. Lipton or Wyler's onion soup mix* (or 1 onion, finely chopped)	1/2 tsp. black pepper
	1 can tomato sauce

Trim fat from meat, cut in small cubes, brown well in fat in heavy pan. Grind or mash garlic and mix with a little water. Add this to meat together with other spices, chopped onion or onion soup mix, tomato sauce and enough water to barely cover meat. Cover pan and simmer on low heat for 30-40 minutes. Blend **1-2 tablespoonfuls flour** with **1/2 cup cold water**. Stir into meat to make gravy. Cook 3-5 minutes. Serves 6-8. *If onion soup mix is used, taste before adding more salt.

Miss Justina Nava
Brooks County

*Tact is the ability to close your mouth
before someone else wants to.*

VENISON SLOW COOKER STEW

1 1/4 lbs. venison, fat removed
  and cut into large cubes
1 16-oz. can tomatoes
1 lg. onion, chopped
2-3 ribs celery, cut into
  1-inch pieces
2 lg. potatoes, pared and sliced
  into 1/2-inch pieces

3 carrots, scraped and cut
  into 1-inch pieces
2 tsp. instant bouillon
1/2 c. water
1/4 c. parsley, chopped
1/4 c. wine (opt.)
Salt and pepper to taste

Place all ingredients into a 3 1/2-quart slow cooker. Cover and cook on High for one hour. Turn cooker to Low and cook 6-8 hours. Season to taste with salt and pepper. Serves 4-6 generously. Good with corn bread!

Brooks County

VENISON SWISS ROAST

3 T. bacon drippings or
  vegetable oil
1 1/2 lb. boneless venison,
  free of fat
1/4 tsp. black pepper
3 T. all-purpose flour

1 c. mixed vegetable juice
1 16-oz. can stewed tomatoes
1 lg. onion, peeled and sliced
  into rings
2 ribs celery, chopped
1/2 tsp. salt

Heat bacon drippings or oil in heavy skillet. Sprinkle venison with pepper an dredge in flour. Brown roast in hot oil. Drain excess oil from pan. Pour vegetable juice in pan and place roast in pan. Pour tomatoes over roast. Top with onion slices and celery. Sprinkle with salt. Cover and simmer 4-5 hours or until roast is tender. If desired, make a sauce by placing 3/4 of the tomato/onion mixture into blender or food processor and puree. Serve roast with remaining tomato/onion mixture on top. Serve sauce on side. To cook in slow cooker: Follow above directions. After browning roast, place in slow cooker with vegetable juice and other vegetables. Cover and cook on High for 1 hour. Turn to Low and cook 8 hours or more.

Brooks County

MAC'S BEER FRIED VENISON

1 1/2 lbs. venison, cut into
  1/4-inch steaks
1 egg, beaten
1 c. beer

1/2 c. Wondra flour
Cooking oil or shortening
Salt and black pepper to taste

Tenderize steaks with meat mallet if desired. Mix egg and beer together. Dip each steak in flour, then egg mixture, and again in flour. Fry in hot fat until done and browned on both sides. Salt and pepper to taste.

Loretta Osborn
Brooks County Agent

CROCK POT BAR-B-QUE BEEF

4 lb. roast	3 T. liquid smoke
1 14-oz. bottle catsup	2 T. mustard
12-oz. Coke	4 T. brown sugar
4 T. Worcestershire sauce	4 T. applesauce

Cook roast in crock pot until well done (falling apart). Drain, remove waste and shred with fork. Set aside. Mix together other ingredients in crock pot, add shredded beef and cook for 3-4 more hours on low or medium setting.

Velna Ormiston

SOUTHWESTERN BEEF BRISKET

1 3-lb. fresh beef brisket	3/4 tsp. cumin
1 tsp. salt	1/2 tsp. garlic powder
1/4 tsp. black pepper	1/4 tsp. salt
2 T. cooking oil	1/8-1/4 tsp. ground red
1 1/2 c. water	pepper
1 8-oz. can tomato sauce	1/8 tsp. black pepper
1 sm. onion, chopped	3 med. sweet red peppers,
2 T. red wine vinegar	cut into strips
1 T. chili powder	1 1/2 c. carrots, sliced into
1 tsp. dried oregano	1-inch chunks

Season beef with salt and pepper. In a Dutch oven, heat oil; brown beef on both sides. Meanwhile, combine all remaining ingredients, except red peppers and carrots. Pour over meat. Cover and bake at 325 degrees for 2 hours. Add red peppers and carrots; bake 1 hour longer or until meat is tender. Remove meat from pan; allow to stand 15 minutes before cutting. Thicken juices with a little flour or cook over high heat to reduce and thicken. Yield: 10-12 servings.

Eulus Damron
Dawson County

HICKORY BRISKET ROAST

4-5 lb. brisket, well trimmed	1/2 c. Worcestershire sauce
2-oz. hickory liquid smoke	1 lg. bottle barbecue sauce

Place brisket in Dutch oven and pierce well with fork. Mix all ingredients together and pour over meat. Allow to marinate overnight. When ready to bake, place in heavy-duty foil, sealing tightly. Cook 2 1/2-3 hours at 325 degrees. Baste once or twice.

Joyce McCoy
Scurry County

Letters are visits when friends are apart.

WILD HOG HAM

Roast, loin or any large piece	Pepper
Lawry's Seasoned salt and	Morton's Nature (opt.)
pepper	Honey
Garlic salt	

Score meat (ham or loin). Season heavily with seasoned salt and pepper, garlic salt, and pepper (also Morton's Nature, if desired). Place large piece of heavy-duty foil in a baking pan. Wet large piece of cheesecloth and place on top of foil. Place meat on top of cheesecloth. Pour plenty of honey over meat. Wrap with cheesecloth and foil. Bake in 400 degree oven for about 30 minutes and for several hours at 325-350 degrees (depending on size of meat). When done, the meat should just fall apart. Don't uncover while cooking. Should make plenty of juice. SUPER GOOD! Good with baked beans.

Linda Sue Barnes
Live Oak County

PORK CHOP CASSEROLE

6 med. potatoes	1 can mushroom soup
1 onion	1 soup can of milk
Margarine	6 pork chops

Arrange thinly sliced potatoes and onions in casserole. Salt and pepper; dot with margarine. Mix mushroom soup with milk. Pour over potatoes. Dip pork chops in **buttermilk**, then in **seasoned flour**. Fry lightly and place on top of potatoes. Cover and bake 2 hours at 325 degrees.

Ruth O'Bannion
Jasper County

CRABMEAT AU GRATIN

1 stalk celery, chopped fine	1 tsp. salt
1 c. onion, chopped fine	1 tsp. red pepper
1 stick margarine	1/4 tsp. black pepper
1/2 c. flour	1 lb. crabmeat (can use canned
1 13-oz. can evaporated milk	if fresh is not available)
2 eggs	1/2 lb. Cheddar cheese, grated

Melt margarine in pan and saute onions and celery until onions are limp. Add flour and mix well. Add milk to mixture gradually and stir constantly. Add eggs, salt and peppers. Cook about 5 minutes. Add crabmeat and mix well. Put into a buttered casserole dish and sprinkle with grated cheese. Bake at 350 degrees for 20 minutes. Serves 6.

Virginia Burks
Galveston County

HERB & GARLIC FISH

1/2 c. Miracle Whip, Light or non-fat dressing
1/2 tsp. dried marjoram leaves
1/2 tsp. dried thyme leaves
1/2 tsp. garlic powder
1/4 tsp. ground celery seed
1 lb. fish fillets

Mix dressing and seasonings. Place fish on greased grill or rack of broiler pan 2 to 4-inches from heat. Brush with 1/2 of the dressing mixture. Grill or broil 5-8 minutes. Turn, brush with remaining dressing mixture. Continue grilling or broiling 5-8 minutes or until fish flakes easily with fork. Makes 4 servings.

Sandra Beasely
Martin County

FAVORITE BROILED FISH

2 lbs. skinned fish fillets
2 T. lemon juice
1/2 c. Parmesan cheese, grated
1/4 c. butter, softened
3 T. mayonnaise
3 T. green onions, chopped
1/4 tsp. salt
Dash of Tabasco sauce

Place fillets in a single layer on a well greased broiler pan. Brush with lemon juice. Combine Parmesan cheese, butter, mayonnaise, green onions, salt and Tabasco sauce. Set aside. Broil fish 4-6 minutes or until it flakes easily with fork. Remove fish from heat. Spread with cheese mixture. Broil 2-3 minutes to until lightly brown. Serves 6.

Rosa Eggemeyer
Concho County

BAKED ALASKAN ORANGE ROUGHY (FISH)

12-oz. orange roughy
1 T. butter
2 T. lemon juice
1 tsp. onion salt
1/4 tsp. lemon pepper
1/4-1/2 tsp. thyme
Paprika

Melt butter in baking pan and add lemon juice. Rinse fish and drain on paper towel. Coat fish on both sides in butter and lemon juice mixture. Mix rest of ingredients, except paprika and sprinkle over fish. Bake uncovered for about 20 minutes in 400 degree oven or until done. Sprinkle with paprika before serving.

Sue Flynt
Gillespie County

The real problem of your leisure
is how to keep other people from using it.

JAMBALYA (Mild)

1 1/2 lbs. chicken breasts,
  cut into strips
Creole Seasoning
1 lb. 90% fat free smoked
  turkey sausage, cut into
  1/4-inch slices
1 med. onion, chopped
1 c. celery, chopped
1 clove garlic, minced
5 c. chicken broth (fat free)
1 c. green onions, sliced (opt.)
2 cans stewed tomatoes
1 T. vegetable oil
1 lg. green pepper, chopped
1 c. carrots, sliced
2 c. rice, uncooked

Season chicken with Creole Seasoning like salting; brown in hot oil in large saucepan or Dutch oven over high heat. Add sausage; cook 2-3 minutes. Remove chicken and sausage from saucepan; set aside. Cook onions, green pepper, celery, carrots and garlic in same saucepan over medium-high heat until tender crisp; stir in rice, broth, stewed tomatoes and reserved chicken and sausage; bring to a boil. Simmer, covered, for 30 minutes. Stir in green onions if used. Makes 12 hearty servings.

Timmie Ciriack
Parker County

SHRIMP ROLLS (Bea Lejsal)

2 8-oz. pkgs. cream cheese,
  softened
1 clove garlic, minced
1/2 c. milk
4 T. mayonnaise
Dash of M.S.G. (opt.)
3-4 fresh green onions,
  chopped
1 T. lemon juice
1-1 1/2 lbs. boiled shrimp,
  chopped
Salt and pepper to taste
2 lg. loaves of Roman Meal
  or wheat bread (can be made
  with white bread)

Combine all ingredients, except bread, adding more milk if needed to make spreadable. Trim crusts from loaves of bread. Arrange each loaf of 20 slices (5 x 4 slices) onto a sheet of heavy foil paper. Dampen edges of bread, overlap slices and press together to form a sheet. Spread one-half of mixture on each sheet of bread, then roll carefully (like jelly roll) and wrap securely with foil paper. Chill well for at least 24 hours before slicing to serve. (Can be made ahead and frozen. Thaw in refrigerator several hours before slicing.)

Brazoria County

Two things are bad for your heart,
running up stairs and running down people.

SHRIMP CASSEROLE

1 1/2- 2 lbs. raw shrimp	1 can Rotel tomatoes
1/2 c. raw rice	1 lg. onion, diced
1 stick butter or margarine	1 bell pepper, diced
1 can French onion soup	2 tsp. black pepper
1 can cream of chicken soup	Dash of red pepper
1 tsp. salt	Dash of dried parsley

Preheat oven to 350 degrees. Melt butter or margarine in casserole dish. In another big bowl, mix well remainder ingredients. Do not cook rice, mix raw; chop tomatoes and add with juice. Cover and cook for 30 minutes. Smells wonderful while cooking. You won't be able to stay out of the kitchen.

Margaret Dwin
Jefferson County

BLEND OF THE BAYOU SEAFOOD CASSEROLE

1 8-oz. pkg. cream cheese	1 can mushrooms, drained
1 stick margarine	1 T. garlic salt
1 lb. shrimp, peeled	1/2 tsp. Tabasco
1 lg. onion, chopped	1/2 tsp. red pepper
1 bell pepper, chopped	1 pt. crabmeat (white)
2 ribs of celery, chopped	1 c. cooked rice
2 T. margarine	Sharp cheese, grated
1 can cream of mushroom soup	Cracker crumbs

Melt cream cheese and margarine. Saute shrimp, onion, pepper and celery in margarine. Add to first mixture. Add soup, mushrooms, seasonings, crabmeat and rice. Mix well. Place in 2-quart casserole. Top with cheese and cracker crumbs. Bake at 350 degrees for about 20-30 minutes or until bubbly. Freezes very well. Serves 8.

Missy Merritt
Lamar County

QUICK JAMBALAYA

1 c. onion, chopped	1 14 1/2-oz. can tomatoes
1 c. green bell peppers	1 lb. ground beef, browned
1 clove garlic, crushed	and drained
1 T. butter or margarine	Dash of red pepper
1 c. rice, uncooked	1 tsp. poultry seasoning
1 1/2 cans chicken broth	

Saute onions, green peppers and garlic in butter until tender. Brown beef, add to sauteed onion and peppers. Stir in rice, broth, tomatoes and seasoning. Bring to a boil, reduce heat, cover and simmer 20 minutes until rice is tender and liquid is absorbed. Fluff lightly with fork and serve.

Johnnie Grayer
Fort Bend County

TUNA PATE

1 8-oz. pkg. cream cheese, softened
2 T. chili sauce
2 T. snipped parsley (opt.)
1/2 tsp. bottled hot pepper sauce
1 tsp. instant minced onion
2 6 1/2-7-oz. cans tuna, drained

Blend all ingredients, except tuna. Gradually stir in tuna, beat until blended. Pack in 4 cup mold or bowl. Chill at least 5 hours. Serve with crackers. Yield: 3 cups.

Suzanne Gaines
Comanche County

TUNA MOUSSE

1 1/2 env. Knox gelatin
1/2 c. cold water
1 can cream of mushroom soup
1 8-oz. pkg. cream cheese
1/2 c. mayonnaise
1/2 tsp. salt
2 tsp. lemon juice
1/4 tsp. prepared mustard
1 c. celery, finely chopped
2 or 3 green onions, minced
(can use 2 T. regular onion)
1 can solid pack white tuna
(do not substitute)

Stir gelatin into cold water. Dissolve over hot water in double boiler. Heat mushroom soup and cream cheese. Remove from heat and add gelatin mixture, mayonnaise, salt, lemon juice, prepared mustard, celery, onions and tuna. Pour into lightly olive oil coated mold or muffin tins that have been lined with foil liners. Refrigerate for at least 2 hours, then unmold on **lettuce leaf**. Note: Ripe black olives may be sliced into bottom of mold before adding mousse mixture.

Lonnie Moore
Washington County

SALMON PATTIES

1 can (tall can) salmon, drained
2 eggs
1 c. rice, cooked
6 soda crackers, crushed
1 T. lemon juice

Combine all ingredients. Chill well. Shape into patties. Roll in flour. Fry in hot oil. Makes a lot! Good hot or cold. (May be baked on "Pam" sprayed baking sheet - but do not flour them.)

Sara Esralian
Collin County

You can't keep trouble from coming,
but you needn't give it a chair to sit on.

SALMON PATTIES

1 tall can salmon	1/2 c. onion, diced
2 eggs or egg substitute	1/4 c. flour
2 T. milk	Cooking oil as needed
1/2 c. bell pepper, diced	Salt and pepper to taste

Remove bones and dark skin. Flake salmon. Whip eggs in bowl, add milk, salmon and all other ingredients. Add more flour if needed, a little at a time if salmon is watery. Heat 2 tablespoonfuls cooking oil. Make patties with serving spoon; fry patties until brown on one side. Turn and brown other side. Drain on paper towel in platter. Makes 10-12 patties.

Jovita Saenz
Brooks County

SALMON ROLL

1/4 c. onion, chopped	2 c. biscuit mix
1/4 c. celery, chopped	1/2 c. yellow cornmeal
1 can salmon, cleaned and boned	2 T. parsley, chopped
1 can cream of celery soup	1/4 c. milk
1 T. butter	2 T. dill pickle, chopped

Cook onion and celery in butter until tender. Add dash of pepper. Stir in salmon. Set aside. Blend biscuit mix, cornmeal and parsley with 3/4 cup water. Knead dough 10-12 times. Roll into a rectangle 12 x 8-inches. Mix half of the soup into the salmon mixture. Spread salmon mixture over dough. Roll as for jelly roll, starting at long end. Pinch ends to seal. Bake at 400 degrees for 20-25 minutes. Combine the rest of the soup, milk and pickle. Heat through and pour over cut slices of roll. Serves 6-8.

Mildred Snow
Cherokee County

COURT BOUILLON

6-8 lbs. fish, cut up	1 c. margarine
1 c. flour	1/2 c. onion tops and parsley
3 c. veg. (garlic, onion, celery,	2 sm. cans tomato sauce
green pepper)	2 qts. water
1 T. Worcestershire sauce	1/2 lemon, sliced

Melt margarine in an iron dutch oven and add flour, stirring until Roux is dark brown. Cut off fire, add vegetables and stir until they stop sizzling. Add tomato sauce and heat. Add water and cook 2 hours. Season with **Tony Chacheres seasoning**. Add fish and simmer 45 minutes. Add onion tops, parsley and lemon. Serve over rice.

Georgia Thomas
Sabine County

SMOKED SAUSAGE HARVEST CASSEROLE

2 T. margarine or butter
5 c. green cabbage, chopped
1 med. onion, cut into halves
   and sliced
1 c. carrots, sliced
1 15.5-oz. drained red beans

1 lb. smoked sausage
1 8-oz. can stewed tomatoes
1 T. vinegar
1/3 c. Parmesan cheese, grated
2 T. flour
Dash of ground black pepper

Heat oven to 350 degrees. Melt margarine in dutch oven over medium-high heat. Add cabbage, onion and carrots; saute 5 minutes. Stir in beans, tomatoes and vinegar. Sprinkle cheese, flour and pepper over cabbage mixture; stir in. Spoon into greased 2-quart casserole. Cut sausage into serving size pieces (or bite size). Arrange on top of cabbage mixture and push down partially. Cover and bake 40 minutes or until hot. Makes 6 servings.

Susie McKamie
Coryell County

COWBOY PEAS

3 c. black-eyed peas, cooked
3 c. cooked sausage (cut into
   bite size pieces)

1 1/2 tsp. chili powder
1 T. flour
1/2 c. water

Cook the above ingredients for about 30 minutes. Mix flour into water. Mix into peas to thicken. Serves 8.

Cookie Murphy
Pecos County

EGG-SAUSAGE CASSEROLE

1 lb. ground sausage
2 1/4 c. milk
8-10 eggs
1 1/2 tsp. dry mustard

1/2 tsp. salt
1 1/2 c. Cheddar cheese,
   shredded
3 slices white bread, crumbled

In large skillet, brown sausage; drain well and set aside. In large bowl, put in milk, eggs, dry mustard and salt. Beat 1 minute on medium speed; stir in cheese, bread and sausage. Pour into greased 13 x 9-inch pan. Bake at 350 degrees for 30-40 minutes until knife inserted into center comes out clean. Can be made with egg substitute, skim milk, and low-fat cheese. Serves 12.

Lee Caruthers
Blanco County

Be patient with the faults of others;
they have to be patient with yours.

BREAKFAST PIZZA

1 lb. bulk pork sausage	5 eggs
1 pkg. (8) refrigerated crescent	1/4 c. milk
rolls	1/2 tsp. salt
1 c. frozen loose pack hash	1/8 tsp. pepper
brown potatoes, thawed	2 T. Parmesan cheese, grated
1 c. sharp Cheddar cheese, shredded	

In large skillet, cook sausage until brown; drain excess fat. Separate crescent rolls into 8 triangles. Place in a greased 12-inch pizza pan with points toward center. Press bottom and sides to form a crust; seal perforations. Spoon sausage over crust. Sprinkle with potatoes. Top with Cheddar cheese. In separate bowl, beat together eggs, milk, salt and pepper. Pour onto crust. Sprinkle with Parmesan cheese. Bake at 375 degrees for 25-30 minutes. Yield: 6-8 servings.

Martha Ables & Brenda Haedge
Erath County

SAUSAGE-EGG CASSEROLE

	To serve approx. 50:
6 eggs	4 doz. eggs
2 c. milk	1 gallon milk
3 slices bread (regular THICK	8 lbs. sausage
slices)	24 slices bread
1 tsp. salt (opt.)	8 c. cheese
1 tsp. dry mustard	8 tsp. dry mustard
1 lb. sausage	Salt (opt.)
1 c. cheese, grated	

Fry sausage (crumbled); drain off grease. Break up bread, pour 1 cup of milk over bread. Beat eggs. Add the other cup of milk, salt, mustard, cheese; mix well. Add bread and sausage. Pour into large baking dish. Refrigerate overnight. Bake 45 minutes at 300 degrees. Yield: approximately 6 servings.

Ina Keeton
Vanzandt County

Begin each day as if it is
the beginning of your life,
for truly it is the beginnng
of whatever is left of your life.

DO AHEAD SAUSAGE SOUFFLE

8 slices bread, cubed
2 c. sharp Cheddar cheese, grated
1 1/2 lbs. sausage, cooked, drained, and in med. sized pieces

4 eggs
2 1/4 c. milk
3/4 tsp. dry mustard
1 can cream of mushroom soup
1/2 c. milk

Place cubed bread in bottom of greased 8 x 12-inch or 9 x 13-inch baking dish. Top with grated cheese. Brown meat; drain well and spread over cheese. Beat eggs with 2 1/4 cups milk and dry mustard. Pour over sausage. Dilute mushroom soup with 1/2 cup milk and pour over mixture. Cover and refrigerate overnight. Next day, place in cold oven and bake at 350 degrees for 1 1/2 hours or until set. (Freezes well and recipe may be doubled.)

Fern Maxwell
Wichita County

RICE CRUNCH

1 lb. Owens sausage (hot if desired)
2 c. celery, chopped
1 c. onion, chopped
1 can water chestnuts, chopped coarsely

1 can mushrooms stems and pieces, undrained
1 tsp. salt
1/4 tsp. pepper
1 can chicken noodle soup
1 c. water
1 c. long grain raw rice

Cook sausage in iron skillet until pink is all gone. Remove sausage with slotted spoon. Saute onion and celery in pan drippings, then add sausage, water chestnuts, mushrooms, salt, pepper, chicken noodle soup and water. Add rice and an additional cup of boiling water. Grease a deep casserole dish and add mixture. Cook at 350 degrees for 1 hour or until rice fluffs up. Stir once during cooking time. Freezes well.

Lucile Snider
Refugio County

HARVEST RICE STUFFING

1 pumpkin
1 lb. sausage
1/2 c. onion, chopped
3 c. rice, cooked
1/2 c. celery, chopped
1 red apple, chopped

1/2 c. raisins
1 T. brown sugar
1/2 tsp. salt
1/4 tsp. allspice
1/4 tsp. cinnamon
1/8 tsp. pepper

To prepare pumpkin, cut top out. Remove seeds and membranes. Saute sausage and onion; drain fat. Add remaining ingredients. Mix and place inside pumpkin. Bake at 325 degrees for 45 minutes or until pumpkin is a delicious harvest gold. Serve stuffing from pumpkin, then serve pumpkin meat.

Shirley Smith, Little Elm
Denton County

AMAZING QUICHE

1 lb. sausage	1 c. Bisquick
1 c. Cheddar cheese	4 eggs
1/3 c. onion	1/4 tsp. salt
2 c. milk	1/8 tsp. pepper

Fry sausage; drain and cool. When cool, crumble into bottom of 10-inch round pie pan with 1 1/2-inch side. Sprinkle grated cheese over sausage, then sprinkle with grated onions. Combine remaining ingredients in blender and process for 2 minutes. Pour over other ingredients in pie plate. Bake in 400 degree oven for 20-30 minutes or until brown on top.

Dorothy Daniel
Tarrant County

UPSIDE DOWN POLENTA CASSEROLE

1 lb. bulk pork sausage	3/4 c. flour
1 c. onion, chopped	3/4 c. cornmeal
1 8-oz. can tomato sauce	3/4 c. Parmesan cheese, grated
1 16-oz. can tomatoes, cut up	1 T. baking powder
1 4-oz. can sliced mushrooms,	1 T. sugar (or 1 1/2 T.)
drained	3/4 tsp. salt
1 tsp. salt	3/4 c. milk
1/4 tsp. dried oregano,	1 egg, well beaten
crushed	1 c. Cheddar cheese, shredded
1/8 tsp. garlic powder	2 T. snipped parsley

In a saucepan, cook sausage and onion until meat is brown and onion is tender; drain off fat. Stir in undrained tomatoes, tomato sauce, mushrooms, 1 teaspoonful salt, oregano, garlic powder, and a dash of pepper. Bring to boil; simmer covered for 5 minutes. In a bowl, mix flour, cornmeal, Parmesan cheese, sugar, baking powder and 3/4 teaspoonful salt; make a well in the center of dry ingredients. Add milk, egg and oil, stirring until combined. Spread in an ungreased 13 x 9 x 2-inch baking pan. Spoon tomato mixture on top. Bake in a 400 degree oven for 20 minutes. Sprinkle with cheese and parsley. Bake about 5 minutes. Serves 8.

Opal Humphrey
Upshur County

I am grateful for my friends.
I take this time now to be aware
of and to give thanks for the
blessings of friendship.

SOUTHWEST STEW

2 lbs. ground beef
1 28-oz. can tomatoes
1 17-oz. can whole kernel corn
  or frozen corn
1 c. picante sauce
1 tsp. garlic powder

Salt to taste
1 1/2 c. onion, diced
1 15-oz. can pinto beans
3/4 c. water
1/2 tsp. ground cumin
1/2 tsp. black pepper

Brown ground beef and onions; drain fat. Add other ingredients. Bring to boil and simmer covered for 15-20 minutes. Garnish with shredded Cheddar cheese, if desired.

June Rea
Oldham County

COWBOY STEW

1 lb. ground beef or chuck
1 T. margarine
1 med. onion, chopped
1/4 c. celery, chopped
1/4 c. bell pepper, chopped
1/2 clove garlic
1 T. chili powder
Salt

Pepper
1/4 tsp. sugar
1 can tomatoes
1 can corn
1 can ranch style beans
  with jalapeno peppers
6 med. potatoes, cubed
2-3 c. water

Brown meat in margarine. Add other ingredients, cover and simmer until potatoes are tender.

Alvena Wenzel
Waller County

SPICY STEW

2 lbs. round steak, cubed
2 14-oz. cans tomatoes, cubed
1 sm. clove garlic or 1/2 tsp.
  garlic, diced
1/4 tsp. black pepper

4 14-oz. cans beef broth
1 lg. onion, chopped
1/2 tsp. cumin
1 7-oz. can chopped green
  chilies

Brown meat in 3 teaspoonfuls olive oil with garlic. Add all other ingredients and simmer 3-4 hours. Best made the day before. Serve with cold avocado, chopped and a dollop of sour cream.

Mary Wayne Spurlock
Sherman County

It is nice to be important,
but it is more important to be nice.

OLE' STEW

2 lbs. boneless beef stew meat,
  cut into 1-inch pieces
2 T. vegetable oil
1 c. hot water
1 med. onion, chopped
1 tsp. salt
2 cloves garlic, minced
3 carrots, cut into 1-inch pieces
4 potatoes
2 T. flour
1 10 1/2-oz. can condensed
  beef broth
1 8-oz. Pace picante sauce
1/4 c. parsley, chopped
1 tsp. comino
1 16-oz. can tomatoes, chopped
2 ears corn or 1 can corn
1/2 c. cold water

Brown meat in hot oil. Add broth, hot water, Picante sauce, onion, parsley, salt, comino and garlic. Bring to boil. Reduce heat and simmer 1 hour. Add tomatoes, carrots, potatoes and corn. Cover and cook until vegetables are tender. Add cold water to flour and stir until smooth. Add to stew and boil 1 minute.

Glenvoir E. H. Club
Caldwell County

BOUMIANE PROVENCALE (FRENCH STEW)

1 lg. onion
9 garlic cloves
2 lg. eggplant
3 zucchini
2 red bell peppers, cubed
4 T. olive oil
2 bay leaves
2 tsp. basil
1 T. fresh parsley
2 lbs. tomatoes (fresh or
  canned)
1 tsp. sugar
Salt

Saute onion and garlic in olive oil. Add tomatoes, cook to reduce some of the liquid, add eggplant, zucchini, red peppers, bay leaves, basil, and parsley. Add sugar and salt. Cook for about 1-2 hours. Cook slowly and stir often. Yield: 8 servings.

Jeanette Alexander
Palo Pinto County

*Charm: the ability to make
someone else think that both
of you are pretty wonderful.*

HEALTHY JAMBALAYA

1 T. Canola oil
1 lb. chicken breast, boneless
and skinless
3 onions, chopped
1/2 c. celery, finely chopped
2 14-oz. cans stewed tomatoes
2 1/2 c. water or chicken broth
1/2 tsp. oregano
1/2 tsp. black pepper
1/2 tsp. cayenne pepper

1 lb. low-fat smoked sausage,
diced
1 1/2 c. long grain rice
3 bell peppers, chopped
2 cloves garlic, minced
2 8-oz. cans tomato sauce
2 tsp. Tony's Chacheres
Seasoning
1/2 tsp. thyme
1/4 tsp. Tabasco sauce
(according to taste, may
want more)

Add oil to a cast iron pot that is very hot (for lower fat, spray with a vegetable spray prior to heating skillet). Add sausage and chicken, stirring constantly for 10 minutes, until browned. Add rice, stirring constantly until rice has browned. Add onions, bell peppers, garlic and celery. Cook for 15 minutes, stirring often. Add stewed tomatoes, tomato sauce, liquids, and seasonings to pan. Lower heat, cover pan and simmer for 45 minutes, stirring often. May need to add more water as the rice absorbs the liquid. Remove from heat. Optional: After removing from heat, you can add 1/4 cup finely chopped green onions and 2 tablespoonfuls fresh parsley. Cover, let stand for 5 minutes before serving.

Covington E. H. Club
Hill County

Life is like an onion,
you peel off one layer at a time
and sometimes you weep.

A loud mouth is often nothing
more than an echo from an
empty head.

MICROWAVE

Microwave

FRESH BLUEBERRY TOPPING

1/2 c. sugar
2 T. cornstarch

1/2 c. orange juice
2 c. fresh blueberries

Combine sugar and cornstarch in a 4-cup glass measure. Blend in orange juice and stir in blueberries. Microwave on High 4-5 minutes or until thickened, stirring once. Cool before topping dessert. Yield: 1 3/4 cups.

Anna Belle Bratton
Hardin County

CHOCOLATE DESSERT SUPREME

<u>Chocolate Filling</u>:

2 c. sugar
3 heaping T. cocoa
2 T. flour or corn starch
2 c. milk

3 egg yolks, beaten
1 T. margarine or butter
2 tsp. vanilla

Mix sugar, cocoa and flour well in a 1-quart microwaveable bowl (I use the popular microwave container with pouring spout and measurements imprinted on the container as it's large enough to contain mixture without boiling over). Add milk and continue to mix well. Place in microwave on High for 5 minutes. Stir, and continue cooking until mixture begins to thicken. Remove from microwave and add a portion of hot mixture to beaten egg yolks. Mix well and add to remaining chocolate mixture. Stir and place in microwave, continue cooking (about 2 minutes on Medium High) or until desired thickness. Remove from microwave and add vanilla and margarine. Mix well. While mixture begins to cool somewhat, prepare crust.

<u>Crust</u>:

1 pkg. Pecan Sandies Cookies
   (use enough for 2 c. of crumbs)

1/4 c. margarine or butter,
   melted

Crumble cookies to a fine consistency, add margarine and mix well. Pat into a rectangular Pyrex baking dish. Microwave on High for 1 1/2-2 minutes. Remove from microwave, add chocolate custard mixture. Let cool and refrigerate. When cold, cover with **Cool Whip**. Place whole cookies around dish and garnish with chocolate curls. Cut into small squares, as it is very rich! Serves 10-12 people.

Georgia Rogers

Blowing out the other fellow's candle
will not make yours shine any brighter.

MICROWAVE CHOCOLATE MARSHMALLOW CAKE

1 c. margarine
1/2 c. cocoa
2 c. sugar
4 eggs
1 1/2 c. flour

1/4 tsp. salt
2 tsp. vanilla
1 1/2 c. nuts
1 c. miniature marshmallows

Microwave margarine and cocoa in a 2-quart casserole dish on High for 2 minutes. Stir in sugar, add eggs; beat well. Blend in salt, flour and vanilla. Pour batter into 2 greased and floured 8-inch round baking pans. Microwave on low for 7 minutes. Microwave on High for 2 or 3 minutes. Spread marshmallows over top of cake. Microwave on High 1 minute longer.

Ruth Redmon

CARAMEL POPCORN

3-4 pkgs. microwave popcorn
2 sticks butter
1/2 c. white Karo syrup

2 c. brown sugar
1 tsp. vanilla
1 tsp. soda

Pop microwave popcorn and set aside in a large bowl. Bring to boil butter, syrup and brown sugar; boil 5 minutes. Remove from heat and add vanilla and soda. Mix well and pour over popped corn. Mix well to coat and bake for 1 hour in a 200 degree oven. Stir every 15 minutes. Remove from oven and cool. Store in a tightly closed container. May add 1 cup toasted pecans and/or peanuts for variation.

Janice Cordray
Angelina County

MICROWAVE PEANUT BRITTLE

1 c. peanuts
1 c. sugar
1/8 tsp. salt
1/2 c. white corn syrup

1 tsp. butter or margarine
1 tsp. vanilla
1 tsp. baking soda

Stir together peanuts, sugar, syrup and salt in a 1 1/2-quart casserole or large measuring cup. Place in microwave and cook 3 minutes on High. Stir and cook 3-4 minutes longer. Add butter or margarine and vanilla and stir well. Return to oven and cook on High 1-2 minutes. Peanuts will be lightly browned and syrup will be very hot. Add baking soda and gently stir until light and foamy. Pour mixture onto lightly greased baking sheet. Allow to cool. Note: If roasted salted peanuts are used, omit salt and add peanuts after first 4 minutes of cooking.

Lyons E. H. Club, Burleson County
Wilma Payne, Titus County

Grace Franklin from Collin County uses unsalted peanuts and does not add salt.

MICRO PEANUT PATTIES

2 c. sugar	1 1/2 c. peanuts
1/2 c. water	2 T. butter
1/2 c. white syrup	1 tsp. vanilla
Dash of salt	Few drops red food coloring

Boil sugar, water, syrup and salt on High for 3 minutes and add peanuts. Cook on High for 9 minutes (soft boil). Add butter, vanilla and red food coloring. Stir until cool and thick. Drop on waxed paper.

Velma Tate
Tarrant County

MICROWAVE PRALINES (Easy)

1 lb. box of light brown sugar	Dash of salt
1/2 pt. whipping cream	Pecans, chopped
2 T. butter or margarine	1 tsp. vanilla (opt.)

Mix brown sugar and whipping cream. Cook on High until rolling boil. Boil 12-15 minutes (varies by microwave output). Add butter and salt. Beat by hand for 1 1/2-2 minutes. Stir in pecans and vanilla if desired. Drop by tablespoonfuls onto foil to cool.

Fern Maxwell
Wichita County

HOT CHICKEN SALAD

3 c. chicken, diced	1/2 c. almonds, diced (or
1 1/2 c. celery, diced	other nuts
1 T. onion, minced	1/2 c. mayonnaise
1/8 tsp. pepper	1 1/2 c. cheddar cheese, grated
	1 1/2 c. potato chips, crushed

Mix all ingredients except chips. Place in greased casserole dish. Put chips on top. Bake until bubbly in microwave or in oven at 350 degrees for 25 minutes.

Mary Smith
Reeves County

When you are angry,
pretend you are a bird,
Sing just a little,
but don't say a word.

POTATO CASSEROLE

2 lbs. frozen hash browns,
  thawed
1/2 c. margarine, melted
1 can cream of chicken soup
1 soup can of milk
1/2 tsp. pepper

1 tsp. salt
1 pt. sour cream
2 c. cheese, grated
2 T. instant onion
2 c. crushed Corn Flakes

Mix together all ingredients, except Corn Flakes and margarine. Place in 9 x 13-inch pan, cover with Corn Flakes mixed with margarine. Bake in microwave until bubbly or in oven at 350 degrees for 45 minutes. This freezes well, but add crumb topping just before heating.

Myrl Soles
Howard County

"KOCH" CHEESE

2 pkg. Swiss cheese
1 stick margarine
1 T. flour

1 lg. can Pet Milk
Dill or caraway seed to taste

Melt margarine in microwave. Add flour and milk to melted oleo. Microwave 3 minutes. Stir and cut up cheese. Microwave 3-5 minutes until cheese is melted. Pour into bowl and add caraway or dill seed according to your taste.

Leanne Fritsch
Fayette County

SOUTHWESTERN CAVIAR

1 15-oz. can black-eyed peas
1 clove garlic, minced
2 green onions with tops,
  chopped

1/8 c. margarine
1 4 oz. can green chilies,
  chopped
1 3-oz. jar Old English Cheese
  Spread

Drain liquid from peas and mash in food processor or blender. Saute garlic and onion in margarine. Add peas and remaining ingredients; cook on low until heated. Serve warm. This recipe doubles or triples easily.
Microwave: Cook onions and garlic in margarine for 2 minutes on High power. Add all other ingredients and microwave on High power for 3 minutes or until heated.

Annetta McIver
Hansford County

Variety is the very spice of life
that gives it all its flavor.

FOOL PROOF PEANUT BRITTLE

1 c. sugar	1 tsp. margarine
1/2 c. Karo syrup	1 tsp. vanilla
1 1/2 c. salted peanuts	1 tsp. soda

Combine sugar and syrup; microwave on High for 4 minutes. Stir in peanuts and microwave for 4 more minutes. Add margarine, vanilla and soda. Stir until foamy and microwave another 2 minutes. Pour into buttered cookie sheet and spread very thin. Cool. Break into pieces.

Ruth Polston
Childress County

CLEAN HANDS

*Once, in my childhood days
gone and dead,
I watched a supper table
being spread.
By busy hands: and eagerly
I said --
Wishing to help, "Please may
I bring the bread?"
Gently, reprovingly, a kind
voice said,
"Are your hands clean?"
Oft, when I see the multitude, unfed,
And waiting hungry for the
living bread
My heart and hands are eager
to be sped
To bring the manna that they
may be fed.
But one voice says, e'en as a
voice once said,
"Are your hands clean?" --
I only bow my head.*

226

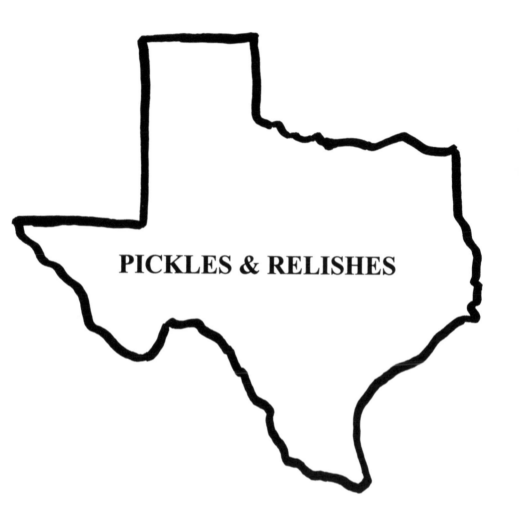

PICKLES & RELISHES

Pickles, Relishes and Appetizers

Pickles

CINNAMON PICKLES

12-16 lbs. lg. cucumbers	1 c. red hot candies
2 c. lime	1 T. pickling salt
2 gal. water	2 1/2 c. red wine vinegar
1 sm. bottle red food coloring	2 1/2 c. water
1 c. white vinegar	8 c. sugar
1 T. powdered alum	3 cinnamon sticks

Peel, core and slice cukes 1/2-inch thick. Soak in lime/water mixture for 12 hours. Wash three times, put in ice water and soak 3 hours, drain. Mix red food coloring with 1 cup white vinegar and 1 tablespoonful alum. Pour over cukes, cover and let set 3 hours; drain. Mix, boil and pour over cukes the red hot candies, pickling salt, red wine vinegar, 2 1/2 cups water, sugar and cinnamon sticks. Let stand 24 hours. Drain off liquid, bring to boil and pour over cukes again. Let stand 24 hours. Bring to boil, pack in hot jars and process 10 minutes in water bath.

Jo Newman
San Patricio/Aransas County

DILLED OKRA

1 qt. vinegar	Dill seed (or fresh dill)
6 c. water	Garlic cloves
1/3 c. salt	Small green chilies

Use sterilized jars. Pack raw okra (3-inches long) into jars. To each quart jar, add 2 tablespoonfuls of dill seed, 1 clove garlic and 1 green chili (garlic and chili optional). Heat the vinegar, water and salt solution to boiling. Pour boiling solution over okra in jars. Seal. Better if kept refrigerated until used.

Billie H. McCraw
Citizenship/Legislative Chairman

DILL PICKLES

1/4 c. salt	Dill heads
1 c. vinegar	Garlic cloves
2 c. water	Cucumbers

Bring salt, vinegar and water to a boil. Put 2 heads of dill and 3-4 cloves of garlic in the bottom of quart jars. Pack cucumbers in jars and pour the boiling solution over the cucumbers and seal.

Mrs. Viola Caffey
Milam County

DILL PICKLES

8 1/2 c. water	Sprigs of fresh dill
2 1/2 c. vinegar (white, 90 grain-barrel vinegar)	Garlic cloves
	Fresh hot peppers (opt.)
1/2 c. pickling salt	Cucumbers

To make brine, combine water, vinegar and salt in a pan and bring to a boil. Yields: 7 quarts brine. Pack washed cucumbers in clean jars placing dill sprigs at top and bottom of jar. Put 4 garlic cloves and 1 small hot pepper (optional) in bottom of each quart jar. Cover with hot brine, adjust lids and process in hot-water-bath for 10 minutes. Let set 4 weeks before eating. Use just-picked pickling variety of cucumbers. Wash cucumbers well especially around stem-end. Sterilize jars in boiling water for 15 minutes. To water-bath pickles, put the hot, packed jars on a rack in the canner filled with simmering water. The water should cover the jar tops by 1 or 2-inches. Start to count processing time when water reaches a boil. Process 10 minutes, gentle boil.

Jane Gault
Bastrop County

SWEET & SOUR DILL PICKLES

1 c. sugar	1 T. salt
3 c. water (enough for 2 qts.)	1 clove garlic
1 c. vinegar	Dill
1/8 tsp. alum	Cucumbers

Bring sugar, water and vinegar to boil. In bottom of quart jar put alum, garlic, salt and dill. Slice cucumbers lengthwise and fill jars. Pour hot juice over and seal. Put in hot water bath for 5 minutes.

Debbie Ferguson
Sherman County

CRANBERRY CHUTNEY

3 c. cranberries	1/4 tsp. ground allspice
1 c. brown sugar	1/2 c. water
1/2 c. cider vinegar	1/2 c. dry sherry
1/2 c. golden raisins	1 c. apple, peeled and chopped
1 tsp. ground cinnamon	1/2 c. celery, chopped
1 tsp. ground ginger	1/2 c. onion, chopped (opt.)
1/4 tsp. ground cloves	1/3 c. walnuts, chopped (opt.)

Combine first 10 ingredients in a Dutch oven or heavy pan. Cook over medium heat approximately 15 minutes, stirring frequently. Add the remaining ingredients, reduce heat and simmer another 15 minutes or until thickened. After cooking, put into clean glass jars and chill. Makes 1 quart and will keep refrigerated up to 2 weeks. Freezes well. Delicious served with turkey, ham, pork and venison. Makes a lovely gift for the holidays.

Florence McDaniel
Gillespie County

PICKLED SHRIMP

1 1/4 c. salad oil	1 button garlic (put through
3/4 c. white vinegar	press)
1 1/2 tsp. salt or more	2 lb. shrimp, boiled
2 1/2 tsp. celery seed	3 med. white onions
2 1/2 T. capers and juice	10 bay leaves
	1 T. whole cloves

Boil and clean shrimp. In a baking dish which has a lid (or use foil), arrange shrimp and thinly-sliced onions in alternate layers. Sprinkle with whole cloves and tuck in a bay leaf now and then. Cover with marinade (first 6 ingredients combined) and allow to stand in refrigerator for several hours. Occasionally drain off sauce and pour back over, as oil rises to top and other seasonings settle.

Margaret Beerwinkle
Hale County

CRISP SWEET PICKLES

1 gal. cucumbers, sliced	8 c. sugar
2 gal. water	5 c. vinegar
2 c. lime	1 sm. box pickling spices

Soak cucumbers, water and lime for 24 hours. Rinse and soak in 2 gallons water for 3 hours. Soak 24 hours in sugar, vinegar and pickling spices. Cook over medium heat for 2 1/2-3 hours. Place in sterilized jars and seal.

Mary Casey
Van Zandt County

Relishes

CRANBERRY RELISH

1 pkg. cranberries, ground	1-2 c. sugar
4 apples, unpeeled, cored, and	1/2 c. walnuts or pecans
chopped	1 c. celery, diced
1 orange, ground (med. size -	
use 1/2 rind)	

Mix cranberries, apples and orange. Add sugar, walnuts or pecans and celery. Makes about 2-quarts. Refrigerate, keeps several weeks.

Margaret Lively
Llano County

When embracing opportunity,
give it a big hug.

GREEN TOMATO RELISH

1 gal. green tomatoes, chopped	1/2 c. salt
1/2 gal. onion, chopped	1/2 tsp. turmeric
1 qt. bell peppers, diced	3 1/2 c. sugar
1 pt. hot peppers, diced	Black and red pepper to taste
1 qt. vinegar	1/2 tsp. cloves
1/2 T. mustard seed	

Cut tomatoes into desired sizes (bite size, quarter, etc.). Sprinkle with salt and let stand while preparing other vegetables. Drain liquid from tomatoes. Put all ingredients together in a large container and let come to a rolling boil. Remove from heat; put in sterilized jars and seal while hot. Makes about 9 pints.

Betty Tidwell
Rains County

TEXAS CAVIAR

2 14-oz. cans black-eyed peas, drained	1 med. sized green pepper, chopped
1 15 1/2-oz. can white hominy, drained	1 jalapeno pepper, chopped (opt.)
2 med. tomatoes, chopped	1/2 c. onion, chopped
4 green onions, chopped	1/2 c. fresh parsley, chopped
2 cloves garlic, minced	1 8-oz. bottle commercial Italian salad dressing

Combine all ingredients, except salad dressing; mix well. Pour salad dressing over black-eyed pea mixture; cover and marinate at least 2 hours in refrigerator; drain. Serve with tortilla chips. Makes 7 cups. *Best of Section - Colorado County Fair

Barbara Prause
Colorado County

*Give no more to every guest,
than he is able to digest.
Give him always of the prime,
and but little at a time.*

ZUCCHINI RELISH

5 lbs. zucchini
6 lg. onions
1/2 c. salt
Cold water
2 4-oz. jars pimentos, chopped
2 c. white vinegar
1 c. sugar
1 tsp. dry mustard
2 tsp. celery seed
1/2 tsp. ground cinnamon
1/2 tsp. nutmeg
1/2 tsp. pepper

Put squash and onions through food chopper, using a medium blade or chop. Mix with salt in bowl and cover with water. Refrigerate for 4 hours or overnight. Drain vegetables, rinse, then drain again. In a 5 to 6-quart pan, combine vegetables, vinegar, sugar, dry mustard, celery seed, cinnamon, nutmeg, pepper and pimentos. Bring quickly to boiling, stirring constantly. Reduce heat and simmer, uncovered, for about 20 minutes or until reduced to about 3-quarts (or 6-pints). Prepare 6 pint size canning jars, process 15 minutes in boiling water bath. Yield: 6-pints.

Myrtle Smith
Gray County

Appetizers

ARMADILLO EGGS

15-17 med. to sm. jalapenos
1 lb. Owen or Jimmy Dean -
    hot or regular pan sausage
1/2 lb. Monterey Jack cheese,
    grated
1 1/2 c. buttermilk Bisquick
    mix
1 box Shake 'N Bake for
    pork (2 packs)
2 eggs, beaten

Wash peppers, then split them and remove seeds. Stuff peppers with part of the grated cheese and place the two halves back together. Add remainder of cheese to the sausage. Knead this mixture; gradually add the Bisquick and mix until well blended. Pat balls of the dough into shape of small pancakes and shape dough around each jalapeno to form egg shape. Roll each "egg" in Shake 'N Bake, then in beaten egg, then in Shake 'N Bake again. Bake on cookie sheet at 300-325 degrees or 20-25 minutes. Serve hot or cold. Good appetizers.

Eloise Denbow
Matagorda County

No soil upon earth is dear to our eyes,
As the soil we first stirred in making mud pies!

ARMADILLO EGGS

1/2 lb. Monterey jack cheese
1/2 lb. cheddar cheese
1/2 lb. bulk hot sausage
1 1/2 c. Bisquick mix

15-20 med. to lg. canned
  jalapeno peppers
1 egg
1 pkg. Shake 'N Bake for Pork

Grate cheese (both kinds) and mix together, then divide in half. Mix together half of the grated cheese, the raw sausage and the Bisquick mix. Knead until stiff dough is formed. Set aside. Slit jalapeno peppers and remove seeds. Do not rinse. Stuff each pepper with remaining cheese. Pinch pepper together to seal. Now pinch off a bit of dough mixture and pat into a pancake approximately 1/4-inch thick. Place stuffed pepper in middle and roll in hand to form egg shape. Roll each ball in beaten egg and then in Shake 'N Bake mixture. Bake at 325 degrees for 20 minutes. These may be frozen and baked later.

Jennifer Starbuck
Austin County

BLUE CHEESE BALL

8 oz. cream cheese
1 oz. blue cheese
1 stick butter (no substitute)

Dash of garlic salt
1/3 c. ripe olives, chopped
1 c. nuts, chopped

Soften cheeses and butter. Cream together. Add garlic salt, mix again. Add olives. Mix and shape into ball. Roll in chopped nuts. Cover in plastic wrap and chill several hours. Serve with assorted crackers.

Charlene McClain
McLennan County

HAM/SPINACH/CHEESE ROLL UPS

1 8-oz. pkg. cream cheese
1/4 tsp. garlic powder
1 pkg. flour tortillas

1 pkg. Danish ham
4 lg. spinach leaves

Let cream cheese set to room temperature; add garlic powder and mix well. Spread heavy layer of cream cheese on tortilla. Add slice of ham and washed and dried spinach leaf. Roll tightly into rolls. Place in refrigerator. Let set overnight. Slice into 1-inch slices and serve.

David Butler
Martin County

A good meal soothes the soul
as it regenerates the body.

CHEESE STICKS

1/2 c. butter or margarine (1 stick)   1/2 tsp. salt
1/2 lb. Old English Cheese   2 tsp. red pepper
2 1/2 c. flour   1 c. nuts, chopped

Mix all ingredients and roll into straws or logs. Bake at 350 degrees for 6-7 minutes for straws and 12-15 minutes for logs. Slice logs and put pecans on top for wonderful appetizers.

Aubrey Sampson
Grayson County

JALAPENO CHEESE ROLL

1 lb. box Velveeta Cheese (at   1 c. pecans, chopped
  room temperature)   1 sm. jar pickled jalapenos
1 8-oz. pkg. cream cheese (at
  room temperature)

Roll out Velveeta cheese on freezer paper or wax paper. Spread cream cheese over evenly, then sprinkle on 3/4 cup of pecans and jalapenos . Roll up and sprinkle with remaining pecans and jalapenos. Slice and serve on crackers.

Carolyn Manville
Fort Bend County

PARTY CHEESE BALL

2 8-oz. pkgs. cream cheese   2 c. (8-oz.) sharp natural
1 T. pimentos, chopped   cheddar cheese, shredded
1 T. green pepper, chopped   1 T. onion, finely chopped
2 tsp. Worcestershire sauce   1 tsp. lemon juice
Dash of cayenne pepper   Dash of salt
Pecans, finely chopped

Combine softened cream cheese and cheddar cheese in bowl, mixing well until blended. Add remaining ingredients, except nuts; mix well. Chill. Shape into ball; roll in nuts. Serve with crackers.

Marian Quinn
Jefferson County

SPAM CHEESE LOG

8 oz. non-fat cream cheese   2 T. Worcestershire sauce
8 oz. light cream cheese   1 T. minced dry onion
8 oz. cheddar cheese, grated   Garlic powder to taste
3 slices of Spam, chopped   Seasoned salt
  (about)   Paprika

Mix all ingredients together. Sprinkle paprika on wax paper. Form log on wax paper. Sprinkle with chopped pecans and wrap in wax paper. Chill. Serve with any crackers.

Jeanine Brunson
Hale County

DRIED BEEF DIP

2 8-oz. pkgs. cream cheese
1 2 1/2-oz. jar dried beef,
  chopped

1 10-oz. can Rotel diced
  tomatoes with chilies
1 bunch green onions, chopped

Soften cream cheese. Mix cream cheese, dried beef and tomatoes with chilies well with a mixer. Stir in green onions. Let set refrigerated several hours to blend flavors. Serve with corn chips.

Joan Plumlee
Bell County

BEEFY DIP

2 8-oz. pkgs. Light, regular or
  "Free" cream cheese, softened
2 pkgs. thinly sliced beef
  luncheon meat, chopped

1 1/2 tsp. Accent or original
  Mrs. Dash
1 1/2 tsp. Worcestershire sauce

Mix all ingredients together. Best if made a day ahead. Serve with crackers or vegetables: celery sticks, carrot sticks, broccoli flowerets, cauliflower flowerets.

Hamby-Ruth Perkins
Taylor County

SPICY BEEF DIP

1 lb. ground beef
3/4 c onion, chopped
1/2 clove garlic
1/2 c. green peppers, chopped
1 tsp. salt
1 18-oz. can tomato sauce

1/4 c. catsup
1 tsp. sugar
3/4 tsp. oregano
1 tsp. pepper
1 8-oz. pkg. cream cheese
1/3 c. Parmesan cheese, grated

Brown beef, onion, garlic, peppers and salt in large skillet. Drain off excess fat. Stir in tomato sauce, catsup, sugar, oregano and pepper. Cover and simmer slowly for 10 minutes. Spoon off any excess fat. Add cream cheese and Parmesan cheese. Heat until cheese is melted and well combined. Serve warm with tortilla chips. Serve in crock pot to keep it hot. This also freezes well.

Nelma Ritchey, Chairman
Cultural Arts & International Understanding
Mitchell County

I am not afraid of tomorrow
For I have seen yesterday
And I love today.

SASSY DIP

1 lb. ground beef
1 lb. Velveeta cheese, cubed
1 lg. onion, chopped
1/2 c. green chilies, chopped
  (fresh or canned)

2 13-oz. cans cream of chicken
  soup
2 13-oz. cans cream of
  mushroom soup
Salt and pepper to taste

Brown ground beef and onion. Drain well. Add cubed Velveeta, soup and green chilies. Cook over low heat until cheese is melted. Use as a dip, pour over fritos, or spread on party rye and pop under broiler for a few minutes.

La Jauna Thames, Director
District 6

EASY SOUTHWEST DIP

1 pt. sour cream
1/2 c. mayonnaise
1 pkg. (4 serving) vegetable
  soup and recipe mix

1 c. chunky salsa
2 tsp. chili powder
1/4 c. cilantro, chopped

In medium bowl, stir sour cream, mayonnaise, soup mix, salsa, chili powder and cilantro until well mixed. Cover, chill 2 hours. Serve with cut-up vegetables or tortilla chips.

Mary Evelyn Steelman
Bovina Club

FRESH FRUIT DIP

1 8-oz. pkg. cream cheese
3/4 c. brown sugar, packed
1/4 c. granulated sugar

1 tsp. vanilla
Fresh fruit

Combine all ingredients in bowl and mix at high speed until smooth and creamy. Chill about 2 hours. Cut fresh fruit, such as bananas, strawberries, apples, grapes, kiwi, and place on a serving tray. Set dip in middle.

Cindy Guest
Oldham County

PEANUT BUTTER FRUIT DIP

1 8-oz. carton non-fat
  plain yogurt
1/2 c. creamy peanut butter
1/4 c. milk

2 T. honey
1 tsp. ground cinnamon
Assorted fresh fruit, cut up

Combine all ingredients, except fruit, in a small bowl, stirring well. Combine and chill thoroughly. Serve as a dip with an assortment of fresh fruit pieces. Yield: 1 2/3 cups dip.

Glenda King
Henderson County

HAMBURGER CHEESE DIP

1 can Rotel tomatoes	1 lb. hamburger meat
1 lb. Velveeta cheese	Salt and pepper to taste
1 roll garlic cheese	1 sm. onion
1 roll jalapeno cheese or	
bacon cheese	

Brown hamburger meat and onion. Melt cheeses with Rotel tomatoes and combine all ingredients. Best if served warm.

Syble Jones
Baylor County

ZIPPY MEXICAN 7 LAYER DIP

1 lg. can bean dip or refried	1/2 c. mayonnaise
beans	2 tsp. lemon or lime juice
1 pkg. taco seasoning mix	2 bunches green onions,
3 avocados, peeled and mashed	chopped (including tops)
8-oz. cheese, grated	3 ripe tomatoes, chopped
1 sm. can black olives, chopped	1 tsp. salt
8-oz. sour cream	1 tsp. garlic powder

In a small bowl, combine sour cream, mayonnaise and taco seasoning. Peel, pit and mash avocados; combine with juice of lemon or lime, salt and garlic powder. In a 9 x 11-inch shallow serving dish, layer as follows: bean dip, sour cream mixture, avocado mixture, green onions, olives and tomatoes. Top with cheese. Serve with tortilla chips.

Carrol Davig, State First Vice President
Victoria County

CARROT SANDWICHES

4 med. carrots, grated	1/2 c. mayonnaise
8-oz. cream cheese	1 c. nuts, chopped

Mix mayonnaise and cream cheese until soft. Add carrots and nuts. Mix well. Spread on rye bread.

Lucille Alford
Hardin County

Forgiveness does not change the past,
but it does enlarge the future.

CHEESE BLITZES

3 8-oz. pkgs. cream cheese
3 egg yolks
3 T. sugar

28 slices thin, crustless
   sandwich bread
3 sticks margarine, melted
Sugar and cinnamon mixture

Mix cream cheese, egg yolks and sugar. Spread on bread slices. Roll up. Dip into melted margarine. Coat with sugar-cinnamon mixture. Place in freezer for 10-15 minutes. Slice each roll into 4 pieces. Freeze until firm. Place in freezer bags and freeze. When ready to serve, thaw 30 minutes. Bake 10-12 minutes in 400 degree oven. Makes 112.

Henderson County

CHEESE PUFFS

1/4 lb. margarine
3-oz. cream cheese
6-oz. sharp Cheddar cheese

2 egg whites, stiffly beaten
Unsliced bread

Melt margarine, cream cheese and Cheddar cheese in double boiler. Add beaten egg whites. Cut bread into 1-inch cubes. Dip bread cubes into cheese mixture. Place on ungreased cookie sheet. Refrigerate overnight. Bake at 400 degrees for 8 minutes. Makes about 50.

Vi Bilbro
Upshur County

CREAM CHEESE SPREAD

1 8-oz. cream cheese,
  softened
1 sm. jar dry beef, rinsed
  and chopped
1/2 tsp. Accent

6-oz. pitted black olives,
  chopped
1 T. mustard
3/4 c. mayonnaise
1/2 c. celery, chopped (opt.)
1/2 tsp. onion salt or flakes

Mix all ingredients together until the mixture will spread smoothly. Makes a great party sandwich spread. I use a food processor to chop beef, celery and olives. Using 1 loaf sandwich bread, this will yield 36 finger sandwiches. For each sandwich, cut in one-thirds. Remove crust.

Mable Voigt
Bastrop County

A grudge is too heavy a load
for anyone to carry.

HI-JINKS

1 lb. ground beef	1 tsp. oregano
1 lb. hot sausage	1 tsp. black pepper
1 lb. Velveeta processed cheese	1 or 2 loaves Party Rye bread

Cook beef and sausage; drain well. Stir in cheese and seasonings. Allow cheese to melt, mix well, and spread mixture on Party Rye bread pieces while still warm. Broil until mixture is bubbly or about 5 minutes. Freeze on cookie sheets and pack in plastic bags for later use.

Pleasant Ridge Club

ROUND-UPS

1 pkg. Hidden Valley Original Salad Dressing mix	1/2 c. Cheddar cheese, shredded
1/2 c. real mayonnaise	1/2 c. assorted toppings - ripe olives, bell pepper,
French bread	mushrooms, green onions, pimentos

Combine salad dressing mix and mayonnaise. Spread thin layer on bread with a little bit of cheese and thinly sliced vegetables. Bake at 375 degrees for 8-10 minutes. Yield: 25.

Pam Bloxham
Knox County

PEANUT BUTTER STICKS

1 loaf bread	Crisco oil
1 c. creamy peanut butter (or more)	

Cut crust off bread and bake until real brown and crispy. Mix peanut butter and enough Crisco oil to make a paste. Put crust in blender until powdery. Cut bread slices into 4 sticks and bake until dry at 350 degrees. Dip sticks in peanut butter mixture; roll sticks in crust powder. Lay on paper towels to drain well.

Edith Belyeu
Stephens County

TORTILLA HORS D'OEUVRES

1 pkg. flour tortillas	Pace picante sauce
1 lg. pkg. cream cheese	1 sm. pkg. sour cream
3 green shallots, cut up	

Take flour tortillas; spread with cream cheese, cut up shallots and a little picante sauce and sour cream. Roll up and wrap in Saran Wrap. Place in freezer or refrigerator until ready to serve. Do not cook. Slice and have picante sauce handy to dip in.

Barbara Caddel
Polk County

TORTILLA PINWHEELS

1 8-oz. dairy sour cream
1 8-oz. pkg. cream cheese,
  softened
1 4-oz. can diced green chilies,
  well drained
1 4-oz. can chopped black
  olives, well drained

1 c. Cheddar cheese, grated
1/2 c. green onions, chopped
Garlic powder to taste
Seasoned salt to taste
5 10-in. flour tortillas
Fresh parsley for garnish (opt.)
Salsa

Mix all of the filling ingredients together thoroughly. Divide the filling and spread evenly over the tortillas. Roll up tortillas. Cover tightly with plastic wrap, twisting ends. Refrigerate for several hours. Unwrap; cut into slices 1/2-3/4-inch thick. (An electric knife works best.) Discard ends. Lay pinwheels flat on serving plate; garnish with parsley, leave space in center of plate for small bowl of salsa, if desired. Yield: about 50 pinwheels. Your guests will love them!

Bernadette Bludau, Lavaca County
Patsy Burleson, Scurry County

TORTILLA ROLL-UPS

20 flour tortillas
1 8-oz. pkg. cream cheese
1 8-oz. carton sour cream

1/4 c. onion, finely chopped
3 or 4 jalapeno peppers, finely
  chopped

Spread tortillas out on waxed paper. When they are at room temperature, mix remaining ingredients; spoon equally onto tortillas, spreading to edges. Roll over 3 times to make roll 1 1/2-inches wide. With waxed paper between layers, chill for 2 hours, then cut tortillas into 4 equal parts and arrange on serving tray.

Evelyn Sherrill
Cheerful E. H. C. T.

FLOUR TORTILLA SNACKS

2 8-oz. pkgs. cream cheese,
  softened
1 bunch green onions, chopped

1 4-oz. can ripe olives, chopped
1 4-oz. can green chilies,
  chopped
2 doz. 6-in. flour tortillas

Mix together the cream cheese, onions, olives and green chilies until well blended. Spread on tortillas. Stack 2 tortillas together with the spread side face up. fold the two tortillas in half creating a half-moon shape of four thicknesses. Cut into finger strips from the folded edge out. Serve with **picante sauce** as dip. Keeps well in refrigerator for 2 weeks.

Kay Chastain, "Messenger" Editor
Rains County

CRAWFISH PIES

1/2 c. celery
2 bunches green onions
1/4 c. green pepper
1 1/2 sticks margarine
1/4 c. fresh parsley
1 tsp. cornstarch
1/4 c. water

25 sm. pie shells, tart size
2 cans cream of mushroom soup
2 cans cream milk (Carnation)
2 lbs. crawfish tails, peeled and
  cooked (frozen works well)
Tony's Creole Seasoning to
  taste

Finely chop celery, green onions, green pepper and parsley. Saute onions in margarine. Slowly add soup and cream to mixture while stirring constantly. Cook 5-7 minutes. Add crawfish tails, seasonings and **pepper.** Stir well. Cook for 15-20 minutes. Mix cornstarch and water; add to mixture. Remove from heat. Spoon into pie shells. Place pies on cookie sheet. Bake at 375 degrees for 20-25 minutes or until bubbling. Crust should be golden brown. You may substitute shrimp for crawfish tails.

Scott and Rebecca Dimak
Lynn County

TUNA STUFFING MUFFIN CAKES

1 1/2 c. hot water
1/4 c. butter or margarine, cut
  into pieces
1 6-oz. pkg. corn bread
  stuffing mix
1 9 1/4-oz. can tuna,
  drained and flaked
2 hard-cooked eggs, diced

3/4 c. green or sweet red
  pepper, diced
1/4 c. green onion, minced
1/3 c. Parmesan cheese,
  shredded
Tartar sauce or commercial
  salsa (opt.)

Combine water, butter and vegetable seasoning packet; stir until butter is melted. Add stuffing crumbs and next 4 ingredients; stir until moistened. Lightly grease muffin pan with cooking spray. Sprinkle cheese evenly in muffin pan. Spoon stuffing mixture over cheese, packing lightly. Bake at 400 degrees for 20 minutes. Cool in pan 5 minutes. Serve with tartar sauce or commercial salsa, if desired. Yield: 6 servings.

NOTE: Substitute 2 5-oz. cans chunk chicken, drained and flaked, for tuna, if desired.

Eva Merino
Kleberg County

Use what talents you possess,
the woods would be very silent
if no birds sang there except
those that sang best.
Henry Van Dyke

SALMON LOG

1 15-oz. can red salmon	1/4 tsp. salt
1 8-oz. pkg. cream cheese	1 T. liquid smoke
3 T. lemon juice	3/4 c. pecans, chopped
2 T. onion, grated or green	8 drops Tabasco sauce
onions, chopped	3 T. fresh parsley, chopped

Drain salmon, remove bone and skin. Flake salmon with fork. Add softened cream cheese, lemon juice, onion, salt, liquid smoke and Tabasco sauce. Mix well. Chill for a few hours or overnight. When salmon is well chilled, shape into a roll. Mix chopped pecans and parsley. Roll salmon into mixture until well covered. Chill again. Serve with crackers of your choice. Makes 1 10-inch log.

Juanita Green
Hunt County

STUFFED MUSHROOMS

2 lg. pkgs. mushrooms	Green onions, chopped
1 pkg. Philadelphia Cream	Parsley, chopped
Cheese	3 sticks butter
1 lb. Velveeta cheese	Parmesan cheese
Garlic powder	

Mix melted cream cheese, Velveeta, garlic powder (to your taste), parsley and onions together. Fill mushrooms, set in shallow trays. Melt butter and pour into trays. Allow to marinate overnight. (Mushrooms will absorb butter.) Sprinkle with Parmesan cheese and broil until brown and bubbly.

Barbara Creager
Loving County

SNACK PLATE

2 apples	2 sticks celery
2 oranges	Pimento cheese
2 bananas	Crackers
2 peaches	Peanut butter
Small jar cherries	Toothpicks (opt.)
Fruit of your choice	

Wash and core apples. Wash and deseed peaches. Slice fruit into bite size pieces. Wash and slice celery into bite size pieces. Fill celery with pimento cheese. Spread crackers with peanut butter. Arrange ingredients onto platter and place in refrigerator until time to serve.

Jason Ridgeway
Winkler County

BARBECUED MEATBALLS

1/4 c. stale bread crumbs	1/4 c. vinegar
1/4 c. milk	1/4 c. ketchup
1 lb. ground beef	1/4 c. chili sauce
1 tsp. salt	1/4 tsp. Tabasco sauce
1/2 tsp. Accent	Flour, small amount
1 onion, diced	4 T. margarine
2 T. molasses	

Soak bread crumbs in milk. Mix ground beef, salt, Accent and onion. Shape into small balls. Roll in flour; brown in margarine. Combine remaining ingredients and pour over meatballs. Simmer 10 minutes. Keep warm while serving. Chafing dish works well. Furnish toothpicks to lift meatballs to plates. Serves 4 amply.

OPTIONAL SAUCES FOR MINI-MEATBALLS

A. **Sweet and Sour Sauce**
   1/4 c. chili sauce
   1/4 c. grape or plum jelly
   Stir in small pan over medium flame until jelly melts.

B. **Honey Soy Sauce**

1/2 c. soy sauce	1/2 tsp. MSG
1/2 c. honey	1/2 tsp. ginger

   Stir over medium heat until blended.

C. **Sauce O'Gold**

1/4 c. prepared mustard	1/2 tsp. salt
1/4 c. honey	1/4 tsp. rosemary leaves
1/8 tsp. pepper	

   Stir over medium heat until well blended.

Winona Baugh, Chairman
Family Life & Resources
McLennan County

PEAR PRESERVES

5 lbs. firm pears	2 lbs. sugar
1/3 c. Karo syrup	Lemon slices, if desired

Wash, peel and slice pears. Put in a large boiler, add sugar, Karo syrup and lemon slices. Cook slowly using medium heat for several hours or until pears are transparent and tender and the liquid is the consistency of syrup.

Anna B. Hall
Harrison County

Nothing ruins the truth like stretching it.

IT CAN'T BE BEET JELLY

3 c. beet juice
4 tsp. lemon juice
1 box powdered pectin

1 sm. pkg. raspberry Kool-Aid
4 c. sugar

Combine juice and pectin. Cook to rolling boil. Add sugar and cook 6 minutes. Skim off foam. Add soft drink powder and mix thoroughly. Pour into sterilized jars. Cover with paraffin. Makes 10 one-half cup portions. Approximate value: 4 grams carbohydrate, 16 calories per teaspoonful.

Betty Wilson
Bell County

CREAM CHEESE STRAWBERRIES

1 8-oz. pkg. cream cheese
1 c. pecans, finely chopped
1 2.25-oz. pkg. coarse red
    sugar crystals

1 3-oz. pkg. strawberry jello
Fresh parsley

Blend cream cheese, nuts, dry jello and 1/2 package red sugar until even color. Refrigerate. Using about 1 teaspoonful mixture, shape into strawberries. Roll in remaining red sugar and top with a sprig of parsley. Refrigerate until ready to serve. Makes about 2 dozen.

Dorothy C. Vails
Travis County

ORANGE PECANS

1 c. sugar
1/3 c. frozen orange juice
    concentrate, undiluted

1 tsp. lemon extract
2 T. butter or margarine
2 1/2 c. pecan halves

Combine sugar and orange juice concentrate. Cook to soft ball stage. Add lemon extract and butter. Beat until creamy. Add nuts and stir until well coated. Place on waxed paper. Separate each pecan.

Johnnie Bussey
Gregg County

*We are either leaving our mark on the world
or the world is leaving its mark on us.*

PIES & PASTRIES

Pies and Pastries

APPLE BURRITOS

1 21-oz. can apple pie   12 flour tortillas
filling (or your choice of
other fruits)

Heat oven to 350 degrees. Spray 9 x 13-inch baking dish with Pam. Fill tortillas evenly with pie filling and roll up. Place in baking dish and cover with sauce.

Sauce:

2 sticks margarine, melted   1/2 tsp. nutmeg
1 1/2 c. sugar   2 c. water
1 tsp. cinnamon   1 tsp. vanilla

Melt margarine in 3-quart saucepan and set aside. Mix spices with sugar and pour into margarine. Add vanilla and water and mix well. Pour over tortillas. Sauce will soak up into tortillas. Bake 40 minutes. After tortillas have baked for 20 minutes, long enough to get crusty, cover with foil and cook rest of time. This keeps them from being hard on top.

Mary Hastings
Tyler County

APPLE STRUDEL

Dough:

1 1/2 sticks margarine   1 c. warm milk
2 egg yolks, beaten   3 c. flour

Filling:

Vanilla wafer crumbs   Coconut
2 apples, shredded   Raisins
1/2 c. sugar   Pecans, chopped
Cinnamon   Butter, melted

Melt margarine, add egg yolks and warm milk. Add flour. Mix well, at least 8-10 minutes, then form into small balls, about the size of half dollar. Cover and let stand about 3 hours or overnight. Then roll out real thin and brush with melted butter. Sprinkle with vanilla wafer crumbs, shredded apples, sugar, cinnamon, coconut, chopped pecans and raisins. Drizzle butter on top. Roll up like jelly roll and place in buttered pan. Bake about 25-30 minutes at 350 degrees.

Olga Kurc
Van Zandt County

Laughter is a tranquilizer with no side effects.

BAKLAVA

Honey:

2 c. honey   1 T. orange rind

1 c. sugar   1 tsp. cinnamon

1 c. water

Pastry:

1/2 lb. unsalted butter, melted   2 tsp. cinnamon

1 lb. phyllo sheets   1/2 tsp. ground cloves

3 c. walnuts or pecans, finely chopped

Brush a 13 x 9 x 2-inch cake pan with some of the melted butter. Fold a phyllo sheet in half and place in pan. Brush with butter and top with another sheet of phyllo and brush with butter. In a bowl, combine nuts, cinnamon and cloves; mix well. Top phyllo with one cup of nut mixture. Top with 4 more sheets of phyllo, brushing each with butter. Repeat this layering process until all nuts are used. Layer 4 sheets for top crust, buttering each sheet. With a sharp knife, cut through top layers into 24 small rectangles. Bake at 325 degrees for 50 minutes. Remove from the oven and with a sharp knife cut through all layers of pastry. Pour the cooled honey over the pastry and cool. Makes 24 pieces of pastry.

Georgia Summers
Midland County

ROLLED BAKLAVA

1 lb. Fillo (Philo or Phyllo)   1 lb. butter, melted

   pastry   2 c. pecans

1 c. sugar

Cut fillo pastry into thirds. Chop sugar and pecans in blender. Picking up 5 pastry sheets at a time, roll with 2 tablespoonfuls nut mixture. Place with open end down on cookie sheet. Pour melted butter over rolled pastries. Bake at 325 degrees turning once. Bake until brown and butter is absorbed, about 10-12 minutes.

Glaze:

1 c. water   2 T. lemon juice

2 c. sugar

Dip pastries in glaze and cut into thirds. Best when served warm. Can be frozen.

Velda Hammons
Angelina County

Praising yourself to the sky will not get you there.

MRS. HUBENAK'S KOLACHE RECIPE

2 cakes yeast or 2 pkgs.
 dry yeast
1/4 c. lukewarm water
1 tsp. sugar
3/4 c. butter, margarine or
 shortening
3/4 c. sugar

2 egg yolks
1 lg. can evaporated milk
 plus hot water to equal 2 c.
6 c. flour (measure by lightly
 spooning into cup and
 leveling off)
2 tsp. salt

Dissolve yeast in the 1/4 cup lukewarm water and sprinkle with 1 teaspoonful sugar. In a large bowl, cream sugar and butter; add yolks, salt and mix well. Add the dissolved yeast and about 1/2 cup of the flour. Mix slowly with electric mixer. Add all the milk and continue adding the remaining flour, stirring with the mixer or by hand until dough is glossy. Cover; let rise in a warm place until doubled in bulk, about 1 hour. After dough has risen, punch down and divide into egg-sized portions. Shape each piece into a ball and place about 1-inch apart on greased pans. Brush well with melted butter or margarine and let rise until light. Using 4 fingers, make a circular indentation in each ball and fill with selected filling, sprinkle with topping and bake at 425 degrees for 15 minutes. Brush kolaches with melted butter as they come from the oven, then sprinkle with superfine sugar, if desired.

Apricot Filling for Kolaches:

1 10-oz. pkg. dried apricots   1 1/2 c. sugar

Place apricots in saucepan and add water to cover. Cook slowly until fruit is soft and water has been cooked out. Take care not to overcook as this darkens fruit. When done, add sugar and mash and mix until well blended.

Posipka (topping):

1 c. sugar   3/4-1 tsp. cinnamon
1/2 c. flour   2 T. butter, melted

Mix all ingredients until mixture resembles coarse meal.

McClellan County

PECAN TARTS

1 3-oz. pkg. cream cheese
1/2 c. margarine
1 c. flour
2/3 c. pecans, chopped
1 egg, beaten

3/4 c. light brown sugar
1 T. margarine, melted
1 tsp. vanilla
Dash of salt

Make pastry of first 3 ingredients. Mix well and chill 1 hour. Shape into balls and put into miniature muffin tins. Press dough into and around the muffin tin. Make bottom thin, but no holes. Partially fill 24 tart shells with the pecan mixture made from remaining ingredients. Bake 20 minutes at 400 degrees or until lightly brown. Cool slightly. Remove from tins.

Elizabeth Todd
Sabine County

KOLACHES

1/2 c. sugar	1 tsp. salt
1 1/2 pkgs. dry yeast	1 egg, beaten
1/2 c. margarine	1/2 c. boiling water
1/2 c. warm water	3-3 1/2 c. flour

Cream sugar, margarine and salt. Add boiling water and stir well. Let mixture cool to lukewarm. Dissolve yeast in warm water. Add beaten egg to yeast mixture. Combine mixtures, add flour and mix well. Let rise to double in bulk in greased bowl. Grease top of dough after placing in bowl and before rising. When doubled in bulk, punch down. Put margarine on hands because dough is sticky. Pinch off a little handful and make into little balls for round kolaches or roll out on floured board for filling kolaches. Place little kolaches in buttered pan and butter tops of each. Then let rise about 30 minutes, make indention in each and add filling and/or streusel and bake in 350 degrees oven until they turn tan, about 15-20 minutes.

Peach Filling for Kolaches:

1 pkg. dried peaches	1 1/2 c. sugar
or any fruit	

Cook peaches with just enough water to cover until tender and most of the water is cooked away. Mash with sugar, add about 1 teaspoonful margarine. Cool before spooning onto dough.

Prune Filling for Kolaches:

1 lb. prunes	1/2 tsp. ground cinnamon
1/2 c. sugar	

In a saucepan, cook prunes in water just to cover until tender. Drain. (Reserve the liquid to mix with fruit juice if you like.) Discard pits. Mash pulp with sugar and cinnamon. Use as directed above. Enough for 3 dozen.

Streusel for Kolaches:

Margarine, melted (enough to	3/4 c. sugar
make mixture crumbly)	1/2 c. flour

Mix together until crumbly and spoon over fruit filling.

Burleson County

PIE CRUST (Food Processor)

1 1/2 c. flour	1 stick butter or margarine
1 tsp. salt	1/4 c. ice water

Add dry ingredients to butter. Blend well in food processor. Slowly add water until dough forms into a ball. Makes 1 crust.

Debbie Ferguson
Sherman County

Speak kind words and you will hear kind echoes.

PIE CRUST

2 c. flour
1 tsp. salt

2/3 c. + 2 T. shortening
1/4 c. cold water

Cut shortening and flour to size of peas; add water and mix until it forms a ball. Divide into 2 balls and use plenty of flour on cabinet and rolling pin. Flatten to pie shape and place in pie pan. Pierce with fork on sides and bottom. Crimp edges and trim with a knife. Bake at 400 degrees for as long it takes crust to brown.

Wanda Walker

NEVER FAIL PIE CRUST

2 c. flour
1/2 c. vegetable oil

1/4 c. skim milk
1 tsp. salt

Mix flour with salt. Make well in flour. Pour oil and milk in at once. **DO NOT mix oil and milk together BEFORE pouring into flour.** Mix into balls. Roll out between 2 sheets of wax paper. Makes 1 double pie crust. This recipe can be doubled. Always tender.

Maxine Taylor
Hood County

PIE CRUST

1 1/2 c. flour
1/2 c. Crisco

3/4 tsp. salt
6 T. cold water

Mix flour, shortening and salt thoroughly until mixture looks like meal, or small granules. Spoon in cold water and mix until it is all in a ball. Roll out and bake. This makes 1 large pie crust. (I have used this recipe for a long time and I do know that it makes a good crust.)

Houston County

LEMON CHESS PIE

3 eggs
1 c. sugar
1/2 c. light corn syrup
5 T. butter, melted
6 T. sour cream

1 tsp. vanilla
1/4 c. lemon juice
2 T. cornmeal
2 T. flour
1 9-inch pie shell, unbaked

Beat eggs. Add sugar gradually and beat until thick. Stir in remaining ingredients for filling. Mix well and pour into pie shell. Bake at 350 degrees for 45 minutes or until firm and brown.

Lois Gray, Ranch Homes
Llano County

Peace is seeing a sunset and knowing who to thank.

CHOCOLATE CHESS PIE

1 c. sugar
3 T. cornmeal
3 T. cocoa
3 eggs, well beaten

1/2 c. butter or margarine,
  melted
1/2 c. light corn syrup
1 tsp. vanilla
1 9-inch pie shell, unbaked

Mix the sugar, cornmeal and cocoa in a bowl. Add the eggs, butter, corn syrup and vanilla and mix well. Pour into pie crust. Bake at 350 degrees for 45 minutes.

Dorothy Richey
Lamar County

CHOCOLATE CHESS PIE

4 T. cocoa
1 1/2 c. sugar
3/4 stick margarine
3 eggs, well beaten

1 tsp. vanilla
1 sm. or 1/2 lg. can evaporated
  milk
1 pie shell, unbaked

Blend well. Pour into pie crust. Bake at 300 degrees until firm.

Bessie Whitley
Menard County

BASIC PIE FILLING

1 c. sugar
2 c. sweet milk
1/3 c. flour
2 egg yolks (save whites
  for meringue)

Pinch of salt
1 tsp. vanilla
1 T. butter

Mix sugar and flour, add enough milk to make a thick paste. Add egg yolks and beat. Ad rest of milk and salt. Mix well. Cook in double boiler until thick. Remove from fire and add butter and vanilla.

For coconut pie, add 1 cup coconut.
For chocolate pie, add 2 tablespoonfuls cocoa to sugar.
For pineapple pie, add 1 cup pineapple.
For raisin pie, cook 1 cup raisins; drain, add to filling.
Also good for banana pie.

Houston County

Forget your mistakes,
but remember what they taught you.

BLACK FORREST PIE

1 chocolate flavored pie crust
1 8-oz. carton whipped topping
1 c. cold milk
1 pkg. chocolate instant
    pudding
1 c. cherry pie filling

Spread 1 cup of whipped topping on bottom of pie crust. Combine milk and pudding mix, blend well with wire whip. Fold in 1 1/2 cups of whipped topping. Spread over topping in crust. Spread remaining whipped topping over top, leaving a 1-inch border and forming a depression in the center. Spoon cherry pie filling in the center. Chill at least 3 hours. Garnish with melted chocolate, if desired.

Joyce Biggs
Lubbock County

CARAMEL PIE

1 c. sugar, divided
2 c. milk
1 T. margarine
3 T. flour
1 tsp. vanilla
3 eggs, separated

Mix 1/4 cup sugar with flour. Add milk, beaten egg yolks and vanilla. Set aside. Melt 3/4 cup sugar and margarine. Cook slowly until brown but not burned. Add milk mixture and cook slowly until thick and all sugar is melted. Pour into a baked pie crust. Top with meringue. Brown.

Ruby Elliston
Throckmorton County

CHOCOLATE PIE

6 T. flour
1 1/2 c. sugar
3 T. cocoa
2 egg yolks (use whites
    for meringue)
1 1/2 c. evaporated milk
1 tsp. vanilla
3 T. butter
1 baked pastry shell
4 T. sugar
Pinch of baking powder

Mix flour, sugar and cocoa together. Add beaten egg yolks. Add evaporated milk. Add flavoring and butter. Cook in double boiler until thick. Pour into a baked pie shell. For meringue, beat egg whites until stiff. Add sugar and baking powder. Spread on pie and bake at 250 degrees for 15 minutes.

Hazel Stevenson
Jasper County

*The best way to succeed in life
is to act on the advise you give to others.*

QUICKIE CHOCOLATE PIE

1 8-oz. Hershey Chocolate Bar (plain or almond)
1 12-oz. carton Cool Whip

1 9-in. graham cracker crust or baked crust
Grated chocolate for garnish

Melt broken up chocolate bar in microwave for 2 minutes. Cool slightly. Stir in Cool Whip. Put into pie crust and top with a thin layer of Cool Whip. Garnish with grated chocolate. Chill. Serves 6-8. Very rich, but oh so quick.

Juanita Green
Hunt County

COCONUT PIE

1/4 c. sugar
2 lg. eggs, lightly beaten
1/2 c. evaporated milk
1/2 c. canned coconut milk or milk

1 8 1/2-oz. can cream of coconut
1/2 c. flaked coconut
1 8-in. graham cracker crust

Combine first 5 ingredients; stir in coconut. Pour mixture into prepared crust. Bake at 350 degrees for 50-55 minutes. Yield: 1 8-inch pie.
NOTE: Canned coconut milk is available in large supermarkets near other canned milk products.

Clarine Gold
Wharton County

COCONUT CREAM PIE

3/4 c. sugar
2 egg yolks
1 tsp. vanilla

3 T. cornstarch
2 1/4 c. milk
1/3 c. coconut

Mix sugar, cornstarch, egg yolks and milk in double boiler; add vanilla and cook until thickened. Add coconut. Put custard into a 9-inch baked pie shell, cover with meringue, sprinkle coconut on top and bake at 350 degrees for 18 minutes or until golden brown.

Never Fail Meringue:
1 T. cornstarch
1 T. sugar
3 egg whites

1/8 tsp. salt
1/2 c. water

Cook until clear, then set aside. Add salt to the egg whites and beat until stiff and stands in peaks. Add sugar and water mixture and beat well, adding 6 tablespoonfuls sugar, 1 at a time, while beating.

Pie Crust:
1 c. flour
3-5 T. water

1/3 c. Crisco

Blend flour and Crisco until coarse, add water and gather dough in ball. Place on lightly floured board and roll out to make a 9-inch pie crust.

Inez Clement
Collingsworth County

COCONUT CREAM PIE

Filling:

1/2 c. sugar	1/2 tsp. butter flavoring
3 T. cornstarch	1/2 tsp. coconut flavoring
1/2 tsp. salt	1/2 tsp. vanilla flavoring
2 1/4 c. milk	3/4 c. angel flake coconut
3 egg yolks, beaten slightly	

Mix sugar, cornstarch and salt in medium Pyrex mixing bowl. Gradually stir in milk. Cook in microwave, stirring well each minute, until custard thickens and boils. Boil 1 minute. Remove from microwave. Gradually stir at least half of hot mixture into egg yolks. Then blend into hot mixture in bowl. Boil 1 minute more. Remove from microwave. Blend in flavorings and coconut. Pour into baked 9-inch pie shell. Prepare meringue.

Meringue:

3 egg whites	3 T. sugar
1/4 tsp. baking powder	1/2 tsp. vanilla

Beat egg whites with baking powder until frothy. Continue to beat until soft peaks form; gradually add sugar and vanilla. Continue beating until stiff peaks form. Spread on top of filling. Sprinkle with 1/3 cup coconut. Brown in 375 degree oven until coconut and meringue is delicately brown.

Stir-N-Roll Pastry:

1 1/3 c. flour	1/3 c. canola cooking oil
1/2 tsp. salt	3 T. cold milk

Mix flour and salt together. Pour oil and milk into measuring cup, but do not stir. Add all at once. Stir until mixed. Press into smooth ball, flatten slightly. Place between 2 sheets of waxed paper (12-inch square). (Dampen table top to prevent slipping.) Roll out gently to edges of paper. Peel off paper. Place over 9-inch pie pan and gently peel off second piece of paper. Flute edge. Prick thoroughly with fork. Bake in 450 degree oven 8-10 minutes or until lightly brown. Cool slightly and add filling and meringue. Yield: 1 9-inch pie.

Erna Thielemann
Fort Bend County

JOSSIE EGG CUSTARD PIE

4 eggs	1/4 tsp. nutmeg
3/4 c. sugar	1 10-inch pie crust, uncooked
3 c. milk	

Beat eggs until yolks are blended with white eggs; add sugar, 1/4 cup at a time. Add milk and stir well so the sugar is dissolved. Add nutmeg. Pour into 10-inch uncooked pie crust. Bake at 400 degrees for 10-15 minutes. Reduce heat to 350 degrees until done. Pie will be done when knife inserted in middle comes out clean.

Leatha Jeffrey
Willacy County

DIET MILLION DOLLAR PIE

1 3-oz. pkg. Instant Jello
    Vanilla Pudding mix (diet
    or sugar free)
1 c. skim milk
1 8-oz. pkg. fat free cream cheese

2 c. unsweetened crushed
    pineapple, drained
1/2 c. pecans, chopped (opt.)
Graham cracker crust

Mix pudding and milk according to package directions. Mix cream cheese and crushed pineapple. Mix prepared pudding, cream cheese mixture and nuts all together. Pour into graham cracker crust and top with 1 cup diet whipped topping. Chill.

Virginia Stevenson
Wilbarger County

GERMAN SWEET CHOCOLATE PIE

14-oz. Baker's Sweet Chocolate
1/4 c. butter
1 2/3 c. (14 1/2-oz. can)
    evaporated milk
1 1/3 c. sugar
3 T. cornstarch

1/8 tsp. salt
2 eggs
1 tsp. vanilla
1 1/3 c. Bakers Angel Flake
    coconut
1/2 c. pecans, chopped

Melt chocolate with butter over low heat; gradually blend in milk. Mix sugar, cornstarch and salt thoroughly; beat in eggs and vanilla. Gradually blend in chocolate mixture. Pour into pie shell. Mix coconut and nuts and sprinkle over filling. Bake at 375 degrees for 45-50 minutes or until top is puffed and brown (filling will be soft, but will set while cooling). Cool 4 hours or more. Makes 10-12 servings.

Hazel Bray, Director
District 12, Brooks County

BAKER'S GERMAN CHOCOLATE PIE

1 pkg. German chocolate
1/4 c. butter
1 2/3 c. evaporated milk
1 1/2 c. sugar
3 T. cornstarch
1/8 tsp. salt

2 eggs
1 tsp. vanilla
1 1/3 c. coconut
1/2 c. pecans, chopped
1 10-in. pie shell, unbaked

Melt chocolate with butter over low heat, stirring well. Remove from heat; gradually blend in milk. Mix sugar, cornstarch and salt in separate bowl; beat in eggs and vanilla. Gradually blend in chocolate mixture. Pour into shell. Mix coconut and pecans. Sprinkle over filling. Bake at 375 degrees for 45 minutes or until top is puffed. Cool at least 4 hours before serving.

Joan Martin
Baylor County

HAWAIIAN DREAM CREAM PIE

1 baked pie crust
1 T. cornstarch
3 T. cold water
1/2 c. boiling water
1 c. sugar
5 T. cornstarch
1/2 tsp. salt
2 c. milk
3 egg yolks, beaten

1 8-oz. can crushed pineapple,
  drained
2 T. margarine
1/2 c. coconut
1 tsp. vanilla
1 1/2 bananas
3 egg whites
6 T. sugar
1/2 c. coconut

In a small pan, mix 1 tablespoonful cornstarch and cold water. Add boiling water and cook until thick and clear; set aside to cool. In a saucepan, combine 1 cup sugar, 5 tablespoonfuls cornstarch, salt, milk, egg yolks, drained pineapple and margarine. Cook until thick; cool slightly. Add vanilla and 1/2 cup coconut; set aside. Slice bananas into baked crust. Pour in the filling. Beat egg whites until stiff. Add 6 tablespoonfuls sugar, 1 tablespoonful at a time, beating well after each addition. Beat in the cooked cornstarch water mixture. Mound meringue on filling; sealing edges. Sprinkle with 1/2 cup coconut. Bake 15 minutes at 375 degrees or until brown. Cool before serving.

Leila Webb
Nolan County

PEPPERMINT ICE CREAM PIE

1 1/2 c. rolled oats
3/4 c. flaked coconut
3/4 c. walnuts, finely chopped
3/4 c. sugar
1/2 c. unsweetened cocoa
  powder
1/2 c. margarine

2 c. vanilla ice cream
2 c. pink or green peppermint
  ice cream
1/4 c. round, stripped
  peppermint candies,
  coarsely crushed

For crust, stir together oats, coconut and nuts in a medium size mixing bowl; set aside. In a small saucepan, melt margarine over medium heat. Add sugar and cocoa powder, stirring until smooth. Pour over the oat mixture. Mix well and reserve 1 cup of the crust mixture. Using the back of a spoon, press remaining crust mixture into the bottom and up the sides of a 9-inch pie pan. Freeze 5-10 minutes or until the crust is firm. Scoop 1/2 of each ice cream flavor alternately side by side into crust using a metal spoon. Smooth surface and swirl gently to marble. Sprinkle with 3/4 cup of reserve crust mixture. Seal and freeze for up to 1 month. Let stand 10-15 minutes before serving. Makes 8 servings.

Virginia Burks
Galveston County

PINEAPPLE CREAM PIE

26 lg. marshmallows
1 c. pineapple juice

1 c. heavy cream
1 pie shell, baked

Melt marshmallows in juice on low heat to dissolve. Cool in refrigerator until thick. Whip cream. Whip pineapple mix and combine with cream. Pour into baked pie shell.

Inez Bayley
Brazoria County

PUMPKIN CREAM PIE

3/4 c. sugar
4 T. cornstarch
2 c. Pet Milk
1/2 c. canned pumpkin

1/2 tsp. nutmeg
1/2 tsp. ginger
1/2 tsp. salt
2 egg yolks, beaten

Mix sugar and cornstarch in heavy pot. Add rest of ingredients, except egg yolks. Cook over medium heat until thick. Remove from heat and pour a small amount of hot mixture into bowl with beaten egg yolks, stirring constantly. Return to stove and bring back to bubble stage. Cool and pour into **baked pie shell or graham cracker crust**. Top with **Cool Whip**. Refrigerate; may be kept for several days.

Never Fail Pie Crust:

3 c. flour
1 1/4 c. Crisco
1 tsp. salt

1 egg
1 T. vinegar
4 T. water

Blend flour and shortening. Beat egg, add liquid. Pour over dry mixture and mix. Roll onto floured board. Easy to work with. Bake at 475 degrees for 8-10 minutes. Yield: 3 single crusts.

Ecey Renken
Medina County

PUMPKIN PIE

1 c. pumpkin
3/4 c. skim milk
1/2 tsp. pumpkin pie spice

1 sm. pkg. vanilla sugar-free
   instant pudding
1 1/2 c. lite frozen whipped
   topping

Mix together pumpkin, milk, spices and pudding with mixer. Then fold in the whipped topping. Pour into **graham cracker crust** and chill.

Crust:

18 2 1/2-in. graham crackers,
   crushed

3 T. diet margarine, melted

Mix together and put into 9-inch pie plate. Each serving counts as: 1 bread, 3/4 fat and 1/4 vegetable. 54 optional calories for diabetics.

Beryl Trew
Ochiltree County

PUMPKIN CREAM PIE

1 1/2 c. white sugar	Butter, size of walnut
1/2 c. brown sugar	2 eggs
1/2 c. flour	1/2 tsp. cinnamon
1 can pumpkin	1/4 tsp. allspice
2 c.milk	2 pie shells, baked

Put sugars and flour in a bowl or heavy saucepan and mix. In blender, mix pumpkin, milk, butter, eggs, cinnamon and allspice. Blend and add to sugar/flour mixture. Mix and cook in heavy saucepan or in microwave until thick. Place in baked pie shells and top with **whipped topping** before serving. Makes 2 8-inch pies. Can be frozen or stored in refrigerator for a few days.

Mozelle Gillit
Lubbock County

RHUBARB CREAM PIE

4 c. rhubarb, cut in 1/2-in. pieces	3 eggs
1 1/2 c. sugar	2 T. butter
1/4 c flour	1 T. orange rind, grated (opt.)

Line pie tin with pastry. Combine sugar, flour, butter and orange rind. Add rhubarb. Put into pan. Top with lattice crust. Bake at 425 degrees for 10 minutes, reduce heat to 375 degrees and bake until knife inserted comes out clean.

Mary Arlene Jurgens
Kaufman County

BUTTERMILK COCONUT PIE

7 T. margarine, melted	1 c. coconut
5 eggs	3/4 c. buttermilk
1 3/4 c. sugar	1 9-inch pie crust, unbaked

Combine all ingredients into a mixing bowl. Beat until well mixed. Pour into crust and bake at 350 degrees for 35-40 minutes or until center of pie is set. Refrigerate.

Vee Gordon
Garza County

How can we judge the deeds of others
when most of the time we can't
understand what we do ourselves?

7 WAYS BASIC CREAM PIE

2/3 c. sugar   1 T. butter
3 T. cornstarch or   1/4 tsp. salt
  1/3 c. flour   1 tsp. vanilla
2 c. milk   3 egg yolks

Mix sugar, cornstarch and salt; add milk and cook, stirring until thickened. Add egg yolks stirring constantly. Continue to cook over medium heat, stirring constantly, until thickened. Remove from heat, add butter and vanilla. Allow filling to cool, then pour into a **pre-baked 9-inch pie shell** and top with **meringue or whipped cream.**

Meringue:

3 egg whites, stiffly beaten   6 T. sugar

Banana: You can either slice **2 large bananas** into the baked shell, then add the filling, or add them to the cream filling before pouring into the baked pie shell. Top with meringue or whipped cream.

Butterscotch: Substitute **1 cup brown sugar** for the white sugar. Increase butter to 1/4 cup.

Cherry: Add **1 cup of sweetened, cooked and well-drained cherries** to the cream filling.

Chocolate: Add **3 tablespoonfuls cocoa** with dry ingredients in basic recipe. Or add **2 squares of melted chocolate** to the hot cream filling. You can also add **semi-sweet chocolate chips** to the hot mixture.

Coconut: Add **1/2 or 1 cup shredded coconut** to the filling just before pouring into the pie shell. Cover with meringue and sprinkle with **1/4 cup coconut,** then brown in oven.

Pineapple: Add **1 cup of drained pineapple** to the cooled pie filling. Top with meringue or whipped cream.

You can create your own special pie by mixing or matching using the BASIC ingredients. Let your imagination run wild - ENJOY!

Sylvia Steen, Director
District 2, Hale County

We may live without friends,
We may live without books,
But civilized man ....
Cannot live without cooks!!!!

BUTTERMILK PIE CRUST AND PIE

Crust:

2 1/2 c. flour	1 tsp. salt
1 stick butter (1/2 c.)	2 tsp. sugar
1/2 c. Crisco	1/2 c. + 2 T. buttermilk

Mix dry ingredients; cut in butter and Crisco; add buttermilk. Makes a sticky dough. Put in refrigerator for 1 hour before rolling out for pie crust. Makes 1 large cobbler or 2 pie crusts.

Pie:

1 1/2 c. sugar	1/2 c. buttermilk
3 T. flour	1/2 tsp. lemon extract
1/2 stick margarine, melted	3 eggs

Mix sugar and flour. Add margarine, buttermilk, lemon extract and eggs. Pour into unbaked pie shell and bake 1 hour at 325 degrees.

Urban Club
Lamar County

APPLE PIE IN A JAR

4 1/2 c. sugar	1 tsp. salt
3/4 c. cornstarch	10 c. water
2 tsp. cinnamon	3 T. lemon juice
1/4 tsp. nutmeg	Apples

Cook sugar, cornstarch, cinnamon, nutmeg and water until thick and bubbly. Add lemon juice. Peel and slice apples. Fill quart jars tightly and cover with syrup. Hot water bath for 20 minutes.

MOTHER'S ALL-AMERICAN PIE

Pour Apple Pie in a Jar into unbaked 9-inch pie crust. Put 2 tablespoonfuls butter or margarine on top of apples. Cover with top crust. Cut slashes and sprinkle with cinnamon and sugar. Bake at 375 degrees for 50 minutes.

Debbie Ferguson
Sherman County

APPLE-SWEET POTATO PIE

1/2 c. brown sugar	Sweet potatoes, partially
1/4 c. flour	cooked
1/2 tsp. cinnamon	Margarine, melted
2 apples, sliced	Pie crust

Mix together brown sugar, flour and cinnamon. Brush pie crust with melted margarine and sprinkle with some of the brown sugar mixture. Place a layer of sliced apples, then a layer of partially cooked sweet potatoes in the crust, sprinkle with brown sugar mixture. Repeat layers ending with brown sugar mixture. Dot the top with margarine. Bake at 400 degrees until apples are tender. Serve with ice cream or Cool Whip.

Edith Stevens
Rains County

9-22-93

DELICIOUS APPLE PIE

Apples	3 egg yolks, well beaten
1 1/4 c. sugar	1/2 c. thick cream
2 T. cornstarch	1/4 c. milk
1/4 c. butter	Juice of 1/2 lemon

Line a deep pie pan with rich pastry. Fill with peeled and sliced apples. Mix well all ingredients. Spread mixture over the apples. Bake in 350 degree oven until done. Beat the **egg whites** until stiff, slowly add **6 tablespoonfuls sugar.** Spread this over the pie. Bake slowly until meringue is nicely browned.

Arvie Schulz
Floyd County

MOM'S APPLE COBBLER

1/2 c. (1 stick) butter or	1/2 c. shortening
margarine	1/3 c. milk
2 c. sugar	2 c. apples, finely chopped
2 c. water	1 tsp. cinnamon
1 1/2 c. Gladiola Self-Rising	
Flour, sifted	

Heat oven to 350 degrees. Melt the butter in a 13 x 9 x 2-inch baking dish or sheet cake pan. In a saucepan, heat sugar and water until sugar melts; set aside. Cut shortening into flour until particles are like fine crumbs. Add milk and stir with a fork only until dough leaves the side of the bowl. Turn out onto lightly floured board or pastry cloth. Knead just until smooth. Roll dough out into a large rectangle about 1/4-inch thick. Sprinkle cinnamon over apples; then sprinkle apples evenly over the dough. Roll up dough like jelly roll. Dampen the edges of the dough with a little water and seal. Slice dough into about 16 slices, 1/2-inch thick. Place in the pan with melted butter. Pour sugar syrup carefully around rolls. (This look like too much liquid, but the crust will absorb it.) Bake for 55-60 minutes. Makes 8 servings.
Mom's Variations: This cobbler may be made with other fresh, frozen or canned fruit such as blackberries, cherries or peaches. Drain liquid from fruit and substitute for part of the sugar syrup. Always use 2 cups of liquid.

Lorene Harris
Haskell County

Life is like a mirror;
we get the best results
when we smile at it.

BANANA APRICOT PIE

2 c. dried apricots
1 1/4 c. sugar
1/2 c. flour

3 egg yolks, beaten
2 tsp. butter
2 sm. bananas, thinly sliced

In saucepan, combine apricots and 1 1/2 c. water. Cover and simmer 10 minutes or until tender. Combine sugar, flour, and 1/4 tsp. salt. Stir into apricot mixture. Cook and stir until thickened and bubbly. Stir in butter; arrange bananas in pastry shell. Pour apricot mixture on top. Prepare meringue and spread over hot filling. Bake at 350 degrees for 13-15 minutes. Serve warm or cold.

Maggie Freemon

FRESH BLUEBERRY-JELLO PIE

1 9-in. baked pie shell
3-4 c. blueberries
3 T. cornstarch
3 T. red raspberry jello

3/4 c. sugar
1 tsp. lemon juice
1 c. water

Line pie shell with blueberries. Combine remaining ingredients in a saucepan in order given. Boil 1 minute; pour over berries. Refrigerate and top with **whipped topping** to serve.

Glenda Partlow
Hardin County

FRUIT SALAD PIE

1 16-oz. can red tart cherries
Hot water
3 T. cornstarch
1 box raspberry flavored jello
1/2 tsp. red food coloring
1 c. granulated sugar

1 15 1/2-oz. can crushed
  pineapple
4 med. sized bananas, diced
1/2 c. pecans, coarsely broken
2 pie shells, baked
Whipped cream

Drain juice from cherries; add enough hot water to make 2 cups liquid. Place in saucepan and stir in cornstarch. Cook over medium flame, stirring constantly until thickened and clear. Remove from heat. Add raspberry jello, red food coloring and sugar; stir until dissolved. Stir in drained pitted cherries and crushed pineapple (drain a little of the juice off). Cool. When just beginning to thicken, add bananas and pecans. Pour into baked pie shells. Chill at least 2 hours. Serve with whipped topping

Verna Brown
Hansford County

Take a rest; a field that has
rested gives a bountiful crop.

ANNIE'S FRIED PIES

Crust:

2 c. flour	1 tsp. baking powder
1/2 tsp. salt	1/2 c. shortening

Mix together flour, salt and baking powder; cut in shortening. Add enough milk to make stiff dough. Roll out like pie crust dough and cut with plastic cereal bowl with sharp edges. Put filling in middle and wet one side with water. Crimp with fork so sides are sealed together. Prick top and deep fry in peanut oil until golden brown. While still hot, drizzle small amount of frosting on top to glaze.

Filling (pineapple):

1 20-oz. can crushed pineapple	1 tsp. margarine
3 T. cornstarch	1 tsp. lemon juice (opt.)
1 c. sugar	

Mix together sugar and cornstarch; add to cold crushed pineapple in saucepan. Add lemon juice and margarine and stir while heating. Bring to boil, then cool.

Frosting:

1 c. powdered sugar	1/2 tsp. vanilla
1 T. margarine, melted	Canned or whole milk or water

Mix together powdered sugar, margarine and vanilla. Add enough milk or water to make a smooth glaze.

Myrtle LaGrange
Atascosa County

LEMON TARTS

4 graham cracker tart shells	1 can Eagle Brand milk
1 can frozen lemonade	8-oz. whipped cream

Mix lemonade and milk. Fold in whipped cream. Spoon into tart shells and refrigerate.

Mary Mizell
Guadalupe County

LEMON MERINGUE PIE

1/4 c. cornstarch	1 T. lemon peel, grated
2 T. flour	6 T. lemon juice
1 c. sugar	1 9-inch pie shell, baked
1/4 tsp. salt	3 eggs (room temperature)
2 c. boiling water	6 T. sugar

Separate eggs. Set whites aside. Mix cornstarch, flour, sugar and salt in boiling water over low heat. Gradually add beaten egg yolks until smooth. Add lemon juice and peel. Stir constantly over low heat until thick. Pour into shell. Beat egg whites into soft peaks. Beat until stiff. Slowly add sugar. Spread over filling to edge of crust. Bake 12-15 minutes at 350 degrees.

Maggie Freeman

GLAZED FRUIT PIZZA PIE

Crust:

1/2 c. butter	1 c. sugar
1 egg	1/2 c. oil
1/4 tsp. salt	1 tsp. vanilla
2 1/2 c. flour	1 tsp. soda
1 tsp. cream of tartar	

Cream butter, oil and sugar. Add eggs and vanilla; mix well. Add dry ingredients and mix well. Pat onto a large pizza pan. Bake at 350 degrees for 10-15 minutes; cool.

Filling:

1 8-oz. pkg. cream cheese	1/2 c. powdered sugar
1 tsp. vanilla	

Combine ingredients and spread on top of cooled crust.

Fruit:

Strawberries	Peaches
Bananas	Pineapple (canned)
Grapes (seedless)	Kiwi

Wash, peel and slice fruits. Using fruits of choice, arrange on top of filling.

Glaze:

1 c. orange juice	3/4 c. water
1/4 c. lemon juice	3 T. cornstarch
1 c. sugar	Dash salt

Dissolve cornstarch in water. Combine orange juice, lemon juice, sugar and salt with dissolved cornstarch. Cook over medium heat until mixture starts to thicken. Remove from heat and cool 5 minutes. Spoon on top of fruit. Refrigerate until ready to serve.

Sue Platt
Bowie County

MANGO PIE

Juice of 2 oranges	1 1/2 c. sugar
2 T. cornstarch	Juice of 1 lemon
4 T. butter	3/4 c. warm water
4 mangoes, peeled and	1/4 T. nutmeg
sliced	1/2 T. cinnamon
1 T. vanilla	1 doubled pie crust

Mix cornstarch, sugar, cinnamon and nutmeg together; add orange juice and lemon juice. Add butter and water, mixing well. Put on stove and stir until thick. Set aside and make crust. Peel mangoes and slice, place in pie crust, 1 layer at a time. Add hot mixture and spoon over layers of mango, then cover with lattice crust. Bake until done and crust is a golden brown. Bake in a 375 degree oven. Makes a very tasty pie!

Loretta Walton

LEMON PIE HAWAIIAN

1 8 1/4-oz. can crushed
   pineapple, drained
1/4 c. brown sugar, packed
1/4 c. flaked coconut
2 T. butter or margarine,
   softened
1 9-inch pastry shell, unbaked
1 4-serving-size pkg. regular
   lemon pudding mix

1/2 c. granulated sugar
1 3/4 c. water
2 egg yolks, slightly beaten
2 T. lemon juice
1 T. butter or margarine
2 egg whites
1/4 c. granulated sugar
Toasted coconut (opt.)

Combine drained pineapple, brown sugar, 1/4 cup coconut, and 2 table-spoonfuls butter or margarine; spread over bottom of pastry shell. Cover edge of pastry with foil. Bake in 425 degree oven for 15 minutes, removing foil after first 5 minutes of baking. Cool. Meanwhile, in saucepan, combine pudding mix and 1/2 cup granulated sugar. Stir in water and egg yolks; cook and stir until bubbly. Remove from heat. Stir in lemon juice and 1 tablespoonful butter or margarine. Cover with clear plastic wrap; cool, stirring occasionally. Beat egg whites on high speed of electric mixer to soft peaks; gradually beat in 1/4 cup granulated sugar to stiff peaks. Fold whites into cooled filling; pile into pastry shell. Chill at least 4 hours. Garnish with toasted coconut, if desired.

MINCEMEAT PIE

1 pt. mincemeat
1 apple, peeled and chopped
1/2 c. sugar

3 T. cornstarch
Dash of salt
9-inch pie shell, unbaked

Mix well and put in 9-inch unbaked shell. Top with strips or double crust. Bake at 425 degrees for 30 minutes.

Mrs. Alice Chaddock
Milam County

TORTILLA FRUIT PIE

Fruit of your choice
6 flour tortillas
1 c. sugar

1 c. water
1 c. butter or margarine

Roll fruit up in tortilla. Place in baking dish. Heat sugar, water and butter or margarine. Pour hot sauce over tortillas and bake 30-40 minutes in 400 degree oven.

Jewel Whitener
Hockley County

The way to keep a boy out of "hot water" is to put soap in it.

PINEAPPLE CHESS PIE

2 c. sugar
1/2 c. margarine, melted and
 cooled
4 eggs
3 T. flour

1 8-oz. can crushed pineapple,
 drained
1 tsp. vanilla
1 9-inch pie shell, unbaked

Combine sugar and margarine. Add eggs and flour, beating well. Stir in pineapple and vanilla. Bake at 350 degrees for about 45 minutes or until knife inserted comes out clean. Cool thoroughly.

Nell Davis
Reeves County

PINEAPPLE DISH

3/4 c. sugar
3 T. reserved pineapple juice
3 T. flour

2 15 1/4-oz. cans pineapple
 chunks
1 c. longhorn cheese, grated

Mix sugar, pineapple juice, flour and pineapple; add cheese.

Topping:
1/2 stick margarine

1 1/2 c. Ritz crackers, crushed

Melt margarine; mix with crackers and put on top of pineapple. Bake for 15 minutes at 350 degrees.

Judy Macha
Hockley County

DANG GOOD PIE

3/4 stick margarine
3 eggs
3 T. flour
1 c. flaked coconuts

1 c. crushed pineapple,
 drained
1 1/2 c. sugar
1 9-in. pie shell, unbaked

Melt margarine and mix with other ingredients. Pour into a 9-inch unbaked pie shell. Bake at 350 degrees for 1 hour or until set.

Shirley Pittman
Brown County

CHEESE PINEAPPLE PIE

3 eggs, beaten
1 1/2 c. sugar
1/4 c. margarine, melted
1/2 tsp. vanilla

1/8 tsp. salt
1 8-oz. can. crushed
 pineapple, drained
1 9-in. pie shell

Mix eggs, sugar, margarine, vanilla and salt; add drained pineapple. Pour into pie shell. Bake for 12 minutes at 400 degrees. Reduce heat to 300 degrees and bake 35 minutes or until set.

Edna Brownlow
Wilson County

TEXAS "GANG GOOD" PIE

3 eggs, slightly beaten
1 3/4 c. sugar
1 1/2 c. coconut
1 tsp. vanilla

1 c. crushed pineapple,
  undrained
3/4 c. margarine, melted
1 10-in. pie crust, unbaked

Mix all ingredients. Pour into pie crust. Bake at 350 degrees until slightly brown and well set.

Arleta Shirey
Eastland County

HONEY RAISIN PIE

2 c. seedless raisins
1 c. water
1/3 c. honey
2 T. flour

2 T. butter
1/2 lemon, juiced and grated
1 pie shell, unbaked

Simmer raisins until plump. Blend honey, flour and butter; then add raisins and cook until thickened. Add lemon juice and grated rind. Cool; pour into pie shell and cover with top crust or lattice crust. Bake at 450 degrees for 30 minutes.

Ruby Harrod
Live Oak County

SOUR CREAM RAISIN PIE

2 eggs
1 c. sugar
1 c. sour cream
1 T. flour
1/8 tsp. salt

1/2 tsp. nutmeg
1/2 tsp. cinnamon
1 c. raisins, chopped
1/2 c. nuts, chopped
1 9-in. pie shell, unbaked

Preheat oven to 350 degrees. Beat together the eggs and sugar until lemony color. Gradually stir in the sour cream. Combine the remaining ingredients in a small bowl and add to the cream mixture, mixing well. Pour into pastry shell. Bake in a moderate oven, 350 degrees, for 40-45 minutes. Cool. Serves 6-8.

Jackie Blaylock
Bailey County

The richest inheritance a grandparent
can leave us is a spiritual heritage --
a godly example.

PECAN PIE

Crust:
1 1/3 c. flour
1/2 c. Crisco
Filling:
3 lg. eggs, beaten
2/3 c. sugar
1/2 tsp. salt
1 tsp. vanilla

1/2 tsp. salt
3 T. ice water

2 T. margarine, softened
1 c. Blackburn syrup
1 c. pecans

Crust: Put all ingredients in food processor. Process until forms ball. Roll out and put in pie pan. Put pecans in crust in pan. Mix rest of filling ingredients together and pour into crust. Bake at 350-375 degrees for 40-50 minutes.

Groves E. H. Club
Jefferson County

CHERRY PECAN PIE

2 c. flour
1 tsp. baking soda
1/2 tsp. salt
3/4 c. sugar
1/2 c. butter
2 eggs

1 tsp. vanilla
1 c. buttermilk
1 c. pecans
1 10-oz. jar maraschino
    cherries, drained and
    chopped

In large mixing bowl, stir together flour and baking soda; set aside. Cream together sugar, butter, eggs and vanilla until light and fluffy. Add flour mixture and buttermilk to creamed mixture. Beat just until blended, after each addition. Fold in nuts and cherries. Turn batter into prepared pan. Bake in 350 degree oven for 55-60 minutes.

Icing:
1 c. powdered sugar
1/4 tsp. vanilla

1 1/2 T. milk

Maggie Freemon

CHOCOLATE PECAN PIE

1 9-in. pie shell, unbaked
1/2 c. sugar
3 eggs
1 c. dark corn syrup
1/4 tsp. salt
1 T. butter

1 T. flour
2 1-oz. squares chocolate
1 tsp. vanilla
1 1/2 c. pecan halves
1/2 c. heavy cream, whipped
    (opt.)

Beat together sugar, syrup, eggs, salt and flour. Melt butter and chocolate. Beat into egg mixture with vanilla. Put pecans into pastry shell; pour egg mixture over. Bake at 300 degrees for 50-60 minutes or until custard is set. Garnish with whipped cream.

Lena Woodrow

268

GRANNY ETHEL'S PECAN PIE

2 T. flour (heaping spoonfuls)
2/3 c. sugar
1 c. white Karo syrup
1 c. pecans, chopped

2 eggs, slightly beaten
3 T. margarine, melted
1 tsp. vanilla
1 9-in. pie shell, unbaked

Mix flour and sugar together, add syrup; stir well. Ad beaten eggs, pecans, margarine and vanilla. Mix well. Pour mixture into pie shell. Bake for 1 hour at 350 degrees.

Perry Keyes
Deaf Smith County

HONEY CRUNCH PECAN PIE

Filling:
4 eggs, lightly beaten
1/4 c. brown sugar, packed
1/4 c. white sugar
1/2 tsp. salt
2 T. margarine, melted

1 T. bourbon
1 tsp. vanilla
1 c. pecans, chopped
1 c. light corn syrup
1 pie shell, unbaked

Topping:
3 T. honey
1/3 c. brown sugar, packed

1 1/2 c. pecans
3 T. margarine

Heat oven to 350 degrees. For filling: combine eggs, brown sugar, white sugar, salt, corn syrup, margarine, bourbon, vanilla and nuts. Mix well. Spoon into unbaked pie shell. Bake for 15 minutes. Cover edge of pastry with foil. Bake 20 minutes. Remove from oven. For topping: combine sugar, margarine and honey in medium saucepan. Cook about 2 minutes or until sugar dissolves. Add nuts. Stir until coated. Spoon evenly over pie. Cover edge of pastry with foil. Bake 10-20 minutes or until top is bubbly and golden brown. Cool before serving.

Ann Johnson
McCulloch County

PINEAPPLE PECAN PIE

1/2 c. sugar
2 T. flour
1 tsp. vanilla
1 c. dark corn syrup (white
    may be used)
1 1-lb. 4-oz. can pineapple
    tidbits, well drained

1/2 tsp. salt
2 T. butter
3 eggs, beaten
1 c. pecans, chopped
1 9-in. pastry shell, unbaked

Cream thoroughly butter, sugar, flour, vanilla and salt; blend in eggs and corn syrup. Fold in pecans and pineapple; pour into pastry shell. Bake in 350 degree oven for 1 hour or until firm.

Ruby Sellers
Victoria County

PECAN PIE

1 c. brown sugar
1/2 c. granulated sugar
1/2 c. soft margarine
1 T. flour
2 eggs

2 T. milk
1 tsp. vanilla
1 c. pecans, chopped
1 pie crust, unbaked

Cream sugars with margarine; add flour and mix. Add eggs, milk and vanilla; beat well. Pour into unbaked pie crust. Put chopped pecans on top. Bake at 325 degrees for 50 minutes.

Ione Hanna
San Patricio/Aransas County

PECAN PIE

3 eggs, beaten
1 1/2 c. white syrup
1 tsp. vanilla

2 T. shortening, melted
1 c. pecans
Pinch of salt

Combine eggs, syrup, vanilla, shortening and salt. Mix **flour** with nuts. Stir into egg mixture and pour into **unbaked 9-inch pie shell**. Bake at 425 degrees for 10 minutes, then lower to 350 degrees for about 45 minutes. When knife inserted comes out clean, the pie is done.

Virginia Horton
Gray County

PECAN CHIFFON PIE

3 egg whites
1 c. sugar
1 tsp. vanilla

1 c. pecans, chopped
1 c. Ritz cracker crumbs
Cool Whip

Beat egg whites until stiff. Gradually add sugar and vanilla. Fold in cracker crumbs and chopped pecans. Pour into greased pie plate. Bake in 325 degree oven for 25 minutes. Cool, then fill with Cool Whip. Sprinkle with chopped pecans and chill.

Doris Griffin
Burnet County

When on vacation,
be with us in spirit.
The rest of the summer,
be with us in person.

SOUTHERN PECAN PIE

1 c. sugar
1 c. light corn syrup
1/3 c. butter
1 9-in. pie shell, unbaked

4 eggs, beaten
1 tsp. vanilla
1/4 tsp. salt
1-1 1/2 c. pecans, halves or
   chopped

Combine sugar, corn syrup and butter in medium saucepan. Cook over medium heat, stirring constantly until sugar dissolves and butter melts. Let cool slightly. Add eggs, vanilla and salt to mixture, stirring well by hand. Pour into pie shell and arrange pecan halves on top. Or stir in chopped pecans and pour into pie shell. Bake at 350 degrees for 50-55 minutes.

Fannie Crawford
San Saba County

PECAN PIE

3 eggs, slightly beaten
1 c. sugar
1 tsp. vanilla

1 c. Karo syrup
2 T. margarine, softened
1 3/4 c. pecans

Mix all ingredients into bowl, except pecans; mix well. Add pecans and pour into an **unbaked pie shell (9 or 10-inch)**. Place pie plate on cookie sheet and bake in a 350 degree oven for 55 minutes. Reduce heat to 300 degrees and bake another 10-15 minutes.

Indian Holiday
Harrison County

"SWEET POTATO" PIE

3 or 4 potatoes (2 1/4 lbs.)
2 c. sugar
1 tsp. cinnamon
1/2 tsp. nutmeg
1 tall can Pet milk (1/2 can
   to start)

1/4 c. butter, softened
4 eggs
1/2 tsp. salt
1/2 c. coconut
2 T. vanilla flavoring
2 pie shells, unbaked

Boil potatoes in water until tender. Pierce with fork. Peel potatoes and put into mixing bowl. Mash until they are lump free; add butter and sugar. Mix well. Put in spices, salt and milk; add vanilla, coconut and 1 egg at a time; beat well. Pour into unbaked pie shells. Bake for 70 minutes or until done at 325-350 degrees. Yield: 2 pies.

B. J. Johnson
Falls County

Anger is a wind which blows out the lamp of the mind.

POPPY SEED PIE

1/2 pt. whipping cream	1 can poppy seed
1 c. sugar	1 tsp vanilla
6 T. tapioca	1/8 T. salt
1 c. milk	1 deep dish pie shell,
4 eggs, beaten	baked

Topping:

1 8-oz. pkg. cream cheese,	1 c. powdered sugar
softened	1 tsp. vanilla
	Milk

Mix the whipping cream, milk, sugar and tapioca. Allow to set for 5-10 minutes. Add beaten eggs; bring to a boil, then add poppy seed and vanilla. Bring to a boil. Pour into baked pie shell. Topping: Mix cream cheese and powdered sugar. Add enough milk to make creamy. Add vanilla. Spread over top of cooled pie.

Connie Taylor, Chairman
Natural/Community Resources

OLD-FASHIONED OATMEAL PIE

2 lg. eggs	3/4 c. sweetened flaked or
3/4 c. honey	shredded coconut
1/2 c. brown sugar, packed	1/2 c. Zante currants
1/2 c. butter or margarine,	1/2 c. walnuts, chopped
melted	1 9-in. pie shell, unbaked
3/4 c. quick cooking oats	Whipped cream for garnish

Heat oven to 350 degrees. Whisk eggs in large bowl. Add honey, brown sugar and butter. Whisk until blended. Stir in oats, coconut, currants and nuts. Pour into pie shell. Bake 45-50 minutes until knife inserted near center comes out clean. Cool on wire rack. Garnish with whipped cream.

Margaret Rutter
Palo Pinto County

SWEET POTATO PIE

2 1/2 c. sweet potatoes (3 med.)	1/2 c. milk
1/2 c. stick margarine	1/2 tsp. nutmeg
1/4 c. flour	1 tsp. cinnamon
1 c. sugar	3 eggs, well beaten
1/2 tsp. salt	1 tsp. vanilla

Cook and mash potatoes. Add margarine and allow to melt in hot potatoes. Mix sugar and flour, add to potatoes. Add salt, milk, spices, eggs and vanilla. Mix and pour into **unbaked pie crust.** Bake at 350 degrees for 30 minutes or until done.

Margaret Lively
Llano County

SOUPS,
SALADS & SAUCES

Soups, Salads and Sauces

Soups

BROCCOLI CHEESE SOUP

2 qts. water
5 chicken bouillon cubes
1 c. celery, chopped
1/2 c. onion, chopped
1 lb. fresh broccoli, chopped
   or 1 lg. bag frozen broccoli

2 c. milk
3/4 lb. Velveeta cheese, cubed
1/2 c. flour (with water)
Salt (if needed)
Dash of pepper, thyme and
   cayenne pepper

Bring water to a boil and add vegetables and cook until tender. Save about 2 cups of this and blend the remainder until smooth. Combine, and then add milk and cheese and heat, stirring often. Thicken with flour and water. Do not boil.

NOTE: You may use 1/2% milk and lite cheese to decrease fat, if desired.

Betty Coffey
Leon County

FRESH BROCCOLI SOUP

3-4 c. fresh broccoli, chopped
1 1/2 c. water
3 chicken flavored bouillon
   cubes
1 10 3/4- oz. cream of chicken
   soup (I sometimes use cream
   of mushroom soup)

1/2 soup can of milk
1/2 soup can of water
3 or 4 flour tortillas, cut
   into strips
Dash of pepper
Cheese for garnish

Combine broccoli, 1 1/2 cups water and bouillon cubes; cook over medium heat until broccoli is tender and the bouillon cubes are dissolved, about 5 minutes. Add soup, milk and remaining water, heat until bubbly, about 3-5 minutes. Reduce to low heat. Add tortilla strips; cook covered 5-7 minutes. Stir, remove from heat and let soup stand covered 5-10 minutes. Ladle into bowls and garnish with cheese. It makes about 4 servings. I usually double the recipe. Lower fat cheese content may be used.

Gayle Odom
Cooke County

A rich relative is described as:
"the kin we love to touch."

HEARTY CHEDDAR CHOWDER

3 c. water
3 chicken bouillon cubes
4 med. potatoes, peeled and
 chunked
1 med. onion, sliced
1 c. carrots, thinly sliced
1/2 c. green peppers, diced

1/3 c. butter or margarine
1/3 c. all-purpose flour
3 1/2 c. milk
4 c. sharp Cheddar cheese,
 shredded
1 2-oz. jar diced pimentos
1/4 tsp. hot sauce (opt.)

Combine water and bouillon cubes in dutch oven; bring to a boil. Add vegetables; cover and simmer for 2 minutes or until vegetables are tender. Melt butter in a heavy saucepan; blend in flour and cook 1 minute. Gradually add milk, cook over medium heat until thickened; stirring constantly. Add cheese, stirring until melted. Stir cheese sauce, pimentos and hot sauce into vegetable mixture. Cook over low heat until thoroughly heated. DO NOT BOIL. Yield: 8-10 servings.

NOTE: To cut down on sodium, lower salt bouillon cubes may be used. To cut fat, use skim milk and Butter Buds.

Gayle Odom
Cooke County

CHICKEN CHOWDER

1 chicken
2 cans cream of chicken soup
1 can cream style corn

1 can whole kernel corn
Salt and pepper to taste

Cover chicken with water in stew pot. Cook until done. Let cool. Take chicken off bone. Mix chicken, soup and corn together. Cook 30 minutes.

Earline Mitchell
Grimes County

CHICKEN CHEESE SOUP

1 c. celery, finely chopped
1/4 c. onion, minced
3 T. margarine
2 c. chicken broth
2 c. milk
1 c. carrot, grated

1 c. cooked chicken, finely
 chopped
1 lb. Velveeta cheese
Cornstarch for thickening
 (if desired)
Salt and pepper to taste

Saute celery and onion about 5 minutes in margarine until soft, but not brown. Remove from heat; add flour and blend thoroughly. Add broth and milk all at once, stirring until creamy. Add carrots and chopped chicken. Cook about 10 minutes. Season to taste with salt and pepper. Serves 6.

Lipscomb County

CHICKEN BARLEY SOUP

1 broiler fryer chicken, cut up (2-3 lbs.)	1 chicken bouillon cube (opt.)
2 qts. water	1 tsp. salt (opt.)
1 1/2 c. carrots, diced	1 bay leaf
1 c. celery, diced	1/2 tsp. poultry seasoning
1/2 c. barley	1/2 tsp. pepper
1/2 c. onion, chopped	1/2 tsp. dried sage

In large kettle, cook chicken in water until tender. Cool broth and skim off fat. Bone the chicken and cut into bite size pieces; return to kettle along with remaining ingredients. Simmer covered for at least 1 hour or until vegetables and barley are tender. Remove bay leaf. Yields: 6 servings - about 1 1/2 quarts. Diabetic Exchange: One serving (prepared without bouillon and salt) equals 2 1/2 lean meat, 1 starch, 1 vegetable; also 259 calories, 127 mg. sodium, 89 mg. cholesterol, 22 gm. carbohydrate, 31 gm. protein, 5 gm. fat

Jackie Hill
Wichita County

HOMEMADE CHICKEN NOODLE SOUP

4 c. chicken stock	1/2 tsp. poultry seasoning
2 c. cooked chicken, diced	1/4 tsp. pepper
1/2 c. celery, sliced	2 c. noodles, uncooked
1/2 c. green onion, sliced	2 T. flour
1/2 tsp. salt	2 c. milk

Add chicken, celery, onion and seasoning to stock. Bring to a boil. Add noodles. Cover and cook until noodles are almost tender, 5-10 minutes. Mix flour with small amount of milk until smooth. Add remaining milk. Stir into soup. Cook to desired thickness. Yield: 6 servings.

Burnelle Knight
Stephens County

If you expect to be gentle,
gracious, lovable, and
appreciated in your old age,
you better start practicing now.

CHICKEN SAUSAGE GUMBO

1-2 1/2 lbs. chicken, cut up
1 lg. onion, chopped
1 med. bell pepper, chopped
1 bunch onion tops, chopped

1 bunch parsley, minced
1 1/2 lbs. pork sausage, cut
 in pieces
Salt, black pepper, red pepper

Roux: 1/2 cup cooking oil and 1 cup flour. Heat oil in a thick iron pot over medium heat. When hot, stir in flour and continue to stir until a deep brown color, about 30 minutes. Be careful; the roux burns quickly once it starts to brown.

Put chicken in large pot with 2 quarts of cold water. Add salt, black pepper and red pepper. Saute large onion and bell pepper in roux until wilted. Add sausage and brown in same pot. Add 1 quart cold water to roux and sausage mixture. Stir and put in gumbo pot with chicken. Cook slowly until chicken is tender. Add onion tops and parsley, cook 15 minutes longer. Bone the chicken before serving. Serve gumbo over rice in individual bowls.

Elsie Belle Lindsay
San Augustine County

CHICKEN AND SAUSAGE GUMBO

6 T. oil
6 T. flour
1 lb. smoked sausage
1 lg. cut up hen
2 gal. water
2 lg. onions
1/4 stalk celery

1/2 bell pepper, chopped
5 green onion tops
Salt
Cayenne pepper
Black pepper
5 sprigs parsley, chopped
2 tsp. gumbo file

Make a fudge looking roux with oil and flour. Boil sausage in separate pot. Combine roux, chopped seasonings, cut up hen, sausage and 1 1/2 gallons of water. Cook 2 hours, adding extra water as needed. During last half hour of cooking, add salt, cayenne and black pepper. As cooking, skim off excess fat. Turn off fire and add 2 teaspoonfuls of gumbo file. Serve over hot rice.

Rita Roeder
Polk County

SAUSAGE, BEAN, VEGETABLE GUMBO

2 14.5-oz. cans no salt tomatoes
2 15-oz. cans no salt pinto beans
1 c. water
1 pkg. taco seasoning

2 16-oz. pkgs. frozen vegetable
 gumbo mixture, defrosted
1 lb. lite Polish sausage, sliced

Combine ingredients in large pot. Simmer 30 minutes. Refrigerate overnight. Reheat.

Gerri Sullivan
Harris County

SHRIMP CHOWDER

1 bunch green onions, chopped
1 stick margarine (1/4 lb.)
2 cans creamy potato soup
1 #2 can whole kernel corn
1 1/2 soup cans of milk
(or water)

8-oz. cream cheese, diced 1/2-in.
2 c. (approx.) frozen shrimp or
may use drained, rinsed
canned shrimp
1/2 tsp. (approx.) cayenne
pepper

Saute chopped onions in margarine; add soup and stir in milk (or water). Add corn and heat. Add creamed cheese and stir until melted. Add shrimp and continue heating until shrimp are done and chowder is hot. Season with cayenne pepper. Serve sprinkled with Pepperidge Farm cheese fish. Doubled recipe serves approximately 20.

Dorothy Brown
Wichita County

SHRIMP SOUP

2 cans cream of shrimp soup
2 cans cream of potato soup
1 c. potatoes, cut small
1 c. whole kernel corn

1 8-oz. pkg. cream cheese
4 soup cans of milk
2 green onions, chopped
1 sm. can shrimp

Mix together, cook on low heat.

Lyons Extension Club

SEAFOOD GUMBO

3/4 c. vegetable oil
1 c. all-purpose flour
2 lg. onions, chopped
4 stalks celery, chopped
1 16-oz. can whole tomatoes,
undrained and chopped
4 cloves garlic, minced
1/2 c. fresh parsley, chopped
1 tsp. dried whole thyme
1 tsp. red pepper
1 bay leaf
4 14 1/2-oz. cans chicken broth

2 lbs. med. shrimp, peeled and
deveined
1 lb. fresh crabmeat
2-3 doz. oysters, shucked
1 lb. fresh crab claws (opt.)
1 1/2 tsp. salt
1/2 tsp. black pepper
Hot cooked rice
Fresh chopped parsley
Chopped green onions
Gumbo file

Heat oil in a large Dutch oven. Add flour and cook over medium heat 10-15 minutes, stirring constantly, until roux is the color of a copper penny. Stir in onions and celery; cook 10 minutes, stirring occasionally. Add next 6 ingredients and cook 10 minutes, stirring occasionally. Add shrimp and crab meat; cover and simmer 15 minutes. Add oysters and crab claws, if desired; cover and simmer 15 minutes. Stir in salt and pepper. Remove bay leaf. Serve gumbo over rice.

Rusk County

CHILI TACO SOUP

2 lbs. ground beef
1 sm. onion, chopped
1 4-oz. can green chilies,
  chopped
1 tsp. salt
1/2 tsp. pepper
3 14 1/2-oz. cans Del Monte
  Mexican Style Stewed Tomatoes

1 15-oz. can jalapeno pinto
  beans
1 15-oz. can white hominy
1 1.25-oz. pkg. taco seasoning
  mix
1 env. Ranch dressing
1 1/2 c. water

Brown beef with onion and chilies in large skillet. Drain fat, if necessary. Place meat in large pot. Add salt, pepper, tomatoes, beans, hominy (do not drain vegetables), dry taco seasoning and dry Ranch dressing. Add water. Bring to boil. Reduce heat and simmer about 30 minutes. Freezes well.

Myrtle Stewart
Nolan County

TACO SOUP

2 lbs. lean ground meat
1 sm. onion, chopped
1 tsp. salt
1 tsp. black pepper
1 1-oz. pkg. Ranch style
  dressing mix
1 1 1/4-oz. pkg. taco seasoning
  mix
3 4-oz. can mild green chilies,
  diced
1 15 or 16-oz. can pinto beans,
  drained and rinsed

1 15 or 16-oz. can kidney
  beans, drained and rinsed
1 15 or 16-oz. can lima beans,
  drained and rinsed
1 14 or 15-oz. can hominy,
  drained and rinsed
3 14 1/2 oz. cans tomatoes,
  diced
1 1/2 c. water
Cheese
Chips

In a large Dutch kettle, brown beef and onion; add salt, pepper, Ranch style dressing mix and taco seasoning mix. Mix well. Add all remaining ingredients, except cheese and chips. Bring to a boil; reduce heat and simmer 30 minutes. When in individual serving bowls, top with cheese and serve with chips. Yields: 10 servings. It's even better the second day. I sometimes add about 2 tablespoonfuls chili powder.

Betti Sheffield
Waller County

If we do what we should,
we will not have time to do what
we should not.

TACO SOUP

2 lbs. hamburger meat
2-3 cans Rotel tomatoes and
  chilies
2 cans pinto beans

1 can white hominy
1 pkg. taco seasoning
1 pkg. Ranch style dressing mix
1 onion, chopped

Saute meat and onion. Add rest of ingredients. Simmer 30 minutes.

Hazel Davis, Comanche County
Barbara Fangmann, Wichita County

TACO SOUP

2 lbs. lean ground beef
1 sm. onion, chopped
1 pkg. Ranch style dressing mix
2 14.5-oz. cans stewed tomatoes
1 15.5-oz. can yellow hominy
1 4-oz. can chopped green
  chilies

1 16-oz. can pinto beans
1 15-oz. can kidney beans
2 c. water
Grated Cheddar or Monterey
  Jack cheese

Brown ground beef and onion in a large skillet until well done. Drain off liquid and stir in the dressing mix. Pour beef mixture into a large stockpot and add the remaining ingredients. Simmer for 30-45 minutes. Serve with grated cheese on top. Good with corn bread, crackers or tortillas. Yield: 6 servings.

Ada Murrah
Bailey County

TACO SOUP

1 1/2 lbs. ground beef
1 onion, chopped
1 qt. tomatoes with juice
1 14 or 15-oz. can kidney or
  pinto beans with juice
1 17-oz. can corn with juice

1 8-oz. can tomato sauce
1 pkg. or 2 T. taco seasoning
1-2 c. water
Salt and pepper to taste
1 c. Cheddar cheese, grated

Brown beef and onions in large heavy pot, drain. Add remaining ingredients, except cheese, simmer for 15 minutes. Ladle into bowls, top with grated cheese. Serve with tortilla or corn chips.

Eva Dillenbeck
Newton County

*It isn't necessary to blow out the other
person's light to let your's shine.*

TEXAS TORTILLA SOUP

1/4 c. oil (may use less)
1 lg. purple onion, chopped
1 fresh jalapeno, seeded and
  chopped (omit for milder
  soup)
4 cloves garlic, minced
2 lg. carrots, diced
6 ribs celery diced
1 lb. raw chicken, diced
4 10 1/2-oz. cans chicken broth

8 corn tortillas, cut in strips and
  fried (or crumble tostito
  chips)
1 tsp. ground cumin
1 tsp. lemon pepper
1 tsp. salt
1 tsp. chili powder (or ground
  red pepper)
1 14-oz. can tomatoes or
  (tomatoes and green chilies)
3 tsp. bottled hot red pepper
  sauce or picante sauce

Garnishes:
1 c. sour cream
3 avocados, diced

1 c. Cheddar or Monterey Jack
  cheese, grated

Heat oil in large kettle. Saute onion, jalapeno, garlic, carrots, celery and chicken. Simmer 5 minutes. Combine cumin, chili powder, salt, hot sauce and flour. Add to the vegetables. Add tomatoes and chicken stock. Simmer 1 hour. Refrigerate overnight. When ready to serve, reheat. To serve, each person adds crumbled tostitos in bottom of bowls. Next add a spoon each of sour cream and avocado. Spoon hot soup over mixture. Top generously with grated cheese. Serve with tortilla chips. This recipe may be tripled for freezing.

Wahnetta Detrixhe
Pecos County

TORTILLA SOUP

2 cloves garlic, crushed
1/4 c. coil
4 corn tortillas (cut in strips)
1 sm. onion, chopped
2 ribs celery, chopped
2 carrots, chopped

1 can chicken broth, plus
  enough water to make 2 c.
1 can tomatoes, broken up
1 tsp. chili powder
1 bay leaf
1 can red kidney beans

Saute garlic in oil until brown; discard. Brown tortilla strips in oil, drain on paper towel; set aside. In food processor, use slicer blade; process and saute onion in same oil until slightly brown. Add to vegetables and simmer uncovered until carrots are tender, about 20 minutes. Add red kidney beans, simmer until heated through. To serve: divide tortillas into 4 bowls, add soup and sprinkle with crushed red pepper, if desired.

Hidaldo County

Anger is a wind which blows out the lamp of the mind.

HILLBILLY BEAN SOUP

2 c. bean mix*
1 T. salt
1 lb. ham, chopped (opt.)
1 clove garlic
1 16-oz. can tomatoes

1 10-oz. can Rotel tomatoes
1 lg. onion, chopped
1 T. lemon juice
1/8 tsp. cayenne pepper
Salt and pepper to taste

Wash beans, cover with water, add salt. Soak overnight. Drain. In 2 quarts of water, add the beans and all other ingredients and cook approximately 4 hours or until done.

*Dry Bean Mixture:

2 T. lentils
2 T. pinto beans
2 T. red kidney beans
2 T. small red beans
2 T. split peas

2 T. black beans
2 T. baby lima beans
2 T. navy beans
2 T. black-eyed peas
2 T. Great Northern beans

Gladys Buchannon
Taylor County

GOLDEN CREAM SOUP

3 c. potatoes, chopped
1 c. water
1/2 c. celery slices
1/4 c. onion, chopped
1 tsp. parsley flakes
1 chicken bouillon cube

1/4 tsp. salt
Dash of pepper
1 1/2 c. milk
2 T. flour
1/2 lb. Velveeta cheese, cubed
1 c. fresh carrots, chopped

In large saucepan, combine potatoes, water, celery, carrots, onion, parsley flakes, bouillon cube and seasonings; mix well. Cover; simmer 15-20 minutes or until vegetables are tender. Gradually add milk to flour, mixing until well blended. Add milk mixture to vegetables; cook until thickened. Add cheese; stir until melted. Yield: 6-8 servings.

Sherry Ward
Comanche County

POTATO SOUP

6 med. potatoes, diced
2 med. onions, diced
1/2 c. celery, chopped
2 qts. water
1/2 tsp. coarse black pepper
Salt to taste

2 T. flour
2 T. butter
1 c. cream
1/2 c. fresh parsley
1/2 tsp. dill seed

Boil potatoes, onions and celery in water until tender. Remove vegetables, reserving broth. Blend in blender; return to broth. Add pepper, salt, flour and butter to cream and stir into soup. Reheat to serving temperature, but do not boil. Makes 6-8 servings. May be frozen.

Beatrice Cartee
Jasper County

POTATO SOUP

6 c. potatoes, cubed
1 c. celery, diced
2 c. water
2 tsp. dried parsley
2 chicken bouillon cubes
1/4 c. flour

1 c. carrots, sliced
1/2 c. onion, chopped
1 tsp. salt
1/2 tsp. black pepper
3 c. milk
3/4 lb. Velveeta cheese

Combine all ingredients, except milk, flour and cheese in a large pot. Bring to a boil and lower heat. Simmer until vegetables are tender. Make a paste of flour and 1/4 cup milk. Add to vegetable mixture and stir. Add remaining milk and cheese. Cook over low heat until thick.

Vicki Wade
Rains County

PUMPKIN SOUP

2 lbs. (approx.) pumpkin or
  banana squash
3 or 4 stalks celery with tops
1 med. onion

2 or 3 med. carrots
1/3 c. instant grits
2 T. oil
Salt to taste

Cut and peel squash, brown in 2 tablespoonfuls oil in large enough soup pot, add enough boiling water to cover. Add celery and tops, chopped onion and sliced carrots. Cook on low heat for 1-1 1/2 hours. About 15 minutes before end of cooking time, add the grits. Stir the soup often; if needed, add more water. Salt to taste.

Phyllis Williams
El Paso County

ZUCCHINI SOUP

3 med. zucchini
1 lg. onion, sliced

4 chicken bouillon cubes
1 c. water

Slice unpeeled zucchini; add to onion and water. Boil 10 minutes. Add bouillon cubes and place in blender. Reheat with equal amount of **milk**. Pour into soup bowls. Garnish with grated Parmesan cheese, if desired.

Myrtle Dutton
Brooks County

There are two kinds of gratitude:
The sudden kind we feel for what we take;
and the larger kind we feel for what we give.

Salads

PASTA SALAD

3 qts. salted water
1 tsp. butter or margarine
12-oz. Curly-Roni (Rotini)
1/2 c. sweet green pepper, minced
1/2 c. carrots, grated
1 sm. jar pimentos, diced
1 c. celery, thinly sliced
1/4 c. onion, minced
3/4 c. Cheddar cheese, cubed small
3/4 c. Ranch style dressing
1/2 tsp. salt
1/4 c. Cheddar cheese, cubed small

Bring salted water and margarine to boil; add rotini and boil uncovered 20-25 minutes. Rinse under cold water and drain well in colander. Mix remaining ingredients, except 1/4 cup cubed Cheddar cheese. Combine pasta and vegetable mixture. Sprinkle with additional Cheddar cheese on top and serve.

Ada Chandler
Ector County

POLYNESIAN SEASHELL PASTA SALAD

1 10-12-oz. pkg. shell pasta
1 sm. can pineapple tidbits, drained
3 Roma tomatoes, seeded and cubed
2 med. carrots, thinly sliced diagonally
1/2 red bell pepper, cubed
1/2 green bell pepper, cubed
3 green onions, thinly sliced
1 2.25-oz. can sliced ripe olives, drained
1/3 c. Kraft Zesty Italian dressing
1/2 tsp. salt
1/4 tsp. white pepper
1/2 tsp. lemon pepper
1/8 tsp. cajun seasoning

Cook shell pasta according to the package directions. Rinse with cold water and drain. In large bowl, stir together all ingredients until well mixed. Cover and refrigerate for 1 hour or longer before serving. Makes 10 cups of salad.

Jean Roy
Wichita County

PRETTY PASTA SALAD

1 pkg. Vegetable Pasta Twists
1 lb. summer sausage, cut into bite size pieces
1 c. mozzarella cheese, cubed
1 cucumber, cut up
1 bunch green onions, cut up
2 c. cherry tomatoes
Italian dressing

Toss in large bowl with Italian dressing (my favorite is Paul Newman's, but low fat is good too).

Nancy Hoedebeck
Cooke County

THREE COLORED SALAD

1 pkg. of 3 colored pasta
1 pkg. pepperoni
1 lb. mozzarella cheese

1 can of black olives
1 bottle Italian dressing

Cook pasta according to package directions. Drain and rinse with cold water. Cut pepperoni into bite size pieces. Grate or cut mozzarella into pieces. Combine all ingredients; toss. Chill in refrigerator 2 hours before serving.

Nancy Philley
Armstrong County

VERMICELLI SPAGHETTI SALAD

1 10-oz. pkg. vermicelli,
  cooked
1 T. Accent
2 T. seasoned salt
3 T. lemon juice
4 T. vegetable oil

1 c. celery, chopped
1/2 c. green pepper, chopped
1/2 c. onion, chopped
1/2 c. black olives, chopped
1 jar pimentos, chopped
1 1/2 c. mayonnaise

Drain cooked spaghetti and rinse well. Break into 1/4-inch pieces. Add Accent, seasoned salt, lemon juice and vegetable oil. Cover and marinate overnight or longer. After spaghetti has marinated, add celery, green pepper, onion, black olives, pimentos and mayonnaise; mix well. This may be made ahead of time. Keeps well.

Winifred Jones
Lubbock County

FRUITED CHICKEN SALAD

4 c. chicken, cooked and
  diced
1 15-oz. can pineapple chunks,
  drained
1 c. celery, chopped
1 11-oz. can mandarin orange
  sections, drained
1/2 c. pitted ripe olives, sliced

1/2 c. green pepper, chopped
2 T. onion, grated
1 c. mayonnaise or salad
  dressing
1 T. prepared mustard
1 5-oz. can chow mein
  noodles
Lettuce leaves

In a large bowl, combine cooked chicken, pineapple, celery, oranges, olives, green pepper and onion. Blend mayonnaise or salad dressing and mustard; toss gently with chicken mixture. Cover and chill several hours. Just before serving, mix in chow mein noodles; turn salad into a lettuce-lined serving bowl. Makes 8 servings.

Take away love and our earth is a tomb.
Robert Browning

CHICKEN PASTA SALAD

1/2 c. Miracle Whip salad
dressing
1/4 c. (1-oz.) Kraft grated
Parmesan cheese
2 T. milk
1/2 tsp. salt
1 1/2 c. chicken, chopped

1 c. (4-oz.) corkscrew noodles,
cooked and drained
1 c. tomato, chopped
1 c. green pepper chunks
1/4 c. onion, coarsely chopped
Lettuce

Combine salad dressing, cheese, milk and salt. Mix well. Add all ingredients, except lettuce. Mix lightly. Chill several hours or overnight. Add additional salad dressing just before serving, if desired. Serve on lettuce-covered platter. Serves 4.

Margarette Jenkins
Quincy

HOT CHICKEN SALAD

2 c. chicken, cooked and
chopped
1 8-oz. or 10 3/4-oz. can
cream of chicken soup
3 tsp. lemon juice
1 c. celery, diced
3 eggs, boiled and chopped

1 tsp. pepper
2 T. onion, chopped
1 c. rice, cooked
3/4 c. mayonnaise
1/3 c. pimentos, chopped
Slivered almonds

Mix all ingredients and pour into a buttered 2-quart casserole dish. Sprinkle with slivered almonds. Bake at 350 degrees for 45 minutes. Serves 10-12.

LaVelle Parsons
Bell County

CHICKEN SALAD

10 lbs. chicken parts
4-oz. slivered almonds
1 can water chestnuts
5 stalks celery

1/2 lb. grapes
36-oz. mayonnaise
1 tsp. lemon juice
2 tsp. water

Cook and dice chicken. Mix water chestnuts, celery and mix all ingredients together in a large bowl. Refrigerate.

Herta Sokolyk
Kerr County

*Mother's write on the hearts of their children
what the world's rough hand cannot erase.*

CHICKEN SALAD
AND/OR CHICKEN SALAD SANDWICHES

3 c. chicken, boiled and cubed
2 eggs, hard boiled and sliced
2/3 c. sweet pickle relish
1 c. celery, chopped

1 tsp. salt
1 tsp. lemon juice
1/2 c. mayonnaise or salad
   dressing

Reserve 4 center slices of eggs for garnish. Chop remaining eggs; mix with other ingredients. Serve on salad greens. Garnish with egg slices and sprinkle with paprika. To make sandwiches: Grind chicken and celery (chopped fine). Chop or mash eggs with a fork. Mix all ingredients and chill. This makes enough sandwich filling for a 1 1/2 loaf of bread.

Ila Robinson
Hidalgo County

HAWAIIAN CHICKEN SALAD

2 c. chicken, cooked and
  chopped
1 c. celery, chopped
1 c. pineapple chunks
1/2 c. coconut
2/3 c. Minute Rice, raw

1 c. mayonnaise
1/2 tsp. salt and pepper
1 tsp. onion
1 T. lemon juice
1/2 tsp. curry powder
1/2 c. toasted almonds

Mix all ingredients. Chill and serve on lettuce leaves.

Juanita Wingo

LUAU CHICKEN SALAD

1 whole chicken + 4 chicken
  breasts
1 15 3/4-oz. can pineapple slices,
  in its own juice and diced
  (drain and reserve juice)
1 c. raisins or grapes
5 stalks celery, diced

1/2 c. coconut
2 c. salad dressing (regular
  or light)
1/4 c. pineapple juice
2 tsp. curry powder
2 tsp. ground ginger

Cook chicken, skin and de-bone. Cool and chop into small pieces. Chop celery and pineapple. Set aside. Mix salad dressing, curry powder, ginger and pineapple juice. If too thick, add more pineapple juice a little at a time. Mix coconut, raisins, celery and pineapple with chicken. Pour dressing over and mix to combine. Chill several hours. Serve on a bed of lettuce. May adjust the curry and ginger to taste.

Lea Cooper
Kent County

Even if I knew that tomorrow
the world would go to pieces,
I would still plant my apple tree.

IRENE HARVEY'S CHICKEN SALAD

1 chicken, cooked and boned
1 c. celery
1/2 c. sweet pickles, chopped
1 c. nuts, chopped
1 c. seedless grapes
3 eggs, hard-boiled
1 sm. can pimentos
3 T. salad dressing
1/2 c. broth
1/2 pt. whipping cream
3 T. vinegar
1 T. sugar
Salt to taste
1 T. onion, finely chopped
2 apples (unpeeled), chopped

Cut chicken into bite-size pieces. Mix vinegar, sugar, salt and broth together. Toss all other ingredients, except whipping cream and salad dressing; add vinegar mixture. Set aside. Whip whipping cream and fold into salad dressing. Fold into salad and refrigerate.

Irene Harvey
Lamar County

CHINESE CHICKEN SALAD

2-3 lbs. boneless chicken
breast
3/4 pkg. Chinese rice sticks
1/3 c. almonds, sliced
1 tsp. sesame seed
3/4 head lettuce, shredded

Boil chicken breast in **water** with a **pinch of ginger** added to it. Break rice sticks into small 2-3-inch pieces. Deep fry in hot oil at 375 degrees. Fry only a handful of rice sticks at a time as they will puff up after only a few seconds. Drain rice sticks on several cookie sheets lined with paper towels. Toast sesame seeds and almonds in oven at 275 degrees for 10 minutes or until light golden brown. Shred lettuce and cut up chicken into bite size pieces. Place the above ingredients in a large bowl. Prepare dressing. Pour dressing over salad and toss lightly.

Dressing:

1/2 c. oil
1 T. salt
1/4 c. sugar
1 tsp. Accent
1/4 tsp. pepper
1/4 c. vinegar

Vennie Dollahan
Midland County

What should not be heard by little ears
should not be spoken by big mouths.

288

TURKEY FRUIT SALAD

1/3 c. plain low-fat yogurt
1 T. honey
1/8 tsp. salt
2 c. turkey or chicken, cooked
  and cubed
1 sm. banana, cut into 1/2-in.
  slices

2 med. oranges
1 T. mayonnaise
1/2 tsp. orange peel, finely
  shredded
1 c. fresh strawberries
1/2 c. celery, sliced
Lettuce leaves

Stir yogurt, mayonnaise, honey, orange peel and salt. Cover and chill. Combine turkey, strawberries, banana and celery and fold in the yogurt mixture, mixing lightly to coat. Cover, chill 2 hours. Peel and section oranges, arrange lettuce and orange sections on plate, mound turkey-fruit in center. Yield: 4 servings - 30 calories and 8 gm. fat per serving.

Opal Gerken
Potter County

HOT TURKEY SALAD

2 c. turkey, cooked and diced
2 c. celery, finely chopped
1/2 sm. onion, thinly sliced
1 6-oz. can water chestnuts,
  drained and sliced
1/2 sm. green pepper, cut in
  short thin strips

2 T. pimentos or stuffed
  olives, chopped
1 c. mayonnaise
2 T. lemon juice
1 c. corn chips, crushed
1 c. sharp Cheddar cheese,
  shredded

Combine turkey, celery, onion, water chestnuts, green pepper, pimentos, mayonnaise and lemon juice in 1 1/2-quart casserole. Cover. Microwave 10-11 minutes on 3/4 power. Add layer of corn chips and cheese and microwave on High power until cheese melts. Yield: 4-6 servings.

Barbara Shaw
Gray County

There is no better exercise
for strengthening the heart than
reaching down and lifting people up.

MACARONI CHEDDAR SALAD

3 c. med. shell macaroni (10-oz.)
1 c. sour cream
1 c. mayonnaise or salad dressing
1/4 c. milk
1/2 c. sweet pickle relish
2 T. vinegar
2 tsp. prepared mustard
3/4 tsp. salt
2 c. Cheddar cheese (8-oz.), cubed
1 c. celery, chopped
1/2 c. green pepper, chopped
1/4 c. onion, chopped

Cook macaroni according to package directions; drain. Rinse with cold water. Drain and set aside. Combine sour cream, mayonnaise and milk; stir in pickle relish, vinegar, mustard and salt. Toss together cooled macaroni, cheese, celery, green pepper and onion. Pour sour cream mixture over all; toss lightly to mix (salad will appear quite moist). Chill several hours or overnight. Makes 12 servings.

Verna Brown
Hansford County

CORN BREAD SALAD

2 pkgs. corn bread mix
8 slices bacon, fried crisp and crumbled
1 med. onion, chopped finely
1 bell pepper, chopped finely
2 lg. fresh tomatoes, chopped
1 1/2 c. mayonnaise
2 eggs, hard-cooked and chopped
Salt and pepper to taste

Prepare corn bread mix as directed on package or use your own recipe. Crumble corn bread. Combine with rest of ingredients. May add 1/2 cup of sweet pickle relish.

Katherine Wedgeworth
Anderson County

Mary Dean from Harrison County uses 1/2 cup baked ham or crisp fried bacon, 1 cup mayonnaise and no hard-cooked eggs.

CRACKER SALAD

1 pkg. Saltine Crackers, crushed (1/4 lb.)
1 sm. jar pimentos, diced
1/2 c. bell pepper, chopped
1/2 c. onions, chopped
5 eggs, boiled
1/2 c. sweet relish
1 c. salad dressing (use more if needed)

Mix all ingredients together and let set in refrigerator for 1 hour.

Mrs. Eunice Lane
Limestone County

CRACKER SALAD

1 tube Saltine Crackers, crushed
1/2 c. onion, chopped
1 c. celery, chopped
3/4 c. sweet pickles, chopped
1 med. bell pepper, chopped

1/2 c. bacon bits
1 2-oz. jar pimentos, chopped
  and drained
4-5 hard-boiled eggs, chopped
1 pt. salad dressing

Mix thoroughly and serve or chill and then serve.

Rhonda Welch
Kent County

GREEN BEAN PICANTE

1 T. margarine
2 sm. onions, sliced
2 cans cut green beans
1/4 c. picante sauce

1/4 tsp. salt
1/4 tsp. pepper
1/4 tsp. lemon juice

In a saucepan, melt margarine. Add onions and saute until tender. Add other ingredients, cover and heat thoroughly.

Anna Marie Kalka
Potter County

POTATO-ENGLISH PEA SALAD

1 16-oz. can whole new canned
  potatoes, drained and sliced
1 17-oz. can drained peas
1/4 c. green onions, chopped
1/4 c. green pepper, chopped
1/4 c. celery, chopped

1/4 c. dill pickle, chopped
2 eggs, boiled and chopped
1 2-oz. jar diced pimentos,
  drained
Salt and pepper to taste
Mayonnaise to your liking

Combine all ingredients. Chill several hours to allow flavors to blend.

Willie Pitts
Kerr County

7-LAYER PEA SALAD

1 head lettuce, torn into small
  pieces
Celery
Bell pepper
Green onion
Frozen peas

Mayonnaise (must use
  mayonnaise)
1 T. sugar
Cheese
Bacon

Layer and let marinate for 2 days (at least 1 1/2 days). Cook decides desired amounts.

Connie Janicek
Austin County

WESTERN SALAD

1 med. head lettuce,
 torn into sm. pieces
2 med. tomatoes, chopped
1/2 onion, cut fine
1/2 lb. Cheddar cheese

1 can Ranch style beans,
 washed and drained
1 pkg. regular size Fritos
1 tsp. salt
1 sm. size bottle Catalina
 dressing

Mix and toss together with dressing. Chill. Serves 8-10.

Elois Retzlaff
Kerr County

VEGETABLE SALAD

3/4 c. vinegar
1 c. sugar
1/2 tsp. pepper
1 can French style green
 beans, drained
1 can whole kernel corn,
 drained

1 can small peas, drained
1 c. celery, chopped
1 2-oz. jar pimentos
1/2 c. salad oil
1 tsp. salt
1 onion, chopped

In a small pan, put in vinegar, sugar, salt, pepper and oil. Bring to a boil.
Put vegetables in a large bowl and mix. Pour hot liquid over the vegetables and
mix. Let salad set in refrigerator overnight.

Alva J. Porter
Navarro County

GREEN VEGETABLE SALAD

1 can English peas, drained
1 can French cut green beans,
 drained
1 can white shoe peg corn,
 drained
1 c. celery, diced

1 c. green pepper, diced
1 sm. can pimentos, diced
1/2 tsp. salt
1/2 c. sugar
1/2 c. vinegar
1/2 c. salad oil

Combine vegetables. Mix together salt, sugar, vinegar and oil. Pour over
vegetable mixture. Chill 5 hours before serving. Will keep several weeks.
(Frozen vegetables could be used instead of canned.)

Mrs. Bernice Randolph
Fisher County

*Only in giving of oneself is enough
taken away to make room for receiving more.*

CHRISTMAS SALAD

1 can French cut green beans, drained
1 can shoe peg corn, drained
1 can small peas
2 stalks celery, chopped fine

1 sm. green pepper, chopped fine
1 lg. red onion, chopped fine
1 T. pimentos, chopped fine

Dressing:
1 c. sugar
1/4 c. oil

1/2 c. white vinegar
Salt and pepper to taste

Mix ingredients together. Boil the dressing and pour over the vegetable mixture. Let stand at least 4 hours. This salad will keep for 2 weeks in the refrigerator.

Almeda Anderson
Denton County

MARINATED VEGETABLE SALAD

1 303-can small LeSeur peas
1 can green beans, cut small
1 rib celery, chopped fine
1 bell pepper, chopped

1 jar pimentos, chopped
1 sm. onion, chopped
1 sm. carrot, grated (opt.)

Sauce:
1/2 c. sugar
1/2 c. white vinegar
1/2 c. vegetable oil

1/2 c. water
1/2 tsp. salt

Mix sauce ingredients; pour over vegetables. Cover and refrigerate overnight. Keeps for several days.

Ruby Allison
Throckmorton County

VEGETABLE SALAD

1 head lettuce
1 c. celery
1 10-oz. pkg. frozen peas
8 slices bacon
4-oz. cheese

4 eggs, hard-boiled
1/2 c. green pepper
1/2 sweet onion
1 tsp. sugar
Mayonnaise

Take lettuce apart in bite size pieces. Chop celery and eggs. Cook peas until done; cool. Then cook bacon crisp. Dice pepper, onion. Place the above ingredients in layers in dish, including grated cheese. Put mayonnaise on top, but don't stir. Let set 8-12 hours in refrigerator before serving.

Irene Humphrey
Falls County

THREE BEAN SALAD

2 cans cut green beans
1 can lima beans
1 can kidney beans
1 onion, chopped fine
1/2 c. oil

1/3-1/2 c. sugar
1/2 c. cider vinegar
1 tsp. seasoning salt
Monosodium glutamate to
    taste

Dressing: Mix together oil, sugar, cider vinegar, seasoning salt and Monosodium glutamate. Pour over beans and refrigerate overnight. Mix 1/2 jar of pimentos, if desired for color.

Ruth Spirek
Kerr County

MISSISSIPPI RICE SALAD

3 c. rice, cooked and cooled
1/2 c. onion, finely chopped
1/2 c. sweet or dill pickles,
  finely chopped
1/2 tsp. salt

1/4 tsp. pepper
1 c. mayonnaise
1 tsp. prepared mustard
1 2-oz. can pimentos, diced
4 eggs, hard-boiled and chopped

Blend all ingredients thoroughly. Chill. Serve on lettuce leaves. Makes 6 generous servings.

Gussie Richardson
Refugio County

POTATO SALAD FOR A CROWD
(Serves 60)

10-12 lbs. potatoes, boiled
  in skins, cooled, peeled
  and diced
2 qts. Miracle Whip
1 sm. carton sour cream
1 c. mustard
1 doz. eggs, boiled and
  chopped fine

1 stalk celery, chopped fine
1 qt. dill pickles, chopped fine
1 qt. sweet pickles, chopped
  fine (can use dill and sweet
  pickle relish)
1/2 c. dry minced onion
Salt and pepper to taste

Mix ingredients well in a large bowl; hand stir - better than a spoon. This is better made 24 hours ahead. Keep refrigerated.

Eager Housewives E. H. Club
Haskell County

You make a living by what you get,
and a life by what you give.

GWEN'S POTATO SALAD

6 med. potatoes, pared, boiled
and sliced
6 eggs, hard-boiled and sliced
1 red onion, sliced and separated
into rings
1 lg. carton cottage cheese

1 pkg. Hidden Valley Ranch
Dressing (dry)
3 tsp. oil
2 c. mayonnaise
Pepper
Lemon juice

Divide into thirds and layer in order above, repeating sequence 3 times. Layers of black olives may be added. Chill thoroughly before serving.

Carolyn Holland
Wilbarger County

POTATO SALAD

1/2 c. plain yogurt
1/2 c. mayonnaise
3 T. cider vinegar
2 T. sugar

1 tsp. salt (or to taste)
1/2 c. green onion
Potatoes

Cook potatoes. Cool and slice. Mix rest of ingredients and pour over potatoes. Let set for 2 hours. Chill.

Pat Bandelman
Travis County

GERMAN POTATO SALAD

1 c. sugar
2 T. flour
2 eggs
1/2 c. cider vinegar
1/2 c. onion, finely chopped

1/4 lb. bacon
3 lbs. potatoes, cooked, sliced
Salt and pepper to taste
2 c. water

In a small bowl, measure sugar and flour together and stir in the eggs. Add the vinegar and onion and let stand. Dice the bacon, fry until crisp. Remove bacon only. Add water to the bacon drippings. Be careful that it doesn't splatter. Let this come to a boil, slowly until it thickens. Add salt and pepper to taste. Pour over the potatoes, add the bacon bits and mix carefully. Should be served warm.

Jean Olsen
Leon County

Discontent makes the rich poor;
contentment makes the poor rich.

MARINATED POTATO SALAD

6-7 med. potatoes (6 c. cubed)   4 boiled eggs, chopped
1 c. mayonnaise   1/2 c. onion, chopped
1 c. French dressing   1/2 c. bell pepper, chopped
2 T. vinegar   1/2 c. sweet pickle, chopped
2 tsp. sugar
Garnish:
2 eggs, boiled   1 bell pepper

Wash potatoes. Cover unpeeled potatoes with water and 1/2 teaspoonful salt. Boil until just fork tender. Remove and cool completely. Stir mayonnaise, French dressing, vinegar and sugar together until smooth; add chopped ingredients. Mix well. Peel cooled potatoes; cut into desired cubes. Pour dressing over potatoes; mix gently. Slice 2 boiled eggs crosswise; slice bell pepper into thin strips. Place on salad in pinwheel fashion. Refrigerate at least 6 hours before serving.

Jan Harrison
Kent County

SWEET POTATO SALAD

3 lbs. sweet potatoes, cooked,   1/2 c. onion, chopped
  peeled and cubed   1 c. bell pepper, chopped
2 c. celery, sliced   1 1/2 c. Miracle Whip
1 1/2 tsp. salt   1/4 tsp. ground black pepper
Few dashes Tabasco

In large bowl, combine all ingredients and mix well. Cover and refrigerate for at least overnight to blend flavors. This is always a big hit when I take it somewhere because it is not only delicious but also unusual.
Tested by: Paula Kemp, Jean Pitcock, Patricia Forrester.

Carolyn Stockton
Wheeler County

LETTUCE AND MANDARIN ORANGE SALAD

1 head leaf lettuce   1/2 c. slivered almonds
1 can mandarian orange slices,   1/2 c. green onion, chopped
  drained
HONEY-MUSTARD SALAD DRESSING
1/2 c. mayonnaise   2 T. mustard
2 T. vinegar   4 T. honey
1/2 c. vegetable oil

Break lettuce into bite-size pieces and add mandarin oranges, slivered almonds and onion; toss. Just before serving, add honey and mustard salad dressing and gently mix.

Faye Howard
Bosque County

MARINATED ORANGE-ONION SALAD

2 c. fresh orange sections
1 sm. purple onion, sliced and
  separated into rings
1/4 c. red wine vinegar
1/4 c. olive oil
2 T. fresh parsley, chopped
8 c. mixed salad greens

Combine orange sections and onion rings in a medium bowl; set aside. Combine vinegar and oil, pour over orange mixture, and sprinkle with parsley. Cover and refrigerate up to 3 hours, tossing occasionally. Place salad greens in a shallow dish; arrange oranges and onions evenly over greens; drizzle dressing over salad. Serve immediately. Yield: 8 servings.

PICKLE SALAD

1 1/2 T. unflavored gelatin
1/4 c. lemon juice
1/4 c. dill pickle juice
1/4 c. pineapple juice
1/4 c. pimento juice
1/4 tsp. salt
1 c. cold water
2 lg. dill pickles
1/2 c. pimentos, chopped
1 c. pecans
1 c. crushed pineapple, drained
1 c. sugar

Dissolve gelatin in cold water. Set aside. Heat sugar, salt and juices together. Add to dissolved gelatin. Place in refrigerator until almost congealed. Then add pickles, pecans, pimentos and pineapple. Pour into ring to mold. Chill. Serve with mayonnaise. Good with barbecued meats and spaghetti.

Helen Blackwell
Ochiltree County

SPINACH SALAD

1 pkg. fresh spinach, broken
  into pieces
Dressing: (enough for 2 salads)
1 med. onion
1 c. salad oil
1/2 c. wine vinegar
5 slices crisp bacon, crumbled
3 eggs, hard-boiled and chopped

3/4 c. sugar
1/3 c. catsup
2 T. Worcestershire sauce

Mix dressing ingredients in blender. Add to salad ingredients just before serving.

McDaniel E. H. Club
Brown County

Counting time is not nearly as important
as making time count.

297

MEDLEY MARINADE

1 1/4 c. fluffy white rice, cooked
1 16-oz. can whole kernel corn,
  drained
1 16-oz. can French style green
  beans, drained
1 16-oz. can small English peas,
  drained
Marinade:
1 c. vinegar
1 c. sugar

1 14-oz. jar diced pimentos,
  drained
1 bunch green onions, chopped
1 carrot, grated
1 green pepper, chopped
1 stalk celery, chopped
1 cucumber, chopped

1/2 c. vegetable oil

Combine all vegetables except cooked rice in large bowl; mix well. Combine marinade in saucepan on stove until sugar is dissolved. Let cool. Pour marinade over vegetables mixing well. Chill 24 hours. Drain and add cooked fluffy rice mixing well. Serve.

Shelley Newsom
Jackson County

SPAGHETTI SQUASH SALAD

1 c. spaghetti squash, cooked and
  cut in shreds
3/4 c. apple, cubed
Dressing:
1/2 c. sugar
1 T. cornstarch

3/4 c. pineapple, drained and
  cubed
1/2 c. coconut

1/3 c. lemon juice
1 egg yolk

In bowl combine squash, apple, pineapple and coconut; set aside. Mix dressing ingredients and cook until it coats spoon. Combine dressing with salad. Chill 2 hours to overnight before serving.

Lela Mae Moore
Coleman County

SPROUT SALAD WITH GARLIC DRESSING

1 sm. head Boston or Romaine
  lettuce
1 c. radishes, sliced
1 med. cucumber, sliced
4 T. white vinegar
1/2 tsp. pepper
1 c. alfalfa sprouts

1 c. bean sprouts
1 c. green onion, sliced
2 T. salad oil
2 tsp. salt
1 to 2 cloves garlic, crushed
  or chopped

Wash and dry lettuce and tear into bite size pieces. Add onions, radishes and cucumber to lettuce; cover and chill. Combine the salad oil, vinegar, salt, pepper and garlic in a jar with a lid. Shake well. Chill. When ready to serve, pour dressing over salad and toss.

Marcillee Goldwater
Harrison County

SAUERKRAUT SALAD

1 qt. sauerkraut, drained
1 c. sugar
1 c. onion, chopped
1 c. green bell pepper, chopped
1 c. red bell pepper, chopped

3 T. olive oil
1/2 tsp. black pepper
1 tsp. caraway seed
1 tsp. ground mustard

Put the sauerkraut in a bowl and sprinkle with sugar. Let set while preparing rest of ingredients. Mix well, cover and refrigerate. Flavor improves with age. Will last up to 1 week.

Dorothy Faas
Wharton County

FROZEN CUCUMBER SALAD

2 qts. cucumbers, peeled and
   thinly sliced
1 lg. onion, sliced thin

2 T. salt
1 1/2 c. sugar
1/2 c. 90 grain vinegar mix

Mix sliced cucumbers, onion and salt. Let stand 2 hours. Rinse and drain. Add sugar and vinegar. Mix and let stand for 20 minutes. Put in plastic bags or juice cartons and freeze. Delicious with meats.

Elsie Prause
Lavaca County

24 HOUR COLESLAW

1 lg. cabbage, chopped
1 sm. jar stuffed olives, sliced
1-2 onions, sliced and separated
   into rings

1 med. bell pepper, sliced into
   rings
1 med. carrot, finely chopped or
   shredded

Dressing:
1 c. sugar
1 c. vinegar
1/2 c. Wesson oil

1 tsp. celery salt
1 1/2 tsp. pepper
1 1/2 tsp. salt

Bring dressing ingredients to boil. Pour over cabbage while hot; stir. Top with pepper and onion rings. Refrigerate several hours.

Barbara Creagor
Loving County

Did you know that a good neighbor
always knocks before she enters,
not after she leaves.

CHOLESTEROL-FREE COLESLAW

1 med. head cabbage, finely
  shredded or chopped
3 med. carrots, finely shredded
Dressing:
1 c. cider vinegar
1 c. sugar
1/2 c. olive oil

1 med. onion, finely chopped
1 tsp. season salt

1 tsp. mustard seed
1 tsp. celery seed

Sprinkle season salt over cabbage, carrots and onion; set aside. Bring dressing ingredients to a boil. While hot, pour over cabbage mixture and let set for 24 hours before serving.

Evelyn Horton
Bowie County

YEAR AROUND CABBAGE SLAW

1 med. cabbage head, shredded
1 med. onion, chopped
1 sweet green pepper,
  chopped (opt.)
1 med. can pimentos, drained

1/2 c. honey
1/2 c. oil
1/4 c. vinegar (or more)
2 T. sugar (or more)
2 tsp. salt

Mix cabbage, onion, green peppers and pimentos; set aside. In a saucepan, combine honey, oil, vinegar, sugar and salt. Boil hard for 1 minute; pour over vegetables mixing well. Pack into a jar with a lid; refrigerate for 3 days. Good until it is used up. *Best of Section - Colorado County Fair.

Mildred Schultz
Colorado County

RUBY'S CABBAGE SLAW

4 c. cabbage, shredded
1 c. fresh mushrooms, diced
  (can substitute drained canned
  mushrooms)
3/4 c. water chestnuts, diced
1/2 c. golden raisins
1 c.mayonnaise

1/4 c. Dijon mustard
1/8 tsp. curry powder
1/4 tsp. lemon pepper
1/4 tsp. black pepper
1/2 tsp. salt
1 T. fresh lemon juice

Place cabbage, mushrooms, water chestnuts and raisins in a large bowl. Mix remaining ingredients and fold into salad. Let stand in refrigerator for a few hours before serving.

Ruby K. Agnew
Travis County

NAPPA CABBAGE SALAD

1 sm. head Nappa cabbage,
  chopped and refrigerated
  overnight
2 pkgs. Ramen noodles

6 oz. almonds, slivered
4 green onions, cut into
  1/2-in. pieces
1/2 c. margarine

Dressing:
1/2 c. sugar
1/4 c. vinegar
1 T. soy sauce

1/4 tsp. salt
1/4 tsp. pepper
1/2 c. oil

Mix dressing ingredients together; set aside. Brown noodles and almonds in margarine in skillet. Just before serving, mix cabbage with noodle mixture and onion. Pour dressing over salad and serve.

Camille Bertinet
Smith County

CAMLACHIE SALAD (Cabbage and Pineapple)

4 c. cabbage, shredded or
  finely chopped
1 can crushed pineapple in light
  syrup, well drained, save juice
1 10-oz. bag small marshmallows

1/2 c. almonds, blanched and
  slivered
1/2 c. maraschino cherries,
  drained, cut in half

Dressing:
Pineapple juice
1 tsp. lemon juice

1 c. Miracle Whip salad
  dressing
1/2 tsp. celery seed

Using the saved pineapple juice, add lemon juice and salad dressing; mix until smooth and creamy. Stir in celery seed. Do not add dressing to salad until shortly before serving.

BLACK-EYE PEA SALAD

1 can black-eye peas
1 rib celery, chopped
1 T. onion, finely chopped
1 T. salad oil
1 T. mayonnaise

1 T. vinegar
1/4 tsp. salt
Dash of cayenne pepper
1 ripe tomato, diced

Drain and rinse black-eye peas with cold water. Drain well. Add remaining ingredients, except tomato. Mix well, stirring gently. Chill well. At serving time, gently stir in tomato. Yield: 4 servings.

Mary Smentek
Austin County

BROCCOLI DELIGHT SALAD

1 lg. broccoli, cut into small
  pieces (4-5 c.)
1 c. golden raisins
Dressing:
3-4 T. sugar
1 T. white vinegar

1/4 red onion, thinly sliced
10 strips crisp bacon, crumbled
1 c. sunflower seeds

1/2 c. lite mayonnaise

    Mix salad ingredients. Make dressing and toss. Chill and serve.

Jennie Kitching
Engedi Parmer, Tom Green County

Phylecia Bailey from Haskell County uses 2 lbs. broccoli flowerettes, 1 pound of bacon, 1 cup mayonnaise, 1/3 cup sugar and 2 tablespoonfuls red wine vinegar.

Norinne Gillespie from Bosque County uses 8 strips of crisp, crumbled bacon, 2 tablespoonfuls vinegar, 2 tablespoonfuls sugar and 3/4 c. lite mayonnaise.

Lipscomb County uses 2 pounds broccoli, 1 medium onion, 1/2 c. raisins, 1 pound bacon, 1/2 cup sunflower seeds, 1 cup mayonnaise and 1/4 cup sugar.

Margaret Beams from Tarrant County uses 8 slices bacon, crumbled, 1 cup salad dressing, 1/4 cup sugar and 1 cup grated Cheddar cheese.

BROCCOLI SALAD

1 head broccoli
1/2 c. red onion, chopped
1/2-1 c. green grapes, halved
Dressing:
1 c. mayonnaise
1/3 c. sugar

12 slices bacon, cooked and
  crumbled
1/2 c. sunflower seeds, roasted

1 T. vinegar

    Cut florets of the broccoli. Toss together with onion and grapes. Cover with dressing. Add bacon and sunflower seeds at serving time.

Virginia Singletary
Cherokee County

BROCCOLI SALAD

2 bunches fresh broccoli
1 sm. onion, minced
1 red tart apple, unpeeled
  and diced
10-12 slices crisp bacon, crumbled

1/2 c. Cheddar cheese, shredded
1/2 c. mayonnaise
1/4 c. sugar
1 T. vinegar

    Wash and drain broccoli. Chop the flowerettes into bite-size pieces into a large salad bowl. Add the onion, apple, bacon and cheese and mix together. Mix the mayonnaise, sugar and vinegar in a 2-cup measuring cup and then pour over the broccoli mixture. Stir to coat. Refrigerate until serving time. It keeps well for several days in the refrigerator. Serves 6-8.

Lavonne Hinkson
Bailey County

BROCCOLI/CAULIFLOWER SALAD
WITH SWEET DRESSING

5 bunches broccoli	1/4 c. orange juice, frozen
5 heads cauliflower	concentrate
5 c. mayonnaise	1/2 c. orange juice,
2 1/2 c. sugar	reconstituted

Chop vegetables to use as much of stem as possible, to small bite size pieces. Add dressing. Yield: 100 servings.

Thelma Wesley
Kaufman County

CAULIFLOWER & BROCCOLI SALAD

1 bunch broccoli	1 sm. bunch green onions
1 head cauliflower	1 green bell pepper

Dressing:

1/2 c. sour cream	1 T. vinegar
1/4 c. French dressing	Dash of Tabasco sauce
1 c. mayonnaise	Dash of Worcestershire sauce
1 T. sugar	

Mix together cauliflower, broccoli, green onions and green pepper (chopped fine). Toss with the dressing. Let stand a few hours. Keeps well all week (covered) in refrigerator.

Helen Hamilton
Guadalupe County

CAULIFLOWER SALAD

2 heads cauliflower	2 ripe tomatoes
2 ripe avocados	1/4 c. ripe olives, chopped
1 8-oz. carton sour cream	Garlic salt to taste

Cut all ingredients fine and mix well. Use garlic salt to taste. This is a pretty and tasty salad.

Etta Lee Gibson
Mitchell County

*Success in marriage is more
than finding the right person;
it's being the right person.*

COPPER CARROT PENNIES

2 lbs. carrots	1 c. sugar
1 sm. green pepper	3/4 c. vinegar
1 med. onion	1 tsp. prepared mustard
1 10 3/4-oz. can tomato soup	1 tsp. Worcestershire sauce
1/2 c. salad oil	Salt and pepper to taste

Slice and boil carrots in salted water until fork tender (should be crisp). When ready, remove from hot water; rinse in ice cold water. Then alternate layers of carrots, peppers and rings of onions cut thin. Cut pepper rings thin also. Make marinade of remaining ingredients, heating until completely blended. Pour mixture over vegetables and refrigerate. Can be prepared several days before using. Keeps in refrigerator for weeks. (Secret in keeping carrots crisp, keep covered in refrigerator.)

Lucille Blassingame
Mitchell County

Pauline Adams from Terry County uses 1 large green pepper, 1 large onion, 1 5 1/2-oz. can tomato juice, 3/4 cup red wine vinegar, 1 teaspoonful salt and 1/4 teaspoonful pepper.

Joann Mandeville, Chairman, Membership/Leadership Committee from Polk County uses 1 large green pepper, 1 cup celery, 1 cup oil, and no Worcestershire sauce.

SHOE PEG CORN SALAD

Vegetable mix:

1 18-oz. can Lesuer English peas, drained	1 2-oz. jar pimentos
1 16-oz. can French style green beans, drained	1 c. bell pepper, chopped
	1 c. celery, chopped
1 8-oz. can white whole kernel corn, drained	1 bunch green onions, chopped

Marinade mix:

1 c. sugar	1 tsp. salt
1/2 c. Mazola oil	1 tsp. black pepper
1/2 c. white vinegar	

Mix together vegetables. Bring marinade mix to boil and let cool. Pour over vegetables; mix and marinate overnight. Serves 10.

Louise Keel
Atascosa County

Inez Lichte from Lamb County uses 1/2 cup chopped green pepper and 3/4 cup oil and does not use green beans.

Without the living bread,
we will die of spiritual malnutrition.

3 PLUS 3

1 c. green pepper, chopped	1 16-oz. can whole kernel corn
1 c. celery, chopped	(or shoe peg corn)
1 c. green onion and tops,	1 16-oz. can sweet peas
chopped	1 sm. jar pimentos

Dressing:

1 c. vinegar	1 tsp. salt
1 c. sugar	1 tsp. pepper
1 c. corn oil	

Boil and cool dressing ingredients. Pour dressing over chopped vegetables and let set at least 2 hours. Keeps well for several days, if it lasts that long.

Argen Draper
Deaf Smith County

FRUITY HAM RICE SALAD

1/4 c. red wine vinegar	1/2 c. carrots, diced
2 T. honey	1/2 c. raisins
1 T. oil	2 c. cooked ham or chicken,
1 tsp. sugar	diced
1/4 tsp. salt	1 c. red or green seedless grapes
1 1/4 c. water	2 T. toasted almonds, chopped
1 1/2 c. Minute Instant Brown Rice	1 T. parsley, chopped

Mix vinegar, honey, oil, sugar and salt in small bowl; set aside. In medium saucepan, bring water, carrots and raisins to boil. Stir in rice. Return to boil, cover, reduce heat and simmer 5 minutes. Remove from heat and stir. Cover and let stand 5 minutes. Stir in remaining ingredients. Pour into serving bowl. Add honey dressing and toss. Refrigerate at least 1 hour before serving.

Judy Johnson
Jackson County

SHRIMP SALAD

1 8-oz. pkg. shell macaroni	4 eggs, hard-boiled
3 cans sm. shrimp	1 c. mayonnaise
4-5 fresh onions	Salt and pepper
1/2 c. sweet relish	

Chop onions and tops and eggs. Clean and rinse shrimp. Cook and cool shell macaroni. Toss all ingredients with mayonnaise, salt and pepper. Cool and serve.

Myrna Allred
Jones County

A man of words and not of deeds
is like a garden full of weeds.

LAYERED MACARONI SHRIMP SALAD

4 c. mixed salad greens, torn
1 7-oz. pkg. or 2 c. elbow
  macaroni, cooked and drained
1 8-oz. pkg. cheese substitute or
  Cheddar cheese, shredded
2 lg. tomatoes, cut into wedges
1 or 2 4 1/2-oz. cans Orleans
  shrimp, drained and soaked
1 10-oz. pkg. frozen green peas,
  thawed
4 c. red/green cabbage,
  shredded
1 1/2 c. mayonnaise or salad
  dressing
1/2 c. bottled Italian salad
  dressing

In large salad bowl, layer greens, macaroni, 1 1/2 c. cheese substitute, tomatoes, shrimp, peas and cabbage. Combine mayonnaise and Italian dressing; pour over salad. Top with remaining cheese substitute. Cover and refrigerate several hours. Toss to serve. Refrigerate leftovers. Yield: 8-10 servings.

Lue Ann Huckaby
Comanche County

TUNA MOUSSE

1 1/2 pkgs. Knox gelatin
1/2 c. cold water
1 can mushroom soup
1 8-oz. pkg. cream cheese
1/2 c. mayonnaise
1/2 tsp. salt
2 tsp. lemon juice
1/4 tsp. prepared mustard
1 c. celery, finely chopped
2 or 3 green onions, minced
  or 2 T. regular onion
1 can solid pack white tuna

Stir gelatin into cold water, dissolve over hot water in double boiler. Heat soup and cream cheese. Remove from heat and add gelatin mixture and remaining ingredients. Pour into lightly olive oil coated mold or muffin tins that have been lined with foil liners. Refrigerate for at least 2 hours, then unmold onto **lettuce leaf.** Do not substitute tuna. Note: Ripe black olives may be sliced into bottom of mold before adding mousse mixture.

Lonnie Moore
Washington County

APRICOT SALAD

1/2 c. sugar
1 3-oz. pkg. apricot gelatin
1 8-oz. pkg. cream cheese
1 20-oz. can pineapple
2 4-oz. jars apricot baby food
1 4-oz. size whipped topping

Bring sugar and pineapple to a boil. Stir in gelatin; cool until partially set. Whip cream cheese and baby food. Fold in cream cheese mixture and whipped topping into gelatin. Top with pecans, if desired. Chill for several hours. Yield: 10-12 servings.

Betty Darby
Gaines County

APRICOT SALAD

1 lg. orange flavored gelatin
3 c. boiling water
2 c. miniature marshmallows
1 20-oz. can crushed pineapple, well drained, reserve juice

1 17-oz. can apricots, diced, well drained, reserve juice
1 egg
1/4 c. flour
1 8-oz. frozen non-dairy whipped topping, thawed

Combine gelatin and boiling water. Add marshmallows. Add crushed pineapple and apricots. Chill until set. For topping: Cook reserved pineapple and apricot juices (about 1 1/2 cups), egg and flour. Cook until thick. Cool and add whipped topping, mix thoroughly. Spread over gelatin mixture.

Dorothy Hutchings
Harris County

FRUIT SALAD

1 can apricots
1 can pineapple chunks
2 bananas

2 apples
1 lg. pkg. vanilla instant pudding mix

Drain apricots and pineapple. Save juice. Cut up bananas and apples. Add pudding whip to fruit juice and mix in fruit. Chill.

Myrtie Sheffield
San Augustine County

CALLIE'S APRICOT SALAD

1 20-oz. can crushed pineapple
1/4 to 1/2 c. sugar
1 6-oz. pkg. apricot gelatin
1 8-oz. pkg. cream cheese (room temperature)

1 c. ice water
1 c. pecans, chopped or canned coconut
1 12-oz. can evaporated milk, chilled and whipped (or 1 12-oz. carton Cool Whip)

Bring pineapple and sugar to a boil. Stir in gelatin and cream cheese and set aside to cool. Add ice water and nuts. Whip evaporated milk and fold into mixture. Pour into a 9 x 13-inch Pyrex dish and chill overnight. Yield: 12 servings.

Jimmie Ryan
Lampasas County

The way we view eternity
will affect the way we live in time.

CHRISTMAS SALAD

3 pkgs. lemon lime and
  strawberry jello
1 8-oz. can crushed pineapple

2 3-oz. pkgs. cream cheese
1 17-oz. can apricot halves

Green layer: Dissolve lime jello in 1 cup boiling water. Add 1/2 cup cold water and pineapple. Refrigerate until firm in 13 x 9-inch serving container.

White layer: Add dry lemon jello and 1 cup boiling water to cream cheese. Add 1 cup cold water and blend. Spoon on green layer and set until firm.

Red layer: Puree apricots in blender; drain juice. Dissolve red jello in 1 cup boiling water. Add apricots. Let cool and spread over white layer.

Gladys Reeves
Blanco County

GRANDMA'S GELATIN FRUIT SALAD

2 c. boiling water, divided
2 c. ice cubes, divided
1 20-oz. can crushed pineapple,
  drained and reserved
1/2 c. Cheddar cheese, finely
  shredded (opt.)

1 3-oz. pkg. lemon-flavored
  gelatin
1 3-oz. pkg. orange-flavored
  gelatin
2 c. miniature marshmallows
3 lg. bananas, sliced

COOKED SALAD DRESSING

1 c. reserved pineapple juice
2 T. cornstarch
1 c. whipped topping
  (I used Dream Whip)

1/2 c. sugar
1 egg, beaten
1 T. butter or margarine

In a mixing bowl, combine 1 cup boiling water and lemon gelatin. Add cup ice cubes, stirring until melted. Add pineapple. Pour into a 13 x 9-inch pan; refrigerate until set. Repeat with orange gelatin, remaining water and ice. Stir in marshmallows. Pour over lemon layer, refrigerate until set. For dressing, combine pineapple juice, sugar, egg, cornstarch and butter in a saucepan. Cook over medium heat, stirring constantly, until thickened. Cover and refrigerate overnight. The next day, arrange banana over gelatin. Combine dressing with whipped topping; spread over bananas. Sprinkle with cheese. Yield: 12-15 servings.

Pat Boydston
Williamson County

A friend is a person who goes
around saying nice things
about you behind your back.

CHERRY NUT SALAD

2 sm. pkgs. cherry jello
1 c. hot water
1 #2 can pitted sour cherries
1 c. sugar

1 #2 can crushed pineapple
1 T. red cake coloring
Juice of 1 lemon
1 c. pecans, chopped

Melt jello with hot water. Cook cherries and sugar 5 minutes. Add melted jello and allow mixture to cool. When completely cool, add remaining ingredients in order listed and refrigerate. Serves 10.

Kathleen Afflerbach
Runnels County

CRANBERRY CREAM CHEESE SALAD

Topping:
1 3-oz. pkg. cream cheese,
  softened

1 c. whipping cream
16 lg. marshmallows, quartered

Whip cream cheese in bowl until creamy using electric mixer at low speed. Gradually add whipping cream (do not whip). Stir in marshmallows. Cover and chill overnight to soften marshmallows.

1 lb. fresh cranberries
1 c. sugar
2 c. boiling water
Red and green candied cherries

1 med. apple, cored and
  quartered
2 3-oz. pkg. cherry jello
1/2 c. pecans, chopped

Grind together apple and cranberries (coarsely). Add sugar and set aside. Dissolve gelatin in boiling water. Chill until thick and syrupy. Fold in cranberry mixture and pecans. Pour into a 9 x 13-inch glass Pyrex dish. Cover and chill until set. Whip topping at high speed until thick. Spread over jello mixture. Cut 8 red cherries in half and place on top for flowers. Add bits of green cherries for "leaves".

Janet Thomas
Eastland County

CRANBERRY SALAD

1 6-oz. pkg. orange gelatin
2 2/3 c. boiling water
2 T. sugar
1/4 c. cranberries, ground

1/2 c. celery, finely chopped
1 c. crushed pineapple
2/3 c. pecans, chopped

Dissolve gelatin in boiling water in large bowl. Stir in sugar, cranberries, celery, pineapple and pecans. Mix well. Pour into an 8-inch square pan. Chill until set. Cut into squares to serve.

Loraine Oakes
Blanco County

309

CRANBERRY SALAD

1 3-oz. box sugar-free lemon
  or orange flavored gelatin
1 3-oz. box sugar-free cherry
  flavored gelatin
2 c. unsweetened apple juice
  or white grape juice, boiling

1 20-oz. can crushed pineapple
  (unsweetened), undrained
2 apples, peeled and diced
1 12-oz. bag fresh or frozen
  cranberries, chopped
1 c. pecans, chopped

Dissolve gelatins in juice. Stir until dissolved. Stir in pineapple. Chill until thickened. Add remaining ingredients. Chill until firm. Yield: 15 servings.

Note: For a sweeter tasting salad, you may want to add artificial sweetener.

Cinda Haisler
Lampasas County

CONGEALED SALAD

1 6-oz. box orange jello
1 10 1/2-oz. can crushed pineapple
2 bananas

2 c. miniature marshmallows
1 pkg. Dream Whip

Dissolve jello in 2 cups hot water. Add 1 1/2 cups cold water. Drain pineapple (reserve juice) and add to jello. Slice bananas over jello. Put marshmallows on top of bananas.

Custard topping:

1 egg
1/2 c. sugar

2 T. flour
Juice from pineapple

Combine and cook until custard is thick. Whip Dream Whip with 1/2 cup cold milk; add 1 teaspoonful vanilla. Combine custard and Dream Whip. Pour over jello mixture and refrigerate.

Mattie Mae Walker
Waller County

CONGEALED SALAD

1 pkg. strawberry banana jello
1 pkg. Dream Whip
1 sm. pkg. cream cheese

1 can fruit cocktail, drained
1 c. small marshmallows
1/2 c. nuts

Dissolve jello in 1 1/2 cups water. Put into an 8 x 8-inch pan and let cool. Cut in small squares when set. Beat Dream Whip and cream cheese together. Add fruit cocktail, marshmallows and nuts. Mix together and refrigerate.

Edith Moore
Hidalgo County

A smile is a light in the window of your face
to show your heart is at home.

310

TASTY CONGEALED SALAD

1 15-oz. can crushed pineapple
1 3-oz. box gelatin, your
  choice of flavor (sugar free)
1 16-oz. carton cottage cheese
1 8-oz. carton Cool Whip

Empty pineapple into saucepan over medium heat. Empty gelatin into pineapple, turn off heat. Mix well. Turn cottage cheese into mixture and blend. Fold Cool Whip lightly into mixture. Do not over mix. Turn into casserole dish and refrigerate. This holds well and is so easy to prepare.

Gladys Meisenheimer
Marion County

ORANGE JELLO

1 6-oz. frozen orange juice
2 3-oz. boxes orange jello
1 sm. can crushed pineapple
1 can mandarin oranges
8 lg. ice cubes or 12 sm.
2 c. boiling water

Add water and jello until well dissolved. Add orange juice and ice cubes. Add well-drained mandarin oranges and crushed pineapple. May add nuts.

Shirley Faukner

JELLO SALAD

1 pkg. lemon jello
1 pkg. orange jello
2 c. hot water
1 1/2 c. cold water
1 can mandarin oranges,
  drained
1 sm. can crushed pineapple,
  drained
About 40 sm. marshmallows

Mix together and put in refrigerator. Let set before putting topping on. Save juice from pineapple and add little of **orange juice** to make 1/2 cup for topping.

Topping:

1 egg, beaten
2 T. flour
2 T. butter
1/2 c. sugar
1/2 c. pineapple juice
1 c. Dream Whip

Cook egg, flour, butter, sugar and pineapple juice until thick; cool. Add Dream Whip which has been whipped and cooled. Spread onto jello mixture; top with grated cheese.

Clarice Miller
Lamb County

All of the really valuable things you own
are things you can't photograph.

DIABETIC JELLO

1 lb. pkg. unsweetened lime jello
2 c. buttermilk
1 sm. can crushed pineapple
1 c. dairy whip

Open pineapple and put into small pan. Pour the jello mixture into the pineapple and bring to a boil. Remove from heat and let cool. Add buttermilk and dairy whip. Place into flat container and allow to set in refrigerator.

Madison County

GRAPE JELLO

1 3-oz. box grape jello
1 c. boiling water
1 15-oz. can pitted black bing
cherries, drained and chopped
1 15-oz. can crushed pineapple
1 3-oz. pkg. cream cheese
1/2 c. pecans, chopped

Dissolve the jello in boiling water. Add softened cream cheese and beat mixture until smooth. Add rest of ingredients and congeal.

Clara Slutz
Oldham County

STRAWBERRY SALAD

2 3-oz. pkgs. strawberry jello
2 10-oz. pkgs. frozen strawberries
1 13 1/2-oz. can crushed pineapple
2 ripe bananas, diced
1 c. sour cream

Dissolve jello in 2 cups boiling water. Thaw strawberries in the jello and add pineapple and bananas. Pour half of the mixture into a dish and gel. Spread sour cream over gelled mixture. Pour the remaining jello over the sour cream. Chill until firm.

Kay Center
Llano County

STRAWBERRY PRETZEL SALAD

2 sm. pkgs. strawberry jello
2 c. boiling water
2 sm. pkgs. frozen strawberries
2 1/2 c. pretzels, crushed
3/4 c. butter, melted
3 T. powdered sugar
1 8-oz. pkg. cream cheese
1 egg
1 c. powdered sugar
1 9-oz. carton Cool Whip

Mix jello, boiling water and strawberries; refrigerate until thick. Mix together pretzels, melted butter and 3 tablespoonfuls powdered sugar; press into a 9 x 13-inch pan. Bake 10 minutes at 350 degrees. Beat cream cheese with egg and 1 cup powdered sugar. Fold in Cool Whip. Spread over pretzel crust. Top with jello mixture. Sprinkle on extra crushed pretzels. Refrigerate.

Trixie Gimnich
Anderson County

312

STRAWBERRY PRETZEL SALAD

2 c. pretzels, crushed
2 T. sugar
1 1/2 sticks margarine, melted
1 8-oz. pkg. cream cheese,
  softened
1 c. sugar

1 8-oz. carton Cool Whip
2 lg. pkgs. strawberry jello
2 c. boiling water
2 10-oz. pkgs. frozen
  strawberries with juice

Combine pretzels, 2 tablespoonfuls sugar and margarine. Pat into a large oblong pan. Bake 8 minutes at 400 degrees. Cool completely. Combine cream cheese and 1 cup sugar. Mix well. Fold in Cool Whip. Spread on cooled pretzel crust. Cool. Dissolve jello in boiling water. Add strawberries. Mix well. When jello begins to thicken, pour over cream cheese layer. Refrigerate until set. Cut into squares to serve.

Sue Maxey
Garza County

Belle Wilde from Willary County uses 3/4 cup margarine and add 1 8-oz. can crushed pineapple with juice.

TOMATO SOUP SALAD

1 sm. lemon jello
3/4 c. boiling water
2 T. lemon juice
1 3-oz. pkg. cream cheese
1 c. mayonnaise

1 can tomato soup
2 T. green pepper
1 c. celery, chopped fine
1 T. onion, grated
Green olives and nuts

Dissolve jello in water. Add lemon juice. When this begins to set, add blended cream cheese and mayonnaise. Add remaining ingredients. Pour into mold and chill. Serves 8-10.

Judy Young
Sabine County

LITE COOL COUNTRY SALAD

1 pt. low fat cottage cheese
1 sm. pkg. sugar free orange jello
1 sm. can crushed pineapple
  packed in juice, drained

1 can mandarin orange slices,
  drained and rinsed twice
1 pt. Cool Whip

Sprinkle jello over cottage cheese and mix well. Add drained pineapple and orange slices and mix well. Fold in Cool Whip. Chill and serve. (Ingredients with sugar and higher fat may also be used.)

Faye Payton
Garza County

No door is too difficult for the key of love to open.

BUTTERMILK SALAD

1 6-oz. pkg. jello
1 15 1/2-oz. crushed pineapple
  or any #2 can of fruit

2 c. buttermilk
1 8-oz. carton Cool Whip
1/2 c. pecans (opt.)

Mix jello and pineapple or fruit; bring to a slight boil. Let cool and add rest of ingredients. Pour into a 9 1/2 x 13-inch pan or equal size mold and chill.

Frances Orton
Dallas County

WHEAT SALAD

1 1/2 c. wheat
1 8-oz. pkg. cream cheese,
  softened
2 lg. pkgs. vanilla instant
  pudding mix

1 15 1/2-oz. can crushed
  pineapple, undrained
1/4 c. nuts, chopped
3 T. lemon juice
1 9-oz. carton frozen whipped
  topping

Clean and wash wheat, soak overnight. Cook 1 hour or until desired crunchiness; drain well. Mix together cream cheese and pudding mix. Add pineapple, nuts, lemon juice and frozen whipped topping. Mix everything together and chill in refrigerator overnight. This makes a large bowl of salad.

Nell Hill
Nolan County

FROZEN BANANA SALAD

5 bananas, mashed
4 T. lemon juice
1 1/2 c. sugar

1 lg. can crushed pineapple,
  drained
1 8-oz. carton sour cream
1 9-oz. carton Cool Whip

Mix and freeze. Decorate with pecan halves and cherry halves or both, if desired.

Thelma Grigsby
Montague County

FROZEN SALAD

5 bananas mashed
1 c. sugar
1 c. buttermilk

1 c. pecans, chopped
1 12-oz. carton whipped topping
Cherries, if desired

Mix together bananas, sugar and buttermilk until well blended. Add pecans; fold in whipped topping. Pour into a 9 x 13-inch dish. Top with cherries, if desired. Cover and freeze. When ready to serve, cut into squares and serve on **lettuce leaf**. Serves 12.

Faye Wilson
San Patricio/Aransas County

CHRISTMAS HOLIDAY FRUIT SALAD

1 15 1/2-oz. can pineapple
  chunks, juice drained and
  reserved
1/2 c. sugar
1 T. all-purpose flour
1 egg, beaten
1 c. pecans, chopped

3 bananas, sliced
2 11-oz. cans mandarin oranges,
  drained
3 med. apples, unpeeled and
  chopped
1/2 lb. red seedless grapes,
  halved

In a small saucepan, combine pineapple juice, sugar, flour and egg. Cook over low heat, stirring constantly until smooth and thickened. Cool. Combine pecans and fruit, add dressing and stir well. Chill before serving. Yield: 10-12 servings.

Bea Crunk
Concho County

FROZEN FRUIT SALAD

1 #2 1/2 can fruit cocktail
1 tsp. unflavored gelatin
2 T. lemon juice
1 3-oz. pkg. cream cheese
1/4 c. mayonnaise

1/16 tsp. salt
2/3 c. whipping cream, chilled
1/2 c. sugar
1/2 c. nuts, chopped

Drain fruit cocktail. Soak gelatin in lemon juice, then dissolve over hot water. Blend cream cheese, mayonnaise and salt. Stir in gelatin. Whip cream until stiff, adding sugar gradually during last stages of beating. Fold in cheese mixture, nuts and fruit cocktail. Pour into a pan lined with wax paper. Freeze until firm. Turn out onto platter, remove paper, cut into thick slices. Garnish with watercress. Serves 8.

Eunice Walker
Montgomery County

PINEAPPLE AND ORANGE SALAD

1 c. sour cream or light
  sour cream
1 sm. can crushed pineapple,
  drained
1 sm. can mandarin orange slices,
  drained

1 c. miniature marshmallows
1 c. coconut, grated
10-12 maraschino cherries,
  chopped

Mix all ingredients in a mixing bowl. Refrigerate overnight for best results. Serves 6-8.

Maurice Browning
Bailey County

Alma Foster from Jones County does not use maraschino cherries in her recipe.

315

ORANGE SALAD

Crust:
60 Ritz crackers, crushed
1 stick butter, melted

1/4 c. sugar

Filling:
1 can Eagle Brand milk
1 6-oz. can frozen orange juice,
   thawed
2 sm. cans mandarin oranges,
   drained

1 sm. can crushed pineapple,
   drained
1 12-oz. Cool Whip

Pack crust into 13 x 9-inch pan. Stir filling gently, do not whip. Pour over crust. Sprinkle crushed Ritz crackers over top when finished.

Marjorie Knowles
Tarrant County

AUNT OMA'S CHAMPAGNE SALAD

1 8-oz. pkg. Philadelphia
   Cream Cheese
3/4 c. sugar
1 lg. can crushed pineapple,
   drained

2 ripe bananas, diced
1/2 c. pecans, chopped
1 10-oz. pkg. frozen
   strawberries
1 14-oz. carton Cool Whip

Cream the cheese and sugar. Add other ingredients except Cool Whip. Fold in Cool Whip at last and freeze. Remove from freezer 30 minutes before serving. Keeps in freezer for weeks.

Gerry Daugherty
Grayson County

BLUEBERRY SALAD

2 3-oz. pkgs. grape jello
1 1/2 c. hot water
1 20-oz. can crushed pineapple
   and juice

1 21-oz. can blueberry pie
   filling (I use lite)

Topping:
1 8-oz. pkg. cream cheese
1 8-oz. carton sour cream
1/2 c. sugar

1 tsp. vanilla
1/2 c. nuts, chopped

Mix the first 4 ingredients and chill until set. Mix topping ingredients together and spread over chilled mixture.

Marjorie Koenig
Victoria County

Doris Snodgrass from Floyd County uses 2 cups hot water and does not use nuts in topping mixture.

LIGHT AND LIVELY SALAD

1 can sweetened condensed milk
1 lg. carton Cool Whip
1 can cherry or apricot pie filling
1 c. coconut

1 c. pineapple tidbits
1 c. miniature marshmallows
1/2 c. pecans
1/2 c. maraschino cherries

Combine first 6 ingredients; put in serving bowl and chill. Garnish with pecans and cherries. Serves 12.

Ann Henderson

CHERRY PIE SALAD

1 21-oz. can cherry pie filling
1 13-oz. carton non-dairy
  whipped topping
1 15-oz. can pineapple chunks,
  drained

1 can condensed milk
Pecans, chopped

Mix pie filling and whipped topping together. Fold in drained pineapple chunks, condensed milk and pecans. Mix well. Chill overnight before serving.

Belinda Woodall
Howard County

JELLO SALAD

1 lg. pkg. cherry jello
1 can cherry pie filling
1 15 1/2-oz. can crushed
  pineapple, drained

2 cartons Cool Whip
1 c. pecans, chopped
4 or 5 bananas, sliced

Mix jello by package directions. Add sliced bananas (they will float), and refrigerate. Chop cherry pie filling. When jello mixture is set, mix other ingredients and spoon over jello. Return to refrigerator until ready to serve. Any fruit or jello may be used.

Inez Clevenger
McCulloch County

FRUIT SALAD

1 lg. can fruit cocktail, drained
1 can pineapple, drained
1 can Comstock apricot pie filling
  Mix all ingredients and chill.

6 bananas
1/2 c. sugar

Madge Wright
Baylor County

Wear a smile and have friends.
Wear a frown and have wrinkles.

FESTIVE FRUIT SALAD

1 21-oz. can peach pie filling
1 11-oz. can mandarin oranges
1 20-oz. can chunk pineapple

2 10-oz. pkgs. frozen
   strawberries
3 bananas

Drain juice from pineapple and oranges. Mix all ingredients. Chill. In this salad, the bananas do not darken.

Toni Jones
Yoakum County

Sauces

MAC'S DRESSING

2 c. salad dressing (Miracle
  Whip)
1 c. thick buttermilk
1/4 c. catsup
1/4 c. sugar
1/2 tsp. salt

1 tsp. paprika
2 T. wine vinegar
1/2 tsp. garlic powder
  (or more to taste) or
1 garlic bud, mashed

Mix all ingredients together. Chill.

Maxine Hoff
Stephens County

BLACK OLIVE SALSA

1 4 1/4-oz. can ripe olives,
  chopped
1 4-oz. can green chilies,
  chopped (mild or hot)

3 Roma tomatoes, chopped
6 sm. green onions with
  tops, chopped
4 T. Italian dressing

Mix all ingredients and chill at least 1 hour. Serve with tortilla chips of your choice. Use spoon.

Lois Brauner
Fayette County

Face powder may catch a man,
but it takes baking powder to hold him.

318

HOT SAUCE

3 lg. onions	2 tsp. dry mustard
3 c. celery	1 tsp. paprika
2 c. bell pepper, diced	1/2 tsp. basil
2 #2 cans peeled tomatoes	1/2 tsp. oregano
1 lg. can V8 juice	2 bay leaves, crushed
1 c. vinegar	4 lg. cloves of garlic
1/4 c. sugar	4 doz. jalapeno peppers,
1 1/2 tsp. salt	ground

Put all ingredients into a large enamel or teflon pan and bring to a full boil, then lower heat and simmer for 1 hour. Put into sterilized jars and seal.

Jane Holubec
McCulloch County

"PEACHES" SPAGHETTI SAUCE

1 lb. ground beef	1 sm. onion, chopped
1 6-oz. can tomato paste	1/2 tsp. oregano
1 8-oz. can tomato sauce	1/2 tsp. basil powder
2 c. hot water	Garlic salt to taste
2 T. beef bouillon powder	
or 6 cubes	

Brown hamburger, drain in strainer and add tomato paste. Add remaining ingredients and cook all together. Let come to a slow simmer. Do not cook further. Use over spaghetti.

Rena Kirk
Eastland County

BUTTERSCOTCH ALMOND SAUCE

1/2 c. butter	2 tsp. lemon juice
2 c. light brown sugar	2 T. blanched, toasted almonds,
1/2 c. whipping cream	chopped

Melt butter in double boiler over simmering water. Add sugar and heat, stirring until sugar has absorbed the butter. Add cream and carefully stir in lemon juice. Cook over simmering water for 1/2-3/4 hour, stirring frequently. Add chopped almonds. Serve hot over ice cream. Makes about 2 cups of sauce.

Dorothy Hesse
Cooke County

I do not go alone through the
hours of this day,
for Thou art with me.

VEGETABLES

Vegetables

AGAPITA'S PINTO BEANS

2 lbs. pinto beans	1 T. salt
4 slices bacon, cooked crisp	3 T. bacon drippings
1 sm. onion, diced	2 tsp. season-all salt
1 lg. bell pepper	1 10-oz. can Rotel
3 lg. green jalapeno peppers, chopped	tomatoes (can use diced tomatoes and
3 ribs celery, sliced very thin	chilies)

Rinse beans with cold water 2 or 3 times. Put in large pot; add 10 cups hot water and cover. Add all ingredients, except salt and season-all salt. Cook on high until water boils, then simmer on low heat for 3 hours. Add salt and season-all salt during the last 30 minutes of cooking. Beans are good to eat with barbecue meat, barbecue chicken and rice and sausage. Enjoy!

Agapita Sauceda Perez
Brooks County

CALICO BEANS

1 lb. ground beef	1 #2 little white navies
6 slices bacon	1/4 c. barbecue sauce
1 med. onion	1/4 c. catsup
1 #2 can pinto beans	1/3 c. brown sugar
1 #2 can pork and beans	2 T. Granmas molasses
1 #2 can ranch style beans	1 T. mustard
1 #2 can butter beans	1 T. chili powder

Cook ground beef and onion until meat is grey and onion is clear; drain fat. Fry bacon until crisp; drain. Break into bite size pieces and add to beef. Add beans and other ingredients; mix well. Bake covered for 1 hour at 350 degrees.

Sybil Woodward
Throckmorton County

The best thing parents can do
for their children
is to love each other.

CALICO BEANS

1/2 lb. bacon, cut into 1-in.
  pieces
1 lb. lean ground meat
1 red onion, chopped
1/2 c. catsup
1/2 tsp. prepared mustard
2 T. vinegar
1/2 tsp. salt
1/4 c. brown sugar

1 16-oz. can pork and beans,
  undrained
1 16-oz. can kidney beans,
  drained
1 16-oz. can lima beans,
  drained
2 16-oz. can barbecue beans,
  undrained

Cook bacon in skillet until crisp; drain keeping 2 tablespoonfuls of grease in skillet. Add ground beef to skillet and cook until brown; remove and add onions and cook until tender. Combine all ingredients in a crock pot and cook on slow for 3-4 hours.

Nadine Weatherford
Smith County

GREEN BEAN BEARNAISE

1 T. butter or margarine
1 sm. clove garlic, minced
1 tsp. salt
Pepper to taste
1/2 c. fully cooked ham,
  finely diced

1 med. tomato, cut into wedges
1 lb. French cut fresh green
  beans or 9-oz. frozen green
  beans or 1 lb. can green beans

Cook green beans according to directions; drain water off. Melt butter or margarine in saucepan. Add ham and garlic; cook until garlic is softened. Stir in beans, salt and pepper. Sprinkle tomatoes on top. Heat until tomatoes are cooked. Serves 4.

Evelyn Miller
Dallas County

GREEN BEAN CASSEROLE

1 can French cut green beans
1 can mushroom soup

1 can casserole onions
8-oz. Cheddar Cheese, grated

Layer half of the green beans, mushroom soup, casserole onions and cheese; then repeat the same layering process, top layer being cheese. Cook in microwave oven 8-9 minutes. Bake in oven 20-25 minutes at 350 degrees.

Barbara Huse
Bosque County

A smile is a language understood by all persons.

GREEN BEAN CASSEROLE

1 qt. green beans, cooked and
drained
1 8-oz. pkg. cream cheese
1 can cream of mushroom soup

1 med. onion, sliced thin
1 stick margarine
1 c. Ritz cracker crumbs

Cook and drain green beans if using fresh. Otherwise drain canned beans. Combine softened cream cheese and mushroom soup. Stir into beans. Saute onions in margarine until transparent. Remove onions from margarine and stir onions into green bean mixture. Pour into oblong baking dish. Bake at 350 degrees for 30 minutes. Meanwhile, stir cracker crumbs into reserved margarine. Sprinkle on green bean mixture last 5 minutes of baking. Let stand briefly before serving. Yield: 6-8 servings.

Lillie Mae Bailey
Gregg County

BROCCOLI CASSEROLE

1 8-oz. pkg. broccoli, cooked
1 1/2 c. rice, cooked
1/2 stick margarine
1/2 c. celery, chopped

1/2 c. onion, chopped
1 can cream of mushroom soup
1 can cream of chicken soup
1 c. Cheddar cheese, grated

Cook and drain broccoli. Combine with rice. Melt margarine in skillet; add celery and saute. After celery has cooked 5 minutes, add onion and cook until tender. Combine cooked vegetables, broccoli and rice with soups and cheese. Pour into a 1 3/4-quart casserole. Bake in preheated oven at 350 degrees for 15 minutes. Makes 6-8 servings.

Lydia Menchaca
Tom Green County

Wanda Floyd from Fisher County uses 1 cup rice and 1 small jar Cheez Whiz. **Evelyn Shifflett** from Scurry County uses 1/3 c. chopped celery, 3 cups cooked rice, 3 tablespoonfuls butter, 1 medium jar Cheez Whiz and 1/2 cup milk. She uses only cream of mushroom soup.
Octavia Sherman from Falls County uses 1 cup Minute Rice, 1 can cream of celery soup, and 1 small jar of Cheez Whiz.

RICE SUPREME

1 stick butter
1/2 onion
1/4 c. green pepper
1 can mushrooms
1 tsp. chili powder

1 c. long grain rice
1 can beef consume
1 can water
Salt to taste

Melt butter. Dice onion and green pepper. Combine all ingredients and bring to a boil. Simmer for 30 minutes.

Mrs. Velma Ransom
Limestone County

MEXICAN RICE

1 c. uncooked rice
1 med. onion, chopped
2 T. shortening
1 green pepper, chopped

1/2 tsp. salt
2 tsp. chili powder
1 c. tomatoes
1 c. boiling water

Brown rice and onions in hot fat. Add green peppers, salt, chili powder, tomatoes and water. Mix well. Cover; bring to a boil. Reduce heat to simmer and cook 30 minutes. Serves 6-8. *Best of Section - Colorado County Fair.

Evelyn Barrett
Colorado County

CHEESE CARROTS

1 8-oz. pkg. cream cheese
3-4 T. chives, chopped
1/2 tsp. salt
1/4 tsp. garlic salt
1/2 tsp. Worcestershire sauce

1/4 tsp. cayenne
1 c. carrots, grated
1/2 lb. Cheddar cheese, grated
Parsley sprigs

Mix and form into 2-inch "carrots". Chill. Put small sprig of parsley into top of each and serve.

CARROT CASSEROLE

3 c. sliced carrots, cooked
1 10 1/2-oz. can cream of
  celery soup

1 c. Cheddar cheese, grated
1 T. butter, melted
1/4 c. dry bread crumbs

Preheat oven to 350 degrees. Mix carrots, soup and cheese in baking dish. Mix bread crumbs and butter. Sprinkle on top of carrot mixture. Bake about 20 minutes or until bread crumbs brown.

Marie Arrott
Coke County

CELERY & CARROTS ALMONDINE

1/3 c. almonds, sliced
2 T. butter
2 c. carrots, diagonally thin
  sliced
2 c. celery, diagonally thin
  sliced

1 chicken bouillon cube,
  crumbled
1 tsp. Accent
1/2 tsp. sugar
1/8 tsp. garlic pod
1/2 tsp. ginger
1 tsp. cornstarch

Saute almonds in butter. Add remaining ingredients. Stir until mixed. Cover and cook 10 minutes or until celery and carrots are tender and crisp. Mix 1 teaspoonful cornstarch with 2 tablespoonfuls water; stir into vegetables to glaze.

Lucille Lutkenhaus
Cooke County

CORN CASSEROLE

1 20-oz. pkg. frozen corn,
    thawed
1 tomato, chopped
1/2 c. milk
1 green pepper, chopped

2 eggs
2 T. sugar
1 T. butter or margarine
2 T. bacon bits
Salt and pepper to taste

    Mix all ingredients, except eggs and milk, in oblong baking dish. Beat eggs and milk and pour over ingredients in dish. Stir and dot with butter. Sprinkle with **paprika** and decorate with **green pepper rings.** Bake at 350 degrees for 30-45 minutes or until set and golden. Serves 6.

Mrs. Jerry Matus
Lavaca County

CORN CASSEROLE

2 11-oz. cans Green Giant
    Mexican Corn
1/2 c. Wesson oil
3/4 c. Mexican cornmeal
3/4 tsp. garlic salt

1/4 tsp. baking powder
2 eggs
1 c. Cheddar cheese, grated
1/2 c. sugar

    Mix all ingredients in a large bowl. Spray 2-quart casserole dish with Pam. Pour in mixture. Bake at 350 degrees for 30 minutes. Reduce heat to 300 degrees and bake 30 minutes more.

Jean Van Vliet
Wichita County

MEXICAN CORN CASSEROLE

1 lb. ground meat
1 onion, chopped
Salt and pepper to taste
3 jalapeno peppers, chopped
1/2 lb. Cheddar cheese, grated

1 c. cornmeal
1 tsp. soda
1 tsp. salt
1 egg
1 c. milk
1 can cream corn

    Saute meat, onions, salt, pepper and jalapeno until completely cooked. Drain well. Make batter with cornmeal, milk, soda, salt, corn and egg. Pour half of batter into greased, preheated 3-quart baking dish which has been sprinkled with cornmeal. Arrange meat in a layer, then sprinkle cheese over meat. Cover with remaining batter. Bake at 350 degrees for 55 minutes.

Askey E. H. Club
Caldwell County

Love never asks how much must I do,
but how much can I do?

BAKED CORN WITH A ZING!

2 c. cream style corn
1/2 c. oil
2 eggs, well beaten
1/2 c. cornmeal
1/2 tsp. garlic powder
3/4 tsp. salt

1 c. Cheddar cheese, grated
1-2 jalapeno peppers, chopped
1/2 med. onion, chopped and sauted

Saute onion in microwave with part of oil. Mix all ingredients together and pour into Pam sprayed casserole dish, about 1 3/4-quart. Bake for 45 minutes at 350 degrees. Reheats and freezes well. Feeds 4 but may be doubled or tripled with same results.

Betty Dismuke
Wilson County

ITALIAN CORN

1 16-oz. can cream style corn
1 16-oz. can whole kernel corn
1 c. margarine, diced
1/4 c. green pepper, diced (opt.)

1 c. dry macaroni
1 c. cheese, diced
1/2 c. onion, diced

Mix all ingredients together and bake in a 350 degree oven for 1 hour. Stir occasionally.

Lipscomb County

CORN PUDDING

4 T. butter or margarine, divided
3 T. all-purpose flour
1 1/2 c. milk
3 egg yolks, lightly beaten
2 oz. chopped pimentos, drained
1 2/3 c. cracker crumbs, divided

1 green pepper, chopped
1 med. onion, chopped
1 tsp. salt
Dash of pepper
2 c. fresh or frozen corn kernels

In a skillet, melt 3 tablespoonfuls butter or margarine over medium heat. Saute pepper and onion until tender. Add flour, salt and pepper; stir until well blended. Gradually add milk; cook and stir until thickened. Slowly blend in egg yolks. Remove from heat; fold in corn, pimentos and 1 cup crumbs. Pour into a greased 1 1/2-quart casserole. Melt remaining butter or margarine and toss with remaining crumbs; sprinkle on top of casserole. Bake, uncovered, at 350 degrees for 30-40 minutes. Yield: 6 servings.

Viola Smith
Bell County

Patience is the ability to put up with
people you'd like to put down.

CREAMY CHEESE CORN CASSEROLE

2 16-oz. cans white corn, drained
1 can green chilies, chopped and drained
1 med. onion, chopped
1 lb. processed cheese food, melted
1/4 c. butter, melted

Combine all ingredients and pour into greased casserole dish. Cook for 30 minutes at 325 degrees.

Pam Redman
Yoakum County

CORN PUDDING

1/2 c. oleo
1/2 c. onion, chopped
1/2 c. green pepper, chopped
2 T. pimentos
2 eggs
1 #2 can cream corn
1/2 c. bread crumbs
1/2 tsp. salt
1/2 tsp. pepper
1/2 c. milk

Mix all ingredients together. Bake at 350 degrees for 1 hour.

Juanita Norton
Hockley County

CORN CASSEROLE

1 lg. pkg. frozen whole kernel corn, defrosted
4 eggs, beaten
1/4 c. sugar
3/4 c. milk
1/4 c. margarine
Salt and pepper to taste
1 c. cracker crumbs

Mix together eggs, sugar, milk and salt and pepper to taste. Mix with corn and top with margarine (cut into pieces). Bake 45 minutes at 350 degrees. Remove from oven and top with cracker crumbs. Brown crumbs for 10 minutes.

Billie Smith
Milam County

CORN CASSEROLE

2 #2 cans cream corn
2 eggs
1 8-oz. carton sour cream
1 pkg. Jiffy corn muffin mix
1 stick margarine, melted

Melt margarine in 9 x 13-inch pan in 350 degree oven. Mix all other ingredients and pour over melted margarine. Bake 45 minutes to 1 hour.

Sylvia Knight
Henderson County

Daily prayers lessen daily cares.

328

BAKED CORN CASSEROLE

4 eggs	2 12-oz. or 16-oz. can cream
1/2 c. oil	style corn
1 8-oz. pkg. shredded Cheddar	1 pkg. Mexican corn bread mix
cheese	

Beat eggs. Add oil and beat well. Stir in corn, corn bread mix and cheese. Mix well. Bake in a greased 13 x 9-inch baking dish at 400 degrees for 30 minutes or until lightly browned.

Dorothy Coker
Grayson County

CORN CASSEROLE

1 16-oz. can cream style corn	1/2 tsp. salt
2 eggs, beaten	1 tsp. sugar
1 c. milk	1 c. onion, chopped
1 c. crackers, crushed	1/4 c. sweet pepper
1/2 tsp. black pepper	

Combine all ingredients in a medium mixing bowl. Put into a buttered 2-quart baking dish. Dot with **butter.** Bake at 400 degrees for 45 minutes. Serves 6-8.

Annie Bell Cloe
Terry County

CORN CASSEROLE

1 can whole kernel corn,	1 can cream style corn
undrained	1 c. sour cream
1 stick butter, melted	2 eggs, beaten
1 8 1/2-oz. box Jiffy corn	
bread mix	

Mix together all ingredients. Pour into a 9 x 13-inch baking pan and bake 1 hour at 350 degrees or until lightly brown on top.

Helen Thompson
Hays County

CORN CASSEROLE

1 med. onion	Dash of black pepper
1 stick margarine	1/2 green sweet pepper,
2 cans cream style corn	chopped
2 c. Minute Rice	1/4 lb. cheese
1/8 tsp. salt	

Saute onion in margarine. Mix with cream style corn, rice, salt and pepper. Chop 1/4 of green pepper into mixture. Pour into buttered casserole dish. Cover with cheese and 1/4 of green pepper. Bake in covered dish at 350 degrees for 30 minutes.

Myrtle Langley
Vanzandt County

BAKED CORN

2 cans cream style corn
3 T. sugar
3 T. flour
1/4 tsp. salt
1/4 tsp. red pepper
1/4 tsp. black pepper

4 eggs, well beaten
1 lg. onion, chopped
1 green pepper, chopped
2 T. pimentos
1/2 stick margarine, melted

Mix flour, sugar, salt, red pepper and black pepper. Add to corn. Stir in beaten eggs, onion, green pepper, pimentos and margarine. Pour into greased baking dish. Bake 45 minutes in a 350 degree oven.

June Brooks
Llano County

WATER CHESTNUT CASSEROLE

1 16-oz. can mixed vegetables, drained
1 can water chestnuts, sliced and drained
1 c. mayonnaise

1 c. processed cheese, grated
1 can white cream style corn, undrained
1 c. onion, chopped (or onion salt to taste)

Mix together. Top with crushed butter flavored crackers. Bake 20-30 minutes at 350 degrees.

Vera Hardy
Ochiltree County

JALAPENO-CORN CASSEROLE

1 c. regular rice, uncooked
1 med. onion, chopped
1 med. green pepper, chopped
1 c. celery, chopped
1/2 c. butter or margarine, melted
1 T. sugar
1/2 jalapeno pepper, finely chopped

2 17-oz. cans cream style corn
1 c. (4-oz.) mild Cheddar cheese, shredded
Green pepper rings (opt.)
Cherry tomato halves (opt.)
Parsley sprigs (opt.)

Cook rice according to package directions; set aside. Saute onion, green pepper and celery in butter until vegetables are tender. Combine rice, sauted vegetables and next 4 ingredients, stirring well. Spoon mixture into a lightly greased 12 x 8 x 2-inch baking dish. Bake at 350 degrees for 40-45 minutes. Garnish with green pepper rings, cherry tomatoes and parsley, if desired. Yield: 10 servings.

Grace Glaze, Director
District 11, Wharton County

HOMINY CASSEROLE

1 c. bell pepper, chopped
1 c. onion, chopped
2 cloves garlic, chopped
1/2 tsp. hot red pepper sauce

1/2 stick margarine (4 T.)
2 cans yellow hominy, drained
1 can cream of mushroom soup
1 sm. jar Cheez Whiz

Saute bell pepper, onion, garlic, red pepper sauce in margarine. Heat hominy, mushroom soup and Cheez Whiz. Combine the 2 mixtures. Pour into a 1 1/2-2-quart baking dish. Top with **1 cup corn flakes**. Bake at 350 degrees until bubbly.

Gretchen Stiles
Cooke County

HOMINY CASSEROLE

2 #2 cans hominy
1 T. butter
1 4-oz. can green chilies

1 c. sour cream
Salt and pepper to taste
Cheese

Boil hominy, butter, chilies and salt and pepper until water is almost gone. Add sour cream. Put into casserole dish and sprinkle with cheese. Bake in moderate oven until cheese is melted.

Shirley Huse and Audra Morgan
Wheeler County

CHEESE HOMINY CASSEROLE

1 stick margarine
1 lg. onion, chopped and
  sauteed in butter
1 can mushroom soup
1 sm. jar jalapeno peppers

Cheez Whiz
1/2 c. milk
1 c. corn chips, crushed
2 cans golden hominy,
  well drained

Mix all ingredients together and bake at 350 degrees for 20 minutes.

Myrtle Wright
Menard County

BAKED HOMINY AND GREEN CHILIES

1 30-oz. can hominy
1 4-oz. can chopped green
  chilies
1 8-oz. carton sour cream

1/2 tsp. garlic salt
1 T. butter
3/4 c. cheese, grated

Season hominy with butter and garlic salt. Bring to a boil; simmer 30 minutes. Drain hominy and mix with sour cream and chilies. Place in a 1 1/2-quart baking dish and cover with grated cheese. Bake at 350 degrees until cheese is melted.

Ava Gay Dill
Terry County

GREEK HOMINY

1/4 c. butter
3 T. Cheez Whiz
1 tsp. Worcestershire sauce
1 2-oz. jar pimentos, rinsed
  and drained
Greek seasoning to taste
  (start with 1 1/2 tsp.)

1/4 c. butter, melted
1/4 c. flour
1 c. milk
1 15-oz. can white hominy,
  drained
1 15-oz. can yellow hominy,
  drained

Combine 1/4 cup butter, Cheez Whiz, Worcestershire sauce, pimentos and seasoning. Cook over low heat until melted. Blend melted butter and flour in small pan. Stir in milk; cook until thick. Combine cheese sauce, white sauce and hominy in a 1 1/2-quart casserole. Bake at 350 degrees for 20 minutes.

Joyce Pool
Kaufman County

HOMINY CASSEROLE

2 #2 cans hominy
1 c. celery, chopped
1 can cream of mushroom soup
Sprinkle of black pepper

1 T. butter or margarine
1 c. onion, chopped
4 slices American cheese

Pour hominy and soup into a large enough baking dish. Spread chopped onions and celery on top of hominy. Sprinkle black pepper over hominy. Cover this mixture with cheese squares. Bake 45 minutes in 350 degree oven. Yield: 8 servings.

Marie Scott
Palo Pinto County

HOMINY

1 can hominy, drained
1/2 can Rotel tomatoes
1 c. cheese, grated
Salt and pepper to taste

1/2 c. green pepper, chopped
2 green onions, chopped
Garlic powder to taste

Mix all ingredients and simmer until hot, bubbly and cheese is melted. (Also can use Italian tomatoes and bake it...Good!)

Hamilton County

Be sure you are right,
then go ahead,
and be sure you are wrong
before you quit.

HOMINY CASSEROLE

1 16-oz. can hominy, drained
1 can cream of chicken soup
1 c. Velveeta cheese
1 sm. onion, chopped

1 bell pepper, chopped
1/2 c. celery, chopped (opt.)
1 5-oz. can chuck hominy,
broken up

Combine soup and cheese in bowl and microwave to melt cheese. Saute onion, pepper and celery. Combine all above ingredients and pour into a 1-quart baking dish and top with **1 cup crushed potato chips**. Bake at 350 degrees for 20 minutes or until golden brown and bubbly.

Lelda Thompson
Titus County

LAYERED CABBAGE CASSEROLE

1 med. head cabbage
1/4 c. butter or margarine
1/4 c. flour
1/2 tsp. salt
1/4 tsp. pepper
2 c. evaporated milk

1/4 c. green pepper, chopped
1/4 c. sweet red pepper,
chopped
1/4 c. onion, chopped
2/3 c. Cheddar cheese, shredded
1/2 c. mayonnaise
3 T. salsa

Cut cabbage into small wedges; cook in boiling salted water until tender; drain. Place wedges in a 13 x 9 x 2-inch baking dish; set aside. Melt butter in a small saucepan; stir in flour, salt and pepper. Gradually stir in milk; cook over medium heat until thickened, stirring constantly. Pour sauce over cabbage wedges. Bake at 350 degrees for 20 minutes. Combine remaining ingredients, mixing well. Spoon over cabbage. Return to oven and bake for 20 minutes. Serves 8.

Helen McIntyre
Howard County

CABBAGE CASSEROLE

1 med. firm head cabbage
1/4 c. flour
Dash of pepper
1 1/2 c. Cheddar cheese, grated

1 stick margarine
1 tsp. salt
2 c. milk

Slice cabbage. Cook in boiling salted water about 8 minutes or until tender; drain. Melt margarine and blend in flour, salt and pepper. Add milk; cook, stirring constantly until smooth and thickened. Add 1/2 of grated cheese and stir until melted. Pour half of cabbage in buttered casserole. Pour 1 cup or half of cheese sauce over cabbage. Sprinkle half of cheese over sauce; add remaining cabbage, then cheese sauce and grated cheese. Sprinkle paprika lightly over top for color, if desired. Bake 15-20 minutes at 350 degrees or until sauce is thick and bubbly. Serves 8-10. (This is great and never any left.)

Ozell Holt, Director
District 9, Polk County

SCALLOPED CABBAGE

1 med. head cabbage   1 1/2 c. milk
3 eggs, well beaten   1 T. butter
1 1/2 packs crackers   Salt and pepper

Cut cabbage into small pieces and boil until tender. Beat eggs well and pour over milk soaked crackers. Mix thoroughly with cabbage. Season with butter, salt and pepper. Pour into baking dish and bake until brown at 350 degrees for about 30 minutes.

Sherri Jennings
Live Oak County

CABBAGE AND GREEN BEANS

3 or 4 slices bacon   2 cans cut green beans,
1 med. onion   undrained
                           Small head of cabbage

In large skillet, fry bacon until crisp; set aside. Saute onion in bacon grease until clear. Add green beans (including liquid). Quarter and core cabbage; add to skillet. Cook over medium-low heat until cabbage is done and most of liquid has cooked away. Crumble bacon on top and serve.

Martha Crawford, State 2nd Vice President
Runnels County

CORN PUDDING

2 lg. eggs   3/4 c. corn muffin mix
1 17-oz. can whole kernel corn,   1/2 c. margarine
   drained   Black pepper to taste
1/2 c. evaporated milk   Paprika

Beat eggs in bowl. Add all corn, milk and muffin mix, folding in these ingredients. Melt margarine in an oblong baking dish. Pour in corn mixture. Sprinkle black pepper and paprika on top. Bake at 350 degrees for 35-45 minutes or until done.

Catherine S. Jackson
Sabine County

*Little things can often be the
biggest things in someone's day.*

CORN PUDDING

1 1/4 c. fine cracker crumbs	2 c. fresh raw corn (2 or 3 ears)
1/2 c. butter or margarine, melted	1/2 tsp. salt
	1/2 tsp. onion salt (opt.)
2 T. butter or margarine	2 T. flour
1 1/4 c. milk	2 eggs, beaten

Combine crumbs and melted butter. Save 1/2 cup for topping. Line a 9-inch pie pan with remaining crumbs. Combine butter or margarine, 1 cup milk, raw corn and salt. Bring to a boil. Reduce heat and cook 3 minutes. Add flour to 1/4 cup milk. Mix to a smooth paste. Add slowly to hot milk-corn mixture, stirring constantly. Cook 2-3 minutes or until thick. Cool slightly. Add onion salt, if desired. Add eggs slowly, stirring constantly. Pour into crumb-lined pan. Top with remaining crumbs. Bake at 400 degrees for 20 minutes. Serves 6.

Rusk County

CORN PUDDING

1 lg. can creamed corn	3 tsp. sugar
1/2 stick margarine, melted	2 eggs, beaten
3 tsp. flour	1/2 c. milk

Mix all ingredients. Place in greased casserole dish. Bake at 375 degrees for 30 minutes.

Nacogdoches County

BAKED ASPARAGUS

1 1/2 lbs. fresh asparagus, thin stalks	3 cloves garlic, thinly minced
2 T. fresh parsley, finely chopped (opt.)	4 T. extra virgin olive oil
	Salt and freshly ground black pepper

Preheat oven to 400 degrees. Break off tough ends of asparagus. Place in baking tray so the stalks do not overlap. Add the oil, herbs and spices. Bake uncovered just until tender, 5-8 minutes. Serve hot.

Betty Clifford

One who uses the Bible as his guide
never loses his sense of direction.

ASPARAGUS CASSEROLE

1 can chopped asparagus, drained
1 stick margarine, melted
1 can English peas, drained

1 can cream of mushroom soup
1 c. water chestnuts, chopped
1 c. Cheddar cheese, grated
4-5 slices white bread

Contains 5 layers.

1st layer: Spread asparagus over surface of a buttered 9 x 13-inch casserole dish.

2nd layer: Cover asparagus with English peas.

3rd layer: Spread mushroom soup over peas.

4th layer: Distribute water chestnuts over soup.

5th layer: Cover with heavy layer of grated cheese.

Trim bread slices and cut into 1-inch strips. Dip strips into melted margarine and place on top of cheese layer. Bake in 325 degree oven until bread is crisp but not brown, about 20 minutes. Yield: 12 servings.

DeLois Duncan
Palo Pinto County

ASPARAGUS CASSEROLE

1 can water chestnuts
12-oz. canned fried onion rings
2 16-oz. cans asparagus

1 can cream of mushroom soup, low sodium
1/4 lb. processed cheese
1/2 c. evaporated milk

Layer 1/2 of water chestnuts, onion rings and asparagus in a 13 x 9-inch casserole dish. Melt cream of mushroom soup, processed cheese and evaporated milk over low heat; pour half over ingredients in casserole dish. Repeat layering. Microwave on Medium to heat through.

Phyllis McMakin
Smith County

GOLDEN EGGPLANT CASSEROLE

2 1/2 c. eggplant, peeled and cubed
18 saltine crackers, crumbled
1/2 c. sharp cheese, shredded
1/4 c. celery, chopped

2 T. margarine, melted
1 T. pimentos, chopped
1/2 tsp. salt
Dash of pepper
1 sm. can evaporated milk

Cook eggplant in boiling salted water for 10 minutes; drain. Combine with remaining ingredients. Bake in 350 degree oven for 45 minutes. Makes 6 servings.

Shelby County

Life is fragile; handle with prayer.

ITALIAN EGGPLANT

1 med. eggplant
3 T. butter or margarine
1/4 c. onion, chopped
1 clove garlic, minced
1 c. mushrooms, sliced
2 8-oz. cans tomato sauce

1/2 tsp. basil
1/2 tsp. oregano
3 T. butter or margarine
4 slices mozzarella cheese
Grated Parmesan cheese

Pare eggplant and cut into 1/2-inch slices. Sprinkle with salt and let stand 30 minutes. Rinse in cold water and pat dry with paper towels. Melt 3 tablespoonfuls butter in skillet; add onion, garlic and mushrooms and cook until onion is tender. Stir in tomato sauce, basil and oregano. Cook 10 minutes, stirring occasionally. Saute eggplant in remainder of butter. In greased 1-quart casserole, alternate layers of eggplant, tomato sauce and mozzarella cheese, ending with tomato sauce. Sprinkle liberally with grated Parmesan cheese. Bake in a moderate 275 degree oven for 20 minutes. Makes 4-6 servings.

Madison County

BAKED EGGPLANT

2 med. eggplants
2 eggs
1/4 c. butter or margarine
1/4 c. onion, finely cut
1 garlic, slivered

1 c. fine cracker crumbs
1/2 c. milk
1 tsp. salt
1/8 tsp. pepper
1 c. mild American cheese, grated

Peel and cube eggplant. Cook over low heat in small amount of water until tender. Add butter and seasonings. Beat eggs with milk. Stir into eggplant mixture. Pour mixture into casserole. Cover with grated cheese. Bake 15 minutes at 300 degrees.

Dorothy Lamont
Collin County

TEXAS FUDGE

1 lb. Monterey Jack cheese
1 lb. Cheddar cheese

6 eggs
2 cans whole (mild) green chilies

Grate both cheeses keeping separate. Spread either one on bottom of a 9 x 12-inch glass baking dish. Remove seeds from chilies and slice thinly. Arrange chilies so they cover top of cheese. Sprinkle second cheese on top. Beat eggs and pour over cheese. Bake at 325-350 degrees for 20-25 minutes or until slightly golden brown. Let cool 10 minutes. Cut into 1 x 1-inch pieces. Serve warm or cool.

Loretta Nail
Montague County

ORIENTAL RICE

3 c. long grain rice, cooked
3/4 lb. fresh mushrooms,
  rinsed, pat dried and sliced
  or 2 cans (6-8-oz.), sliced
  and drained
1/4 c. salad oil (for frying
  vegetables)
2 c. celery, sliced
2 lg. green peppers, sliced
2 lg. onions, sliced
1 sm. can water chestnuts,
  sliced
1 c. beef broth
1 sm. garlic clove, mashed
1/2 c. soy sauce (light)
1 T. honey or sugar
1 T. dry cooking sherry
1 tsp. white pepper
1 1-lb. pkg. frozen shrimp
  or 1 sm. can (opt.)

Cook rice and set aside 3 cups. Saute celery, green peppers, onions and water chestnuts for about 4 minutes. Add mashed garlic clove and continue to saute about 3 more minutes or until onions are pale gold. In a large pot, combine broth (1/2 cup to start with); add soy sauce, sugar or honey and sherry. Bring to a boil. If using fresh shrimp and mushrooms, add to sauce now and simmer until shrimp turn pink. Otherwise, just add canned shrimp and mushrooms and simmer a few more minutes. Thicken the sauce with 1 tablespoonful cornstarch and 1 tablespoonful water. Blend the cooked rice first into sauce, then the vegetables. More broth may be needed to blend well. Can be served immediately or baked in a 300 degree oven for about 20 minutes for flavor to set. The sauce may also be used separately to serve over the rice and vegetables instead of blending.

Madison County

TROPICAL GLAZED SWEET POTATOES

4 lg. sweet potatoes
1 8 1/2-oz. can crushed
  pineapple, undrained
1/4 c. brown sugar, firmly
  packed
1 1/2 T. cornstarch
1/4 tsp. salt
1/8 tsp. ground cinnamon
2 T. butter or margarine,
  softened
1 c. canned apricots,
  undrained and pureed
1/2 c. pecans, chopped

Cook sweet potatoes in boiling water 20-25 minutes or until tender. Let cool. Peel and cut into 1/2-inch slices. Arrange slices to overlap in a lightly greased 12 x 8 x 2-inch baking dish. Set aside. Drain pineapple, reserving 1/3 cup. Combine pineapple juice, sugar, cornstarch, salt, cinnamon and apricot puree in heavy saucepan. Cook, stirring constantly until smooth and thickened. Add butter, pecans and pineapple. Pour over potatoes and bake 20-25 minutes at 350 degrees. Yield: 8 servings.

Vivian Curtis
Floyd County

SWEET POTATO CRUNCH

3 c. sweet potatoes, cooked
   and mashed
1/2 c. sugar
1/2 tsp. salt

1/2 stick butter
2 eggs
1/2 c. sweet milk
2 tsp. vanilla

   Mix and place in baking dish.

Topping:

1 c. brown sugar
1/2 stick margarine, melted

1/3 c. flour
1 c. pecans, chopped

   Mix and spread over potato mixture. Bake 30 minutes at 200 degrees.

Inez Ogletree
Lamb County

SWEET POTATO CARROT TOSS

2 med. sweet potatoes, peeled
   and grated (2 1/2 c.)
2 med. carrots, peeled and
   grated (1 1/2 c.)
1 lg. apple, unpeeled and
   grated (1 c.)
1/4 c. prunes, chopped
1 tsp. lemon juice
2 T. margarine

1/2 tsp. cinnamon
3 T. apple juice concentrate
1 c. toasted whole wheat
   bread crumbs
2 T. golden raisins
1 T. brown sugar
1 tsp. lemon peel
1/2 tsp. salt

   Use food processor with grater blade for grating potatoes, carrots and apple. Combine with lemon juice and stir fry in margarine 5-7 minutes in large skillet until crisp. Add remaining ingredients, except crumbs, and simmer about 10 minutes. Place in casserole dish and top with crumbs. Bake at 375 degrees for 10 minutes or until heated.

Peggy Lockley
Parker County

YUMMY SOUTHERN SWEET POTATOES

2 16-oz. cans yams, drained
   or 3-4 fresh yams cooked
   and drained
1 c. sugar
2 eggs, slightly beaten
1/2 tsp. salt

1/2 c. flour
8 T. margarine
1/2 c. milk
1 tsp. vanilla
1 c. brown sugar
1 c. pecans, chopped

   Mash yams, then add milk, eggs, vanilla, salt and pour into greased 9 x 13-inch casserole. Mix brown sugar, flour and 4 tablespoonfuls margarine and crumble on top of potatoes. Sprinkle with pecans. Pour the other 4 tablespoonfuls melted margarine on top. Bake 30 minutes at 400 degrees. Yield: 6 servings.

Dorothy Sirney
Bell County

SWEET POTATO APPLE CASSEROLE

3 lbs. sweet potatoes, peeled
4 med. apples
3 c. marshmallows
1 c. white corn syrup

3/4 c. sweet potato water
1 tsp. salt
1 tsp. cinnamon
2 tsp. cornstarch

Precook the sweet potatoes with 1 cup of water. Save the water after cooking. Mix the corn syrup, salt, cinnamon and cornstarch with the water. Layer the sweet potatoes, apples, marshmallows in a large casserole. Save 1 1/2 cups marshmallows for the top during the last 15 minutes of baking. Pour the corn syrup mixture over the sweet potatoes. Bake 1 hour. After the first 30 minutes of baking time, uncover casserole. Then bake uncovered and during last 15 minutes, add marshmallows. Leave casserole in oven after turning off heat for 20 more minutes until set.

Ella Zmolek
Dallas County

SWEET POTATO CASSEROLE CRUNCH

1 1/2 c. sweet potatoes, mashed
  or 1 29-oz. can yams, drained
1 stick margarine, melted
2 eggs
Topping:
1 c. self-rising flour
3/4 c. sugar
1 stick margarine, melted

1 tsp. vanilla
1 c. sugar
1 c. coconut

1 c. pecans, chopped
2 T. water

Mix mashed sweet potatoes, margarine, eggs, milk, vanilla, sugar and coconut together. Pour into a buttered 2 1/2-quart casserole dish. Mix topping ingredients and sprinkle on top of sweet potatoes. Bake at 350 degrees for 45 minutes.

Margaret Dwin
Jefferson County

Help me to live from day to day,
in such a self-forgetting way
that even when I kneel to pray,
my prayer may be for others.

SWEET POTATO CASSEROLE

3 c. sweet potatoes, mashed	1/3 c. milk
1 c. sugar	1 c. light brown sugar
1/2 c. butter	1 c. flour
2 eggs, beaten	1 c. nuts, chopped
1 tsp. vanilla	

Mix all ingredients, except brown sugar, flour and nuts and put in baking dish. Mix brown sugar, flour and nuts; sprinkle on top of potato mixture. Bake in a 350 degree oven for 25 minutes.

Madison County

Alma Smith from Dallas County uses 1/4 cup butter or margarine, 1/4 cup milk and 3/4 c. coconut. For topping: 1/2 stick or 4 tablespoonfuls butter or margarine and no flour.

Bitsy Martin from Yoakum County uses 3 medium sweet potatoes, 1/2 cup brown sugar, 1 1/3 teaspoonfuls vanilla, 1/2 cup milk and 1/2 teaspoonful salt. For topping: 1/2 cup brown sugar, 1 cup pecans, 1/2 cup flour and 3 tablespoonfuls margarine.

Mary Youngblood from Young County uses 1 lg. can sweet potatoes and 1 stick melted margarine. For topping: 1/3 c. flour and 1/3 cup margarine.

Vee Gordon from Garza County uses 2 cups mashed sweet potatoes and 1/2 cup milk. For topping: 1/2 cup firmly packed brown sugar, 1/4 cup flour, 2 1/2 teaspoonfuls melted margarine and 1/2 cup chopped pecans.

Evelyn Petree from Taylor County uses 3 1/2 cups cooked sweet potatoes, no eggs, 1/2 cup milk, 1/2 teaspoonful vanilla and 1/2 teaspoonful salt. For topping: 1/3 cup flour, 1/3 cup margarine and 1/2 cup chopped pecans.

SWEET POTATO CASSEROLE

1/2 c. brown sugar, divided	1 tsp. salt
2/3 c. orange juice, divided	1/4 tsp. cloves
1/3 c. margarine, melted and divided	1 tsp. cinnamon
	1 c. pecans, chopped
2 1-lb. cans sweet potatoes, drained	Peeled orange slices
	Marshmallows
2 eggs	

Combine 1/4 cup brown sugar, 2 teaspoonfuls orange juice and 2 teaspoonfuls margarine. Mix and set aside to use for glaze topping. Whip potatoes until smooth; beat in eggs. Add remaining sugar, orange juice and margarine. Add salt, cloves and cinnamon. Mix well and pour into a 1 1/2-quart greased casserole dish. Sprinkle pecans on top. Pour glaze topping over pecans. Bake at 350 degrees for 40 minutes. Top with orange slices and marshmallows. Place under broiler until marshmallows are delicately browned. Yield: 6 servings.

Joyce Cabe, Chairman of Health/Safety
Terry County

OLD FASHIONED SWEET TOMATOES

1 qt. home canned tomatoes
  or fresh cooked
1 1/4 c. sugar

2 T. flour (rounded)
1/4 c. water
1/4 tsp. cinnamon

Heat tomatoes and 1 cup sugar until boiling. Add flour to water and stir smooth. Add flour mixture to tomatoes and cook 5 minutes at low heat. Pour into dish, sprinkle with remaining 1/4 cup sugar and cinnamon. Let cool and serve.

Evelyn Fuchs
Washington County

NOPALITOS

2 c. nopalitos (tender baby
  prickly pears)
1 T. cooking oil
1 sm. clove garlic, mashed
2 eggs

1/2 c. salt pork, diced
1/4 c. onion, diced
1 tsp. chili powder
1/2 tsp. cumin powder
Salt and pepper to taste

Remove prickly pear thorns, rinse thoroughly. Dice. Cook diced prickly pears in 4 cups boiling water for 15 minutes. Rinse. *Drain. Grind garlic and spices and add a little water; set aside. Brown salt pork in oil; add chili powder, stirring constantly (do not scorch!). Add spices and diced prickly pears. Simmer 5-10 minutes. Add salt and pepper. Add eggs and fold into mixture until cooked. May be served with flour or corn tortillas. *If canned prickly pear is used, begin recipe at *.

Belia Barrera
Victoria County

OKRA CASSEROLE

1/4 c. oil
1/2 c. onion, chopped
2 c. okra, cut up
1 15-oz. can tomatoes or
  tomato sauce

Water
Grated cheese (opt.)
1/2 c. raw rice
Salt and pepper
Garlic

Cook okra and onion in oil about 10 minutes or until onion wilts. Spread in baking dish. Pour tomato sauce over the top. Sprinkle on raw rice and seasonings. Cover with water; top with cheese. Bake at 325 degrees for 45 minutes.

Madison County

*Prayers should be the key of the day
and the lock of the night.*

POTATO CASSEROLE

2 lbs. frozen hash brown
  potatoes
1 can cream of chicken soup
2 c. sour cream
1/2 c. onion, chopped
1 c. margarine, melted and
  divided

2 c. sharp Cheddar cheese,
  grated
1 tsp. salt
1/2 tsp. pepper
2 c. corn flakes, crushed

Defrost potatoes. Mix with 1/2 cup margarine, soup, onion, sour cream, cheese, salt and pepper. Put into a greased 3-quart casserole dish. Mix corn flakes with remaining 1/2 cup margarine. Put on top of mixture. Bake 1 hour at 350 degrees.

Juanita Pool
Floyd County

Myrtle Phemiser from Haskell County uses 1 8-ounce carton sour cream, no onion, 1 stick margarine, 1 cup grated Cheddar cheese and salt and pepper to taste.

Pat Northcutt from Hockley County uses 1 can cream of mushroom soup, 1 8-ounce carton sour cream, 1/2 small chopped onion, 12-ounces grated Cheddar cheese.

Ruth Stone from Throckmorton County uses 1 can cream of celery soup, 1/2 cup sour cream, 1 cup grated Cheddar cheese and 3 tablespoonfuls butter.

Becky Tucker from Swisher County uses 2 tablespoonfuls dried onion, 1/2 cup melted margarine, and garnishes with paprika.

TEXAS STYLE POTATOES

8 med. potatoes
2 bunches green onions
1 8-oz. carton sour cream

15 slices bacon, fried crisp
1 c. cheese, grated

Boil potatoes. When tender, prepare as mashed potatoes (put in milk, butter, salt and pepper to taste; mash potatoes). Pour into a 9 x 13-inch Pyrex dish. Layer rest of ingredients in order as listed above. Bake at 350 degrees for 25 minutes.

Margaret Beerwinkle
Hale County

If you walk with the Lord,
you'll never be out of step.

VEGETABLE KATOVAL 'N' GLAZE

5 med. potatoes, pared
  and diced
1 c. green onions, chopped
1 8-oz. carton sour cream
1/2 c. margarine

1 1/2 c. flour
1/2 tsp. salt
2 tsp. baking powder
1-1 1/2 c. water
Salt and pepper to taste

In a large saucepan, put potatoes and water to cover. Cook until tender, do not drain. Mix flour, salt, baking powder and water until smooth. Drop by teaspoonfuls into boiling potatoes. Cover and cook 15 minutes. Remove from heat. Add onions, margarine, sour cream and salt and pepper to taste.

Frances Fischer
Hunt County

SPANISH TORTILLA

8 potatoes
1/3 c. olive oil
1 tsp. garlic salt

1 T. dried minced onion
1 tsp. salt
6 eggs

Peel and dice the potatoes. In skillet (other than teflon), put olive oil, potatoes, garlic salt and dried onion; cook until very done but not brown. Cook on low heat for 1 hour. In a bowl, beat the eggs very well. Add the potatoes and mix well. In the teflon skillet, put in 3 tablespoonfuls olive oil, heat and spread oil. Put egg/potato mixture in skillet. Set edges with a rubber spatula. Move skillet back and forth. When almost cooked through but still liquid, invert onto plate. Slide tortilla back into skillet and cook 4 or 5 minutes more. Good hot or cold.

Annie Brown
Collingsworth County

CHEESY POTATO CASSEROLE

5 lg. potatoes
1 lg. can evaporated milk
1 stick margarine
8-oz. Velveeta cheese

1 8-oz. carton sour cream
1 T. salt
5 or 6 slices bacon, fried
  crisp (can use bacon bits)

Boil potatoes in jackets and cool overnight. Peel and slice in a 9 x 13-inch greased baking dish. Heat margarine, milk, salt and cubed cheese. Pour the melted mixture over the potatoes and bake at 350 degrees until bubbly, about 10-15 minutes. Remove from oven and spread sour cream over top. Sprinkle crumbled bacon (or bacon bits) over top and reheat until sour cream is hot. Note: For a large gathering - double the recipe.

Mary Crider
Ector County

BAKED ONIONS

12 med. onions

1/2 lb. mild cheese

1 bag potato chips (3 3/4 bag)

1/8 tsp. cayenne pepper

1/2 c. milk

2 cans mushroom soup

In 9 x 13-inch buttered casserole dish, place alternate layers of thinly sliced onions, crushed chips and grated cheese. Pour soup and milk over top and sprinkle with pepper. Bake 1 hour at 350 degrees.

Faye Mohon
Castro County

SPINACH CASSEROLE

2 pkgs. chopped spinach, cooked and well drained

1 can cream of mushroom soup

2 3-oz. pkgs. cream cheese

1 can Durkee onion rings

1/2 stick margarine

Ritz crackers, crushed

Melt cheese in soup first. Mix spinach with soup, add onions and place in casserole. Melt margarine and pour over crushed crackers. Mix together and sprinkle on top. Bake at 350 degrees for 20-30 minutes.

Eloise Stafford
Bosque County

WANDA'S PICANTE SPINACH CASSEROLE

2 10-oz. pkgs. frozen chopped spinach

1/3 c. onion, minced

2 T. butter or margarine

2 T. flour

1/2 c. milk

6-oz. pasteurized process cheese spread, cubed

1/2 c. picante sauce

1 tsp. Worcestershire sauce

Crushed tortilla chips or toasted bread crumbs

Cook spinach according to package directions. Drain well, reserving 1/2 cup cooking liquid. In large skillet, cook onion in butter until tender, about 4 minutes, stirring occasionally. Add flour; cook and stir until bubbly. Gradually add reserved spinach liquid and milk; cook and stir until thickened. Stir in cheese, cook and stir until cheese melts. Stir in picante sauce, drained spinach and Worcestershire sauce; mix well. Transfer to greased 1 1/2-quart baking dish. Bake at 350 degrees for 25-30 minutes or until hot and bubbly. Sprinkle with tortilla chips; serve with additional picante sauce. Makes 4-5 servings.

Renee Sanders, County Agent
Wise County

Seven days without prayer makes one weak.

SPINACH CASSEROLE

2 10-oz. boxes frozen chopped
  spinach
1 pkg. dry onion soup mix

1 c. sour cream
Grated cheese

  Cook spinach according to directions on box. Don't add salt. Drain well, but do not press spinach. Combine spinach, dry onion soup mix and sour cream in casserole. Top with cheese. Bake at 350 degrees for 30 minutes or until hot and bubbly.

Dorothy Thompson
Armstrong County

MEXICAN STIR FRY SQUASH

3 T. Wesson oil
8 med. yellow squash,
  chopped
1 lg. onion, sliced thin and
  separated
1 lg. red bell pepper, sliced
  thin

4 lg. Roma tomatoes,
  quartered
Salt and pepper to taste
1/2 tsp. chili (opt.)
1/2 tsp. sugar

  Saute squash, onion and pepper in Wesson oil just until tender crisp. Add tomatoes and seasoning; toss lightly about 1 minute. Serves 6.

Mabel Helton
Montgomery County

JALAPENO SCALLOPED SQUASH

1 3/4 lbs. yellow squash or
  mix yellow and zucchini
1 med. onion, diced
2 eggs, beaten
1/2 c. rich cream

1/4 c. cheese, grated
1/4-1/2 jalapeno, chopped fine
Salt
Pepper

  Salt and pepper to your own taste. Cook squash in salted water. When tender, drain off liquid and mash. Mix all ingredients in buttered casserole. Top with **buttered bread crumbs**. Bake at 350 degrees for 30 minutes.

Maymie Wikoff
Refugio County

The family that prays together,
stays together.

ZUCCHINI CASSEROLE

2 med. onions, chopped
1 clove garlic, minced
2 T. olive oil
8 zucchini, sliced

1/4 tsp. nutmeg
1/3 lb. mozzarella cheese, grated
Salt and pepper to taste

Brown onions and garlic in olive oil. Cut zucchini into 1/4-inch rounds with peel left on. Add zucchini to onions and garlic. Cook over medium heat for 20 minutes, or until tender, stirring occasionally. Add nutmeg and stir in mozzarella cheese. Let cheese melt. Garnish with 2 tablespoonfuls chopped parsley.

Darlean Holeva
Midland County

SUMMER SQUASH CASSEROLE

1/2 lb. yellow squash
1/2 lb. zucchini squash
1 lg. green pepper
1 T. butter
2 lg. tomatoes (I have used canned)
1 lg. onion

1 stalk celery and chopped tops
1 tsp. dried sweet basil
Salt and pepper
1 T. brown sugar
2 T. uncooked rice

Butter a 2-quart casserole dish. Put the rice in the bottom. Cut squash into 1-inch pieces and chop the celery fine. Cut other vegetables in good size pieces. Layer with onions, squash, pepper, tomatoes and celery; repeat layer. Sprinkle with seasoning and brown sugar. Dot with butter. Cover and bake at 350 degrees for 1 1/2 hours. Stir once after about 1 hour of cooking. Serves 6.

People who usually HATE squash have been known to eat 2 or 3 helpings of this recipe. It is delicately flavored and so good; it is inclined to steal the show from the rest of the meal.

Nell Pope
Deaf Smith County

SQUASH CASSEROLE

1/2 c. onion, chopped
1/2 c. bell pepper, chopped
1/2 c. celery, chopped
1/2 c. butter or margarine
1 T. salt
3 c. yellow squash, cooked and drained

5 c. corn bread, crumbled
2 c. milk
1 can cream of mushroom soup, undiluted
1/2 T. pepper

Saute onion, pepper and celery in butter until tender. Add to corn bread and mix well. Stir in remaining ingredients, mixing well. Pour into greased 13 x 9 x 2-inch baking dish. Bake at 400 degrees until lightly browned.

Juanita Montgomery
Grayson County

SQUASH CASSEROLE

4 med. squash
1 sm. onion, chopped
2 eggs, hard-boiled and chopped
1 tsp. salt
1 T. sugar

4 slices crisp bacon, crushed
1/3 c. margarine
1/2 tsp. black pepper
1 c. cracker crumbs

Cook squash in small amount of water; mash. Add salt, pepper, sugar, eggs and bacon. Saute onions in small amount of bacon fat; add and mix well. Place in casserole. Cover with cracker crumbs. Place margarine on top of cracker crumbs. Bake at 375 degrees for 45 minutes.

Corinne Evans
Marion County

TURNIP CASSEROLE

6 turnips
2 T. onion, chopped
2 cubes chicken bouillon
1 c. evaporated milk
Salt and pepper to taste

4 T. butter
2 T. flour
3 T. sugar
1 c. turnip liquid

Prepare and cook turnips; drain and save liquid. In separate pan, saute onion in butter, do not brown. Add flour, bouillon cubes, sugar, milk, turnip liquid. Add more milk if needed. Add salt and pepper to taste. Add sauce to mashed turnips and place in buttered 7 x 12 x 11-inch baking dish. Top with **Pepperidge Farm dressing mix** and **corn bread crumbs**; bake approximately 20 minutes at 350 degrees.

Freddie Spradley
Refugio County

BROCCOLI MACARONI CASSEROLE

2 10-oz. pkgs. frozen
   chopped broccoli
1 med. onion
1 lg. jar Cheez Whiz

1 stick butter or margarine
2 cans cream of mushroom soup
1/2 c. milk
1 12-oz. pkg. macaroni

Saute frozen broccoli and chopped onion in margarine until broccoli thaws and onion is tender; set aside. Cook macaroni; drain water. Mix mushroom soup and milk. Spray 13 x 9-inch baking dish with Pam. Layer 1/2 of the macaroni, 1/2 of the broccoli mixture, 1/2 of the soup mixture and 1/2 of the Cheez Whiz. Layer again in that order. Bake in 350 degree oven until bubbly and cheese begins to brown, about 45 minutes.

Annetta McIver
Hansford County

BREAD STUFFING

1 med. onion, chopped	1 tsp. pepper
1 stalk celery, chopped	2 tsp. poultry seasoning
9 c. homemade corn bread	1-2 T. sage
7 c. bread, cubed	4 eggs, hard-boiled
1 T. salt	

Let bread set out for 2 days to dry. Use homemade corn bread recipe. Let corn bread set out for 1-2 days to dry. Put dry bread and corn bread in food processor and mix well. In a large mixing bowl, add bread and corn bread mixture, onions, celery, salt, pepper, poultry seasoning, sage and eggs. Mix well. Add enough broth to mixture until moist. Put this mixture into a large glass casserole dish. Bake at 350 degrees for 1 1/2 hours or until light brown.

CORN BREAD

2 c. yellow cornmeal	2 eggs
1 c. flour	3 tsp. baking powder
1/2 c. shortening	Salt
1/2 c. sugar	2 c. milk

Combine all ingredients together in large bowl. Mix well. Heat cast iron skillet in oven with 2 tablespoonfuls oil. Pour mixture into pan. Bake at 350 degrees for 30-40 minutes or until golden brown.

Carma Dorton
Hansford County

CROWD-PLEASING VEGETABLE BAKE

1 20-oz. pkg. frozen cauiflower	1 4-oz. can sliced mushrooms drained
1 10-oz. pkg. cut frozen broccoli	2 c. Swiss cheese, shredded (8-oz. - I use Cheddar)
1 17-oz. can cream style corn	1 1/2 c. soft rye bread crumbs (2 slices)
1 17-oz. can whole kernel corn, drained	2 T. margarine, melted
1 10 3/4-oz. can condensed cream of celery soup	

Cook cauliflower and broccoli according to package directions; drain. Cut up any large pieces. Combine cream style corn, drained whole kernel corn, cheese and soup. Fold in cooked vegetables and mushrooms. Turn mixture into a 13 x 9 x 2-inch baking dish. Toss bread crumbs with melted margarine; sprinkle on top casserole. Bake, uncovered, at 375 degrees for 30-35 minutes. Let stand 10 minutes before serving. Makes 10-12 servings. (I used a can of onion rings, crushed, instead of the bread crumbs.)

Kathleen Finger
Medina County

GREEN CHILI RICE

1 c. onion, chopped
1/4 c. butter or margarine
3 c. rice, cooked
2 c. dairy sour cream
1 c. cream style cottage
cheese
1 bay leaf, crushed

1/2 tsp. salt
1/8 tsp. pepper
3 4-oz. cans whole green
chili peppers
1 c. Cheddar cheese,
shredded
Snipped parsley

In a small saucepan, cook onion in butter or margarine until tender, but not brown. In a large bowl, combine onion, rice, sour cream, cottage cheese, bay leaf, salt and pepper. Quarter green chili peppers lengthwise; rinse and seed. Chop half of the chili peppers. Stir chopped peppers into rice mixture; turn into a 12 x 7 1/2 x 2-inch baking dish. Place quartered chili peppers diagonally on top of casserole; sprinkle with Cheddar cheese. Bake, uncovered, in a 375 degree oven for 30 minutes. Sprinkle with parsley. Makes 8-10 servings.

Lisa Royal
Atascosa County

THE KITCHEN PRAYER

Lord of all pots and pans and things
Since I've not time to be
A saint by doing loving things
Or watching late with thee
Or dreaming in the dawn light
Or storming Heaven's gates
Make me a Saint by getting
meals and washing up the plates
Although I must have Martha's hands
I have a Mary mind
And when I black the boots and shoes
Thy sandals, Lord, I find
I think of how they trod the earth
What time I scrub the floor
Accept this meditation, Lord
I haven't time for more
Warm all the kitchen with thy love
And light it with thy space
Forgive me all my worrying
And make my grumbling cease
Thou who didst love to give me food
In room or by the set
Accept this service that I do
I do it unto thee.

---Kiara Munkres

Please send me_____ copies of TEXAS TEMPTATIONS

@$12.00 each_____

per book Postage & Handling @$ 2.00 each_____

Total_____

Enclosed is my check or Money Order
made payable to TEHA Treasurer for $ _____

Name_____

Address_____

City_____ State_____ Zip Code_____

Mail to: Fern Maxwell
1050 Jan Lee Drive
Burkburnett, TX 76354-2942

— —

Please send me_____ copies of TEXAS TEMPTATIONS

@$12.00 each_____

per book Postage & Handling @$ 2.00 each_____

Total_____

Enclosed is my check or Money Order
made payable to TEHA Treasurer for $ _____

Name_____

Address_____

City_____ State_____ Zip Code_____

Mail to: Fern Maxwell
1050 Jan Lee Drive
Burkburnett, TX 76354-2942

— —

Please send me_____ copies of TEXAS TEMPTATIONS

@$12.00 each _____

per book Postage & Handling @$ 2.00 each_____

Total_____

Enclosed is my check or Money Order
made payable to TEHA Treasurer for $ _____

Name_____

Address_____

City_____ State_____ Zip Code_____

Mail to: Fern Maxwell
1050 Jan Lee Drive
Burkburnett, TX 76354-2942

Panhandle
1

South Plains
2

Rolling Plains
3

North Central
4

5
Northeast

West Central
7

Far West
6

Central
8

9
East

South Central
10

11
Upper Coast

Southwest
13

14
Coastal Bend

South

12

● **District Headquarters**
✪ **Texas A&M University**

Lillian
You are a
wonderful lady. Very
"Waco 93" was very
enjoyable. See you in
Lubbock "94". In His Love,
Tammy Todd
Potter County

Juanita Anderson